THE ART AND SCIENCE OF MEDIATION

Cheryl Picard, Peter Bishop,
Rena Ramkay, Neil Sargent

2004
EMOND MONTGOMERY PUBLICATIONS LIMITED
TORONTO, CANADA

Printed in Canada.

Edited, designed, and typeset by WordsWorth Communications, Toronto.

We acknowledge the financial support of the Government of Canada through the Book Publishing Industry Development Program (BPIDP) for our publishing activities.

The events and characters in this book are fictitious. Any similarity to actual persons, living or dead, is purely coincidental.

Library and Archives Canada Cataloguing in Publication

The art and science of mediation / Cheryl Picard ... [et al.].

ISBN 1-55239-095-0

1. Mediation—Textbooks. I. Picard, Cheryl Ann

HM1126.A78 2004 303.6′9 C2004-904327-7

Contents

CHAPTER SIX
Opting for a Guide: The Mediation Process

CHAPTER SEVEN
Deciding On and Preparing the Path: Convening a Mediation

CHAPTER EIGHT
Packing Your Toolkit: Communication Skills

Preface

Over the past few years, mediation has been brought into the mainstream of dispute resolution in Canada. All levels of government are now using mediated processes to resolve workplace conflicts; regulatory agencies invariably offer mediation, among other processes, to resolve disputes; tribunals provide mediation as one avenue through which complaints are resolved; and the court system diverts particular cases to mediated processes. Less formally, individuals and groups employ mediation principles to develop contracts, plan for future development, resolve conflicts in neighbourhoods and communities, and make consensus-based decisions. In families, classrooms and playgrounds, neighbourhoods, church organizations, small businesses, large corporations, and international economic and political relations, mediation processes can be found. Mediation is used for private, as well as public, disputes and for interpersonal, group, organizational, and inter-, as well as intra-, state conflicts. Today there are few contexts in which mediation is not considered an option for resolving disputes.

The rapid growth of the field, coupled with the fact that conflict will not cease to exist, has led to a great deal of interest in mediation and its applications. Potential users of mediation, people interested in becoming mediators, and individuals who will be referring others to mediation are among those seeking more knowledge about the field. Training courses, professional development workshops, and university and college classes and programs in mediation have seen a sharp increase in enrollment. While some excellent Canadian texts are available for law students who wish to study mediation, few interdisciplinary texts offering Canadian perspectives are readily accessible to non-legal students. As mediation instructors, we lamented that we had to put together course materials, selecting articles from a variety of sources and compiling them in a single package, in order to provide our students with a "text" on mediation. This gap sparked the idea for this book.

As the four of us began the project of writing an interdisciplinary, Canadian textbook, the book's scope shifted slightly. In addition to students, we wanted to meet the needs of others who were interested in expanding their knowledge of mediation—future mediators, mediation referral agents, advisers of clients in mediation, and people with a general interest in the field. There are places in the book where we identify one or more of these audiences specifically, and we address both theory and application to meet the diverse needs of these various audiences. We also attempt to be inclusive of the different contexts where mediation is found—our case studies represent a variety of practice areas.

The central theme of this book is that mediation is both art *and* science. Science is the theory and the method. We study the world and derive general principles and concepts that we call knowledge. On the basis of that knowledge, we develop a method or a plan of action for a given case. Carrying out the plan involves "art"—the spontaneity, intuition, and inspiration involved in bringing a plan to fruition.

There is art and science in almost everything we do. To play the piano, we start by learning the theory of music—the do, re, mi. The theory and structure of music can be explained in terms of frequencies, intervals, mathematical structures, and progressions. Most students have to work for years to learn and develop the techniques, as well as master the theory and the method. They do repetitive exercises—scales, intervals, and chords—to master the scientific aspect.

Gradually, the musician becomes able to "make music"—to express, through musical sounds, the emotions, images, and ideas that come from within. The artistic experience involves the imagination and creativity of both the musician and the audience. We understand this at a deep, intuitive level.

We see mediation in similar terms. To deal with conflict, each of us needs to learn mediation methods, models, and techniques. Through repetitive practice with exercises that isolate and develop facility with individual skills and tools, we develop our technique. At some point, however, we take all of our technique and methodology and strive to apply it in a way that encompasses diverse needs, behaviours, attitudes, and values. We use intuition, induction, and experience to uncover insights embedded in conflict. We read between the lines. Body language and "unconscious" and implicit facts are just as important as concrete and explicitly expressed meaning. We "hear" with our eyes and our bodies, not just our ears. We know that the important interests of the heart and soul cannot be fully or adequately expressed in concrete, explicit terms. These often require expression through metaphor, ritual, image, and narrative.

Our search for understanding and insights is undertaken with inquiring, open, and non-judgmental minds. We must accept contrasting, conflicting ideas. We need to embrace paradox and become comfortable with ambiguity. The "universal logic" of conflict requires an integrative approach, which engages our senses and is essential to developing mediation artistry. By using creative, right-brain, lateral thinking, we can generate options and develop potential solutions that can satisfy conflicting interests and conflicting realities. We use a holistic approach, which accepts the validity, merit, and "truth" of conflicting realities and perspectives, without judging either as right or wrong.

We believe that all people have varying talents, scientific and artistic, for constructive human interaction. These need to be developed and realized to their full potential through education, training, experience, reflection, and experimentation.

The holistic nature of conflict led us to adopt a mediation approach that fits with our perspectives about conflict. This approach is called *insight mediation*. The theoretical foundations of insight mediation are laid out in chapter 4, while its practice skills and applications are the emphasis of chapter 6.

Earlier chapters provide a general framework for understanding conflict (chapter 1), surveying dispute resolution processes (chapter 2) and conceptualizing the advantages and limitations of negotiation (chapter 3). Chapter 4 reviews the current approaches to mediation—interest-based, narrative, transformative, and insight—comparing their world views, practice objectives, and the roles that mediators and participants play in the process. The art and science of mediation is conceptualized in chapter 5. The first half of the book sets the context for mediation practice—where mediation has come from—through an examination of its theoretical precepts.

The focus then shifts from the *what* and the *why* of mediation to the *how* in chapters 6, 7, 8, and 9. These chapters deal with the techniques, strategies, and skills of intervening in conflict—how to conduct a mediation, how to prepare parties for mediation, how to communicate effectively as a mediator, and how to manage interaction between the parties.

Chapter 10 consolidates the links between justice and mediation in retributive, corrective, distributive, and restorative models. This relationship is touched on again in our final chapter, where we survey trends and challenges in the field. The final chapter also responds to the many questions people have asked us about becoming mediators or using mediation processes.

The themes we have highlighted throughout this book are a reflection of our world views of conflict and resolution. First and foremost, we view conflict as a relational phenomenon that centres on communication. This means that we study individual responses to conflict at the same time that we are seeking to understand the relational dynamics between or among the parties in conflict. In our approach to conflict intervention, we consider the context and systems within which people operate—and their individual psychological responses to what is going on around them. We recognize that understanding conflict, including the roles that people adopt in it, requires accepting some actions as explainable, and others as non-rational and unpredictable. Nonetheless, we believe that people do strive to connect and relate with one another—we are bound by our humanity, and that makes us seek opportunities to repair broken bonds.

Interaction through communication provides a solid starting point through which to seek reintegration with others. For this reason, we emphasize that improving communication can benefit us all. The skills and techniques outlined in chapters 6 through 9 are life skills, not just mediation techniques. Learning to really listen to one another and assert needs respectfully enhances all of our relationships, not only the conflictual ones.

Because communication is so culturally rooted, we discuss the cultural assumptions embedded in various processes and skills of mediation, leaving the reader to ponder whether more culturally appropriate interventions can be developed. One of our objectives in including creative strategies and techniques was to provide a means to tap into alternate sources of knowledge and understanding when working across cultures.

Finally, we believe that our book has benefited immensely from our collaborative efforts. Our regular discussions required the skilled use of many of the mediation tools outlined in this book. Our different perspectives, strong personalities, and commitment to work collaboratively and inclusively posed challenges. Initial agreement on how we would proceed by chapter was rare. Yet, having finished the book, none among us would not do it again—we gained so much more through the integration of our ideas. In fact, we are proud to tell you that, as often as not, we used non-linear and non-rational methods in developing ideas and consensus. The process of completing this book was a model for a holistic and artful approach to conflict resolution.

But we are also grateful to many others who helped us with this project. Our students have always pushed us to improve and refine our knowledge through their enthusiasm for the subject. We have also benefited from the insights and ideas that have been freely shared among family, colleagues, and students. We especially thank the parties in conflict who have allowed us to learn, as mediators, through their process of becoming self-aware and reconnecting with others. Finally, we appreciate that Emond Montgomery had the confidence to encourage us to write this book.

As collaborators, we welcome your feedback and suggestions. We also wish you the very best in your journey with mediation—whether you wish to become a mediator or gain more knowledge about its workings.

Cheryl Picard
Peter Bishop
Rena Ramkay
Neil Sargent

About the Authors

DR. CHERYL PICARD, Associate Professor, Department of Law, Carleton University, is a practitioner, educator, and researcher in conflict management and mediation, as well as director of the Graduate Certificate in Conflict Resolution and academic director of the Centre for Conflict Education and Research. She has been mediating one-on-one and group conflicts since 1978, and brings a relational ideology to her work, which means viewing people as connected to each other by a shared desire for self-determination and social harmony. Her writings include a mediation primer and numerous journal articles. She is active internationally and locally; is a regular presenter at conferences; and has served as board member for various professional associations.

PETER BISHOP is an Ottawa-based mediator, lawyer, and conflict management practitioner, trainer, and consultant. He has extensive experience with conflict intervening and learning, particularly in the context of organizations in the public, private, and non-profit sectors. Much of his practice has been concerned with the application and integration of mediation methods within established formal resolution systems. He is a sessional instructor in mediation at Carleton University.

RENA RAMKAY is a practitioner, trainer, and researcher in conflict resolution both locally and internationally. She has been teaching in Carleton University's Department of Law and the Graduate Certificate Program in Conflict Resolution since 1996. As the director of special projects at the Canadian International Institute of Applied Negotiation (CIIAN), she assists local partners in implementing conflict programming all over the globe. Her interest in mediation was nurtured when she began coordinating Carleton University's Mediation Centre in September 1992. Her current activities in conflict resolution include local mediation, training and research, and peace building and conflict prevention work internationally.

NEIL SARGENT has been a member of the Department of Law at Carleton University since 1974. He received his LLB from Nottingham University; his LLM from Osgoode Hall Law School; and a Graduate Diploma in European Integration from the University of Amsterdam. Trained as a lawyer, he has been associated with Carleton University's Mediation Centre, Graduate Certificate in Conflict Resolution, and Centre for Conflict Education and Research, and he has been a participant and organizer of the Annual Ottawa Symposium on Conflict Resolution. His research and teaching interests focus on the relation between law and mediation, and mediation and justice.

CHAPTER ONE

Opening Pandora's Box: Understanding Conflict

There are more things in heaven and earth, Horatio, than are dreamt of in your philosophy.

William Shakespeare, Hamlet

Conflict—one of the preconditions for mediation—is the subject of this first chapter. In it, we examine how conflict affects people, their relationships, and their interactions. We discuss how conflict arises from various sources and how people experience conflict and respond to it. Our aim is to help you understand how different people in different circumstances need different ways to deal with conflict. We also want you to become familiar with the basic concepts, methods, and frameworks for analyzing conflict—essential tools for the journey.

WHAT IS CONFLICT?

Conflict—an inevitable and integral part of social and political life—happens in and between families, neighbourhoods, organizations, and governments. Any day's news reports on a wide array of conflict situations. Well-known examples include custody battles, proposed building developments, union–management issues, and wars. A comprehensive list would be endless.

Conflict, however, also serves to enhance relations, increase productivity, and create new understandings, as well as reinforce societal standards and provide opportunity for growth and moral development. The idea that conflict is not always dysfunctional is relatively new. Classical philosophers such as Plato and Aristotle viewed conflict as a threat to the success of the state, a view that led to the belief that conflict needed to be kept to a minimum, if not totally eliminated. The 17th-century philosophers Hobbes and Locke posited the social contract theory, in which order was seen as essential for a proper society. More contemporary theorists such as Simmel and Dahrendorf argue the contrary. In their view, it is the absence of conflict, not its presence, that is surprising and abnormal. Hence, there is good reason to be suspicious if we find a society or social organization that displays no evidence of conflict. Both Marx and Coser argue that conflict is an important aspect of group formation and that group conflict helps establish or re-establish cohesion. Coser (1956) in his book *The Functions of Social Conflict* positions conflict as a constructive form of socialization, telling us that a certain degree of conflict is an ally in the formation and satisfactory continuation of group life. Coser is often cited as the father of current theories of social conflict. As we can see, social phenomena change when viewed from the perspective that conflict is positive.

CONFLICT'S VARIETY

Sometimes conflict is viewed simply as a clash of personalities. At other times it is seen as a struggle over values and needs, or contention over claims to resources, status, and power. Sometimes it means only a disagreement or a difference of opinion. At other times it is viewed as an argument or fight, perhaps the result of antagonistic perceptions or interpretations. Descriptions of conflict often include reference to strong negative emotions such as anger, hatred, and fear, along with hostile actions such as war, violence, injustice, and inequity.

Conflict also generates a variety of responses. At times we might forget or ignore it; it becomes accepted as a normal part of life. At other times, conflict impels us to take action to defend ourselves or to preserve or promote our well-being or our relationships with others. In these cases, we can decide to compromise, compete, collaborate, litigate, or fight.

This whole book is about managing and resolving conflict more efficiently and effectively, both for ourselves and as intervenors in conflict situations. Understanding the nature of conflict, analyzing conflict behaviours, and responding in collaborative rather than competitive ways are what help us to do this. We will explore the many nooks and crannies of conflict in a host of different situations, to help you appreciate its complexities. To help resolve your own conflicts better, we encourage you to listen closely to what others say, to appreciate how they might perceive and understand conflict differently. We ask you to listen with both your eyes and your ears. And we ask you to accept the fact that conflict can mean completely different things to different people in the same situation, let alone in different situations.

DEFINING CONFLICT

There are many definitions of conflict. For instance, Boulding defines conflict as "a situation of competition in which the parties are *aware* of the incompatibility of potential future positions and in which each party *wishes* to occupy a position which is incompatible with the wishes of the other" (1962, p. 5). According to Coser, "Conflict is a struggle over values or claims to status, power, and scarce resources, in which the aims of the conflicting parties are not only to gain the desired values but also to neutralize, injure or eliminate their rivals" (1968, p. 232). Himes defines conflict as "the purposeful struggles between collective actors who use social power to defeat or remove opponents and to gain status, power, resources and scarce values" (1980, p. 14). And Hocker and Wilmot say that conflict is "an expressed struggle between at least two interdependent parties who perceive incompatible goals, scarce resources, and interference from others in achieving their goals" (1995, p. 21).

A number of scholars distinguish between what is referred to as *latent* conflict and *manifest* conflict (Boulding, 1962; Rummell, 1976; Moore, 2003). If at least one of the parties is unaware of the incompatibility of their goals or interests, the conflict is latent. On the other hand, when *both* parties are aware of the incompatibility of their goals and interests and consciously adopt incompatible positions toward each other, their conflict becomes manifest. Manifest conflict usually involves some communication or interaction between the parties; it results in a *struggle*.

Deutsch (1973) uses a somewhat different distinction between manifest and latent conflict. For him, manifest issues are expressed, or at least known by both parties, whereas latent issues are hidden and unknown by one or even both of the parties. Many conflict situations involve an issue or several issues that are manifest as well as others that are underlying or latent. We often refer to manifest conflict as the *presenting problem* and latent conflict as the *underlying problem*.

Contrary to definitions where conflict is defined in terms that include manifest conflict but exclude latent conflict, we prefer to use a broader definition that includes both. Accordingly, we use the following definition: Conflict exists when at least one party believes that the other party's actions or intended actions threaten to harm his or her interests. We find this definition useful because there are situations where one person feels threatened or adversely affected by another person, yet the second person is unaware of this. A classic example of this exists in Shakespeare's play *Hamlet.* During much of the play, Claudius and Gertrude are largely unaware of Hamlet's feelings toward them—an underlying problem that certainly has consequences for the people involved. We use Shakespeare's *Hamlet* to help illustrate some of the key concepts of conflict and our discussion of its resolution.

SCENARIO: Hamlet I

Consider the characters and events of Shakespeare's play *Hamlet.*

As of act 1, scene 4: Hamlet's father, the former king, has been dead about two months. Hamlet's mother, Gertrude, the queen, has married Hamlet's uncle Claudius—the former king's brother. Claudius is the new king. Hamlet is still grieving his father's death and is upset that his mother has remarried so soon.

In act 1, scene 5, the ghost of the former king (Hamlet's father) tells Hamlet that he didn't die from a snake bite, as some people think, but was murdered by his brother Claudius. Hamlet believes the ghost and wants revenge. But no communication results between Hamlet and Claudius about Hamlet's beliefs, emotions, wishes, or intentions in this matter, and Claudius does not know or suspect that Hamlet now suspects him of murder, nor does the queen. Hamlet does not act on his desire for revenge.

1. As of the end of act 1, is there conflict between Hamlet and Claudius? What do we mean by that? What do we mean by "conflict" in this situation?
2. From Hamlet's perspective, is there a conflict between him and Claudius?
3. From Claudius's perspective, is there a conflict between him and Hamlet?
4. What if Hamlet was wrong? What if Claudius did not murder the king? What if the ghost is a delusion of Hamlet's?

ANALYZING CONFLICT

Conflict analysis helps us to gain insights so that we can deal with conflict competently and constructively. As part of this process, we apply the scientific method, using known principles and deductive reasoning to establish facts in order to arrive at verifiable conclusions on which we act.

By way of illustration, a doctor, using the scientific approach to treat a patient's illness, will

- observe and examine all of the patient's symptoms;
- gather further data through tests and diagnostic instruments;
- consider current medical knowledge, which explains in great detail the categories, characteristics, and symptoms of various diseases;
- apply the knowledge to the data to diagnose the illness, including the root cause, severity, and likely consequences of the disease; and
- apply the latest medical knowledge to prescribe the correct treatment or cure for the illness.

To some extent, when dealing with conflict, we can apply a similar scientific approach. We can think of ourselves as a "conflict doctor." A fundamental premise of this book, however, is that the scientific method is *never* sufficient to give us everything we need to deal with conflict. It can give us *some* understanding of the conflict, *some* insights into its nature, causes, and likely effects, but it cannot give us *all* we need. (In chapter 5, we contrast this "old science" method of deductive reasoning to a "new science" method.) It is our strong belief that it is necessary to rely on many sources of knowledge to be conflict competent.

Conflict analysis begins by gathering and examining information about the situation. We obtain factual information—recent and historical—about the people and events. We inquire about the relationships between the people involved in the conflict, including their legal relationships (e.g., marriage) or their status (e.g., employment). We ask questions about the behaviour and interactions of the parties, especially the nature of their communications. We want to understand each person's emotions and get insight into their perceptions of the conflict, as well as their assumptions and attitudes toward everyone involved. We apply social science theories and laws from disciplines such as psychology, sociology, anthropology, economics, and law.

Many questions need to be considered when analyzing a conflict situation. The list below provides a sample of what one would likely want to know before deciding how best to intervene. Remember that conflict changes over time, so answers to these questions may need to be reviewed, especially in deep-rooted conflict and multi-party conflict. At best, responses to these questions provide a perspective, not definitive answers.

Questions To Consider When Analyzing Conflict

1. What factors, such as financial, emotional, relational, legal, procedural, and systemic, have caused or contributed to the conflict?

2. What triggered the conflict to come into the open? How long has it been brewing?
3. What is the background to this conflict? How might culture, gender, class, or power be contributing to the conflict?
4. Who are the parties, both primary and secondary? What is their relationship? How does trust factor into the conflict?
5. What attitudes toward conflict do the parties hold?
6. What are each person's perceptions and interpretations of the conflict?
7. What are the perceived incompatible goals and scarce resources?
8. What are the parties' positions and interests? What interests are in common?
9. What values, needs, and beliefs are motivating the conflict?
10. What conflict styles are the parties using?
11. How is power being used in this conflict? What unused sources of power are present?
12. What are the consequences of the conflict?
13. What options have already been explored? What has been the result?
14. What are the possible responses to this conflict?

SCENARIO: Hamlet II

Until the final scenes of the play, Hamlet never acts on his desire (motivation) to avenge the murder of his father. Hamlet's emotional crisis is reflected in one of the most famous passages in English literature, in his soliloquy that begins with the words: "To be or not to be ..." (act 3, scene 1).

In act 3, scene 4, Hamlet kills Polonius (Laertes's father). This sets off a sequence of events that leads to the death of all of the central characters.

1. In his depiction of Hamlet, what is Shakespeare revealing to us about conflict, its nature, and its effects? What does it mean to say that Hamlet is stricken with "internal conflict"? In that regard, what would we say is *the* conflict? What are its manifestations?
2. *Hamlet* is a tragedy. The conflict is destructive and has destructive consequences for Hamlet and others (Queen, Claudius, Polonius, Ophelia, Laertes). Why is that? What does that tell us about conflict? What does that tell us about people—and about ourselves?

We use the play *Hamlet* to point out five dimensions of conflict: (1) perceptions, assumptions, and interpretations; (2) values and principles; (3) goals and interests; (4) communications; and (5) actions or behaviours.

Conflicting Perceptions, Assumptions, and Interpretations

Polonius is a trusted minister and adviser to the king and queen. However, Hamlet (and through Hamlet's eyes, the audience) sees Polonius as an old fool, a sycophant, a hypocrite, and a meddler.

In acts 2 and 3, Polonius does several things to try to bring Hamlet out of his state of grief and apparent madness—and to restore relations between Hamlet and his mother (the queen) and stepfather (the king). On one hand, the efforts of Polonius can be interpreted as a well-intentioned and good-faith attempt to help Hamlet and serve the best interests of Hamlet and the king and queen. On the other hand, we can also appreciate the very different and conflicting perception that Hamlet has of Polonius and his efforts to intervene in the situation.

Conflicting Values and Principles

We are confronted by a fundamental conflict of values between Hamlet and his mother Queen Gertrude. Clearly, Hamlet feels very strongly that his mother's marriage to Claudius, so soon after the death of her former husband (Hamlet's father) was wrong and immoral. It is important for us to recognize that Hamlet feels this way before his father's ghost visits him and Hamlet discovers that Claudius murdered his father. Even though we can appreciate that Hamlet's grief and his feelings of love and loyalty to his father influence Hamlet's view of his mother's marriage to Claudius, nevertheless we realize that, apart from those feelings, there is fundamental conflict between the values of Hamlet and his mother.

Conflicting Goals and Interests

A central conflict in the play is between Hamlet and his uncle Claudius. We may describe this as the conflict between Claudius's ambition to be accepted by all as the legitimate King of Denmark and Hamlet's desire for revenge, his desire to expose and punish or even destroy Claudius. As observers and students of conflict, it is fascinating to realize how strong and powerful this conflict is. Yet, for the most part, it stays beneath the surface, with minimal overt conflict communications or interactions between Hamlet and Claudius.

Communication in Conflict

When conflict communications occur, they may be either direct and overt or indirect and covert. Hamlet's meeting with his mother in act 3, scene 4 is an example of the former. At the beginning of the scene, Gertrude chastises Hamlet for his offensive conduct over the past few weeks. At the same time, Hamlet accuses his mother of scandalous and disgraceful conduct in marrying Claudius. They clash, although the scene ends with the queen expressing her guilt and remorse.

On the other hand, as the plot unfolds, there are indirect, covert conflict communications between Hamlet and Claudius. Claudius detects double meaning ("method in his madness") in some of Hamlet's ironic or sarcastic comments. In act 3, scene 2, Hamlet arranges for theatre players to act out a play in which a king is poisoned and, subsequently, the poisoner woos and wins the queen. In effect, Hamlet is communicating to Claudius that he knows all about Claudius's foul deeds.

Conflict Actions and Behaviours

Similarly, conflict actions or interactions may be overt or covert. When Laertes, the son of Polonius, returns to Denmark to discover that Hamlet has killed his father, albeit accidentally, Laertes challenges Hamlet to a duel. They fight and both men die.

Hamlet's conflict behaviour is a central feature of most of the play. His conflict interactions with Claudius, Polonius, and Gertrude are mostly covert and indirect. Although driven by strong emotion, we see Hamlet mired in avoidance and other dysfunctional behaviour. Why Hamlet behaves that way—in spite of his frustration and disgust with himself and what he considers to be his own cowardice—has fascinated playgoers and scholars for centuries.

SOURCES OF CONFLICT

While we often ask, "What caused this conflict?" identifying the exact source of the conflict is usually very difficult and sometimes impossible. As well, the event that pushed the conflict into the open, that made a latent conflict become manifest, is rarely the real cause of the conflict. Underlying factors—often hidden beneath the presenting problem and triggering event—are usually what influence a person's conflict behaviour. An important task in conflict analysis is to uncover the underlying source of the conflict.

There are different ways to organize sources of conflict, but here are five categories to think about.

Competition for Scarce or Limited Resources

A common source of conflict between both individuals and groups is over actual or perceived scarce resources. Two teenagers fight over who gets to use the bathroom first in the morning; two directors fight over who takes the larger share of the budget; or two countries fight over a disputed territory.

Conflict Over Procedures

Here are three scenarios to illustrate this category: Two spouses argue about how to carry out the task of renovating the backyard. How will public consultations take place between the police and citizen groups over 911 calls? What process will be used for resolving workplace harassment disputes?

Human Needs Conflicts

According to Maslow (1987), needs motivate our actions, and when they are not met we struggle to achieve them. Human needs include identity needs such as recognition, respect, status, self-esteem, and self-actualization, as well as physiological needs such as nutrition, shelter, and sleep. Here are two examples: parental conflict over custody of the children, and a dispute about English- and French-language signs.

Conflicting Values and Beliefs

These conflicts can arise from differing personal priorities, as well as religious, political, and cultural beliefs. When our values are challenged, we often feel our whole sense of self is threatened. To illustrate, a teacher, a student, and the student's parent may disagree about the appropriate action to take when the student is caught cheating on an assignment. Also, think about a civil war when citizens hold different religious beliefs.

Conflicts Caused by Structure

Examples of this source of conflict might include the fear and disruption from downsizing a company due to shrinking markets, or the changing of government policies and leadership, or social action to protect the rights of the homeless.

Interests as Sources of Conflict

To understand people's behaviour in a particular conflict situation and to determine how best to resolve the conflict, we need to discover each person's interests. Interests are contrasted with positions, which are the demands or ideal outcomes from one party's point of view. Interests motivate people to want these outcomes. In fact, the mantra for principled negotiation is "focus on the parties' interests, not their positions" (Fisher and Ury, 1981). As a way to help determine some of what a person's interests might be, we use the mnemonic device CHEAP BFVs.

Concerns
Hopes
Expectations
Assumptions
Priorities
Beliefs
Fears
Values

This device reminds us to be curious and ask parties about these factors, given that they can be strong motivators.

As a tool, the concept of interests enables us to analyze conflict situations more competently and constructively. Discovering the interests of a person helps us make sense of the behaviour and demands around an issue.

By way of illustration, let us return to *Hamlet*. In act 3, scene 4, Hamlet chastises his mother for marrying Claudius. That is the conflict issue between them. Hamlet, in effect, implores his mother to leave Claudius. This is his position. What are Hamlet's key interests? Is he motivated primarily by his love and respect for his dead father? Does he want to protect the dead king's status as father and husband? Are Hamlet's feelings of revulsion and shame at the thought of his mother with Claudius motivated by his loyalty to his father? Perhaps Hamlet's resentment or even hatred toward Claudius is primarily because he feels his mother's attention toward him will be threatened by Claudius's coming on the scene. Another potential interest is Hamlet's sense of filial obligation toward his dead father, which in turn may be fuelled by his own shame, aggravated by his ongoing passivity or cowardice. This question has fascinated commentators for centuries: Why did Hamlet behave as he did? The question we pose, in more conflict resolution terms, is: What were Hamlet's underlying interests?

Remember that one person's interests in a particular situation may be very different from another person's interests in exactly the same situation. The reasons may derive from the parties' different backgrounds, psychological makeup, education, culture, and social class. If people hold particular values, that may lead us to assume that their interests are good and pure, whereas, in fact, they may not be. Returning to *Hamlet*, we might imagine that in wanting Hamlet to accept her marriage to Claudius, Gertrude's primary interest is her son's love. However, it could also be that Gertrude cares little for how Hamlet feels toward her; instead, what could be most important, her primary interest, is maintaining her reputation with her subjects, the people of Denmark, and her position and wealth as queen.

THE COMPLEXITY OF CONFLICT

Not all conflicts are created equal. There are as many different sources of conflict as there are responses to it. Some conflicts affect a great number of people; others exist between only two individuals. People's interaction in conflict depends on a number of variables, such as how many people are affected by it, how the conflict evolves, cultural norms, the length of time the conflict has persisted, and the stakes involved.

Conflict and its various manifestations and impacts are an inevitable fact of life. Until humans, as social beings, started to develop constructive ways of responding, conflict between all creatures, including humans, instinctively elicited adversarial emotions of hostility, aggression, fear, and defensiveness, leading to the "fight or flight" response. Unless you were particularly good at running and hiding, the only alternative was to "kill or be killed." Given our evolutionary path, it is not hard to understand why conflict often has destructive consequences. We also can appreciate why many people are uncomfortable with conflict, have a negative attitude toward it, and prefer to avoid it.

Conflicts Categorized by Type

In addition to analyzing the sources of conflict, mediators might categorize conflicts into various types or kinds. For example, conflicts can be viewed as relational, operational, or systemic. Keep in mind that conflicts are rarely simple; as with sources of conflict, categories can also overlap.

Relational Conflict

A relational conflict is primarily fuelled by interpersonal frictions in which the parties' basic needs, values, or beliefs are being threatened, denied, or violated. Such conflicts often involve strong emotions, poor communications, and negative behaviour.

Operational Conflict

An operational conflict usually stems from a disagreement relating to a task, transaction, procedure, responsibility, goal, or objective (among other things)—whose turn it is to take out the garbage; what procedure to use for a specific task; how much money or resources should be allocated to a particular objective.

Systemic Conflict

Systemic conflicts affect an entire group, organization, community, or state. They often have causes or effects that are beyond the control of individual parties. They may result from unfair or unintended consequences of authoritative action. Workplace discrimination may be systemic if it extends beyond a specific conflict between a small number of individuals. However, there may be any number of specific conflicts among various individuals and within various sections of an organization that are not systemic.

Conflicts Categorized by Who Is Involved

Rubin and Levinger (1995) articulated four different types of conflict, based on who is involved, in order to determine the level of complexity.

Interpersonal Conflict

Interpersonal conflict refers to conflicts involving a small number of people. A family divorce or a small-group workplace conflict would be examples of this type of conflict. These are considered to be low-level conflicts—they involve the least number of people, identities, issues, and interests.

Intergroup Conflict

Management–union disputes, for example, involve more complex identity issues because people in groups tend to influence each other's perceptions and attitudes, resulting in prejudices and biases toward people outside the group.

Interorganizational Conflict

Disputes at this level are even more complex because there are usually a number of issues, including economic, social, and legal ones, which affect a fairly large number of people. An example of a conflict between organizations could be an environmental dispute that involves a manufacturing company, a municipality, an association of neighbourhood residents, and an environmental lobby group. There is often a public interest at stake, and media coverage is common in these disputes.

International Conflict

This is the most complex level of conflict. These conflicts are found within, between, and among states. Current examples could include disputes between Taiwan and mainland China, the Israeli–Palestinian conflict, and conflict in Iraq. There are usually many issues and sources involved. The history of the conflict, over its many years, must first be examined, analyzed, and understood. Thousands or even millions of people might be affected on both (or all) sides, bringing many different perspectives, interpretations, attitudes, and beliefs about the conflict and how it should be handled. Power and politics outside and within these states affect the conflict, as does public opinion and media coverage. Accordingly, many political leaders have tried to use propaganda to gain a strategic advantage.

The Escalation of Conflict

Another way of looking at the complexity of conflict is by tracing its development. Conflict is never static; a conflict's intensity and complexity can increase through a number of stages. Rubin, Pruitt, & Kim (1994, pp. 60–72) describe five types of transformations that occur during conflict escalation. They agree that transforming the dispute from *the few* to *the many* exacerbates the situation. Finding others willing to attach themselves to the dispute lends additional support to a party's claim. It also increases the stakes and complexity of the conflict because additional parties add new issues and claims. As parties attempt to influence the other in order to get their way, they move from *light* to *heavy* tactics, beginning with persuasive arguments and guilt trips and moving toward threats and undermining actions that cannot be taken back.

Issues also tend to proliferate as a conflict escalates, transforming from *small* to *large*. As more and more resources are committed on each side, an initial disagreement can become a series of problems; parties start to see every action by the "other" as a new grievance. While conflicts usually begin over something quite concrete, they can soon move from *specific* to *general* as the relationship between parties deteriorates. Small, tangible problems then become generalized, intolerant, and all-encompassing positions against the "other." Each party to a conflict is initially trying to just do as well as she or he can for her or himself. As a conflict escalates, however, competition increases and parties move from *wanting to do well*, to *winning*, then to *hurting the other*. When more resources are committed to the conflict, the parties' desire to do well gets displaced by their need to do better than the other. This intensifies as the costs for parties mount and their goals shift to hurt the other party more than they have been hurt themselves.

Picard also uses a scale to describe the escalation of conflict. She says that conflict escalation begins at the problem-solving stage where parties disagree but share the problem. If left unresolved, it moves from the disagreement to personal antagonism stage, in which people, rather than issues, become seen as the problem. From this stage, the conflict moves to issue proliferation, where issues change from being specific to general, then to the triangle stage, where parties talk to others but not to each other. The final two stages of escalation are the antagonism-to-hostility stage (eye for an eye) and the polarization stage, where a change in social structure starts to occur (2002, p. 58).

Conflict will likely de-escalate when those involved focus on the problem rather than each other; emotions are spoken directly rather then demonstrated indirectly; threats are reduced or eliminated; those involved cooperate; needs are openly expressed; and those involved use conflict management skills or get help applying them (2002, p. 55).

Conflict and Cultural Norms

A conflict will also become much more complicated if differing cultural norms are present. In these situations, the potential for misunderstanding is much greater than when behavioural norms and cultural interpretations of events are shared. Some of the ways in which differences are articulated have been dealt with earlier in this chapter. As Ting-Toomey (1985, p. 72) states:

> What constitutes an appropriate conflict topic, whether the conflict should be overtly expressed or harmoniously sublimated, what serves as the proper conflict attitude, and how the conflict ultimately should be resolved—all of these take on particular nuances within the larger webs of a cultural system.

The nature of the conflict will also influence its intensity. Conflicts originating from different sources engage parties in varying degrees of intensity. Picard discusses the impact that three conflict sources are likely to have on a party. First, competition over limited resources are easiest to resolve if they are caught at an early stage. Second, basic human needs conflicts, which challenge a party's identity and self-concept, tend to be more difficult to resolve because they are often not expressed openly and they are at the core of one's existence. Third, conflicts over values and beliefs, which are central to one's understanding of the world and are formed and reinforced over time, are seen to be most difficult to resolve. They do not change quickly and are not likely to be "given up" by an individual in conflict. These conflicts tend to be firmly entrenched and often cannot be simply resolved—rather they need to be mutually understood by all parties in dispute. Value conflicts often present themselves initially as resource conflicts, and only after much discussion and exploration do they become clearer (2002, pp. 52–53).

Duration of Conflict

Finally, the element of time is critical to the development of conflict. Protracted social conflict, intergroup conflict that has persisted for a long time, is extremely complicated to resolve. Azar (1990) believes that this type of conflict arises in multicommunal societies where one or more community has been deprived of or denied its needs. Conflicts are driven and exacerbated here by the various needs of different groups and subgroups and the perceived incompatibility of those needs among the groups. Time makes disputes more complex because it enables other factors to influence the conflict, such as increasing numbers of people involved, the proliferation of issues, the increase in negative tactics, and many other factors we have discussed previously. Even simple interpersonal disputes become more entrenched when they have existed for a long time.

HOW PEOPLE BEHAVE IN CONFLICT

What do people do in conflict situations? Do they run? Do they fight? Do they look the other way? Do they try and work it out? How do they communicate? Are their words easily understood, accusatory, or do they primarily express themselves in non-verbal language? Is what they say and do constructive or destructive? Are they passive, aggressive, or assertive? These elements, and many more, are aspects of conflict behaviour.

Although a person's behaviour may be viewed in isolation, usually we consider it in the context of the conflict relationship. That relationship will have a history, a status (as in marriage, in families, in the workplace), with typical attributes and dynamics of power and patterns of behaviour.

Consider your relationship with a person close to you—a spouse, partner, friend, sibling, parent, or child. How do you usually behave in conflict situations when you disagree with that person? Do you argue? Do you give in? How do you tend to respond to different things that person might say or do? What emotions do you feel? What emotional behaviour do you display? How would a third-party observer describe your emotions and your emotional behaviour at such times? How would you characterize your behaviour? Is it aggressive or passive or some combination of those? What aspects of your behaviour would you say are constructive and which could be destructive? What are the elements of power between you and the other person? How do you influence each other? What are some typical patterns of behaviour in this relationship?

Being able to analyze and understand conflict behaviour is a very valuable tool for successful mediation. We gain useful insights by considering why people behave and interact as they do. We may consider various factors that influence behaviour in a particular context such as culture, social influence, economics, law, and the media. However, no matter how and to what extent we rationalize conflict behaviour and seek to understand it in scientific terms, there are many times when conflict behaviour seems to defy such analysis.

A psychologist may have various answers to this dilemma. Humans are conditioned or preprogrammed. We have instincts of aggression and fear. We have developed coping mechanisms—behaviours that at times may be counterproductive. Or, as we learned from Freud, we all have repressed memories, anxieties, and fears that sometimes result in subconscious drives and forces that are beyond our control. Therefore, in conflict situations, there are internal instincts, emotions, or drives that we can't detect but that may cause us to behave in ways that are counterproductive, even destructive.

HOW CULTURE INFLUENCES CONFLICT BEHAVIOUR

Given the myriad of possible interpretations of conflict, it follows that its causes and consequences may also not be clear. As Faure has pointed out, how conflict is perceived, interpreted, and defined varies from one culture to another (Faure, 1995, pp. 39–55). While culture alone does not determine individual behaviour in conflict, it certainly provides one "lens" through which conflict is understood. Conflict attitudes are linked to the social traditions, relationships, and values of a culture.

Hofstede (1980) identified four areas based on dimensions of differences that are specific to culture. The first is whether individualist or collectivist identities are evident. If we think of identity as a spectrum—from egocentric to sociocentric—where do you think Canadian culture would fall? Most of the literature would consider our culture to be more egocentric, because we privilege the self over the community and believe independence to be more worthy of praise than interdependence. However, if different cultural groups were polled within Canada, you would find less egocentricity. Cultural dimensions have an impact on conflict, because someone with sociocentric values is likely to understand conflict from a perspective that considers the impact on the whole community and seeks solutions that benefit more than the individual. A person with more egocentric values, on the other hand, is going to be more aware of individual needs. He or she is also likely to seek outcomes that have personal benefit.

The second area of cultural difference that affects how conflict is perceived is a society's tolerance for change. Most cultures have either a tolerance for ambiguity and change, like Canada, or a need for harmony and predictability, as is the case in some Asian countries. The effect of this on conflict behaviour will depend on which values take precedence. Someone raised in a country with low tolerance for change will not be likely to confront conflict directly, display high levels of emotion, or communicate directly with the other party. Covert communication, often non-linear and indirect, as well as face-saving behaviours, such as communicating through someone else, will be more commonly noted in cultural groups with low tolerance for change.

Hofstede's third dimension of cultural difference is power distance—whether vertical or horizontal relationships are more evident. This is connected to the previous difference, because societies composed of more horizontal relationships often have a higher tolerance for change. Societies with rigid hierarchies and traditions are less welcoming to change. This area of difference can affect attitudes and styles for dealing with conflict. For example, someone from a culture predisposed toward vertical relationships may prefer that conflict resolution be undertaken by someone else in a position of authoritative power. Where hierarchies are accepted, power imbalance is much less of a concern in conflict, because it is perceived simply as a normal part of life. In cultures with more horizontal power relationships, equality is a big issue to consider in deciding how to resolve conflict. In addition, someone from a society with flexible power relations will prefer informality over formal ritual and process.

Finally, cultures respond differently to conflict, depending on whether masculine or feminine values are present. If the society values nurturing over assertive behaviours, preserving relationships with other ingroup members is going to be essential in deciding how to approach conflicts. More important, caring will be a large part of interactions with others, whether or not in conflict. The process for determining conflict outcomes will be more important than the actual outcome for feminine-oriented cultural groups. The opposite will be true for societies with a greater emphasis on masculine values.

How we perceive, process, and respond to conflict is interlinked with our cultural values. In a Western society, we believe that some conflict is essential to our way of life. Being able to hold and express different and, at times, diametrically opposed viewpoints is a fundamental principle of our democratic way. Tolerating, respecting, and even integrating diverse opinions, practices, and ways of living is an important social value, which is a fundamental premise of our government and other public institutions. Voltaire's adage, "I may disagree with what you have to say, but I shall defend to the death your right to say it," is an important democratic principle.

In relation to public matters with which we have some distance and objectivity, most of us exercise some degree of tolerance and respect for diversity. However, when it comes to conflict situations in which we are directly involved, we are likely to perceive and interpret conflict in a subjective, partisan way. Therefore, when seeking to understand and define a particular conflict, it is essential to consider the perspectives of all the people involved; the different *possible* perceptions, assumptions, and interpretations of these people and observers; and the emotions, beliefs, interests, values, and other factors that shape the participants' views.

SCENARIO: Workplace Conflict

Mark is a clerical worker in a busy office. He is from a wealthy English family who has lived in Canada for generations. Louisa, the office manager, is Mark's supervisor. Louisa is a second-generation Canadian who grew up in a family in which conflict was not openly expressed. Mark has had a lot of difficulty working with Louisa and, as a result, he has been more aggressive than assertive in his dealings with her. Mark is very organized and methodical and he finds Louisa to be "all over the map" in terms of directions and priorities. He is very conscientious and gets upset with what he finds to be a carefree and lackadaisical approach by Louisa. He tried to speak to Louisa several times, but got nowhere. Now his anxiety and stress are affecting his health enough that he is frequently off work on sick leave.

You are one of the company's human resource advisers and Mark has spoken to you about this situation. To be better able to advise Mark, you want to analyze the conflict and gain a deeper and fuller understanding of the situation.

1. What further information would you want to know?
2. How, and from whom, would you get it?
3. What questions would you ask?
4. What are the possible sources of conflict here?
5. How might you assess the conflict behaviour in this situation?
6. On the basis of your conflict analysis, what approach would you recommend be taken in this situation?

RESPONSES TO CONFLICT

People deal with conflict in five basic ways: (1) they *ignore* it and thus tolerate the continuing conflict; (2) they *withdraw* by removing themselves from the conflict situation (the "flight" response); (3) they *fight* by taking unilateral action by way of physical force, coercion, intimidation, or threats to get what they want; (4) they *litigate* and appeal to a "higher" authority to decide what will be done to respond to and change the conflict situation; or (5) they *negotiate* by communicating with others about the conflict in order to effect some change that will improve or resolve the conflict situation.

Mediation, the topic of this book, is a form of negotiation. Mediation is a process in which a person not directly involved in a conflict (the "mediator") interacts with the people who are in conflict (the "parties") to help them resolve the conflict. On one hand, mediation is as old as civilization itself; on the other hand, mediation as we know it in mainstream North American society has really only come to the fore since the mid-1960s.

The action that a person takes, or does not take, to deal with conflict can be any one or a combination of the above five types of response. In most situations, any one of the five responses is possible and may be useful, depending on all of the circumstances. With each response, we may consider two factors that are present in every conflict. The first factor is the degree to which a party tries to achieve his or her goal, which is characterized as "assertiveness." The second factor is the degree to which a party tries to satisfy the other person's goal, which is characterized as "cooperativeness." Let us examine more closely these five basic ways of responding to conflict.

Ignore

Perhaps the most frequent response to a conflict situation is to *ignore* it, and thus avoid dealing with it. People avoid conflict for different reasons and in different ways. For example, a young female employee may be experiencing heightened levels of tension with a male supervisor at work, but may seek to avoid confronting her supervisor about it because she is concerned about the possible implications of doing so. The supervisor may be in a position to write a negative employment review, which could limit her chances for promotion. Any benefit to other approaches she could take, such as confronting her supervisor personally or complaining to someone else in authority, may seem to be outweighed by the risks of doing so. So, she tries to ignore his behaviour and continue her job as if the conflict situation does not exist. In choosing to ignore this conflict, the female employee may "smooth over" the differences or tensions between her supervisor and her and, in so doing, suppress the conflict and accommodate the other party's needs and expectations.

Withdraw

Another response to a conflict situation in which a person seeks to avoid confrontation is to *withdraw* from the situation. After not being able to ignore her supervisor's conduct toward her, the employee in our example may decide that it is just easier to leave the organization, even though she would prefer to keep her job. By deciding to leave, the young woman has removed herself from the conflict situation, but the conflict itself has not been resolved. Withdrawal is an avoidance strategy, rather than a response to conflict that is aimed at addressing the issues that caused the conflict. *Ignore* and *withdraw* are passive responses—parties do not engage with the conflict.

Fight

When parties seek confrontation, they act in an active, aggressive manner known as the *fight* response. In using the term "fight," we are not just referring to a physical contest of strength. However, a fight response to conflict normally does involve a test, in some form, of the relative strength, resources, or willpower of the parties involved.

For example, a labour dispute between a union and management over the terms of a proposed collective bargaining agreement may result in a threat of a strike by the union—or a lockout by management. Perhaps management wants to introduce flexible working hours as a way of ensuring just-in-time delivery to its customers. The union negotiators, on the other hand, want to keep the existing system of compensation based on fixed weekly hours, with double pay for overtime. If management cannot convince the union negotiators of the benefits of the new, flexible compensation system for workers, then management may seek to impose this new system on the union by threatening a lockout—a fight response. The union's response to management's fight threat may be to refuse to accept management's proposed compensation plan, even if this involves a protracted work stoppage that costs both sides a considerable amount.

A fight response to conflict typically involves a unilateral action or threat of action by one party, with the objective of pressuring the other party to accede to its position—to unilaterally impose its will. In the context of the threatened lockout, management acts on the assumption that the union negotiators will consent rather than be locked out. A fight response is both unilateral (initiated by one side with the aim of producing a response by the other) and coercive (involving the exercise, or the threat of exercise, of power).

Power is exercised in many ways in conflict situations. In the context of a fight response to conflict, power is defined by Ury, Brett, and Goldberg as "the ability to coerce someone to do something he would not otherwise do" (1988, p. 7). This implies the capacity to impose costs on another party—costs that can be imposed in financial or economic terms, in physical threats, and in material costs, such as the threatened loss or destruction of something of value to the other party. We can also include costs to a person's reputation, relationships, or psychological health.

We often think that the disputant with the greater resources or capacity to impose costs will be more likely to win in any extended power struggle. Sometimes, however, the disputant with the greater capacity to absorb costs will ultimately prove to be the more powerful. Whatever the relative power balance between the disputants, it is important to realize that a fight response tends to result in escalating costs for all parties the longer the conflict goes on.

By its very nature, a fight response tends to result in winners and losers, since each disputant engaged is seeking to unilaterally impose its will on the other. If one side wins, the other side is not likely to be happy about the outcome. If neither party is sufficiently powerful to obtain a clear victory, a stalemate results in which neither party is satisfied with the outcome. In these circumstances, disputants may seek another approach to resolving the conflict, or they may agree to a truce only to resume their fight at some time in the future. If fight is the only response, the conflict will never be resolved satisfactorily for all parties.

Litigate

The fourth response to conflict is *litigate*. This involves submitting the issues in dispute to an authoritative third party to determine who is right. Here is an example. A professional sports player and the team he is under contract with may not be able to reach agreement on the amount he should be paid under his next contract. The player is not eligible for free agency, and thus cannot test his or her value on the open market. But under the terms of the players' collective agreement, the team cannot simply impose a new contract on the player with terms dictated by the team. Rather than accept the team's offer, the player chooses arbitration, in which a neutral third party determines the value of the player's next contract, after hearing arguments about the player's relative value in the marketplace from both sides.

Alternatively, two divorcing spouses may be unable to agree on the arrangements for custody of and access to their two children, following the divorce. Should the couple's two children live with their mother, with the father spending time with them only on weekends, as the mother insists? Or should the parents try to arrange their lives so that the children spend roughly equal time with both mother and father, as the father wishes? If the parties fail to reach an agreement on the issue of custody, it is likely that they will to go to court to have these questions determined by a judge. In a formal court hearing, the judge will listen to arguments from both parties' lawyers about the issues in dispute between them, and will then hand down a judgment that is legally binding. The parties may appeal the judge's ruling to a higher court, which may overrule the trial judge's decision and substitute its own decision. But in either event, it is the court's decision, rather than that of the divorcing spouses themselves, that will ultimately determine which parent will have legal custody of the children, or how much financial support should be paid.

The introduction of an authoritative, third-party decision maker may alter the dynamics of a conflict in several important respects. Instead of a test of who has the most power or resources, as we saw in the fight response, the focus within a third-party decision-making process such as arbitration or litigation shifts to the question of who has the better argument or claim. Ury, Brett, and Goldberg refer to this as a shift away from a focus on power to a focus on rights (1988, p. 7). The two parents locked in a custody battle will each try to persuade the judge that their own proposed arrangements for the custody of the children satisfy the requirement that such arrangements are in the children's best interests, while those proposed by the other parent would not be. The judge then has to decide which side to believe, and which set of proposed custody arrangements would most likely benefit the children (or, more frequently, least likely to be disruptive to the children's well-being).

In the case of the salary arbitration dispute, the process would be similar. The player or his agent would present his case by comparing his statistics over the past one or two years with those of comparable players, arguing that he should be paid at the same level as these other players. The team might challenge the player's statistical comparison group, with the object of establishing a different salary comparison basis for determining his pay. Or the team might argue that other teams are in a wealthier market and must pay higher salaries than those players' performance actually justify. The arbitrator would then make a ruling based on the arguments and evidence presented by each side in support of its position.

A key element of any rights-based approach to resolving conflict is that, in deciding between the disputants' competing claims, the third-party decision maker should use an independent standard that all parties can accept as legitimate (Ury, Brett, & Goldberg, 1988, p. 7). In the case of the parental custody dispute, the judge's decision will be based on what would be in the "best interests of the children." In ruling on the player's salary, the arbitrator relies on the salary scale for equivalent players, established by the market. Depending on whether the player's side or the team's side wins the arbitration hearing, the other side is likely to be disappointed in the result. But if the arbitrator is impartial in evaluating the two side's arguments against an independent standard established by the market, neither side can complain about the unfairness of the result.

This is one of the strengths of a rights-based approach to conflict, as compared with a power-based or fight response. A fair application of an appropriate rule or standard will lead to a just result. At the same time, however, a rights-based approach to conflict also tends to result in win–lose or zero-sum outcomes, in which any gains achieved by one side are perceived as having been gained at the expense of the other side. In other words, there is often relatively little opportunity for collaborative or win–win outcomes within most rights-based approaches to conflict resolution.

Negotiate

The fifth and final response to conflict, *negotiate*, is a sizable topic; in fact, it informs the bulk of chapter 3. Therefore, we will only highlight some of the key concepts in this discussion.

Negotiations may involve two parties, or they may involve several parties. They may take place between individuals or between groups of individuals, between formal organizations (such as corporations or municipalities) or between countries. Negotiations may be informal (such as a family discussing its vacation plans) or they may be very formal indeed (such as two or more countries negotiating the terms of a peace treaty or an international trade agreement). They may be conducted in public or in private, by the parties themselves, or by representatives who negotiate on behalf of the parties (such as a lawyer, a player's agent, or a union bargaining team). They may take place with the aim of preventing a future conflict or they may occur in response to an existing conflict. In short, negotiation provides an extremely flexible communication process by means of which parties may attempt to resolve situations of potential or actual social conflict.

Negotiation is essentially a communication process through which the disputants seek to find a way of reconciling their competing interests in a manner that allows each disputant to achieve his or her goals. If you think about this idea for a moment, you realize that the dynamics of negotiation suggest that the disputants are in a relationship of *interdependence*. Neither party can act completely independently of the other (Gulliver, 1979, pp. 5–6). The parties enter the negotiating process with competing interests or objectives—neither wants exactly the same thing. At the same time, each negotiating party needs the agreement of the other in order to achieve his or her conflict objectives. If either party is in a position to obtain what he or she wants without the agreement of the other, there would be no need to negotiate. Yet, in most cases at least, neither party is in a position to compel the agreement of the other party. (A peace negotiation after a defeat in war might be one example where one party is able to compel the agreement of the other.) Consequently, the process of negotiation involves a complex dynamic in which each party seeks to influence the beliefs, expectations, or preferences of the other, with the aim of reaching an agreement that satisfies his or her own interests on the best possible terms.

It is in the nature of negotiation that the parties may not always be able to reach an agreement that satisfies their different interests. Incompatible positions, different communication styles, unresolved or unexpressed emotions may all present obstacles. In such circumstances, the parties may seek the intervention of a neutral third party. Mediation, a form of third-party intervention, happens when a mediator assists the disputants in negotiating a resolution to the conflict. The mediator's role is to facilitate the process by helping the parties exchange information and learn more about each other's positions and interests. However, the presence of a mediator does not remove the parties' responsibility for making their own decisions and reaching their own agreement.

CONFLICTS AND CHOICES

In the real world, people do not always respond to conflicts in ways that correspond neatly with the categories we have set out. People rarely choose one particular response to a conflict situation and then pursue this course regardless of other considerations. As individuals—and as members of larger groups and organizations—our behaviour is often contingent on the responses of those around us. In many conflict situations, our responses vary at different times; we decide whether to fight, withdraw, negotiate, or litigate, depending on a host of factors, not least of which is our own perception of the responses of the other party to our own behaviour. By way of illustration, the young female employee who initially sought to avoid a confrontation with her supervisor may subsequently lay a complaint against her employer for failing to protect her from sexual harassment at work, after talking to friends or family members. What began as a strategy of avoidance on her part may shift to a more rights-based response to conflict after obtaining advice from others, who are not direct participants in the conflict situation. In turn, her formal complaint may also result in a shift in response to the conflict by her employer, who is then faced with the consequences of a formal, legal investigation—and the possibility that the organization could be held legally responsible for the conduct of the supervisor. How the conflict is eventually resolved—whether through negotiation, litigation, or otherwise—depends very much on how the employer responds or deals with the complaint laid by its employee.

SCENARIO: The Band Next Door I

It is late Tuesday evening and Farah is trying to relax. She is keyed up about an important presentation that she has to give the next morning. Suddenly, Farah hears loud, pounding rock music coming from the apartment next door. Her neighbour Rocky—and some of his friends—are playing electric guitars and drums. As it goes on and on, Farah wrestles with what she will do about this.

Imagine that you are Farah.

1. What actions would you as an individual be inclined to take at the time, while the band music is continuing?
2. What actions, if any, would you take subsequently—the next day or later?
3. How do you think your neighbour might respond to any of the actions you might take? What effect, if any, would that have on how you would immediately respond to the situation?
4. What other actions might you take either while the music is going on or subsequently?

Imagine that you are Rocky. There are only a few times during the week that you and your mates can get together to practise.

1. How would you feel and how would you respond to various actions that Farah might take with respect to your band practice?

After considering the above scenario from both Farah's perspective and Rocky's perspective, you will realize that there is a wide spectrum of possible responses by both parties, responses that likely involve actions that fall within one, several, or a combination of the five response types presented.

Your various choices for action in the Band Next Door scenario will also show how different responses by people in conflict lead to different outcomes—some good, some not so good. We may say that some responses by Farah and by Rocky are *functional* and will likely lead to beneficial or productive outcomes and to a resolution of the conflict. Other responses may result in no improvement or resolution—or they may make the situation worse and cause the conflict to escalate. These outcomes are *dysfunctional*.

THE RELATIONSHIP BETWEEN POWER, RIGHTS, AND INTERESTS

Another way of looking at how conflict is resolved is by examining the parties' power, rights, or interests (Ury, Brett, & Goldberg, 1988). In a power-dominant system, power is generally confined to coercive power and does not include other more positive or cooperative forms of power such as restorative or creative power.

During the so-called Dark Ages and Middle Ages (about 400 to 1500 CE) in Western civilization, the use of force or power-based methods was common. Rights-based and interest-based methods existed, but without a well-established system of laws and functioning government to implement them, people resorted more to power-based methods to deal with conflict.

In the last half of the second millennium, emerging Western nations developed the laws and the government institutions required to implement what is referred to as the "rule of law." By the 20th century, Canadian society, along with most other Western nations, recognized the legitimate power or authority of the state to establish and apply an elaborate system of laws for regulating virtually all aspects of our lives. The rights-based system and rights-based methods for dealing with conflicts became all-pervasive. Rights-based methods for dealing with conflict require a well-established and well-functioning government, including courts, tribunals, and police forces—and the government departments and agencies to administer and support them. Rights-based methods are established on a foundation of authoritative power. This concept applies in private contexts as well. Within any community, organization, or family, people have recognized rules or norms that govern their interactions—and the persons with legitimate authority or power to apply them. For example, a university student residence will have rules that govern both the activities between 11:00 p.m. and 7:00 a.m. and the person with the recognized authority to enforce those rules. However, as many university dons, school teachers, and parents have experienced, having the authority to enforce standards of good behaviour and having the power to actually do it are often very different.

As discussed previously, the interest-based approach to conflict is one that seeks to resolve the conflict by satisfying the interests of each party. Recall that "interests" are the parties' needs, concerns, desires, and values. Subsequent chapters include discussions of negotiation and mediation as interest-based processes where parties seek to reach a resolution that satisfies the interests of all parties in conflict.

Very few conflicts are unidimensional—power, rights, and interests are elements that are interconnected in many conflict situations. As Ury, Brett, and Goldberg remind us, even in negotiation and mediation, where the emphasis is placed on reconciling the *interests* of the disputants, the relative bargaining *power* of the parties may often play a significant role in the negotiation process (1988, p. 6). Indeed, these authors suggest that some negotiations, which they refer to as "power-based negotiations," may be explicitly concerned with establishing who is the more powerful party. Examples can be found of this in the negotiations over the terms of a peace treaty between two countries that have recently been at war, or the negotiations between management and a union over the terms of a new agreement. Other negotiations, such as an out-of-court settlement negotiation between two parties involved in a lawsuit, may be explicitly concerned with the *rights* of the parties and how a judge would likely decide the case should negotiations fail. In this negotiating context, the rights of the parties, their relative strength or bargaining power, as well as the interests of the parties in reaching a settlement are all likely to be factors in the negotiation process and will influence the final outcome of the conflict.

Ury, Brett, and Goldberg believe that contemporary society is dominated by power, then rights, and, to a lesser extent, interest-based dispute resolution processes. These authors call this a "distressed system"; and they suggest that a better model would be one where interest-based processes are more commonplace than either power or rights processes. Their vision for an "interests dominant system" is depicted in figure 1.1.

FIGURE 1.1 Moving from a Distressed to an Effective Dispute Resolution System

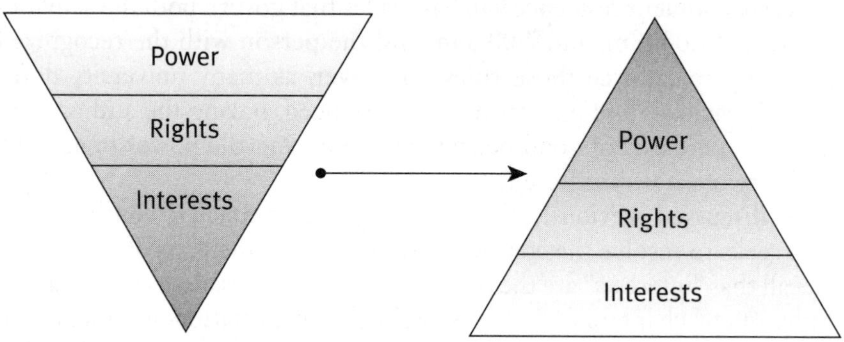

Source: Ury, Brett, and Goldberg (1988, p. 19).

SUMMARY

Conflict practitioners generally begin their work by hearing about the surface problem or "presenting problem"; seldom is the real problem first presented. For this reason, the first task is to probe deeply for the "underlying problem." Underlying problems stem from various sources, including perceived threats to human needs, challenges to beliefs and values, poor communications and incorrect assumptions, as well as behaviours, feelings, and interests. People respond to conflict differently—by fighting, avoiding, withdrawing, negotiating, or litigating. Conflict responses can be rights-, power-, or interest-based, with power- and rights-based responses being the most commonly used. Our hope, along with many others, is that society will come to focus more on interest-based responses.

In this chapter we examined several conflict analysis methods, because it is important to analyze situations through various lenses. Only then can we appreciate the nature and extent of the conflict and enable participants to truly resolve the conflict, rather than simply reach a Band-Aid settlement. However, remember that *no* analytical approach, model, or framework will give a complete or absolute answer in every case. With conflict, there are no complete, absolute, or final answers.

In a conflict situation, we want to discover the parties' "underlying interests," rather than what may be assumed from first impressions. To do that we need to discover their thoughts (perceptions, interpretations, and conclusions) and their feelings, along with how those interact with their wants and needs. In subsequent chapters, we go into detail about the different strategies, techniques, and skills for discovering and working with interests.

We need to learn more about the nature of conflict and the people involved in disputes. Understanding the different dimensions of conflict helps us appreciate its complex, elusive, and paradoxical nature. We start to realize that conflict, like human nature, is beyond the ability of the human mind to fully comprehend and predict. We believe that it will always defy our attempts to define, analyze, and process in a scientific way. For this reason we say that mediation, our most advanced method of responding to and dealing with interpersonal conflict, is both an art and a science.

FURTHER READING

Bunker, B., Rubin, J., & Associates. (1995). *Conflict cooperation and justice*. San Francisco: Jossey-Bass.

Folger, J.P., Poole, M.S., & Stutman, R.K. (1993). *Working through conflict* (2nd ed.). New York: Harper Collins College Publisher.

Hocker, J., & Wilmot, W. (1995). *Interpersonal conflict*. Madison, WI: WCB Brown and Benchmark.

Mayer, B. (2000). *The dynamics of conflict resolution*. San Francisco: Jossey-Bass.

Ury, W., Brett, J., & Goldberg, S. (1988). *Getting disputes resolved: Designing systems to cut the costs of conflict*. San Francisco: Jossey-Bass.

CHAPTER TWO

Choosing a Path: Methods for Resolving Disputes

There is nothing more difficult to carry out, nor more doubtful of success, nor more dangerous to handle than to initiate a new order of things, for the reformer has enemies in all who profit by the old order, and only lukewarm defenders in all those who would profit by the new order. This luke-warmness arises from fear of their adversaries, who have the law in their favour, and partly the incredulity of mankind, who do not truly believe in anything new until they have had actual experience of it.

Machiavelli

In chapter 1 we looked at the subjective ways in which individuals or groups respond to conflict. Our focus now shifts to considering the types of processes or techniques that can be used for resolving conflict. This chapter examines the differences between power-based, rights-based, and interest-based processes for resolving conflict and locates these various methods on a dispute resolution spectrum. We will also ask what is mediation? and what are the values and process advantages that make this particular approach to dispute resolution effective?

All societies develop social arrangements for dealing with conflicts, since no society could function for very long without doing so. Indeed, the success of a society is often contingent on its capacity for developing fair, just, and efficient methods for resolving disputes among its members. Without effective institutional arrangements for managing conflicts peacefully, social conflicts can escalate and become destructive and unmanageable.

We are all familiar with the feud between the Hatfields and the McCoys. The original cause of the conflict was long forgotten as the conflict generated its own momentum, drawing in new members of both families in a never-ending cycle of grievance, hostility, and counter-aggression. We can observe similar patterns of destructive behaviour in many conflict situations, from small, interpersonal, family disputes, to long-standing interethnic or interregional conflicts involving entire communities. Therefore, a primary goal in designing dispute resolution methods is to manage conflict peacefully. As we will see, there are many different ways to achieve this goal.

As discussed in chapter 1, the different methods for dealing with disputes can be categorized as either power-based, rights-based, or interest-based.

POWER-BASED METHODS

Jessie and her younger brother Tim are fighting over a toy. Tim says he had it first, but Jessie says it belongs to her. Who will get the toy? How will their argument be resolved? One method is by *unilateral action*—one of them will physically take the toy and keep it from the other. Since Jessie is bigger and stronger than Tim, she would have the power to do that.

Unilateral Action

Unilateral action happens when one party acts to achieve a desired outcome without the cooperation or participation of the other party. This may involve force or coercion. Of course, all sorts of unilateral action is illegal: theft, hostage taking, or intimidation—getting a thug to call on a delinquent debtor. However, various types of unilateral action are legitimate, acceptable methods for seeking to resolve conflict: strikes, lockouts, peaceful protest, and boycotts. Military or armed intervention, including involvement of peacekeeping forces, or action by a coast guard unit to protect local fisheries are other examples.

Authoritative Command

Another type of power-based method for dealing with disputes is *authoritative command*. Let's return to Jessie and Tim. Their mother hears their argument and intervenes. Each child claims the toy. Tim pleads, "I had it first"; Jessie counters, "I don't care, it belongs to me." They are both right—it does belong to Jessie, and Tim did have it first. The mother listens to the two children and then considers what to do. She may decide that since it belongs to Jessie, she can have it. On the other hand, the mother may say, "Young lady, in this house we share our things, so you are going to have to let Tim keep it, at least for the rest of the morning." Or, she may be so exasperated by their "constant fighting" that she decides to "teach them both a lesson" and takes the toy away so that neither child can have it. The mother's decision-making power derives from her position of authority over the children. In making her decision, the mother is not constrained by the arguments made by the two disputing children. There is no particular standard or rule that she is supposed to rely on in making her decision. She does not have to listen to all the facts before making up her mind, or give each child the opportunity to introduce evidence or cross-examine the other. Even more significantly, the mother does not have to justify her decision to the two squabbling children; she can even make a decision, such as confiscating the toy, that satisfies neither. Finally, of course, the children have no right of appeal against the mother's decision if they consider it unfair or wrong.

Authoritative command, a *power-based* dispute resolution method, is used to resolve various types of conflicts and issues within all kinds of groups, organizations, and institutions. Consider the following example. Two managers from different departments within a corporation are involved in a conflict about how the corporation's budget should be allocated. Manager A wants to see more money spent on research and design of new products; manager B wants more money spent on marketing and sales. The corporation's budget is limited, and neither manager has sufficient authority within the corporation to overrule the other. Such a conflict is likely to be resolved by the authoritative command of a senior manager who is in a position of authority over both of these managers. The senior manager decides the issue based on what she considers to be best for the corporation. The decision is not based on either the rights or the interests of the disputing managers. Rather, we might call this a "management decision."

In a public or government context, "policy" or "administrative" decisions are another form of authoritative command. In Canada's government, the authority of the Queen, as head of state, is exercised through the principles and practices of our parliamentary democracy.

One of the most common democratic processes used to resolve public policy conflicts is the principle of majority vote. Consider the following scenario. City council is considering a request from a developer to rezone a parcel of land in a residential area, to permit the building of a new shopping mall. The developer argues that the mall will bring new jobs and new residents to the area, and will contribute to the process of urban regeneration. A neighbourhood coalition, concerned about the increased traffic that the mall is likely to bring into the area, seeks the support of a city councillor to prevent the development from going ahead. Council listens to arguments both for and against the proposed development, and then votes on the rezoning application. In the end, the policy dispute will be decided by which side is able to obtain the most votes on council. If a majority of the city councillors vote in favour of the motion, the rezoning application will be approved. If, however, a majority of councillors are opposed to the rezoning application, the motion will fail, and the developer will have to reconsider its plans for the shopping mall, perhaps cancel the project altogether. The councillors do not have to justify their individual decisions to vote in favour or against the proposal.

The principle of majority vote is considered to be an effective process for resolving many kinds of public and private policy disputes because it is fair, just, and efficient. It is *fair*, because each party in the process has an equal opportunity to present arguments in support of its position to the voters. (This applies whether the vote is a council decision on a rezoning application or a municipal election to decide who will be the next mayor.) It is *just*, because all the participants accept that this is a legitimate way to decide the outcome of the dispute, and thus are unlikely to contest the outcome even if they are disappointed in the result. Finally, it is *efficient*, because the outcome of the voting procedure is final and will be determined as soon as the votes are counted and the result is announced.

Authoritative command is often an efficient mechanism for resolving organizational conflicts, but it may not always be fair or just. Consider the situation of the young female employee who is subjected to harassing behaviour from her supervisor, which we discussed in chapter 1. She may be justifiably concerned about submitting her complaint to a senior manager in the organization. What if the senior manager favours the supervisor, with whom he or she may have had a working relationship over a number of years? Are there any assurances that the employee's complaint will be listened to seriously or investigated? Even if the senior manager does take the complaint seriously, what criteria should govern the manager's decision? Does the manager have the authority to suspend the supervisor for his improper behaviour, or even to dismiss him on disciplinary grounds? Or could this action by the manager expose the organization to a potential lawsuit by the supervisor for wrongful dismissal? What if the manager responds to the employee's complaint by transferring the supervisor to another position in the organization, or by suggesting to the employee that perhaps she should transfer to another position in the organization?

We can quickly see that relying on a power-based process to resolve workplace harassment disputes may sometimes produce very unjust outcomes, not only for the complainant but also, potentially, for the supervisor. In these circumstances, it may be preferable for all those directly involved in the conflict situation (and this includes not only the complainant and the supervisor but also the manager and the organization as a whole) to utilize a different type of dispute resolution mechanism. The two major categories of dispute resolution techniques that can be used in such a situation are *rights-based processes*, such as adjudication or arbitration, and *interest-based processes*, which are based on negotiation. In chapter 1 we referred to these two modes of responding to conflict as a choice between litigating and negotiating.

RIGHTS-BASED METHODS

Most rights-based processes for responding to conflict typically have a number of common features. These include (1) an objective fact-finding process that is often adversarial in form; (2) relatively formal procedural rules governing the disputants' participation in the fact-finding process; (3) a third party with authority to make a decision that is binding on the disputants; (4) zero-sum outcomes, with a clear winner and a loser; and (5) an expectation (or requirement) that the third party should provide reasons for his or her decision.

We will see all five of these elements at work in the litigation process, in which a judge *adjudicates* a legal dispute between two litigants, as well as in the *arbitration* process, which involves a less formal adjudicative mechanism for deciding a dispute between two parties.

Adjudication

Adjudication is a formal, rights-based process in which an impartial third party (adjudicator), with no personal interest in the outcome of the dispute, makes an authoritative ruling on contested questions of law or fact. Adjudication differs from authoritative command. In the cases of the mother and the senior manager, their decision-making power is based on their pre-existing position of authority over the disputants. An adjudicator, by contrast, has no authority over the disputants except insofar as he or she is required to make a decision about the issues in dispute. This means that the adjudicator's decision-making power is restricted to the specific questions of law or fact that are presented by the parties for decision, and cannot normally extend beyond this. Put simply, unlike the mother dealing with her two squabbling children, an adjudicator has no power to confiscate a contested piece of property, or to send the parties to their rooms if they are too noisy! (For a classic discussion of the elements of adjudication, see Fuller, 1978, pp. 353–409.)

The most familiar context for adjudication is the court system. Here, the judge, a state-appointed official, has the primary responsibility to decide the issues in dispute between the litigants in accordance with formal rules of law. However, as Fuller (1978, p. 354) points out, adjudication is not restricted to the courtroom; it may also be used as part of a private dispute resolution process in which the adjudicator is selected by the parties. Adjudication is also frequently used in the context of rights-based administrative tribunal proceedings, such as an immigration review board hearing, a municipal board hearing, or a complaint before a human rights tribunal. In such circumstances, the adjudicator's decision does not have the same legal authority as the decision handed down by a judge in a formal court hearing. The judge's decision is binding not only on the immediate parties to the legal dispute, but can also be used as a legal precedent to guide the decisions of other judges in future cases that involve similar questions of fact and law.

Strictly speaking, adjudication includes arbitration, which we describe below as a separate dispute resolution method. For our purposes—in considering and comparing these different methods—we generally use the term *adjudication* when referring to processes in which the adjudicator is a publicly appointed official like a judge or a member of a statutory tribunal. An arbitrator is any non-official third party selected by the disputants.

In any adjudication proceeding, the adjudicator can only make a decision on the issues presented by the parties for adjudication. Consequently, adjudication requires that the issues in dispute be *narrowly defined* so that the adjudicator can make a decision. Within the litigation process, this means that the dispute becomes translated into a set of legal and factual issues that the adjudicator rules on. Aspects of the conflict that cannot be narrowly defined tend to be treated as irrelevant to the adjudication process, no matter how important they may be to the disputants (Emond, 1989, pp. 8, 9; Boulle & Kelly, 1998, p. 41). One consequence of this process is that the disputants may feel they have lost control over their own conflict. In most contexts, the disputants have no right to participate directly in the adjudication process. Instead, their lawyers represent them in the legal proceedings and make arguments and present evidence on their behalf. Frequently, the only opportunity most disputants have to participate directly in the adjudication process is if they are called to testify as a witness. Indeed, if one of the parties tries to directly intervene in the court proceedings without being called as a witness, that person may be ejected from the courtroom and found to be in contempt of court.

The adversarial nature of the adjudication process also influences the ways in which the parties are able to participate. In order for the adjudicator to make a fair and impartial decision, each party is given the opportunity to present proofs and evidence in support of its position. Each party is also given an opportunity to challenge the proofs and evidence presented by the other party. The adjudicator is then required to make a decision on questions of fact or law that are in dispute, based on the evidence and proofs that have been presented by the parties. The adjudicator must decide in favour of one or the other party. The result is a zero-sum outcome—one party wins, the other party loses. The adjudicator cannot normally try to find a compromise outcome, or to base his or her decision on any external factors or information that was not presented by the parties themselves. Consequently, the parties tend to adopt a very adversarial approach; each party seeks to emphasize the strength of its own claims or arguments, and tries to discredit or to undermine the weaknesses of the other side's arguments. As a result, the adversarial nature of the adjudication process is often costly, and preserving or maintaining relationships between the parties is not an issue.

Adjudication provides an effective means for resolving conflicts in which issues of fact or legal rights are in question. The formal rules of procedure and evidence are designed specifically to enable the court to perform its primary function of fact finding (Brooks, 1976). Even the adversarial structure of the common law trial process has been designed with this aim in view. Henry Wigmore, a famous American legal scholar, once called cross-examination "the greatest legal engine ever invented for the discovery of truth" (quoted in Emond, 1989, p. 4). In addition, the adjudicator's decision on the issue determines the respective legal rights and entitlements of the disputants. Let's assume that two corporations are involved in a commercial dispute over payment for delivery of merchandise. One corporation, the seller, insists on payment for delivery on first shipment. The other corporation argues that payment is not due until delivery is completed. The contract is not clear on this vital issue, so the parties go to court to have their legal rights under the contract decided by an adjudicator. Once the judge has decided the case, the judge's ruling will be binding on both corporations, and can be enforced by the officers of the court. Moreover, as we have seen, the judge's ruling may also be used as a legal precedent that governs future legal cases. Consequently, the adjudicator's decision may also have an effect that is felt far beyond the immediate parties to the conflict. Indeed, for some commentators, it is the judge's norm-creating or rule-making capacity in setting new legal precedents that is the most distinctive feature of the public adjudication process, and that distinguishes it from more informal dispute resolution processes such as arbitration or mediation (Fiss, 1982, 1984).

Arbitration

In many respects, arbitration is akin to a private form of adjudication (Sander & Goldberg, 1994, p. 50). Like the formal court system, arbitration is a process in which the parties submit their conflict to an impartial third party who is authorized to provide a binding resolution to the issues in dispute. However, unlike a judge, an arbitrator is not a state-appointed official or an officer of the court. Instead, the arbitrator is usually selected by the parties, who are responsible for paying the arbitrator's fees (McLaren & Sanderson, 1995, p. 104). Arbitration is therefore a *private dispute resolution process*, in which the proceedings are informal and confidential. Also, the arbitrator's decision, while providing a final resolution of the issues in dispute, does not become a legal precedent. The result of the arbitration process, even if publicized, remains private since it is binding only on the parties to the dispute.

Arbitration is frequently used for resolving interest-based disputes, such as a deadlocked labour–management negotiation over a collective agreement, or the salary dispute (discussed in chapter 1) between a professional sports player and his team. But arbitration can also be used for resolving rights-based disputes, in which the parties need an authoritative ruling over a contested issue, but do not wish to take their dispute to the courts. Arbitration provides a more *flexible dispute resolution process* than the court system, since it is not bound by the same formal rules of fact finding and procedure as the courts. In addition, the parties are able to select an arbitrator with expertise in a particular area, such as labour–management relations or international commercial arbitration, rather than having an appointed judge who may not be an expert. Arbitration is generally quicker and cheaper than the court system, since the parties are able to arrange the timing of the arbitration hearing by agreement, rather than being forced to wait until their case comes up on the court docket (McLaren & Sanderson, 1995, p. 105; Stitt, Handy, & Simm, 1996, p. 455).

While the parties can select a non-binding arbitration process, it is more common for the disputants to choose binding arbitration, since the primary objective of arbitration is to have the issues decided by an authoritative third party. But while the outcome of binding arbitration may be coercive, the process itself is voluntary, since it is chosen by the parties, rather than being imposed on them by the state. In this sense, arbitration can be viewed as a more consensual process of third-party decision making than most forms of adjudication. Often, parties may select arbitration even in advance of any dispute arising. A partnership agreement, for example, may provide a clause specifying that disputes between partners be settled by arbitration, rather than the courts. Or two corporations with a mutual contract may include a clause in which the parties agree to submit any contract dispute to an arbitrator, to be chosen by agreement from a panel of commercial arbitrators. Such a clause means that the parties agree, in advance, about the process they will use in resolving any dispute that they cannot settle through negotiation. Similarly, for the professional hockey player who cannot agree on the financial terms of his next contract with the team, the option of arbitration is provided for under the terms of the players' collective agreement with the league.

Finally, we should note that the *outcome* of the arbitration process is often more flexible than the court system can provide. While a judge is required to make a decision based on the factual evidence and legal arguments presented to the court, an arbitrator's decision-making authority may be more flexible. In a contract negotiation between labour and management, or between the hockey player and the team, the parties may opt for what is called *final offer arbitration*, under which the arbitrator must choose one or other of the outcomes proposed by the two parties—for example, either the player's suggested contract figure or the team's proposed figure. Alternatively, the parties may agree to conventional arbitration, under which the arbitrator has more discretion to make an award that could be somewhere between the two positions proposed by the parties. The arbitrator could award a contract of a specific amount that seems closer to the player's relative position within the market. Thus the parties (or the rules of an arbitration association) can determine how much scope the arbitrator has in reaching a final decision on the matter in dispute between the parties (Armstrong & Hurley, 2003).

INTEREST-BASED METHODS

Arbitration and adjudication are both rights-based processes. Each involves the active participation of a third-party decision maker who has authority either to determine the outcome of the dispute, or to make a binding decision that affects the rights and entitlements of the parties.

In some conflict situations, the decision of an adjudicator or arbitrator may provide a final, binding resolution of all the outstanding issues in dispute. In other situations, the decision of the adjudicator or arbitrator may only address some of the issues in dispute, leaving the remaining issues to be resolved by the parties through other means, frequently negotiation. For example, in the case of the two corporations that could not agree about the interpretation of their contract, both parties had an interest in obtaining a clear ruling on their respective rights and entitlements. This could be provided either through arbitration or by adjudication, depending on whether the parties prefer the private, confidential nature of arbitration over the formal, public litigation process.

However, usually an arbitrator's or court's ruling does not resolve the whole conflict. Let us suppose that the timing of payment is crucial to the seller because the seller is afraid that the buyer is running into financial difficulties, and might not be able to pay for the goods delivered. If the seller is required to make full delivery before the buyer has to pay, this would expose the seller to a risk of non-payment. Even worse, if the buyer turns out to be bankrupt, the seller would not be able to recover any goods delivered to the buyer, because these would now form part of the assets of the bankrupt buyer, and would be administered by a trustee, to be distributed among all the buyer's creditors. So the seller may not get paid, and may not be able to get its goods back from the buyer.

Even if an arbitrator or adjudicator interprets the contract in the buyer's favour, so that the buyer does not have to pay for the goods until they are fully delivered, this does not solve the seller's problem. In fact, it makes it worse, because now, if the seller halts delivery, the seller may be subject to a breach-of-contract lawsuit from the buyer for non-delivery! In these circumstances, what should the seller do to protect itself against the risk of the buyer's bankruptcy? What options does the seller have?

In chapter 1 we considered five possible responses that a person confronting a conflict situation might have: to avoid or withdraw, to fight, to litigate, or to negotiate. The seller has already tried litigation, which has not resolved the conflict. To avoid the problem, and act as if it does not exist, would be to risk delivering the goods and then not getting paid if the buyer does go bankrupt. To withdraw from the conflict by walking away from the contract would be to risk a lawsuit for breach of contract from the buyer, which is also a highly risky strategy. To fight or threaten to refuse delivery unless the buyer pays is not really an option, because the buyer can respond by threatening to sue for breach of contract—and would probably win the lawsuit! So, the only option left is to negotiate with the buyer and try to find a mutually acceptable resolution that satisfies both parties' interests.

As we saw in chapter 1, negotiation is an *interest-based process* for resolving conflict. Other interest-based processes are mediation and conciliation. The distinguishing feature of interest-based processes is the high degree of input and control over outcomes that the parties themselves have. In a negotiation, the parties may negotiate directly with each other, or they may negotiate through representatives, such as lawyers or agents. Mediation and conciliation are both assisted negotiation processes involving the intervention of an impartial third party who helps the parties reach a negotiated agreement (Boulle & Kelly, 1998, p. 74). In some respects, the role of a conciliator is somewhere between that of a mediator and an arbitrator. A conciliator may actively assist the parties in reaching a settlement, by creating proposed terms of settlement, which the parties are then free to accept or reject. In most forms of mediation, the mediator may explore various settlement options with the parties, but will leave it to the parties to generate their own terms of settlement. As Boulle and Kelly (1998, p. 74) observe, there is a lot of overlap between the role of a mediator and that of a conciliator. In this book we focus on mediation as the most common form of assisted negotiation process.

The key presumption underlying all interest-based processes for resolving conflict is that a decision that satisfies the interests of all the disputants is likely to provide a better resolution to the conflict than a decision imposed by a third party. Why is this? The answer is relevant to everything we will have to say about mediation, so it is useful to stop and reflect on this question now. A number of arguments can be made in support of this presumption:

1. Interest-based processes for resolving conflict tend to promote integrative or win–win outcomes, as compared with the tendency of rights-based or power-based processes to result in zero-sum or win–lose outcomes.
2. A decision that is made by the disputants themselves is more participatory and democratic than a decision imposed by a third party. Interest-based processes, therefore, encourage greater autonomy and self-determination by disputants than rights-based processes.
3. By focusing on the disputants' *interests* rather than on their *rights*, a wider range of potential settlement options may be opened up. Interest-based processes, therefore, tend to promote more creative decision making than rights-based processes.

4. In reaching a decision, or choosing between a range of settlement options, the disputants are likely to be better judges than a third party of their own interests (Mnookin & Kornhauser, 1979).
5. Collaborative or joint decision making, by its very nature, requires the voluntary participation of the disputants. A decision that is arrived at voluntarily is likely to result in a more *satisfying* outcome for all disputants, and, consequently, one that is likely to be more stable and long-lasting than a decision that is externally imposed and does not necessarily satisfy all parties' interests.

Mediation

Mediation is a very flexible form of dispute resolution process that is used in a wide variety of disputing contexts. From remote village communities to the United Nations, from community youth justice programs to labour–management disputes, from international peacekeeping efforts in war-torn countries to interpersonal family conflicts, the value of mediation as a non-coercive process that empowers the disputants to resolve their own conflicts has made it the fastest growing dispute resolution method in the whole alternative dispute resolution (ADR) field (McLaren & Sanderson, 1995, p. 56).

At the same time, the flexibility of this process and the diversity of the contexts in which it can be used make it difficult, if not impossible, to provide a single comprehensive definition of mediation that embraces every dimension of its practice. What a community elder does in mediating a community dispute in Nigeria may be very different from the practice of a professional family mediator in Canada. The role of peacekeeping troops as mediators in the aftermath of an interethnic conflict will look very different from the role of a commercial mediator in settling a dispute between an insurance company and a claimant who has been injured in an automobile accident. A mediator who adopts an evaluative model of practice may define mediation in very different terms from those used by a transformative mediator (see chapter 4). Professional mediators who are paid for their services may have a very different way of describing their work from volunteer peer mediators in a community program.

Part of the difficulty in defining mediation is due to the diversity in models of practice within the mediation community, and also, in Canada, because mediation is still in its "defining phase" (Boulle and Kelly, 1998, p. 4). Although mediation is one of the oldest and most traditional forms of dispute resolution, with roots extending back in many cultures for many thousands of years (Picard, 2002, p. 19; Folberg & Taylor, 1990, pp. 1–5; Moore, 2003, pp. 20–22), the modern mediation movement in Canada and the United States has only emerged in the past 30 to 40 years, and in many ways is still in its infancy. As Picard (2002, pp. 40, 41) has observed, the rapid development of mediation practice has outstripped the capacity of mediation theory to catch up. As a result, there is no generally accepted "standard" definition of the process and goals applicable to all forms of mediation practice. Some definitions place more emphasis on the practical techniques for managing conflict, while de-emphasizing the goals of collaborative decision making and conflict resolution. Others take a normative approach to defining mediation, viewing it as a field of practice that is based on principles that emphasize collaborative decision making, interconnectedness, and self-empowerment of disputants (Boulle and Kelly, 1998, pp. 4–6). As the American scholar Lon Fuller explains, what makes mediation different from other forms of dispute resolution is "its capacity to reorient the parties towards each other, not by imposing rules on them, but by helping them to achieve a new and shared perception of their relationship, a perception that will redirect their attitudes and disposition toward one another" (Fuller, 1971, p. 325; cited in Picard, 2002, p. 22).

Picard (2002, p. 21) says that mediation is

> a form of assisted negotiation where an impartial person facilitates the negotiation process while the parties determine the outcome. The goal is to help the parties gain insight into the cares and concerns that underlie the conflict situation and that are affecting their lives and the lives of others. This insight enables parties to reach consensual decisions that accommodate their needs. It is a self-empowering process that emphasizes self-determination and interconnectedness.

Along similar lines, Kruk (1997, p. 4; cited in Picard, 2002, p. 22) defines mediation in normative terms as

> a collaborative conflict resolution process in which two or more parties in dispute are assisted in their negotiation by a neutral and impartial third party and empowered to voluntarily reach their own mutually acceptable settlement of the issues in dispute. The mediators structure and facilitate the process by which the parties make their own decisions and determine the outcome, in a way that satisfies the interests of all parties in the dispute.

The Elements of Mediation

A number of the core elements of mediation are common to many forms of mediation practice:

1. The process is normally private and confidential.
2. The process is consensual in that the parties must be willing to accept the intervention of a mediator to assist them in the negotiating process (Moore, 2003, p. 16). If one of the parties is unwilling to accept the intervention of a mediator, then the mediator can do little to facilitate a joint resolution of their dispute. In this sense, the mediator's authority is always contingent on the consent of the parties, even if the mediation process is made mandatory.
3. The mediator plays an active role in facilitating the negotiation process between the parties but remains impartial as to the outcome.
4. Any agreement reached in mediation is based on the decision of the parties. The mediator has no authority to impose a decision on them, against their will.
5. The objective of the mediator is to facilitate the parties in reaching a joint resolution of the issues in dispute through a collaborative decision-making process.
6. Mediation is an interest-based process in which it is up to the parties to determine the issues in dispute and how these issues might be resolved.

A number of these points require further elaboration.

CONFIDENTIALITY

While confidentiality is usually a feature of the mediation process, the parties may decide, in consultation with the mediator, how far the process should be confidential, or whether anything said in the mediation process can be used in any other process. For example, one party in a mediation session may admit to having said or done something that could result in legal or disciplinary consequences for them outside the mediation room. It is important for the parties to discuss this in advance, since mediation promotes disclosure between disputants. It is an improper use of mediation to enter the process in the hope of having information disclosed by the other party that can then be used in another process. (For an extended discussion of the legal protection of confidentiality in mediation, see Boulle & Kelly, 1998, pp. 300–314.)

Consensus

The process is consensual, but that does not mean that the parties always voluntarily choose to enter into mediation. There may be situations in which the disputants are required by law to accept the mediation process. A government may pass legislation forcing striking workers back to their jobs, and appoint a labour mediator to assist in the negotiation between the disputants. Ontario's court-connected mediation program for civil litigation is another example in which participation in the mediation process is made mandatory, rather than left to the choice of the parties. But the mediator cannot compel the parties to negotiate if they are not prepared to talk to each other. A mediator can assist the dialogue between the parties to increase the chances for a successful resolution of the conflict. But the mediator cannot create a dialogue where none exists (Moore, 2003, p. 16).

Impartiality and Neutrality

Although the mediator's impartiality is a central element of the mediation process, it is a complex concept and there is little consensus on what it means to be impartial. As with impartiality, there is no shared meaning about neutrality—quite the contrary—and there is much debate about the plausibility as well as suitability of the notion of the "mediator as neutral" (Rifkin, 1996). Michel Foucault and other postmodernists would argue that it is impossible to be neutral, given that our background and culture create a lens through which we make sense of the world around us. Our lens is part of who we are and cannot be put aside when taking on different roles. Whole books go into depth on this topic; however, for our purposes an overview of some of the tenets of these two concepts will suffice.

Impartiality does not mean that the mediator is unknown to the disputants or that he or she plays a passive role in the negotiation process. In fact, in some models of mediation, such as the social network mediator (described in chapter 4), the parties know the mediator, and the mediator is expected to offer opinions. As we emphasize throughout this book, mediation is a dynamic process in which the mediator is actively engaged at all stages of the process. Sometimes the mediator may let the disputants talk directly to each other. At other times, the mediator may actively intervene to disrupt a pattern of communication between the parties that the mediator feels may be destructive or unhelpful. At times, the mediator may concentrate more on one disputant than the other.

However, the mediator must ensure that he or she does not favour one party over another or allow personal preference or bias to influence the negotiation process. This is what we mean by *impartial*. Moore (2003, p. 53) defines impartiality similarly: "[I]mpartiality refers to the absence of bias or preference in favor of one or more negotiators, their interests, or the specific solutions that they are advocating." Acting impartially and ensuring a perception of impartiality is vital if the mediator is to build trust with both parties. If one party believes, correctly or incorrectly, that the mediator is showing bias or undue sympathy for the position of another disputant, then the party who believes this is likely to withdraw his or her trust from the mediator; and this will inevitably interfere with the mediator's ability to facilitate an agreement between the parties. So the mediator must be mindful of this responsibility at all times.

The requirement of impartiality involves a number of competing considerations. For example, how far should a mediator go in trying to treat the parties with strict equality? If one disputant is less skilled in negotiation than the other disputant, or if there appears to be an imbalance in bargaining power between the disputants, how far is it permissible for the mediator to depart from the principle of strict equality—to try to balance the power between the parties, or to influence the negotiating style of the less experienced disputant? A good example of how different views of equality influence mediation approaches is found in the work of Waldman (1996). She found that mediators attend to social norms in different ways. Some mediators leave total responsibility for decision making to the parties (norm-generating), while others require mediators to ensure that parties are informed of their rights and entitlements (norm-educating). Still others view the role of a mediator as one who must advocate for those who, in the future, may be affected by decisions reached in mediation. We go into detail about these approaches to mediation in chapter 4.

Switching now to the concept of neutrality and again drawing from Moore (2003, p. 52), we find that "neutrality refers to the relationship or behavior between intervenor and disputants." He goes on to say that mediators "have often not had any previous relationship with disputing parties, or at least have not had a relationship from which they could directly and significantly benefit." Moore also defines neutrality as the precondition that "the mediator does not expect to obtain benefits or special payments from the parties as compensation for favors in conducting the mediation." Two other conceptions of mediator neutrality commonly found in the field are as follows:

1. A neutral mediator is one who does not allow his or her values, opinions, or preferences to influence his or her interaction with the parties or the mediation process.
2. A neutral mediator does not control or substantively influence the parties' determination of the mediation outcome; he or she is guided by the principle of party self-determination and interacts with the parties in a way that maximizes this principle.

Government agency mediation is an example of where the concept of "mediator as neutral" does not readily fit. Mediators in these programs are expected—and often required—to ensure that core principles and values of the agency's statutory scheme are upheld in mediation discussions and in any agreement reached. For example, a Canadian Human Rights Commission mediator will ensure that parties are aware of the principles, values, and statutory requirements of the *Canadian Human Rights Act* and that any agreement reached is consistent with these policies. When a mediator applies statutory principles, values, or requirements, they are no longer considered neutral by some definitions of neutrality.

Taylor (1997) suggests that the requirement of mediator impartiality and neutrality should be viewed in contextual terms. For example, when the emotional or relational content of the mediation is high, as with many family mediation situations—and especially if the mediator adopts a transformative or facilitative orientation toward practice—then the practitioner may often be working with an expanded concept of neutrality or impartiality, compared with the strict concept of impartiality more familiar to many legally trained mediators. Impartiality or neutrality is thus best viewed on a continuum that reflects the variety of mediation practice itself. At one end of the continuum are mediators who are more strict about their neutrality. They would not find it necessary to balance the power between participants in mediation, but rather would leave the playing field as it is and expect the participants to negotiate without much intervention. They would also not be educational and would stay primarily with a rational-analytic mode. At the other end of the continuum are mediators with a more expanded notion of neutrality. They would feel a need to empower and balance power between clients in mediation, and actively intervene between clients to help bargaining. They would also deal with emotions and interpersonal conflicts during the session, and feel free to use any of the following modes: educational, rational-analytic, and therapeutic, even occasionally the normative-evaluative mode (Taylor, 1997, pp. 226–227, 232–235).

Problems occur when a particular mediator or writer does not clarify what he or she means by neutrality and impartiality. This leads to confusion and contradiction within the field, because the meanings of these terms change, depending on the context and the mediator.

DECISION-MAKING POWER

Mediation is an assisted negotiation process in which it is the parties who retain final authority over the outcome of the conflict. As a third-party intervenor, the mediator may be called upon to play many different roles at different stages in the negotiation process. Building trust between the disputants, clarifying the issues that need resolution, helping the parties to learn more about each other's interests, designing a negotiation process, creating options for settlement, even assisting the parties in drawing up a final agreement—all these are part of the normal functions of a mediator. Yet these functions are incidental to the mediator's primary role in helping the parties reach their own decision. One of the normative values underlying the definition of mediation is the value of self-empowerment of the disputants. By modelling good communication skills, acting as an agent of reality, and helping the parties to identify areas of common interests, a mediator may influence the parties' willingness to reach a negotiated agreement. Ultimately, however, this must remain the parties' decision. As is often stated, in mediation it is the mediator who has the responsibility for the process of the negotiation, while the parties retain control over its outcome. If one party feels pressure from a mediator to settle on terms that he or she would not otherwise accept, that person is likely to feel aggrieved by the outcome and hence less likely to comply with the settlement over time.

The mediator's lack of authoritative decision-making power differs from that of a judge or an arbitrator in a rights-based process. The judge or arbitrator is required to make a binding decision on the particular facts or issues that are in dispute. The role of the judge is not to reconcile the interests of the disputants, but to determine who is right (Eckhoff, 1969). The judge's decision looks back at the past conduct of the parties—who did what to whom, when, and with what justification or lack of justification? The judge does not examine the causes of the conflict, except as they are relevant to reaching a judgment about whether the alleged conduct of either of the disputants violated any legal rule. Nor does the judge inquire into the motivations or beliefs that lie behind the actions of the disputants—or the nature of their relationship. The only question for the judge to decide is whether any legal wrongdoing has been proven, and, if so, what legal consequences should follow from this. As a result, all too often, the root causes of the conflict are left unresolved (Irving & Benjamin, 1987, p. 39).

By contrast, a mediator seeks to uncover the sources of the conflict and to explore the reasons, beliefs, and motivations that underlie the parties' behaviour. A mediator looks to the past, not to judge the parties' conduct, but to gain insight into the conflict and to understand the nature of the relationship between the disputants. Often the key to helping the parties reach a joint resolution to their dispute lies in the ability of the mediator to build a relationship of trust with each of the disputants. Both parties need to feel that they are being listened to by the mediator, and that their interests are regarded as legitimate and worthy of attention. Consequently, the mediator needs to be non-judgmental, and to create an environment in which all parties are able to express their fears, concerns, and emotions to a sympathetic and curious, but impartial, third party.

Contrasted to the role of a judge or arbitrator, the role of the mediator is more facilitative and future-oriented. The mediator seeks to open lines of communication between the disputants, and to promote a constructive dialogue through which the parties may come to a joint understanding of the issues that divide them, as well as the interests they may have in common. A mediator also acts as a problem solver, helping to find creative ways around some of the obstacles that impede progress or inhibit the parties' ability to reach a consensual resolution. The mediator may also act as a sounding board, against which each party can test the accuracy of his or her perceptions of the actions and motives of the other, as well as the reasonableness or feasibility of his or her own claims and demands in response. The mediator must also be a skilled negotiator, who is able to help the disputants in setting their negotiating priorities, evaluating options, and creating an agreement that is capable of satisfying all parties' interests. In all these ways the mediator acts as a facilitator who seeks to reconcile the competing interests of the disputants, and thereby assist them in reaching a negotiated resolution that is tailored to fit their own particular needs.

SCENARIO: Sonata Development I

Haven Homes owns 200 acres of raw land adjacent to a suburban community called "Sonata." Five years ago, this community was taken over (amalgamated) by the city. Most residents value and want to preserve its small-town character and ambience. Haven Homes has applied to the city to rezone the land from agricultural to residential. It has plans for a new, high-density subdivision with semi-detached and row housing and two apartment buildings that would add up to 5,000 people to the population of Sonata. Strong opposition to the proposed development is led by the Sonata Preservation Society (SPS). The two opposing views are presented at a public meeting.

Alex (president of SPS): "This is ridiculous. There is no bloody way we're going to let them do it. It will destroy our community. We might as well be in the middle of the city. There is a perfectly good place for this kind of high-density development in the south end, beside the industrial sector."

Grant (president of Haven Homes): "Our proposed development will be very beneficial for this community. There is a real shortage of lower-cost, affordable housing—especially for younger families. In trying to block this, the SPS is considering only their own selfish interests and couldn't care less about the well-being of the wider community."

Questions

1. What different possible methods might the parties use for dealing with the disputed issues in this case?
2. If you were Alex or Alex's adviser, what would you need to consider in deciding what method or methods to use?
3. If you were Grant or Grant's adviser, what would you need to consider in deciding what method or methods to use?

Having considered some of the primary power-based, rights-based, and interest-based methods of dispute resolution, we are now in a position to consider them in the context of the *dispute resolution spectrum*.

THE DISPUTE RESOLUTION SPECTRUM

Figure 2.1 is a "resolution wheel," showing the spectrum of dispute resolution methods with three basic segments: power-based, rights-based, and interest-based.

The three segments and six methods shown are not mutually exclusive compartments. In a given case, although one of the methods on the spectrum may be chosen as the primary dispute resolution method, parties can use some or all of these methods, with different combinations, variations, or hybrids. Indeed, in many cases, the practitioner may use various methods in order to meet the needs of the parties in a particular dispute.

FIGURE 2.1 The Dispute Resolution Spectrum

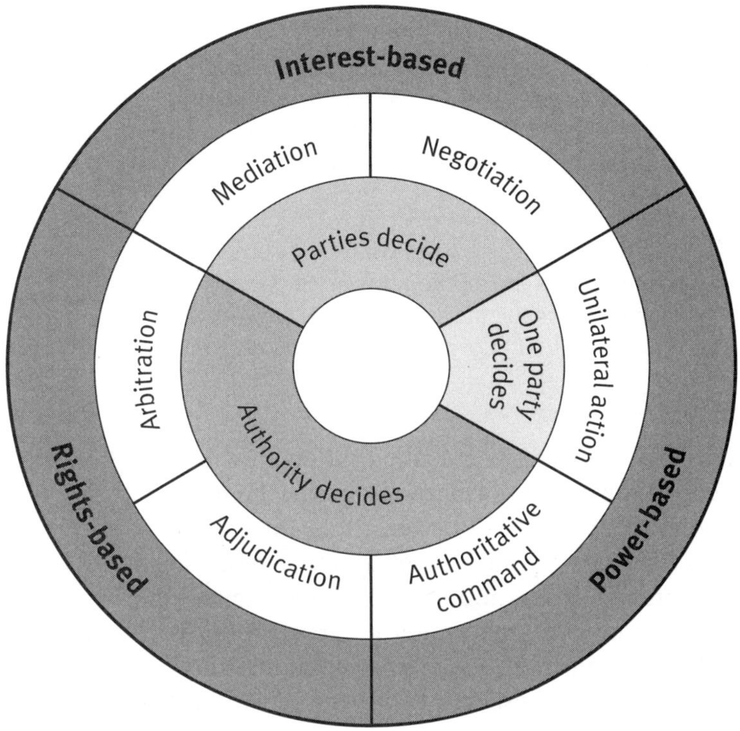

As you can see, the resolution wheel consists of three concentric circles. The outer circle shows the three basic approaches—power, rights, and interests—and the middle circle has the six methods. The inner circle indicates the "nature" of the decision maker for each method—who decides the outcome. In negotiation and mediation, the parties decide the outcome. For arbitration, adjudication, and authoritative command, the authority decides. And for unilateral action, one party decides. It is interesting to note that the methods on the lower half of the wheel are those in which "Authority Decides"; the methods on the upper half are ones in which "Parties Decide," either together or unilaterally. Also remember that with arbitration the parties decide on the authority (they select the arbitrator) and the arbitrator decides the outcome.

SCENARIO: Band Next Door II—Resolution Methods

In the Band Next Door scenario from chapter 1, think of the six different specific resolution methods shown on the resolution wheel: unilateral action, negotiation, mediation, arbitration, adjudication, and authoritative command. Now compare different attributes of each of those methods by considering the following questions:

1. To what extent do the parties control the outcome?
2. To what extent do the parties control the process?
3. To what extent is the method private or public?
4. To what extent is the method formal or informal?
5. How long would it take and how much would it cost?

Mediation, arbitration, and adjudication are the three primary methods used for third-party dispute resolution. Figure 2.2 illustrates some of the chief characteristics of each.

As this figure clearly shows, mediation can be distinguished from both adjudication and arbitration in several important respects, such as the nature of the process, the mode of participation by the parties, their mode of communication, and who has responsibility for the outcome of the conflict. In other respects, however, mediation shares some significant characteristics with arbitration, such as its private character, the selection of the third party, and the consensual nature of the process. Mediation and arbitration are also less formal than adjudication, which normally takes place within the public court system. At the same time, however, mediation is beginning to be used as a dispute resolution process within the formal court system, as well as outside it. Consequently, it is not as easy as it may seem at first to draw clear distinctions between these three methods of third-party conflict intervention.

Hybrid Methods

Dispute resolution practitioners use the basic methods of dispute resolution in various combinations or "hybrids." The possible variations or combinations are limited only by the imagination of the participants. For example, a hybrid method known as *neutral evaluation* is a cross between evaluative mediation and arbitration. Here, the neutral third party considers all the facts and evidence and expresses an opinion as to the likely outcome of an adjudication. The parties then seek to negotiate or

FIGURE 2.2 Comparison of Adjudication, Arbitration, and Mediation as Third-Party Conflict Resolution Techniques

	Adjudication	Arbitration	Mediation
Nature of process	Rights-based	Rights-based	Interest-based
Appointment of third party	Appointed by the state	Selected by the parties	Selected by the parties
Mode of participation	Indirect—parties are represented by legal advisers	Indirect—parties are normally represented by an agent or lawyer	Direct—parties participate directly in the process
Degree of formality of the process	Process is adversarial—with formal rules of procedure and evidence	Process is adversarial—with informal rules of procedure	Process is non-adversarial—ground rules are informal and consensual
Mode of communication between parties	Closed—issues are narrowly defined, and information is presented in the form of facts and arguments	Closed—issues somewhat less narrowly defined, but information is presented in the form of facts and arguments	Open-ended—parties define what issues are relevant and need to be discussed
Role of third party	Authoritative—third party is responsible for the outcome	Authoritative—third party is responsible for the outcome	Facilitative—parties are responsible for the outcome
Outcome	Coercive—outcome is binding, regardless of parties' consent	Neutral—parties determine in advance whether outcome shall be binding or non-binding	Consensual—no agreement without parties' consent

settle their differences based on the opinion expressed by the neutral evaluator.

In some cases, parties and their advisers may combine different methods in different ways. For example, in a divorce dispute, the parties may start with mediation and use that process entirely to deal with the issues between them over child care and parenting and sharing child-care expenses. However, at some point, they may involve their lawyers when dividing their property and agree to jointly select a neutral business evaluator to arbitrate in the valuation of the wife's business.

We will now consider two combinations of mediation, arbitration, and adjudication that have resulted in hybrid forms of mediation practice.

Mediation-Arbitration ("Med-Arb")

One hybrid combines elements of both mediation and arbitration. Mediation-arbitration is a two-stage process in which the parties attempt, first, to negotiate a resolution to their conflict with the assistance of a mediator. Those issues that cannot be resolved through mediation will then be submitted to arbitration (McLaren & Sanderson, 1995, p. 192). In effect, the parties have agreed in advance to a two-step process for resolving their conflict. Once the mediation stage is completed, the parties may agree that the same person who acted as mediator will then act as arbitrator in the second stage of the process. However, this is not necessary; the parties could select a different person to arbitrate the outstanding issues. The advantage of using the same person to act as both mediator and arbitrator is that the third party will already be familiar with the issues remaining to be resolved (McLaren & Sanderson, 1995, p. 193).

Mediation-arbitration shares with both mediation and arbitration the fact that it is a private, informal process based on the consent of the parties. By combining two distinct resolution processes into a two-stage hybrid, the parties are just making the decision in advance as to what will happen if the mediation is unsuccessful, or only partly successful. Both the disputants and the mediator will be aware of the process to be used in resolving the outstanding issues. In short, the parties assure themselves of the advantages of using arbitration for the second stage, and avoid the costs and risks of litigation.

Realize, however, that the nature of mediation and arbitration as dispute resolution techniques remain distinct in important respects. While both an arbitrator and a mediator act as impartial third parties, the roles of a mediator and an arbitrator are very different. A mediator tries to assist the parties in reaching their own negotiated settlement. Frequently, this will involve the mediator in exploring the parties' options for settlement. But it is the parties who remain in control of the outcome; the mediator cannot impose any terms of settlement. However, in the second stage of med-arb, this is exactly what the third party is required to do. If the same person who acts as a mediator in stage one is to take on the role of the arbitrator in stage two, will it be possible for that person to be non-judgmental and impartial as a mediator? The significance of this question will become clearer in chapter 4 when we look at different mediator orientations or approaches to mediation. For the present, it is enough to observe that there is likely to be a tendency within mediation-arbitration for the first-stage mediator to adopt a problem-solving or settlement orientation toward mediation, in the hope of narrowing the issues that remain to be decided by arbitration. The question this raises for mediation theorists and practitioners is whether the hybrid nature of med-arb will indirectly pressure mediators to become more settlement-oriented, rather than adopting a more transformative or facilitative orientation to mediation practice.

Another potential concern with med-arb is that parties may be constrained in what they say and reveal in the mediation stage, if they know that the mediator will be their arbitrator, and if the process moves into that phase. Open, honest, unguarded communication is an important goal of mediation. The concern is that this may not be achieved in the med-arb process.

Court-Connected Mediation

The development of another hybrid form of mediation, court-connected mediation, has also led to some concerns (Picard & Saunders, 2002, p. 231; Welsh, 2001). This form is a hybrid because the mediation process takes place within the institutional confines of the court system. Most court-connected mediation programs have been introduced as part of a institutional court reform process designed to reduce the delays, complexity, and costs of litigation. Under the rules of practice governing Ontario's mandatory mediation program (OMMP), for example, litigants engaged in a private, non-family, civil lawsuit are required to try mediation at an early stage in the trial proceedings, in the hope of arriving at a mediated settlement, before being permitted to continue with the litigation process.

The costs of these mediation sessions are divided between the two parties, with the mediator being selected from a court-approved roster. While there is no requirement that all mediators on the roster have legal training, the majority are lawyers. Their legal training and expertise often enable them to provide a "reality check" for the parties about the likely costs and outcomes of further litigation, which, in turn, may provide a significant stimulus to a negotiated settlement. If the dispute is settled with the assistance of a mediator, the case is withdrawn from the court's trial docket. If the parties are unable to resolve their dispute through mediation, the case will then continue through the normal litigation process until it is heard by a judge (or settled out of court).

While the Ontario civil mediation program is mandatory, other court-connected mediation programs offer more flexibility, allowing the parties to select between mediation and adjudication, often after consulting with a court official who may have the authority to refer the parties to mediation (Boulle & Kelly, 1998, pp. 203, 206). Increasingly, judges in provincial family courts and small claims courts are taking on active case management roles, in which they may even discuss settlement options with the parties, in an effort to promote early settlement. If no settlement is reached, the same judge will formally adjudicate the dispute. Additionally, in cases heard before many administrative boards and tribunals, settlement conferences and other mediation-type procedures are being introduced as a more flexible alternative to a formal adjudicative process. Likewise, many professional associations, such as the Canadian Bankers Association, the Canadian Medical Association, and even provincial law societies, are encouraging the use of informal, non-adversarial processes based on mediation, in responding to professional–client disputes over issues such as complaints of professional misconduct (Boulle & Kelly, 1998, pp. 213, 217; McLaren & Sanderson, 1995, pp. 414–417).

The rapid growth of such court-connected and voluntary professional mediation programs is, in part, a response to a public perception that the courts have become too costly and inaccessible to the average litigant. The *Report of the Ontario Courts Inquiry* into court reform in Ontario found that the average legal costs incurred by a successful litigant in a civil trial often total more than half of any damages awarded. In family law, the situation is even worse, since the costs of continuing to litigate are potentially unlimited, while the assets accumulated by the separating couple are always finite (1987, p. 52). This means that for many litigants, the costs of going to court may exceed the amount claimed, especially if the court case involves any contested legal issues that may be appealed by the unsuccessful litigant. Even if the parties are able to reach an out-of-court settlement agreement before going to court, the legal fees incurred by both sides in preparing for trial are often significant, especially since most cases settle only at a relatively late stage in the proceedings, often on the very steps of the courthouse (Stitt, Handy, & Simm, 1996, pp. 459, 464). Court-connected mediation programs are therefore designed to provide the parties with a relatively low-cost alternative to the court system, but one that preserves their rights to sue if the mediation process proves unsuccessful.

Some mediation practitioners and theorists are concerned that the close link between mediation and litigation (within most court-connected mediation programs) may serve to diminish the process differences between these two dispute resolution techniques. Within many of these court-connected programs, mediation is not so much viewed as an alternative to the formal legal system as an integral part of it. In many ways akin to the mediation-arbitration process, court-connected mediation programs can be seen as a two-stage dispute resolution process, with mediation as the first stage and adjudication as the second stage. Because adjudication is a rights-based process, court-connected mediation programs also tend to adopt a rights-based, or evaluative, orientation, in which the third-party mediator encourages the parties to settle, by discussing the likely outcomes if the case goes on to trial. This tendency may be increased if most court-connected mediators have training or experience as practising lawyers. In an ironic twist of fate, the very success of court-connected mediation programs raises questions about the effectiveness of this form of mediation practice to transform the ways in which we approach and understand conflict (Picard & Saunders, 2002; Bush & Folger, 1994; Welsh, 2001).

CHOOSING A DISPUTE RESOLUTION METHOD

Given the wide choice of dispute resolution processes discussed in this chapter, how should one decide which dispute resolution method is most suited for responding to a particular conflict? Who should make this decision? What method or methods would you advise the young female complainant in the workplace harassment dispute we looked at earlier to use for resolving her conflict? What about two spouses involved in a dispute over post-divorce parenting arrangements for their two children?

One of the most important questions is when and how to use mediation effectively. In some cases, mediation is the best option for disputing parties to use. In family or divorce disputes, for example, mediation is frequently ideally suited to the parties. In other cases, it may not be suitable or appropriate, for various reasons. Therefore, the question is not *whether* mediation is a good method for divorce disputes, but rather *when*. A starting point for considering when and how to use mediation effectively is to review both the *potential* benefits of mediation and its limitations. We emphasize that there are potential benefits because, as with any process, the benefits will only be achieved if the process is applied in a competent and skilled manner. Every process is at risk if it is applied incompetently or in some corrupted way, and risks may also need to be considered in deciding what method or methods to use in a given case.

Process Benefits of Mediation

There are many reasons for the growing popularity of mediation over other methods such as arbitration and litigation. Mediation is informal and not bound by the procedural requirements of a trial or an arbitration hearing—and is often quicker and less expensive. A mediation session can be held wherever the disputants and mediator are prepared to meet to facilitate a resolution to the conflict.

The process is also more flexible, because there is no procedural limit on the number of parties who can participate, as there often is in a formal adjudication process (Emond, 1989, p. 8). It can be used in two-party conflicts, such as a commercial dispute between two individuals or a divorce mediation, or in multi-party disputes involving many different stakeholders. Mediation can be used in disputes with high or low legal content. An example of a dispute with low legal content is a volunteer peer mediation program for dealing with schoolyard bullying. The mediation process can be designed with a single mediator or with co-mediators. The parties can bring representatives (such as lawyers or a close family friend) into the mediation process, or they may participate directly, on their own. The parties may meet together or separately with the mediator. In some international mediations, the process is structured in the form of separate meetings between the mediator and representatives from each country, often in different locations, with the parties only coming together at a later stage in the mediation process, if sufficient progress is being made. This example also shows that the mediation process is flexible enough to respond to changing circumstances, even within the context of a single mediation.

The process is also more informal and encourages direct participation by the parties in conflict. Mediation allows the disputants to retain ownership of their conflict, both in terms of defining the nature of the conflict and in controlling the outcome. The litigation process requires the conflict to be translated into a legal dispute, involving technical questions of fact and law, that can only be fully understood and determined by legal professionals. Consequently, disputants tend to lose control over their own disputes. Even the language in which the dispute is described undergoes a translation into technical legal jargon that most non-legal professionals cannot understand. Litigants therefore rely on their lawyers to navigate these unknown waters for them. Christie (1977, pp. 1–12) goes so far as to call lawyers "professional thieves" who rob disputants and communities of the opportunity and the skills to resolve their own conflicts peacefully.

In mediation, the parties define the nature of the dispute and the issues that need to be discussed. In a sense, the mediator acts as a moderator between the disputants, rather than as an umpire or referee. The mediator has no power to make a decision about what information or issues are relevant. What is relevant depends on the needs of the parties—and these needs may differ at different times during the mediation process. Mediators recognize that conflicts are often multidimensional, and therefore allow space for the parties to address the psychological, relational, and emotional dimensions of the conflict, dimensions that would not normally be addressed in litigation or in an arbitration hearing. In many respects, mediation is unique in its capacity to incorporate the human and relational dimensions of a conflict into the dispute resolution process itself (Boulle & Kelly, 1998, p. 41; Bush & Folger, 1994, p. 2).

The mediation process is non-adversarial and facilitates open communication between the disputants, a critical advantage over litigation and arbitration. In an adversarial process, disputants tend to view information as a resource that becomes less valuable the more it is shared. (If I have more information than you, I should be able to extract a higher price from you for the value of my information.) Information is viewed as a commodity to be carefully hoarded, never shared for free. The litigation process tends to reinforce this view of information. Lawyers discourage their clients from communicating directly with the other party, lest they inadvertently make an admission they should not make, or give away information about the strength of their case.

Unlike litigation, a mediator tries to create a non-adversarial environment, so that the parties communicate openly with each other about the issues in dispute. Ultimately, mediation, like negotiation, can be seen as a communication process in which the parties try to reach a mutually acceptable agreement that is capable of satisfying their separate interests. Any negotiation involves a tension between the parties' desire to reach an agreement and the existence of their competing interests. A mediator often "adds value" to the negotiating process by creating a non-adversarial environment that encourages joint decision making and collaborative problem solving. A basic premise of mediation is that the better the quality of the information jointly available to the participants in mediation, the better the outcome of any joint decision-making process. The mediator therefore focuses on trying to improve the quality of the information jointly available to the disputants by probing their interests and looking for creative options that could provide the basis for a mutual agreement. Information is therefore viewed as a common resource that increases in quality—and therefore also in value—the more it is *shared* between the parties.

The emphasis on open communication and collaborative decision making also opens the door to more creative outcomes than are normally possible in arbitration or litigation. The role of a mediator is not to hand down an authoritative decision on the issues in dispute but to assist the parties in crafting their own resolution to the conflict. The parties are responsible for the outcome of the conflict, not the mediator. This means that the mediator has much more flexibility than either a judge or an arbitrator in examining settlement options, and in encouraging the parties to become joint decision makers in resolving their conflict. The range of potential outcomes is not constrained by legal precedents or by the particular facts of the conflict. Nor are the outcomes restricted to a limited number of specific legal remedies, as would be the case in litigation. Instead, the parties are free to craft outcomes that are uniquely tailored to their own particular needs and circumstances. In a workplace harassment mediation, for example, the parties could reach an agreement that responds to the complainant's interest in having the harassing behaviour of her supervisor acknowledged and stopped. But the outcomes could also extend to a broader organizational commitment to create a harassment-free workplace for the future. Mediation is thus a norm-creating process in which the parties themselves agree on the norms or standards used in settling their dispute and governing their future relationship (Boulle & Kelly, 1998, p. 42; Sander & Goldberg, 1994, p. 52).

Also, because it is a consensual process, mediation often avoids many of the costs and risks of losing associated with more adversarial processes. In litigation and arbitration, the decision of the third party is imposed on the disputants, who are then expected to comply with the ruling of the third-party decision maker. Because litigation and arbitration tend to result in winners and losers, the costs for the loser may often be substantial. The unsuccessful disputant may have invested significant resources in the expectation of obtaining a favourable outcome. If the outcome is unfavourable, not only does the disputant have to accept the result, but also the costs (such as legal fees) of pursuing the litigation or arbitration process, which may be very high.

By contrast, since mediation is based on reconciling the parties' interests rather than determining who is right (or who is in the wrong), the risks and costs of "losing" tend to be significantly reduced. Even if mediation does not result in a negotiated settlement of all the issues that are outstanding between the parties, neither party will have "lost"—they cannot be forced to comply with a ruling that they disagree with. The consensual nature of the mediation process, therefore, also has a tendency to lower the risks of non-compliance that are sometimes associated with more coercive decision-making processes like litigation. The limits of the courts' coercive jurisdiction is indicated by the problem of non-compliance with support and custody awards in family law, which sometimes results in child kidnapping, or child abduction, where one parent rejects the ruling of a court over custody and access. Of course, we do not suggest that the consensual nature of the mediation process is likely to prevent any future disagreement between the parties over such contested issues. But the point is that the coercive nature of the litigation process does not prevent the costs of future conflict between the disputing parties in such circumstances. Indeed, it is arguable that the adversarial and coercive nature of the litigation process may sometimes accentuate the risks of future conflict (Irving & Benjamin, 1987, pp. 36–43).

Less obviously, mediation also reduces the costs of winning that are associated with more adversarial decision-making processes. In a legal process, the costs of being vindicated are sometimes quite high. Following an adversarial workplace harassment proceeding, for example, it may be difficult for a complainant to re-establish relationships with other co-workers or supervisors who were not directly involved in the complaint. Likewise, a business that becomes involved in highly publicized litigation with a customer or client may be concerned about the effect on its reputation, even if it wins its lawsuit. In such circumstances, the privacy and confidentiality of mediation offer significant process advantages over litigation. Where future relationships are important to the disputants, mediation can often minimize the collateral damage that may result from engaging in a hostile adversarial process (Sander & Goldberg, 1994, p. 52).

In addition, mediation also educates the parties in collaborative decision making and constructive conflict management. For Bush and Folger (1994, pp. 2, 4–5), the educative function of mediation is its most important characteristic, and what makes it qualitatively distinct from all other dispute resolution processes. Mediation achieves this, they assert, through the experience gained by disputants in responding to conflict in more constructive ways. Instead of seeing the other disputant as an adversary who must be defeated, mediation teaches us the twin values of *empowerment* and *recognition*. As individuals, we are empowered when we learn to solve our problems through our own efforts, rather than relying on outside agencies or the threat of force. Recognition involves seeing our own image reflected in the eyes of the other disputant, and thereby discovering our common humanity. For Bush and Folger (1994, pp. 2, 4–5), it is this discovery of a shared humanity through mediation that is more important than the actual results of any mediation process for the disputants. Even if the mediation does not result in a negotiated settlement, the experience of mediation is likely to equip the parties with improved communication skills, and thus greater capacity to resolve their own conflicts in the future.

Limitations of Interest-Based Processes

Having identified the potential benefits of mediation and other interest-based processes, we also need to be aware that interest-based processes have their limitations and will not be appropriate for every dispute. These limitations may be summarized as follows:

1. Collaborative decision making is only possible where all disputants are willing to participate in the decision-making process. Where that commitment is lacking, interest-based processes such as mediation and negotiation are unlikely to result in an integrative resolution.
2. Not all conflicts can be resolved through collaborative decision-making processes. Value conflicts are notoriously difficult to resolve through negotiation. People's values often go to their core sense of identity, of who they are as individuals or members of a group. Consequently, they may be unwilling to compromise their "values" in an attempt to reach a negotiated or mediated resolution to the conflict. As well, in some cases, there may be public values at stake that a private, interest-based process may not adequately address.
3. In a conflict in which the rights of the parties are uncertain, one or more of the parties may prefer to rely on a rights-based process in order to clarify their legal rights or entitlements.
4. Where there is a large power imbalance between the disputants, interest-based processes may lack sufficient procedural safeguards to ensure that the weaker party is protected from exploitation by the stronger party (Grillo, 1991).
5. Because they rely on consent, interest-based processes may lack sufficient enforcement "teeth" to ensure that the disputants will actually comply with their agreements.
6. Interest-based processes are typically private and informal, and therefore incapable of generating new, public, legal norms or precedents. Where one of the conflict goals of a disputant is to create new legal rights or precedents, generally this cannot be achieved through an interest-based process (Fiss, 1984). This generally arises in cases where the interests of others—or of a class of people or even of the public—may be at stake.

These six critiques or limitations of interest-based dispute resolution processes have generated a lively debate in the conflict resolution literature, over how and by whom the method of dispute resolution should be determined in a given case. Should this decision be left to the disputants themselves? Are they in the best position to decide what is in their own best interests, as much of our conflict resolution theory would suggest? Are the parties able to make that decision? In many cases, the parties will probably need assistance in deciding how best to deal with their conflict or dispute. We will come back to this question in our discussion of mediation and justice in chapter 10, and also in our discussion of the process of convening a mediation in chapter 7. As mediation theorists and practitioners, we generally favour a self-determination approach, which leaves it to the disputants to ultimately decide which dispute resolution process is most suitable for their own conflict. For illustrative articles on this debate, see Chornenki & Hart (1996, pp. 1–17); Sander & Goldberg (1994, pp. 49–64); Fiss (1984); McThenia & Shaffer (1985); Bailey (1989); and Bush (1989).

SCENARIO: Sonata Development II

Reread the Sonata Development case study earlier in this chapter and reconsider your answers to the questions in light of the discussion in the last half of this chapter.

ASSESSING DIFFERENT DISPUTE RESOLUTION METHODS

Chornenki and Hart (1996, pp. 10–11) review various types of dispute resolution methods and then present a detailed analytical framework that may be used for assessing and determining an appropriate dispute resolution method in a given case. Here are some of the questions they pose:

- What are the costs and consequences of the dispute for the parties—both positive and negative? What is their relative effect on the parties?
- To what extent is the parties' tolerance for these consequences greater or lesser than their desire for resolution? How important is it for each party to find a resolution to the dispute and for what reasons?
- What level of trust is there between the parties and what impact will that have on their process interaction?
- To what extent do the parties expect and to what extent are they willing and able to be active participants in the resolution process?

- For what purposes and to what extent do the parties need outside assistance (either impartial or partisan or both)?
- To what extent are the parties ready, willing, and able to take responsibility for determining the outcome of their dispute?
- To what extent does the organization or culture from which the parties come support the disputants' involvement and participation in the resolution process?
- To what extent is it likely or even intended that the resolution process or its outcome may affect others who are not participating directly in the process? To what extent may the process or its outcome affect the interests of a group, organization, community, or the public at large?
- How will the outcome be used? How can it be implemented or enforced?
- To what extent are the parties able and willing to give "recognition" to each other? To what extent are they willing and able to accept the legitimacy of the other's perspective, even though they may not agree with it?
- To what extent do the parties have the facts, expertise, and opinions needed to deal with the issues in dispute? If necessary, how can these be obtained and at whose cost?
- What standards or norms, if any, are appropriate for the dispute? How or by whom are they to be determined? How are they to be applied or enforced?

Likewise, Sander and Goldberg (1994, p. 50) suggest that a party-centred approach that focuses on identifying the parties' objectives is a useful way of approaching the question of process determination. Here is a synopsis of the types of questions they suggest might be asked before deciding or giving advice about the various dispute resolution methods that may be available.

1. What does each disputant want to achieve? What are their conflict goals?
2. Which dispute resolution process appears best suited to achieving these conflict goals?
3. If the disputants appear to be open to settlement, are there any impediments that need to be overcome, and what process is likely to be best suited to overcoming these impediments to settlement?
4. Are there any other factors, such as the public interest or the need to establish a new legal precedent, that may also affect the parties' decision?

One of the biggest challenges for the conflict practitioner is to determine (or help the parties determine) the best method or methods for dealing with their conflict. This cannot be determined scientifically by some formula or a set of rules or guidelines that one can apply in a given situation. In other words, determining the "best" method in a particular case is an art and a science.

SCENARIO: Divorcing Spouses

Paul and Jo-Anne are going through a divorce after a nine-year marriage. They have two children: Riley, seven, and Brianna, five. Paul works as a bureaucrat with the provincial Department of Health, while Jo-Anne has just gone back to work as an elementary school teacher after putting her career on hold until the children reached kindergarten age. Paul has moved into his own apartment, which is outside the school district where Jo-Anne works and where both children attend school. But there are good elementary schools in Paul's new neighbourhood, and he thinks the kids would do well in a new school environment where their mother is not a teacher. Paul is especially concerned about Riley, who has been getting into trouble at school since his mother and father decided to divorce. Jo-Anne, on the other hand, wants to keep the children at their present school, and living with her in the house where they have grown up. She is concerned that Paul will contest custody of the children, which she feels would make it even harder for the children to adjust to their parents' divorce. For his part, Paul feels that Jo-Anne is putting her anger with him at getting involved with another woman over what is best for the children. He is concerned that Jo-Anne blames him for the divorce, and may try to alienate the children from him. So he wants to make sure, if it is legally possible, that Jo-Anne will not be in a position to jeopardize his future relationship with the children.

As a convenor or mediator:

1. What questions would you ask Paul and Jo-Anne?
2. What factors would you suggest they consider in deciding what method or methods to use for trying to resolve their dispute?

SUMMARY

There is a wide spectrum of power-based, rights-based, and interest-based dispute resolution processes. As we have seen, there are primary processes, such as adjudication and mediation, and there are hybrid processes, such as mediation-arbitration ("med-arb"), which has characteristics of both rights-based and interest-based process. Of course, the focus of this book is mediation. In this chapter, we have considered the benefits of mediation and why it may be such an effective and satisfying mechanism for resolving conflicts in many cases. However, we also realize that mediation and interest-based processes generally have various limitations. Therefore, in every case, it is important to consider and assess process options and choose the dispute resolution method, or combination of methods, that will best meet the diverse needs of the people involved in the conflict situation.

FURTHER READING

Boulle, L., & Kelly, K.J. (1998). *Mediation: Principles, process, practice.* Toronto: Butterworths.

Chornenki, G., & Hart, C. (1996). *Bypass court.* Toronto: Butterworths.

Emond, D.P. (1989). Alternative dispute resolution: A conceptual overview. In D.P. Emond (Ed.), *Commercial dispute resolution.* Aurora, ON: Canada Law Book.

McLaren, R.H., & Sanderson, J.P. (1995). *Innovative dispute resolution: The alternative.* Toronto: Carswell.

CHAPTER THREE

Trading Lemons for Something Sweeter: Mediation as Assisted Negotiation

Know how to listen, and you will profit even from those who talk badly.

Plutarch (AD 46–120)

This chapter looks at some of the different behaviours in negotiation and examines how negotiation is approached—through a positional or principled lens, using cooperative or competitive tactics, or claiming or creating value. Although a principled approach seems eminently sensible—and the way that people should *always* deal with issues and conflicts—we will see that there are tensions and challenges in this type of negotiation. We will also consider the dimensions of gender and culture in conflict. Given that mediation is a process of assisted negotiation, most of this chapter focuses on negotiation and its dynamics; mediation is examined only toward the end of the chapter. Let's begin with some definitions.

WHAT IS NEGOTIATION?

Negotiation is when people communicate for the purpose of reaching agreement on some action that one or more of them will take. By this definition, negotiation includes a discussion you may have with a friend about what to watch on TV, what to have for dinner, what movie to go to, or who will do the laundry, wash the dishes, or clean the bathroom. In the workplace, we negotiate deadlines with our bosses, the division of tasks with our colleagues, and the details of a project's scope with our clients. Living and working with other people requires that we be able to negotiate.

Often negotiation occurs without any *apparent* conflict, without any disagreement, argument, or the usual sorts of conflict emotions, communications, and behaviour typically associated with disagreements or fights. Yet, there is always the potential for a negotiation to become a full-blown conflict if we do not meet one another's needs in a satisfactory way. Think of how easily a negotiation over who will do the dinner dishes can escalate into a shouting match, where each party parades a list of past grievances and instances of unfairness to make his or her point. Negotiation, like mediation, requires a good deal of skill and artistry, particularly in situations where the potential for negative conflict is high.

Any negotiation includes several essential elements. First, negotiation is a process of communication, direct or indirect (where a party communicates through an agent or representative), between two or more parties. Second, in negotiating, the parties communicate for the purpose of trying to reach an agreement. Third, the subject matter of their negotiation must be some proposed *joint or reciprocal action* by the parties. Joint action is an activity in which both parties are active participants—for example, going to a movie together. Reciprocal action implies that one person does something for another and the other does something in return. For example, in a workplace negotiation, one person might agree to draft the content of a project proposal if the other takes on the task of developing a budget. Discussions in which one person attempts to convince another about who the greatest hockey player of all time was or what caused the decline and fall of the Roman Empire are not negotiations.

Negotiation is defined by Pruitt and Carnevale (1993, pp. xv, 2) as "a discussion between two or more parties aimed at resolving incompatible goals." Likewise, Fisher and Ury (1991, p. xvii) define negotiation as "back and forth communication designed to reach an agreement when you and the other side have some interests that are shared and others that are opposed." Accordingly, we have developed the following definition. Negotiation is a process of communication between two or more parties seeking to reach agreement on some joint or reciprocal action to be taken by them. Negotiation is used both to enter into contractual relations (such as to sell an asset or begin employment) and to deal with issues or disagreements that may arise within existing relationships. Disagreements arise within contractual relationships (buyer–seller, employer–employee, partners) and other types of relationships, such as family relationships, where divorcing spouses try to divide assets; community relationships, where neighbours might have disagreements over noise or property use; and tort relationships, where accident victims and other involved parties (or their insurance companies) contest damages sustained in a car accident.

HOW DO PEOPLE NEGOTIATE?

Negotiations occur informally every day; often, the parties do not even think about their actions as negotiations because their discussions are so natural. Yet, there are other times when we know, clearly, that we are about to engage in negotiations. When we want to talk to our bosses about getting a raise or when we purchase a car, we prepare more formally for negotiations. We practise our arguments and gather all the information we need to sound informed, organized, and knowledgeable. Between groups, negotiations are always occurring—in corporate transactions, collective bargaining, federal–provincial relations, and international trade discussions, to name a few. It is these more formal instances of negotiation that are the focus of this chapter, although the informal type can also benefit from the same knowledge and principles.

To understand the ways people negotiate, we begin by looking at negotiating or conflict behaviours. Conflict behaviour includes the perceptions, emotions, thoughts, attitudes, communications, and actions of people in conflict. The more we can understand conflict behaviour in a given situation—our own and others'—the better we can respond to and deal with the conflict constructively.

In chapter 1, we considered some aspects of conflict behaviour in the *Hamlet* and the Band Next Door scenarios. We discussed how people respond differently, based on their feelings and thoughts, and that this leads them to communicate and act differently in certain conflict situations. Some people are more assertive or aggressive than others, and some are more passive. Some people may be passive or even timid in some situations, but can become "tigers" in others. Thomas and Kilmann (1974) identified five key types of negotiating behaviour: competing, accommodating, avoiding, compromising, and collaborating.

Competing

A person who is competing is pursuing his or her own demands, wants, or claims at the expense of the other. They engage in adversarial, aggressive actions such as attacking and criticizing the other's position, exaggerating their own position, blaming, threatening, intimidating, or manipulating the other party. They give the impression that their primary motive is to defeat their opponent. Fisher and Ury (1991, pp. 7–9) call this type of behaviour "hard bargaining." Lax and Sebenius (1986, p. 34) refer to this as "claiming tactics," which will be discussed later in the chapter. Additional traits of this behaviour include insulting or demeaning the other party; displaying impatience, irritation or disgust; interrupting, tuning out, or responding in a negative way; being stubborn and rigid; and bluffing or bottom-lining. Competing is considered *win–lose*—the outcome results in one person gaining at the expense of the other.

Accommodating

A person who is accommodating tends, at his or her own expense, to surrender to the other's demands or wants. An accommodator accepts the other's views and tends to go along with proposals that satisfy the other party's interests, without pursuing or asserting his or her own. Fisher and Ury (1991, pp. 7–9) consider this behaviour to be "soft bargaining." It includes making excessive concessions, being overly agreeable and trusting, being too flexible and "nice," as well as giving in. Accommodating is considered *lose–win*, since the accommodator gives up his or her goals and the other party gains everything.

Avoiding

A person who is avoiding tends to suppress or conceal feelings and concerns that may create conflict. Avoiders do not raise or discuss issues, fearful of what others may say or do. Avoiding behaviour prolongs problems to everyone's detriment, and is considered a *lose–lose* proposition because no one's goals can be met through this approach.

Compromising

A person who is compromising seeks an outcome that partly satisfies each party's demands or wants. They "split the difference," looking for fairly quick and easy solutions somewhere between the two positions of the conflicting parties. Compromising is *win–lose-for-all*, because both the compromiser and the other party end up giving a little to get a little.

Collaborating

A person who is collaborating is being assertive, expressing his or her own interests, while, at the same time, seeking to understand and respond constructively to the interests of the other person. By using creative problem solving, they seek an outcome that maximizes their own interests while also satisfying, as much as possible, the other's interests. Fisher and Ury coined the term "principled bargaining" to describe this behaviour. They consider this approach to be assertive. This does not mean being nice and polite, while someone else dominates the discussion. Collaborating requires that all parties be assertive in expressing their concerns and beliefs, especially those that differ with others. In other words, the expression of disagreement, concerns, or beliefs that seem to be in conflict is essential to engage in a collaborative interaction. It is important that parties discuss contentious issues in a mutually respectful and assertive manner—not in an insulting, intimidating, or aggressive manner, which would be typical of a competing or hard-bargaining style. Collaborating is viewed as *win–win*, in that all parties to the negotiation achieve their goals.

SCENARIO: Open House I

Sam and Terry have joint responsibility to organize an "open house" for current and potential corporate sponsors of their non-profit organization. They have been working on the project for six weeks and the event is four weeks away. They meet with Maria, the organization's executive director, for a project status review and the following exchange occurs:

Terry: "By the way, Sam, when are you going to give me the final list of corporate contacts?"

Sam: "What do you mean? That's not my job."

Terry: "We talked about it three weeks ago. You were supposed to get the old list, make corrections and additions, and get the final list back to me a week ago."

Sam: "No way! We never said that."

Terry: "That was the understanding. How could you screw this up? You knew that I was waiting for the list—that I couldn't do the invitations until I got it!"

Sam: "I didn't screw up. You weren't waiting for me. That's a bloody lie and you know it! This is so typical of you! Drop the ball and then come up with some hogwash to blame somebody else."

1. What specific aspects of competitive behaviour can you identify or infer for each (including their thoughts, emotions, perceptions, communications, and actions)?

Sam and Terry's competing behaviour could continue. Sam may recount his version of their earlier meeting, trying to convince Maria that Terry is wrong. He may list all the things he is doing in comparison with Terry, attempting to prove how unreasonable it would be for him to have this additional responsibility. On the other hand, Terry might try to point out inconsistencies in Sam's version of events. Also, she might recall other times when Sam was unreliable or "dropped the ball." Clearly, such actions by Terry and Sam, with the thoughts and emotions that go with them, will take a real toll on their relationship. Regardless of what they do to complete this project, if they continue working together, they will likely clash again.

Let's consider how this scenario would have played out differently if one or both of them had behaved differently. For example, if Sam had been accommodating, it might have gone like this.

> Terry: "By the way, Sam, when are you going to give me the final list of corporate contacts?"
>
> Sam: "What do you mean? I didn't think that was my job."
>
> Terry: "We talked about it three weeks ago. You were supposed to get the old list, make corrections and additions, and get the final list back to me a week ago."
>
> Sam: "Sorry, I don't recall that at all. I don't know where my head was at. Obviously I've messed up. I'll get right on it and get it to you by Wednesday."

What specific aspects of Sam's accommodating behaviour can you identify in this version?

What are some possible consequences of Sam's accommodating response for Sam and his ongoing relationship with Terry? What are some possible consequences for Terry? What if Terry's recollection or account was inaccurate?

An avoiding response would occur if Sam thought that Terry could be wrong but says nothing. He has doubts that it was ever agreed that he would prepare the corporate contact list. However, rather than "cause trouble" between Terry and him, he responds as follows:

> Terry: "By the way, Sam, when are you going to give me the final list of corporate contacts?"
>
> Sam: "I'm working on it. I'll get it to you tomorrow or Wednesday at the latest."

The avoiding response is different from accommodating in that there is no communication of any conflict, disagreement, or misunderstanding between Sam and Terry. What are some possible consequences of Sam's avoiding response for each individual at the meeting, and for their working relationship? How might those differ from the consequences of the accommodating response?

In terms of negotiation, Sam's avoiding response precludes any negotiation of the issue of who prepares the corporate contact list. With the accommodating response, the issue does get discussed—although there is a brief exchange that we could call a negotiation between Sam and Terry. However, with Sam accommodating or giving in to Terry, they quickly come to an agreement that Sam will do the work. In this scenario, it would be compromising or collaborating behaviours that would lead to significant negotiation between them. The next two variations show how compromising and collaborating might occur. Pay particular attention to the differences between them and their consequences.

A compromising approach by Sam might have gone something like this:

> Terry: "By the way, Sam, when are you going to give me the final list of corporate contacts?"
>
> Sam: "What do you mean? I didn't think that was my job."
>
> Terry: "We talked about it three weeks ago. You were supposed to get the old list, make corrections and additions, and get the final list back to me a week ago."
>
> Sam: "That's not how I recall it. There seems to have been a misunderstanding between us. But I don't think there's much point in going back and rehashing it. The important thing now is for us to get the job done."
>
> Terry: "I suppose. What do you suggest?"
>
> Sam: "What do you say we split the list in two—you take A to L, I'll take M to Z, and we get it done by tomorrow?"
>
> Terry: "Yeah, okay. I'll have to adjust my schedule, but I guess I can do it."

What specific aspects of each person's compromising behaviour can you identify in this version? In this approach, there is some negotiation between Sam and Terry, but without much discussion at all of the issues between them, their concerns, or of the various options they may have for resolving their issues. For example, the issues of misunderstanding, miscommunication, or breakdown in their working relationship (whatever may have caused this task to have been missed) are not really addressed or discussed. Whatever one or both of them did, or failed to do, is not addressed. Therefore, we can expect that similar problems may arise in the future. Conflictual perceptions, doubts, irritations, and attitudes that either one may have of the other are not discussed. If such feelings or concerns exist and continue to be unresolved, they may affect their ongoing relationship or even escalate, to cause more trouble in the future.

The disputed issue between Sam and Terry was how the contact list would be done. Without more discussion of that issue, each person's relevant interests and the various options for resolving it, we have no way of knowing whether their agreed outcome (to split the list) is the best one. However, it may be that some other solution would be better all around, given how much work each of them has, as well as the skills, abilities, and resources each may have to draw on—and how this contact list is actually going to be used.

A collaborative approach, which would probably take more time than a compromising approach, might start off like this:

> Terry: "By the way, Sam, when are you going to give me the final list of corporate contacts?"
>
> Sam: "Terry, I don't know what you're referring to. I don't recall us deciding that I would do that. I think there may have been a misunderstanding between us."
>
> Terry: "Yes, so it seems. I'd suggest we talk about that to see how that might have happened. What do you think?"
>
> Sam: "Yeah, I think we should."

What specific aspects of each person's collaborating behaviour can you identify in this version?

If both Sam and Terry take a collaborating approach to this conflict, they will identify and discuss the issues between them more thoroughly. They will recognize and discuss the issue of miscommunication, both accepting some responsibility for contributing to it and for having to interact differently in the future. They will discuss and explore each person's perceptions, assumptions, expectations, and concerns, each of them wanting to understand the other's differing perspective and experience. By discussing and resolving any concerns or issues between them, they recognize that this will help them to have a good working relationship in the future. This approach to the issue of the contact list requires that they discuss and explore each of their relevant interests and then consider various options for meeting the interests of both. Through collaborative negotiations, it is likely that Sam and Terry would devise a solution that would be better for both of them.

While we have presented all five behaviours as distinct, rarely do we adopt a single behaviour when in negotiations. Instead, we likely use all five or some of the five in a single negotiation, depending on what is happening at the moment. In the Open House scenario we have been using, there might be some "tit for tat" employed in the negotiation. If Terry becomes blaming, Sam may respond in kind, adopting a more competitive approach to assert his needs. When Terry again seems accommodating, Sam may open up and become more collaborating. It is important to recognize that each of the five conflict behaviours has advantages and is a more appropriate response in some circumstances than in others.

Conflict Behaviours Exercise

Under what circumstances might each of the five conflict behaviours be appropriate and what would the advantages of such approach be in such circumstances? Here are five conflict situations. Try to decide which behaviour you would use—and why.

- Your seven-year-old child wants to stay up past her bedtime.
- You are confronted by a man who demands your money. He has no weapons. There's no one else nearby.
- You're fairly sure you gave a cashier a $20 bill. She insists it was only $10.
- You and another customer reach for the last copy of a newspaper. It includes an article written by a friend of yours.
- You and a close friend each have a favourite performer. These performers are each giving a concert on the same evening—to which you both have bought two tickets (to treat the other)—and each event is for one night only.

Understanding people's behaviour is but one component of the negotiation process. We need to also look at the types of negotiation that exist—and the tactics that are employed in each.

TYPES OF NEGOTIATION

There are many different ways to approach negotiations. Fisher and Ury (1981) describe two distinct types of negotiation: positional and principled. After describing each approach, a case study illustrates how that approach might proceed.

Positional Negotiation

You have experienced positional negotiation countless times since you were a child. You want someone to do something, and you try to persuade them to agree to your proposal. You want the family car for the weekend or you want your roommate to clean the kitchen. Any time you try to persuade someone to agree to your proposal, you are engaged in positional negotiation. Your position is your desired outcome—what you want, and your demands—what you want the other person to do. This is a distributive approach to negotiation. The English legal system uses this adversarial principle, pitting opposing positions against each other to determine the truth by choosing the "best" or the strongest. Forceful advocacy and debating prowess are major assets in this system.

SCENARIO: Garage Sale

At a garage sale, Mario sees a white pine cabinet that he'd like to buy. The sticker price is $400, but he wants to get it for no more than $150. He initiates the negotiation by saying to the vendor, Nadia, that he would pay $80 for the item. That is Mario's position, which, in his mind, is his "opening position." Nadia frowns, shakes her head, and says that she might accept "a bit less than $400, but not $80—no way." She shows and describes several features of the piece and says how and when it was made. Mario shrugs his shoulders and decides to leave and come back later in the day. When he returns, the item is still there, but now the price tag is $300 (Nadia has changed her position from $400 to $300). Mario says: "I'll take that thing off your hands for $120." Nadia says: "It's worth three times that—I'd accept $260, but that'd be highway robbery." They continue to haggle, eventually agreeing that Mario will buy the cabinet for $215.

Positional negotiation typically involves strategies and tactics that most of us are familiar with. Competing behaviour will likely be present. In our garage sale example, Mario makes a "lowball" offer as his opening position, concealing the extent of his interest in the piece and his desire to have it. Nadia responds, insisting on her original price, and conceals any willingness to take less. What are some other strategies and tactics employed by Mario and Nadia that you can identify in this example?

Principled Negotiation

In their seminal book *Getting to Yes*, first published in 1981, Fisher and Ury develop an approach to negotiation that is fundamentally different from positional negotiation. They call it "principled negotiation," which is based on the assumption that it is possible to integrate the needs of all parties in determining best outcomes. Principled negotiation is sometimes called "interest-based negotiation," "integrative negotiation," or "collaborative negotiation." In this book, we use these terms interchangeably.

According to Fisher and Ury, principled negotiation is based on four essential principles: (1) separate the people from the problem; (2) focus on interests, not positions; (3) generate options for mutual gain; and (4) use objective criteria. We will examine each of these principles by using the scenario Car Repair Blues.

SCENARIO: Car Repair Blues I

Chris is the owner-operator of the ARCO service station. Dale lives in the neighbourhood and occasionally she gets her gas at the ARCO station, but she has never had her car fixed there—until yesterday. Early in the morning, she comes to the station with her six-year-old Buick. She tells Chris that it needs its six-month check, and that it is running a bit "rough" and probably needs a tune-up. She asks Chris if he could do her a real favour and fix it by the end of the day—she needs her car for work and really can't be without it. Chris says he'll have to "move things around" but he will try to accommodate her. He says a tune-up is likely to run her about $100.

When Dale returns later that day, she hits the roof when Chris gives her a bill for $750. He tells her that their "thorough" inspection revealed that her radiator was almost shot. He is saying that they had been able to locate a rebuilt radiator when Dale blurts out:

Dale: "What is this, a licence to print money?"

Chris: "What do you mean? You wanted me to fix your car right away and I did."

Dale: "I don't think so. I never agreed to this—there is no way I can, or will, pay that kind of money."

Chris: "Well, you're not going to get your car until you do."

Chris refuses to release the car until Dale pays the bill. She storms out.

Dale and Chris have a dispute over what Chris is going to do with Dale's car and what she must do to get it back. After Dale leaves the ARCO garage and is walking home, she may cool down enough to decide to negotiate further with Chris, in an attempt to get her car back. At this point, Dale can pursue one of the following two approaches.

Car Repair Blues: The Positional Approach

Dale takes the position that Chris should return her car upon payment by her of $100. She argues that Chris was wrong in charging her $750 for work he did (or claims to have done)—and, as a result, that she is entitled to get her car back upon payment of a fair and reasonable amount for the repair. Dale believes that Chris was unreasonable and inconsiderate (she may even have doubts about his honesty and business ethics). Clearly, she is very upset with what Chris did, and her behaviour toward him is angry and somewhat sarcastic. In pressing her position with Chris, Dale not only presents her arguments as to why she is right, but attacks Chris's position, his actions toward her, and even his character. Whether she really intends it, her words and manner come across to Chris as being insulting and hostile. Dale hopes that Chris will feel bad about what he did and even afraid of what she might do and give in to her demands.

Car Repair Blues: The Principled Approach

Instead of a positional negotiation approach, Dale could pursue principled negotiation. To do that, Dale would prepare for and approach her negotiation with Chris in accordance with the four principles explained in *Getting to Yes* (Fisher & Ury, 1991).

1. SEPARATE THE PEOPLE FROM THE PROBLEM

Although she feels very strongly about what Chris did, Dale accepts that Chris probably sees the situation quite differently. Although she doesn't necessarily agree with it, Dale is willing to respect and listen to his view of the situation. She wants to have a meaningful dialogue to enable her to get a better understanding of Chris's experience and his perspective of the situation. She also hopes that Chris will be able to understand and respect her perspective. She gives considerable thought about how she can express that in a way that Chris will hear and appreciate. Dale realizes that the negative perceptions and feelings she has toward Chris (and that he probably has toward her) will affect their negotiation. She resolves to do what she can to overcome the negative impact they may have.

Early in their discussion, Dale might say something like,

> I recognize that your view of this situation is very different from mine. We just see things differently. I want to give you a chance to talk about how you see the situation. Then I'd like to do the same. I would like each of us to talk about our hopes and concerns and, in particular, what is really important to each of us. If we do this, I think we'll be able to figure out the best way to resolve our differences.

The purpose of this approach, by Dale, is to overcome any tendency for either party to attack the other—to blame, insult, or intimidate—resulting in an escalation of the conflict. By such an approach, the parties can "attack the problem, not each other"—they can be soft on the people and hard on the problem. Successful application of this principle will enable parties in conflict to move on to the heart of the interest-based negotiation process, the next principle.

2. Focus on Interests, Not Positions

"Positions" are what people say they want—their preferred outcomes. In Car Repair Blues, Chris wants Dale to pay him $750 for the repairs to her car. His position is that Dale must pay him $750. He can present various reasons or arguments why she should do that. On the other hand, Dale's position is that Chris should let her have her car for payment of $100, his original estimate for a tune-up. She also has arguments in support of her position—why she thinks her outcome is the right one.

What are Chris's and Dale's "interests"? What do they really need in this situation? What is really motivating them? What is most important to each of them in relation to the settlement of this issue? Why do they really want what they say they want? According to the theory of interest-based negotiation, discovering each party's interests—the underlying needs or motivation beneath their positions—is the key to unlocking their dispute. It is these "key interests" that we want to discuss. In any conflict, each party usually has a number of interests; some are apparent and some are hidden. In many cases, it may not be at all clear to a party what his or her most important interests are in relation to the disputed issue. How then do we discover the parties' key interests?

In pursuing the interest-based approach, Dale's goal would be for both Chris and her to receive all relevant information, including a full understanding of the true perceptions, needs, expectations, beliefs, and concerns of each of them. To do that she would give Chris a full opportunity to express his perspective, and she would ask appropriate questions to clarify and probe for his concerns, assumptions, and expectations. Then she would invite Chris to give her the opportunity to fully express her perspective and to answer any questions he might have about her concerns.

Dale's objective would be that the understanding and insights they gain from this interest-based discussion would enable them to go on and reach an agreement that fully satisfies both of their interests. The terms of this *win–win* agreement would come from application of the next principle.

3. Generate Options for Mutual Gain

A vitally important component of the collaborative or interest-based negotiation process—one often neglected or avoided—is generating options. After the parties have gained a full understanding of each other's perspectives and key interests, they need to move on to a discussion and negotiation of what actions and agreements will satisfy their interests. As Fisher and Ury explain (1991, pp. 57–59), at this point, most people are inclined to move directly to a discussion of their proposed solution. One or both parties will want to discuss what they believe is the *best* way to resolve their disagreement, to solve their problem. However, such an approach invariably will lead to a narrow, positional negotiation. Instead, Fisher and Ury want negotiators to brainstorm options—to seek all possible actions or agreements that could be part of the agreed outcome—and to do that without judgment or evaluation. Only through such a process can the parties find a broad, integrative, and creative negotiation.

For example, in Car Repair Blues, when the negotiation process has reached the point where Dale and Chris have a good understanding of each other and their key interests, they could move directly to a narrow negotiation of how much money Dale should pay Chris. Imagine, for example, that Chris has acknowledged that he should not have done the work without Dale's authorization and has already apologized for doing so. Likewise, Dale has acknowledged that Chris was well intentioned and did work that was of some value to Dale, although she would not have had the work done at that point. Based on that, they might quite quickly come to an agreement that Dale pay some compromise amount, say $500, to settle their dispute.

However, if instead they use a brainstorming process to think of all possible options before they try to make their deal, they might come up with the following list of options:

- Dale will agree to say to others (friends, associates, etc.) that Chris is a competent, honest, and reliable mechanic, and that she will never make disparaging comments about his work or customer service;
- Dale will make an initial payment of $100 and will pay the balance of the agreed invoice amount in monthly installments of, say, $50 per month;
- Chris will give Dale a credit note (or even two or three) for routine six-month servicing of her car (including the labour for routine checks, oil changes, and the like);
- Dale will agree to give Chris at least two days' notice before bringing her car in for service, and Chris will agree to take Dale's car any time on two days' notice.

We can see that, by taking the time and effort to generate options, Dale and Chris would clearly end up with a better agreement, one that is fully responsive to their needs. They would have achieved a truly win–win outcome.

4. Use Objective Criteria

In every dispute, there are issues and questions that must be answered to resolve the dispute. In Car Repair Blues, we might frame the issues as follows:

- What action should Chris have taken in the circumstances?
- What action by Chris would have been in Dale's best interests?
- What would have been a fair and reasonable price for such work by Chris?

The answers to each of these questions would be based on relevant objective criteria—standard practices, recommendations, and values of the local car repair industry. In most cases, the difficulty would be to identify and obtain such information that both parties find acceptable. In this case, Chris would be able to answer each of these questions based on his experience, and Dale could probably judge for herself how fair and reliable Chris's information was.

We can appreciate the benefits of principled negotiation, provided that both parties actually engage in that process. However, people in conflict may not always be inclined to pursue principled negotiation or will have substantial difficulty with it. Indeed, this is why people often need the assistance of a mediator—to enable them to engage in a process of principled negotiation, when, without such assistance, they would be inclined to revert to positional negotiation. Let's examine the tension between principled and positional negotiating.

THE NEGOTIATOR'S DILEMMA

As students of mediation and conflict resolution, we must be aware of the fundamental reality of every negotiation, which Lax and Sebenius, of the Harvard Program on Negotiation, call the "Negotiator's Dilemma." In their book *The Manager as Negotiator*, Lax and Sebenius explain how all negotiation involves different degrees of cooperation and competition. As they point out, most of us tend to see human interaction as *either* competitive *or* cooperative (1986, pp. 30–33). Yet, our behaviour is rarely consistent throughout a negotiation, as we alluded to in the section on negotiating behaviours. The central hypothesis of Lax and Sebenius (1986, p. 30) is that in every negotiation both cooperation and competition exist between the parties:

> A deeper analysis shows that the competitive and cooperative elements are inextricably entwined. In practice, they cannot be separated. This bonding is fundamentally important to the analysis, structuring and conduct of negotiation. There is a central, inescapable tension between cooperative moves to create value jointly and competitive moves to gain individual advantage. This tension affects virtually all tactical and strategic choice. Analysts must come to grips with it; negotiators must manage it. Neither denial nor discomfort will make it disappear.

Lax and Sebenius go on to say that there is an "essential tension in negotiation ... between cooperative moves to create value and competitive moves to claim it" (1986, p. 33). This tension leads to two principles that give rise to the negotiator's dilemma. The two principles are "claiming tactics"—tactics for claiming value, which will impede or stifle action to create value; and action to create value, which will tend to leave that party vulnerable to the other party's claiming tactics (1986, p. 34).

Using the language of Lax and Sebenius (1986, p. 34), parties' claiming tactics may include overstating the value of their holdings (goods, services); understating or distorting their preferences or needs; minimizing or discounting the value of the other party's holdings; minimizing, downplaying, or worsening the other party's alternative; bargaining hard—start high, concede slowly; exaggerating the value of concessions; bluffing; attacking the other with threats, intimidation, criticism, and ridicule; and deceiving. On the other hand, action to create value may include sharing information; revealing preferences and needs; revealing your honest opinions, doubts, and uncertainties; discussing your past contributions to the problem (admitting your mistakes); looking for a better way, rather than "your" way; and being cooperative by looking for ways that you can help each other.

Figure 3.1 depicts the negotiator's dilemma. If both negotiators cooperate to create value, which they share fairly, they both achieve a "good" result from their negotiation. However, each party faces a risk: if party B is primarily competing and claiming (especially if done in a secretive, deceptive way), party A faces the prospect of a "bad" result. In that case, party B gets a "great" result at party A's expense. To avoid that risk, there is a tendency for both parties to compete and pursue mainly claiming tactics, which puts them in the lower right quadrant of figure 3.1, with a result that is mediocre for both.

Even though, in theory, parties may use principled negotiation to create value and achieve an overall better result, a party may believe, for various reasons, that he will be better off by pursuing a positional, adversarial approach. That party may believe that his maximum benefit will be achieved by making demands, applying pressure, opposing or resisting the other, and generally trying to achieve a good outcome at the expense of the other party. One of the reasons for not pursuing a principled approach could be because one party has better options for resolving the situation, what Fisher and Ury refer to as the party's "best alternative to a negotiated agreement"—BATNA (1991, p. 97). Each party's BATNA is the best, most advantageous course of action they may pursue if no agreement is reached with the other party. In a conflict situation, a claimant's BATNA may be to proceed with litigation—going to court.

FIGURE 3.1 The Negotiator's Dilemma

		Party B's choice	
		CREATE	CLAIM
Party A's choice	CREATE	Good (B) Good (A)	Great (B) Bad (A)
	CLAIM	Bad (B) Great (A)	Mediocre (B) Mediocre (A)

For example, a plaintiff claiming compensation from an insurance company for personal injuries in a car accident may believe that, if the case goes to court, she will likely achieve a net monetary recovery (after all legal costs) of between $20,000 and $50,000. If the plaintiff has accurately assessed the merits, costs, and risks of her court action, she may well be advised to accept a negotiated settlement that would provide her with a net recovery of between $20,000 and $50,000. If the most she can achieve by negotiating is less than $20,000, she should proceed with her best alternative action, her BATNA, and take the case to court. On the other side of the table, it is because the plaintiff could recover $50,000 or more by going to court that the insurance company would be willing to negotiate a settlement of between $20,000 and $50,000 (plus legal costs). That is why we say that a party's BATNA is a substantial component of their negotiating power.

In addition to BATNAs, various other factors (discussed at greater length in later chapters) may contribute to a belief that principled negotiation is not the best option. These include perceptions, emotions, the history of the relationship, and contextual or systemic influences. A major challenge typically experienced by people in conflict is strong, adversarial emotions. These are a barrier to collaborative interaction. How mediators deal with strong emotions and help people to overcome such barriers is the subject of chapter 9. As we discuss in chapters 5 and 6, responses to conflict are not always rational, and people do not necessarily choose options that make logical sense. Intuition and knowledge may also inform the approach taken by individuals.

The negotiator's dilemma is but one reason why people tend not to engage in collaborative negotiation. It also explains why there must be substantial trust between parties before they are willing and able to engage in collaborative interaction. In many conflicts, people need a mediator to help them use cooperative tactics. By managing the tension inherent in the negotiator's dilemma, a mediator can assist parties who are generally motivated to engage in principled negotiation to do so. (The mediator's strategies, tools, and skills are discussed in chapters 6 through 9.) There are often clear benefits to proceeding with a principled negotiation, not the least of which is the potential to create value, which was briefly alluded to earlier. Let's look more closely at this potential.

Creating Value

The positional negotiation approach generally leads to an outcome where a "fixed pie" is divided between the parties. It is known as a "distributive" process, in which things of value are divided between the parties.

As Lax and Sebenius say (1986, pp. 32–33), positional negotiation is primarily a process of "value claiming." In our earlier garage sale example, before their negotiation, Nadia has the pine cabinet, and Mario has some money. Mario wants the cabinet, and the main question is how much he will pay for it. They negotiate, haggling over the price, and the outcome is that Mario gets the cabinet for $215. Nadia may believe it is really worth between $275 and $300, in which case she would believe that Mario has claimed value from her of between $60 and $85. That is, she has lost that amount, which, in turn, Mario has won. For this reason, we refer to positional negotiation as a *win–lose* process.

On the other hand, principled negotiation is said to be a *win–win* process—a process in which value is created, the "pie is expanded." As Lax and Sebenius say (1986, p. 32): "We create value by finding joint gains for all negotiating parties." To do that, negotiators need to be "inventive and cooperative" (p. 30). We will use the following example of kids with fruit, as did Lax and Sebenius, to illustrate the basic principles behind creating value.

SCENARIO: Fruit Exchange

Sally has six apples. Her friend Marc has three pears, and her other friend Judy has four bananas. Sally prefers pears to apples and doesn't like bananas at all. Marc likes bananas the most and pears second, and eats an apple only once in a while. Judy likes all fruit about the same.

If Sally wants one of Marc's pears, it seems unlikely that Marc will agree to trade a pear for one or more of Sally's apples. It seems unlikely that Sally could persuade Marc to trade one of his pears for one or more of her apples. In other words, there is a problem in the negotiation that Sally would like to have with Marc. It appears unlikely that either Sally or Marc will be able to achieve their negotiation goals of trading some of their fruit for other fruit they prefer.

However, if Sally discovers that Marc prefers bananas to pears, and that she could trade with Judy for a banana, then all of a sudden more possibilities open up for each of them to achieve their negotiation goals. This illustrates the theory of mutual gains. Sally trades with Judy, an apple for a banana. Since Judy already has four bananas, she probably prefers getting an apple for one of her bananas. Then Sally trades her banana (which she doesn't like at all) to Marc for a pear. Marc is happy that he now has a banana instead of his pear, and Sally is happy that she now has a pear for one of her apples. Everybody is better off. The two negotiated exchanges have created value for all three of them.

The Fruit Exchange negotiations have created value, produced "mutual gains" for everyone—Sally, Marc, and Judy. Yet this could happen only if Sally knows that Marc likes bananas and that Judy likes apples. As the example illustrates, value creation occurs only if parties have good information about one another's preferences or interests. In fact, if you work through the Fruit Exchange example some more, you will find that if each person has complete information about everyone's interests or preferences, they can make more trades to achieve even more joint gains and all be even better off.

This scenario illustrates a basic principle of value creation, that cooperation among negotiating parties—and open and honest communication of their interests by all parties—will lead to mutual gains.

Another classic example is two sisters fighting over an orange. Gail has the orange, but Glenda is yelling at her: "Give it back, it's mine. I put it in the fridge and you knew it." They argue on and on until finally their mother comes in, cuts it in half, and gives each of them half of the orange. While the mother thinks the solution was fair, both children go away angry and dissatisfied, without saying anything more. However, if their mother had intervened as mediator, rather than as arbiter, and asked each of them why they wanted the orange, the result could have been very different. In fact, Gail wanted the rind from the orange peel to make an orange cake, whereas Glenda wanted the pulp to make juice. Therefore, by discovering their interests—what they really needed with this orange—they could have come up with a solution that fully satisfied both of their interests. They could have realized greater value from the orange.

As the orange example illustrates, "creating" value really means finding ways to realize the potential value inherent in a conflict situation. By discovering the parties' compatible or common interests, the way to expand the pie and "create" value becomes apparent.

To the extent that principled negotiation creates value, it results in *better outcomes* than positional negotiation. That is what "creating value" means: the overall value or well-being realized by *both* parties is greater than it would otherwise be.

In comparing principled and positional negotiation, we also need to consider the costs or negative effects of positional negotiation. As a "value-claiming" process, the parties use positional negotiation to divide their existing value or assets. Through negotiation, they simply redistribute what they both already have. It is what game theorists refer to as a *zero-sum game*—one person gains what the other gives up. However, the competitive positional bargaining process has costs and negative effects that may result in it being a "value-negating" process. Whereas value claiming divides a fixed pie and value creating expands the pie, value negating *shrinks* the pie. The costs and negative effects of positional negotiation may reduce the overall value available to the parties (Bishop 1995).

Comparing Principled and Positional Negotiation

Time and Expense

Fisher and Ury (1991, pp. 5–6) say that "arguing over positions is inefficient ... by starting with an extreme position, by stubbornly holding to it, by deceiving the other party as to your true views, and by making small concessions only as necessary to keep the negotiation going." It may take longer to reach agreement, or may be not reached at all, when an agreement is possible. In many cases, the disagreement will proceed to litigation, with the positional or adversarial negotiation continuing until a settlement agreement is reached before the case goes to court. In such cases, the legal and other costs may be very high.

Quality of Outcome

In competing over their positions, and by not exploring and even concealing their true interests, the parties likely will be misinformed about each other's interests and goals. As a result, their final agreement will probably not include the provisions it could have to meet all the interests of the parties.

Effect on Relationship

As discussed earlier in this chapter, positional bargaining often involves competing or adversarial behaviour, including insults, personal attacks, intimidation, threats, or deception. As a win–lose process, the object may be to "beat" or "defeat" the opposing party or adversary. Regardless of a party's intent, if the other perceives that the party is trying to cheat or "beat" them, then the long-term relationship costs may outweigh any gain from the bargain.

In learning and working with the principles of principled negotiation, we find that there are many reasons to prefer it to positional negotiation. As Fisher and Ury (1991) articulate, principled negotiation will be most successful and will achieve maximum value for the parties when they are able to

- interact with civility, mutual respect, and trust;
- communicate relevant information openly and honestly;
- reveal their genuine interests—their hopes, concerns, preferences, and values;
- seek to understand the other's needs, concerns, and different views and perspective;
- generate a variety of options from which they can fashion a resolution agreement that substantially satisfies the interests of both parties; and
- develop and apply objective criteria in reaching a final agreement that is mutually beneficial, fair, and sustainable.

Having viewed negotiation from both the positional and the principled approach, let's examine another perspective on the process. Gender and culture will provide distinct lenses through which people can and will view conflict, and approach its resolution. Both gender and culture influence negotiations. Let's look at the ways in which this can occur.

GENDER AND NEGOTIATION

Do women negotiate differently from men? Some people argue that this is indeed the case. Others say no, that there is little difference. Those who say no claim that gender is a poor predictor of conflict management style. They say that stereotypes about men and women's negotiation styles persist because of the influence of social situations, not gender alone. Because this is such an important topic for mediators, as well as those who participate in mediation, it is worthwhile to discuss some of the differing viewpoints. Let's begin with those who believe men and women do negotiate differently.

Kolb (1993) outlines a number of gender differences that may affect conflict situations. First, women have a relational view of others, while men tend to have a more individualist view. This means that women are oriented toward nurturance and affiliation, and that they expect emotional connection, empathy, shared experiences, and responsibility in their interactions. Second, unlike men who stereotypically focus on their own individual achievements and tasks, women have an "embedded" sense of their own interactions with others, which blurs the boundaries between themselves and others and between their tasks and the broader environment. This makes separating people from conflict issues enormously difficult. Third, women exercise "control" or influence through mutual empowerment. They take a collaborative approach, rather than a competitive one. Fourth, women engage in problem solving with dialogue, rather than debate. Fifth, women's preference for harmony can dominate other interests, and they will do what they can to smooth over differences, even if it means making sacrifices. Sixth, women speak with qualifiers, to show flexibility and an opportunity for discussion, while men use confident, self-enhancing terms. Finally, because women are expected to act passively and attend to the socio-emotional needs of those present, when they act competitively, it invites criticism. Other aspects of the female approach are said to include a greater expression and experience of feelings—and a reliance on intuition and creativity.

It is wrong to say that all women use the relational, empathic, cooperative approach to negotiating and that all men use the individualist, argumentative, competitive approach. Many people do not fit into these stereotypes. That being said, the majority of people's understanding of the traditional female approach is that of cooperation and harmony, and that the "male" approach is competitive and individualistic. In their critique of mediation, feminists say these patterns of behaviour result in women being more vulnerable in conflict situations with men—and less able to assert and satisfy their own interests.

Most people agree that gender influences the way we process information. In turn, this influences communication in and about conflict. For example, female talk has been found to be inclined toward intimacy and inclusion, while men's talk is more competitive (Gourley 1994). Gilligan (1982) also revealed a tendency for females to value relationships, cooperation, and an ethic of care (from early childhood), whereas males tended to value rules, rights, competition, and an ethic of justice. Other studies show that women often talk in depth and at length about the context of the dispute, whereas men use more rational, linear, and legalistic language to talk about their disputes. Women also talk more about fairness, in a way that includes both their material and relational interests in the dispute (Birkhoff, 2000). Finally, they talk of feeling more disempowered and disadvantaged when dealing with their conflicts with men.

Some people, however, argue that other variables besides gender account for differences in conflict behaviour. Based on a review of several empirical studies on gender and conflict, Keashly (1994) says that processes and outcomes of conflict depend on the nature of the relations between conflicting parties. These relations include intimacy and status, the specific context in which the conflict occurs, and the beliefs the parties hold about conflict. Others argue that power based on social roles is a better predictor of the feelings, behaviour, and outcomes of managerial negotiations than is gender. Participants in high power roles, regardless of gender, were found to be more competitive before the negotiation, to expect greater cooperation from their opponents, and they felt more powerful, more in control, and more satisfied with decisions reached than those in low power roles (Watson, 1994).

The issue of gender difference also gives rise to the question whether men and women mediate differently. Current research has yet to find evidence that male and female mediators differ in perceived effectiveness. It does show, however, that in unresolved disputes, men are thought to be somewhat more competent than female mediators, but that greater satisfaction with the process is expressed when mediators are female. Others support the idea that male and female mediators do interpret conflicting parties' communication differently. For example, Weingarten and Douvan (1985) found that male and female mediators differ in their interpretation of the mediation process. Female mediators envision the mediator role as collaborative, and the process as one of transformation and change affecting all the parties, including the mediators. Male mediators evaluate their personal performance and envision their role as one of acting *on* the other parties. Men use "neutral" and "objective" to define themselves, whereas women see themselves as a "bridge" between the parties. Maxwell (1992, p. 353) suggests that gender may be a surrogate variable for style, and that some elements of style have a latent impact on the effectiveness of mediation. He says that "male and female mediators are equally effective at reaching an agreement; however, female mediators are significantly more effective at mediating binding settlements. The greatest gender difference occurs in emotionally charged disputes."

So why is it important to know that there may be differences in male and female negotiating behaviour and in the way male and female mediators perceive and respond in mediation? We believe that mediators should know that gender, along with other contextual variables such as race and class, can influence parties' negotiating behaviour, as well as their own behaviour as mediators. Thus, they need to be alert to instances of disempowerment as a result of gender or culture, and to personal bias in favour of more familiar negotiating styles. They also need to be sure that their personal upbringing does not create a tendency to prematurely "put the lid on things" when emotions escalate, and relations look like they will be jeopardized. Just as important, we are reminded that generalizations about gender and negotiation are not straightforward and that they often lead to the reinforcement of stereotypes. The following suggestions for a different way of negotiating that does not place either men or women in the role of victim come from Barbara Grey (1994, pp. 27–30):

- change the focus of negotiation from trading on differences to learning to appreciate and honour the differences with the aim of deepening the connection between the parties;
- embrace rather than curtail emotion;
- reconceptualize power from that of "power over" to that of "shared power"; and
- incorporate an ethic of care into the negotiations so that behaving in a supportive way is valued and rewarded.

Gender and Negotiation Exercise

Based on your experiences and views, consider the following questions. We are not asking you to stereotype men and women as behaving in the way you see them. What we hope is that you will become more aware of your perceptions of their behaviours.

1. Do men and women negotiate differently? In what ways?
2. Are men and women treated differently in negotiations? In what ways and in what situations?
3. Do men and women mediate differently? How?

CULTURE AND NEGOTIATION

In many situations, cultural differences can have a significant effect on conflict communications and interactions. Indeed, different cultural groups may perceive and define conflict differently and may have very different interpretations of what constitutes a conflict and its implications (Faure, 1995; LeBaron, 1997). The dominant North American model of mediation rests on culture-bound values and assumptions, such as

- communication should be direct and forthright with confrontation seen as a sign of strength in negotiation;
- there should be full and open disclosure of relevant facts and feelings;

- individual rights and interests are paramount;
- the process should be short-term, task-focused, and future-oriented (Kruk, 1997, p. 12).

LeBaron (1997, p. 324) summarized three frameworks for understanding cultural differences in experiencing and interacting in conflict situations.

Individualist Versus Collectivist Societies

Individualist cultures found in mainstream North America emphasize individual interests, valuing individual freedoms, achievement, and self-reliance. Collectivist cultures emphasize family or community, valuing harmony, face saving, and group relations. Collectivists take the obligations of being in community seriously, while individualists tend to take relationships more casually.

Traditional Versus Modern Societies

Modern societies tend to be rational and task-oriented, focusing on professional and technical achievement. Traditional societies tend to be more holistic, intuitive, and relation-oriented, focusing on community well-being and group achievement.

High-Context Versus Low-Context Societies

Low-context cultures generally refer to groups characterized by individualism, overt communication, and heterogeneity. Communication in low-context cultures tends to focus more on the written/spoken word and takes the message at face value. High-context culture features collective identity-focus, covert communication and homogeneity. In high-context cultures, communication tends to be associative. This means that more attention is paid to the context of the communication, including behaviour and environment, the relationship between the messenger and the receiver, the messenger's family history, and so on.

In a low-context culture, communication will be explicit, following the credo: "Say what you mean and mean what you say." In a high-context culture, communication will be more implicit, requiring communicators to "read [and listen] between the lines."

People in every culture have both collectivist and individualist tendencies, but those from Western cultures tend to be more individualist, while those from Eastern and Southern cultures are more collectivist. It has been argued that women are more collectivist in orientation than men.

Cultural differences, then, have some implications for intercultural negotiations and interactions. LeBaron (1997, p. 326) has conveniently summarized many of the factors we need to consider in such situations:

- the importance of harmony and face saving;
- the potential adverse consequences of being blunt or confrontational;
- the significance of past events, practices, and traditions—and of the future;
- an inclusive definition of parties (for example, extended family);
- the importance of healing and the role of time in that process;
- the importance of symbolism and ritual;
- the need (or not) to respond to visual and non-verbal cues;
- the significance of elders, "gatekeepers," and "wise ones" in dealing with conflict;
- the place of advice giving;
- the honour attached to indirectness and subtlety in various cultural contexts;
- the varying needs for formality or informality; and
- the meaning or significance of requiring a written contract.

Categorizing how people from differing cultures behave is problematic and often abets racist attitudes, due to stereotyping. However, we need to recognize that patterns of communication and behaviour do differ among cultures because of different values about social relations. Yet, it is important to reiterate that not everyone with the same cultural background behaves in the same way or shares the same values; therefore, to label and stereotype people is not constructive. Rather than assuming similarity or difference, we just need to be curious and open-minded about others.

The culturally competent mediator begins by reflecting on his or her own culture and culturally based values, assumptions, and biases. He or she also recognizes the importance of understanding the worldviews of culturally diverse parties. When negotiating or mediating in cross-cultural situations, the process is elicitive and consultative, rather than prescriptive. In other words, it is custom-designed from the bottom up, rather than being imposed from the top down. Being an effective negotiator or mediator in cultural conflict necessitates that, in addition to being elicitive, we be genuine, creative, sensitive, collaborative, and humble (LeBaron, 2003, p. 284).

SCENARIO: The Band Next Door II

Imagine that the parties from the Band Next Door (see chapter 1) have agreed to try mediation to resolve their dispute. Farah arrives at the mediation with her parents, grandparents, three siblings, and one close friend. Rocky, the other party, arrives alone. What do you imagine is happening? Why do you think that is? Which of your own values led you to expect Farah to come alone?

Using this same case, imagine that Rocky is very quiet during the mediation and does not disagree with anything Farah says. What do you think is happening? Why? Which of your own values led you to expect Rocky to be assertive and confrontational?

What do these two scenes tell you about your own biases and potential limitations as a mediator?

To understand conflict and conflict interaction, "culture" needs to be defined broadly. That means that all possible cultural groups and categories should be considered, including racial or ethnic groups, religions, families, gender and age groups, geographic communities, professional and trade organizations, and any other identifiable group.

It is important to recognize how culture may cause or contribute to conflict and how culture influences how people behave and respond in conflict situations. Being aware of how differences in culture and gender may influence a negotiation process will help us to develop our cultural competence, whether we are negotiators or mediators.

A MEDIATOR'S INTERVENTION IN THE NEGOTIATION PROCESS

Now we move to the process of mediation, discussing how a mediator can help parties who want to—but are unable to—collaborate in a principled way.

Mediation can be simply described as "assisted negotiation"—a mediator intervenes to help disputing parties negotiate a resolution of the issues between them. There are many different approaches to mediation and, in each approach, a mediator will have different goals. In this book, we mainly discuss interest-based mediation and use a model called Insight Mediation (see chapters 4 and 6). In this approach to mediation, one of the mediator's primary goals is to help the parties *collaborate*. In many conflict situations, without a mediator's intervention, parties will compete, avoid, accommodate, or compromise, leading to an inferior outcome for one or both of the parties. In situations where the parties would otherwise be inclined to be adversarial and engage in positional bargaining, the mediator will strive to empower and enable them to collaborate. To apply some of the concepts of this chapter, the mediator will seek to move the parties from a distributive approach to an integrative one; and from a competitive, positional orientation to a cooperative, principled one.

There are many challenges and difficulties to achieving genuine collaboration between parties in conflict. In some cases, there are significant risks. Effective mediator intervention requires an understanding of these challenges, difficulties, and risks—and the need for mediator strategies, tools, and skills to meet them. We examine these in more detail in chapters 5 to 9.

This chapter concludes by examining a key element of a mediator's intervention strategy that is particularly important—discovering and working with interests.

Discovering and Working with Interests

Let's return to the Car Repair Blues scenario and consider a discussion that a mediator might have with Dale to explore her interests. First however, reread the scenario and answer the following questions:

1. What are Dale's perceptions of and assumptions about Chris?
2. What are Dale's expectations of Chris?
3. What are Dale's key needs relating to this dispute?
4. What are Dale's primary concerns?
5. What is most important to her?

Interests are the needs, desires, fears, and motivations that drive negotiations. Interests motivate us to take certain positions in a given situation. A position is a means, not an end—and it is often one way to satisfy our interests. Interests reveal *why* we want what we say we want. In the dispute the sisters had over the orange, each of them had the same position: "I want the orange"; but their reasons for wanting it were different. Their *interests* were compatible: one sister's interest was in making a cake and needing the rind from the orange; the other wanted to make juice and, hence, needed the pulp.

Interests tend to emerge from some of our basic human needs. They are composed of what is influencing a person's thinking and behaviour in that situation. You may recall from chapter 1 the useful acronym for considering and identifying different types of interests: CHEAP BFVs—concerns, hopes, expectations, assumptions, priorities, beliefs, fears, and values (Picard, 2002, p. 106).

In exploring interests, a mediator may not need to identify all possible interests a person may have, but will need to discover the person's *key interests*—what is primarily motivating this person in this situation in relation to a particular conflict issue. To do this, the mediator will need to consider several important interest-based principles:

1. Different people in the "same" situation will have different motivators.
2. People are rarely fully aware of their own key interests, let alone the other's. (Each party's key interests are often hidden.)
3. A person's key interests will be associated with the emotions he or she presents. To discover a party's key interests, we need to explore these emotions.
4. Key interests emerge as a function of the relationship that the parties have.

In other words, we cannot determine a person's important interests by just knowing the "facts" of the situation or by simply asking the parties what their interests are. Indeed, in some cases, extensive questioning and probing by a mediator will not necessarily reveal a person's key interests. Sometimes, adversarial emotions and behaviours will conceal a person's key interests; however, such emotions and behaviours usually are indicators, which, if pursued, will provide useful information.

In order to bring interests to the surface, a mediator's exploratory discussion with Dale in the Car Repair Blues scenario might go something like this:

SCENARIO: Car Repair Blues II

Mediator: Dale, you're very upset about what happened last week between you and Chris.

Dale: Yes, very much.

Mediator: What happened to make you feel that way?

Dale: He just went ahead. He didn't ask me. He figured he could just do whatever he wanted to, and charge whatever he wanted. I'm sure he figured, "What does she know?" Then I get stuck with a bill five times more than it should be.

Mediator: Sounds like you're angry because you think that Chris overcharged you.

Dale: That's part of it, I guess.

Mediator: What do you mean, "part of it"?

Dale: For all I know, what he charged might be more or less right for what he did. But, who's to say that the work had to be done?

Mediator: So, you're wondering if Chris did work on your car that was unnecessary.

Dale: Yes, definitely.

Mediator: What do you believe Chris's thinking was in doing this work?

Dale: He probably figured my car needed a new radiator. He probably thought the car would be in better shape if the work was done. I mean, I don't think he's a fraud artist or anything.

Mediator: Dale, are you saying that Chris was wrong in his assessment that this work needed to be done?

Dale: I don't know. As I see it, he thought the car would be better off with the work he did and maybe it would be. But that doesn't mean it had to be done. And it doesn't mean that I wanted the work done on my car at that point in time.

Mediator: So, if Chris had spoken to you after he assessed the situation, but before he did any work, what might you have said?

Dale: I would have asked him if the car could still run without that work being done. If the answer was "yes"—which I think it would have been—I would have told him not to do the work.

Mediator: It was very important that Chris provide you with his findings and his assessment and let you decide what would get done.

Dale: Yes, exactly.

Let's reconsider the questions we posed at the beginning of this section:

1. What are Dale's perceptions of and assumptions about Chris?
2. What are Dale's expectations of Chris?
3. What are Dale's key needs relating to this dispute?
4. What are her primary concerns?
5. What is most important to her?

Are your answers different now from before? As we discovered through the mediator's intervention, Dale's key interest was having the ability to make her own decisions, to be in control. She was not upset because she believed that Chris cheated or took advantage of her, nor because she thought he overcharged her. She was upset because he chose a course of action for her, one that she probably would not have chosen for herself.

Discovering and working with interests is an essential element of the interest-based mediation process. Parties discover their key interests *only* through direct, interactive communication with each other. (In this case, this was facilitated by a mediator.) In most conflict cases, it will be useful to discover both *common* interests and different *individual* interests.

Figure 3.2 illustrates how, in many cases, people in conflict see only their differences, and discuss the situation in terms of their conflicting positions. However, in most cases, by exploring beneath the surface, it is possible to discover and formulate individual as well as common interests that may be used as a basis for collaboration.

In the Car Repair Blues scenario, Dale and Chris have interests in common—they both want Dale to be a "satisfied customer" and to have a reliable, well-running car. It is important that such common interests

FIGURE 3.2 Exploring Positions and Interests

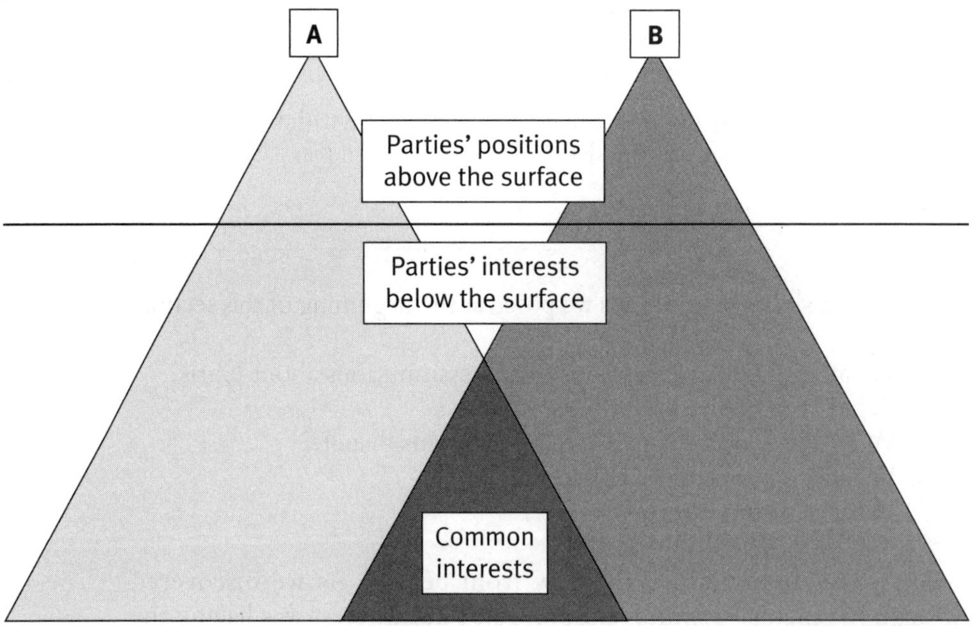

are named—and used—in a way that the important individual interests of each party are not ignored or minimized. A mediator's objective is to find *both* the common interests *and* the key individual interests that will help to unlock the conflict. In most cases, such key interests are an integral component of the parties' relationship and will be revealed only *in the context* of that relationship. In later chapters, we discuss what a mediator and the parties may do with the interests they discover and how they can work with those interests within a truly integrative mediation process.

SUMMARY

In this chapter, we have considered a variety of approaches that people adopt in negotiations. Negotiating is a complex undertaking that is influenced by parties' behaviours, interactions, and tactics. Gender and culture also affect perceptions of conflict and ways of responding to it. We examined both the traditional approach to negotiation, known as positional, and the approach that Fisher and Ury developed, known as principled, which has become the basis for modern interest-based negotiation processes, including mediation. Value-creating tactics were contrasted to value-claiming, competitive strategies, and the latter were found wanting. However, despite the many advantages of principled negotiation over positional negotiation, we also found a number of challenges and obstacles to principled negotiation. This is where the intervention of a skilled mediator can be enormously helpful in moving parties toward a collaborative approach in negotiations. Indeed, as we will explore further in subsequent chapters, in order to work through these challenges and overcome these obstacles, we need the full range of capabilities in both the art and science of mediation. The next chapter delves deeper into the theory of mediation and the many approaches that mediators take in their work. Value creating and promoting cooperative negotiation is key to all these approaches.

FURTHER READING

Fisher, R., & Ury, W. (1991). *Getting to yes* (2nd ed.). New York: Penguin Books.

Lax, D., & Sebenius, J.K. (1986). *The manager as negotiator*. New York: Free Press.

LeBaron, M. (2003). *Bridging cultural conflicts: A new approach for a changing world.* San Francisco: Jossey-Bass.

Raifa, H. (1982). *The art and science of mediation*. Cambridge, MA: Harvard University Press.

Ury, W. (1993). *Getting past no: Negotiating your way from confrontation to cooperation*. New York: Bantam Books.

CHAPTER FOUR

Weaving the Stories: Approaches to Mediation

Postmodernism refuses to privilege any one perspective, and recognizes only difference, never inequality, only fragments, never conflict.

Elizabeth Wilson

This chapter contrasts various approaches to the practice of mediation. The approaches we examine are transformative, evaluative and facilitative, social norm, restorative justice, and narrative. We also introduce you to an approach we use, called "Insight Mediation," outlining the underlying assumptions, roles, and strategies embedded in this model.

Current Conflict Exercise

Recall a conflict from a newspaper report, a television show, or a personal situation. Based on the information you have, consider whether a power, rights, or interests approach was used? Then, while reading about the different mediation approaches discussed in this chapter, reflect on which approach you would choose to resolve this dispute, and why. How is your choice connected to your values and beliefs about conflict and its resolution?

CONTRASTING MEDIATION APPROACHES

The consensus among professionals in this discipline is that there is no one theory of mediation process and outcome, and that mediators lack explanatory models to enable them to be more strategic intervenors (Folger

& Jones, 1994; Kressel & Pruitt, 1989). Instead, professional mediation practices have been based on various social, psychological, economic, and political theories about conflict. Ways of mediating vary from having clearly defined pragmatic problem-solving process goals to broadly articulated social and individual transformation process goals. It is our belief that mediation has the potential to achieve both of these ideals.

The preceding chapters have shown how an individual's background, culture, values, and world views shape his or her beliefs about the nature of conflict and how it should be dealt with. In turn, this grounds the person's approach to mediation in ideological views of what should happen and why. These organizing frameworks are acquired through interactions with others (Folger & Bush, 1994, p. 7).

Two ideologies currently dominate the mediation discourse: individualistic and relational (Folger & Bush, 1994). An individualist view sees the world as made up of separate beings of equal worth but different needs, whose human nature it is to seek satisfaction of their needs and desires. Later in this chapter, we will look at the problem-solving and evaluative approaches to mediation, both of which are based on this view. The relational ideology views the world as made up of persons with diverse needs and desires who possess a common form of consciousness that connects them to each other. We will also examine the transformative, facilitative, narrative, and insight models of mediation, which are based on this ideology.

THE "STORIES" OF MEDIATION

Bush and Folger (1994) help us understand how different perspectives on mediation create different accounts about its effect. They articulate these different accounts in the form of four mediation "stories," pointing out that each story gives a valid account of the different practices of mediators working today—and that none is the "true story" of mediation. The presence of these "stories" underscores the point made earlier that there are many ways to practise mediation and that the process can have different goals and outcomes.

Satisfaction Story

The satisfaction story depicts mediation as a powerful tool to satisfy human needs and reduce the economic and emotional costs of formal dispute settlement processes. Mediation is presented as more flexible, informal, consensual, and collaborative than processes restricted by legal rules and precedents. It is said to facilitate integrative problem solving rather than adversarial distributive bargaining, thus producing *win–win* outcomes and a greater overall satisfaction for disputing parties, regardless of the context of the dispute. We know that child custody mediation has produced better results for children and parents; small claims mediation has resulted in more satisfaction and higher rates of compliance; and environmental and public policy mediation has avoided years of delay and enormous expense, while producing creative and highly praised resolutions.

Fisher and Ury (1981), in their seminal book *Getting to Yes*, did much to advance this story when they set out guidelines for principled negotiation, as was discussed in chapter 3. Court-mandated mediation services and the proliferation of dispute resolution offices in both private and public spheres are products of this story.

Social Justice Story

The social justice story views mediation as a vehicle for organizing people and communities to obtain fairer treatment and build stronger community ties and structures. In this story, mediation is seen to reduce dependency on existing social and legal agencies by encouraging self-help and the establishment of grassroots structures. Relatively powerless individuals are turned into communities of interest, enabling them to pursue common needs, participate in civic life, and achieve a sense of greater social justice. Community-based and neighbourhood conflict resolution programs—such as the San Francisco Community Boards program, St. Stephen's House in Toronto, and Winnipeg Mediation Services—help residents negotiate with landlords and city agencies to pursue both individual and common interests.

Transformation Story

The transformation story holds the promise of fostering a positive change in individual disputants and society at large. Mediation, it is said, facilitates self-determination for parties because they define the problem and decide what to do about it themselves. Mediation helps parties mobilize the necessary resources to achieve their goals. Empowerment is achieved when participants gain a greater sense of self-respect, self-reliance, and self-confidence. Empowerment is not the only important dimension in the transformation story; the other is recognition. Recognition requires that the mediator help parties strengthen their capacity for understanding, acknowledgment, and concern for others. This approach to mediation views conflict as an opportunity for individuals to develop both strength of self and concern for others. This is distinct from the problem-solving approach, which conceives of conflict as an obstruction to self-interest.

Transformation is thought to be important not only in disputes of human relationships but also in organizational and systemic relations. For example, if a transformative model of mediation were to be used in consumer disputes, Bush and Folger believe it has the potential to transform the character of commercial transactions and institutions. If used in divorce disputes, it has the potential to transform the character of male–female interaction generally. The transformation story is receiving a lot of attention today. Specialized training is being conducted across North America to teach mediators how to practise in the transformative way. (See the Institute for the Study of Conflict Transformation Web site at the end of this chapter.)

Oppression Story

The oppression story tells a different tale, because it sees only a covert means of social control and oppression in mediation. It acknowledges that while mediation may have started out with good intentions, it has become an instrument for increasing the power of the strong to take advantage of the weak. Lack of procedural rules is thought to magnify already existing power imbalances, and the private nature of mediation weakens class and public interest matters, thus neutralizing social justice gains achieved through civil rights and women's and consumers' movements. Perhaps the best example of the oppressive nature of mediation comes from those who question whether mediation is appropriate for women because their bargaining power is not equal to that of men. According to the oppression story, the very nature of mediation is oppressive for women because it reinforces patriarchal values. The report published by the Status of Women Canada (1998), *Family Mediation in Canada: Implications for Women's Equality*, is one source to find out about these concerns and about recommendations for the use of mediation in family law cases. (See Goundry, Peters, Currie, & Equity Matters Consulting, 1998.)

MEDIATION DICHOTOMIES

In some early conceptions of mediation, approaches were often classified as being either *content* or *process* interventions. Content interventions focused on resolving the substantive issues in dispute; process interventions focused on communication and the relationship between the parties. Presenting mediation approaches as divergent opposites has become common practice for setting out differences found in a mediator's role. To cite some examples: Kolb (1983) characterized mediators' opposing functions with the metaphors "dealmaker" and "orchestrator," while Silbey and Merry (1986) used the concepts of "bargaining" and "therapeutic." Kenneth Kressel and his colleagues (1994) identified the settlement-oriented style and the problem-solving style. Kressel and Pruitt (1989) developed the task-oriented and socioeconomic mediation approaches, and, while working with Kolb (1994), Kressel determined that mediation espouses either a transformative vision or a pragmatic problem-solving vision. Bush and Folger (1994) contrasted styles of mediation as transformative or problem solving; Schwerin (1995) dichotomized mediators as being either facilitator or activist; and Riskin (1996) described mediators as facilitative or evaluative. Other dualistic classification systems include broad versus narrow, open versus closed, positional versus interest-based, settlement versus process-oriented, and individualist versus relational. In most cases, these typologies depict a mediator as being either a passive facilitator or an active shaper of solutions. This style of contrasting the functions of a mediator into bipolar views still dominates much of the existing literature on mediation. To illustrate this dichotomous positioning, we have clustered the different labels and characteristics of the pragmatic problem-solving and the social and individual transformation goals in figure 4.1. More recent thinking suggests that mediation approaches are likely more integrated than the figure depicts.

FIGURE 4.1 Continuum of Mediation Goals

Pragmatic problem-solving process goals	⟷	Social & individual transformation process goals
• content		• process
• positional		• interest-based
• dealmaker		• orchestrator
• bargaining		• therapeutic
• problem solving		• transformative
• facilitator		• activist
• evaluative		• facilitative
• passive		• active
• individualist		• relational

CONTRASTING TYPES OF MEDIATORS

One way to characterize mediators is by the type of relationship they have with the parties. The three types identified by Moore (1996)—social network, independent, and authoritative—are useful in helping to make the point that mediators can have very different roles, depending on the context and culture in which they work.

Social Network Mediator

A social network mediator is generally part of an ongoing and shared social network—a friend, a family member, a colleague, a neighbour, a religious leader, or an elder. All parties involved in the conflict know this person. Often, the mediator has an ongoing relationship with one or all of the parties and the issues in dispute. A social network mediator does not have to be a neutral party; however, it is expected that he or she will be fair and trustworthy.

Here is an example from our experience, working in a community-based and multicultural conflict resolution program in Ottawa. While explaining how mediation works to a group of Somali newcomers, we learned that mediation is a common form of dispute resolution in their home country; however, there it looks much different. The mediator is not a distant or neutral party; he or she is a member of the community and is well known and respected by all parties. This person is considered to be very knowledgeable, influential, and powerful. They would not trust someone they did not know. The concept of confidentiality is also very different. Not only is the mediation session not considered a private matter, everyone who is connected to the parties attends, from siblings to distant relatives. On many occasions, the mediation room is not large enough to hold all the participants. It was only when we understood the role of a mediator in the Somali tradition that we understood why our North American model, which rests on the principles of impartiality and confidentiality, would not meet their expectations. (See the discussion of neutrality and impartiality in chapter 2.) Their experience of a mediator was that of a social network type.

Independent Mediator

Independent mediators are perceived to have no vested interest in the dispute and are not connected to the parties in any way. They are considered impartial, objective, and outside the dispute. They have no decision-making power and no authority to oversee or enforce any agreements that might be reached through the mediation process. People seek this kind of mediator because they want procedural help that will enable them to negotiate a resolution to the dispute. Independent mediators are often considered specialists or professionals in dispute resolution. The independent mediator is by far the type most Canadians are familiar with as they increasingly turn to them for help in a wide range of marital, civil, and legal disputes.

Most First Nations communities in North America, however, practise a form of dispute resolution that closely resembles that practised by the social network mediator.

Authoritative Mediator

In some ways, authoritative mediators are a combination of social network mediators and independent mediators. They are often known to the parties and have some form of relationship with them. Generally, they are in a more powerful position relative to the parties. For example, an authoritative mediator may be the parties' supervisor or employer. Even though the mediator has authority over the parties, he or she does not make decisions for them. To be sure, authoritative mediators have a vested interest in the mediation's outcome; however, they believe that a solution reached by the parties has more value than an imposed one. While authoritative mediators may have given up their decision-making prerogative, they often exercise some influence over the outcome. In this case, they are not as concerned with getting their interests met as they are with ensuring fairness, efficiency, economy, and minimization of conflict.

The clearest examples of vested-interest mediators are found in the international arena. We are reminded here of the work done by President Carter in the Camp David talks between President Sadat and Prime Minister Begin to construct a general framework for achieving peace between Egypt and Israel. Carter used his influence (material aid and diplomatic relations) to entice both leaders to accept his invitation to join him at the presidential retreat in Maryland. As the story is told, President Carter made it "very clear that the Americans would be playing a very active role in the negotiations, feeling free to set forth their own proposals on the main issues at any time" (Schellenberg, 1996, p. 74). (For more information about the former president's initiatives, the Carter Center's Web site is listed at the end of this book.)

The authoritative (vested-interest) mediator is becoming more commonplace in large organizations, both government and private industry. Managers and senior executive officers undertake training in mediation so they can intervene early, before disputes turn into formal grievances.

Type of Mediator Exercise

Think again about the Current Conflict exercise at the beginning of the chapter. Which type of mediator (social network, independent, authoritative) would be most appropriate for intervening as a third party? Why?

APPROACHES TO MEDIATION

To examine various approaches to mediation, we begin with a discussion of the interest-based approach, followed by the transformative approach set out by Bush and Folger (1994) and Riskin's (1996) comparison of the facilitative and evaluative approaches. Next, we look at the social norm approach put forth by Ellen Waldman (1996). We then go on to describe the restorative justice approach and victim–offender mediation, followed by a new approach to mediation, the narrative model, popularized by Winslade and Monk (2000). Finally, we present the model of mediation that we use—insight mediation.

Interest-Based Approach

This approach became prominent in the 1980s, based on the elements of principled negotiation set out by Fisher and Ury (1981). Principled negotiation focuses on interests or needs. This distinguishes it from positional negotiation, which focuses on positions or demands. One of the first, and perhaps the most widely known, applications of interest-based approach was set out by Christopher Moore (2003) in *The Mediation Process: Practical Strategies for Resolving Conflict*. His book has been updated and revised twice since 1986, when it was first published.

In the interest-based approach, the mediator's primary goal is to help the parties reach an agreement that settles the issues between them in a way that satisfies the interests of all parties. The theory of principled negotiation (Fisher and Ury, 1991) and collaboration (Lax and Sebenius, 1986) says that, under the "right" conditions, collaborative interaction will produce a better outcome than competitive interaction.

The interest-based approach underpins the problem-solving model, which views conflict as a problem to be solved. Folger and Bush characterize the problem-solving approach as one where "conflict is seen as the manifestation of a problem in need of satisfaction" (1994, p. 9). Mediators who take a problem-solving approach see their role, first and foremost, as helping parties to reach an agreement to their dispute. This approach is based on the individualist view, central to mainstream North American culture, where conflict is seen to emerge as a result of unmet and incompatible needs between individuals. Disputes are viewed as problems to be solved, and solutions are sought that maximize joint satisfaction. Mediators use their knowledge and skills to direct parties toward the "best" outcome. The interest-based, problem-solving approach is commonly found in court-connected mediation models, where the goal of mediation is case management, expediency, and efficiency—and success is measured by reaching an agreement. Mediators try to help parties succeed by directing them toward outcomes in which both parties have some of their needs met. Bush and Folger (1994) believe that this is the dominant practice of mediation today. They also believe, as do we, that too much of what passes for mediation today is more of a hybrid settlement process than a transformative process.

From an individualist perspective, collaborative interaction is considered the best way to achieve a good agreement—one that Fisher and Ury (1981) say is wise, efficient, and enduring. Collaborative interaction is a means to an end—an objective that, if achieved, can help parties reach their goal: a good agreement. According to Folger and Bush (1994), some mediators engage in influencing and controlling behaviours because they see conflict as problems—obstacles to satisfying incompatible sets of needs—and see their primary mandate as finding the best solutions to those problems. Mediator influence is justified implicitly by the individualist value of providing maximum satisfaction.

The description of mediation presented by Moore (1996) supports the idea that the mediator's goal is to reach agreement and settle disputed issues. Moore uses a 12-stage mediation model. The first 5 are preliminary stages, part of the convening process, which we detail in chapter 7. One of the mediator's objectives in these early stages would be, in the language of Fisher and Ury, to "separate the people from the problem." The final 7 stages of Moore's model follow closely the elements of Fisher and Ury's principled negotiation method: begin the mediation session, define issues and set an agenda, uncover hidden interests of the parties, generate options for settlement, assess options for settlement, complete final bargaining, and achieve formal settlement (Moore, 1996, pp. 32–33).

Most North Americans understand and apply the interest-based, problem-solving mediation approach, lauding its value in helping to solve problems, negotiate agreements, and settle disputes in a way that satisfies the parties' interests—as well as being more humane than adversarial forms of dispute resolution such as litigation. While some mediators may expressly reject evaluative or directive mediation models in favour of facilitative models based on the principle of self-determination, the fact that their goal is for parties to reach agreement distinguishes them as problem-solving mediators, regardless of how facilitative their approach may be.

Contemporary mediation advocates have begun to connect mediation to a relational ideology. While this ideology also sees people as having individual needs and desires, it emphasizes that people have an inherent form of consciousness that connects them to each other, thus allowing them to realize that others have similar needs and desires. It is this human capacity for relating to others that, it is argued, should underpin a mediator's actions, not settling a dispute. The application of relational ideology becomes evident when we examine the transformative, narrative, and insight models of mediation.

Transformative Approach

Bush and Folger (1994) set out the basic tenets of the transformative approach. Mediators following this approach aim to foster, in the disputing parties, a greater sense of their own efficacy and a greater openness to others, based on a relational ideology. In other words, these mediators try to "improve the parties themselves from what they were before" (Bush & Folger, 1994, p. 84). In this approach, disputes are viewed as opportunities for moral growth and transformation, rather than as problems to be solved.

Two dimensions make up the transformative approach: empowerment and recognition. These are thought to be the most important outcomes mediation can achieve. Empowerment involves strengthening individuals' abilities to reflect, make choices, and act in a conflict situation. Recognition means becoming more sympathetic and responsive to the other party's situation. Empowerment is realized when people understand more clearly their goals and their importance. It also means that parties increase their skills in conflict resolution, gain a new awareness of their resources, and are able to make deliberate, conscious decisions about what they want to do. Bush and Folger tell us that, when this happens, parties experience a greater sense of self-worth, security, self-determination, and autonomy (1994, p. 87). Empowerment is independent of any particular outcome of the mediation. Solving problems for parties is *not* transformative mediation. Parties achieve recognition in mediation when they are able to feel less threatened and more open to the other party. As well, they become sympathetic and have the desire to be responsive to the other party in their thoughts, words, and actions.

Bush and Folger (1994, p. 94) provide a concrete definition of successful mediation:

> A mediation is successful (1) if the parties have been made aware of the opportunities presented during the mediation for both empowerment and recognition; (2) if the parties have been helped to clarify goals, options, and resources, and then to make informed, deliberate and free choices regarding how to proceed at every decision point; and (3) if the parties have been helped to give recognition wherever it was their decision to do so.

These authors make it very clear that, for them, the transformation approach does not mean institutional restructuring; it refers only to changes in the consciousness of the individual. Among mediation practitioners, the transformative model has become a popular and valued approach.

To highlight the differences between an interest-based, problem-solving approach and the transformative model, let's return to the Band Next Door scenario from chapter 1. Recall that the issue was a band practising their music, resulting in complaints of noise from the neighbour. A problem-solving approach would likely seek a compromise to the situation, negotiating days and times for the band to practise that did not interfere with the neighbour's need to relax from the stresses of work. A transformative approach would focus on ensuring that the parties reduce their hostility toward each other by coming to understand the motives behind each person's behaviour, and to relate to one another as individuals. For example, Chris could discover the importance that playing in a band has for the neighbour's self-worth, while the neighbour could discover the importance of performing well at work for a similar reason. It would also focus on allowing the parties to decide for themselves how the issue could be solved, keeping in mind their individual and relational needs. Outcomes reached through the transformative approach may not be all that different from the problem-solving approach;

however, it is the process of getting there that is so different and that distinguishes itself from approaches that emphasize problem solving and settlement. In order to differentiate their approach from other approaches, transformative mediators have articulated specific hallmarks of their practice (Folger & Bush, 1996, pp. 263–278).

Facilitative and Evaluative Approaches

Riskin (1996) created a grid to show what mediation is and what mediators do. (See figure 4.2, opposite.) His typology of mediation styles was designed to help disputants determine what type of mediation they wished to undertake and what type of mediator to use. An important finding from Riskin's work is that mediation approaches are not tightly contained and that there is fluidity within the concepts. That being said, Riskin says that mediators usually have a predominant orientation that is based on a combination of factors: his or her personality, experiences, education, and training (1996, p. 113). He also suggests that mediators may depart from their orientation to respond to the dynamics of the conflict situation. This was also identified in Picard's (2000) research, when mediators stated they change their style based on the nature of the dispute and the parties.

Riskin's grids emphasize two contrasting features: how mediators view their role (evaluative or facilitative) and how mediators define the problem (narrow or broad). Each of the various quadrants reflect a mediator's belief about the nature and scope of mediation and his or her assumption about the parties' expectations.

An evaluative mediator assumes that the participants want and need the mediator to provide direction. An evaluative-narrow approach would involve a mediator assessing the strengths and weaknesses of parties' claims, predicting court outcomes, developing and proposing a settlement, and pushing parties to settle, based on his or her assessment of their claims. An evaluative-broad perspective also seeks settlement, but uses a process that emphasizes interests over positions, with the mediator attempting to accommodate these interests with proposed solutions.

A facilitative mediator assumes that the parties are capable of developing better solutions than those a mediator might create. A broad, facilitative approach helps the parties to understand and define the problems they wish to address, including a discussion of underlying interests, rather than positions. The parties are encouraged to generate and assess proposals designed to accommodate those interests. A facilitative-narrow mediator helps parties become "realistic" about their situation, doing

FIGURE 4.2 Mediator Techniques

The following grid shows the principal techniques associated with each mediator orientation, arranged vertically with the most evaluative at the top and the most facilitative at the bottom. The horizontal axis shows the scope of problems to be addressed, from the narrowest issues to the broadest interests.

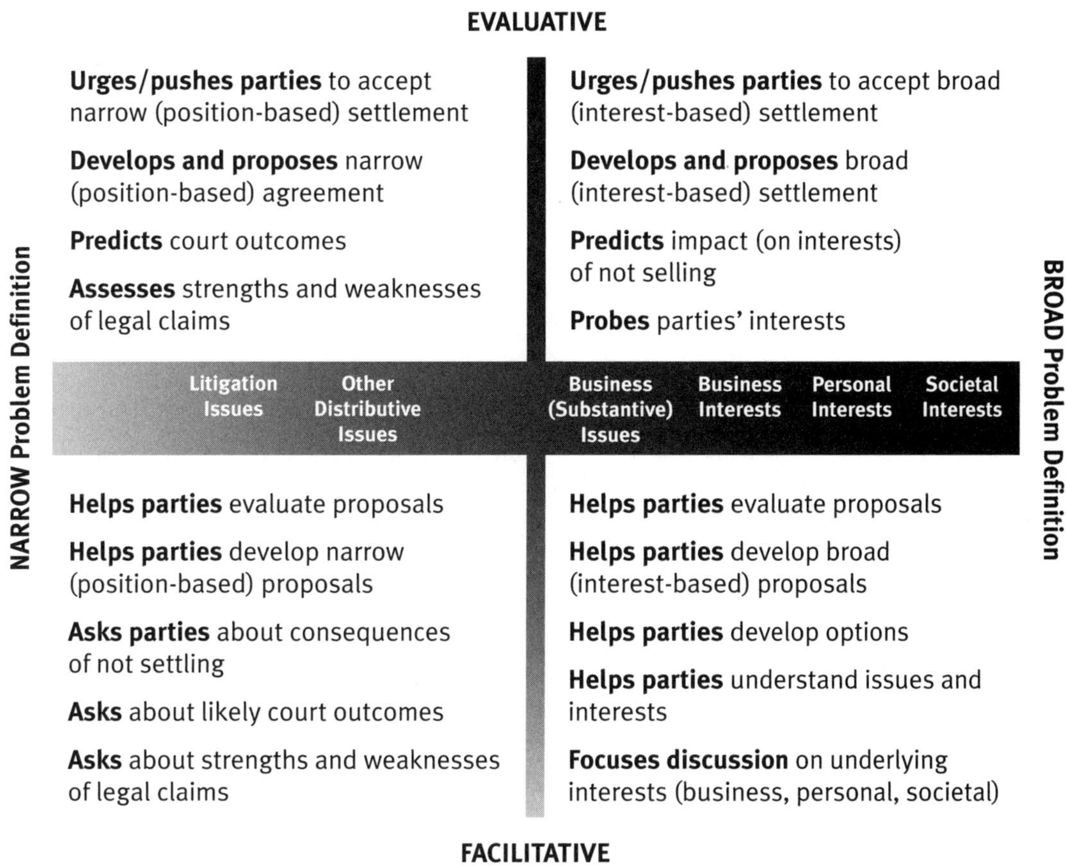

Source: Riskin (1996). Reprinted with permission.

some reality testing based on their knowledge and experience, but does not use his or her own assessments, predictions, or proposals to construct agreements. At the broad end of the facilitative continuum, mediators see their role as helping parties communicate and understand one another. At the broad end of the evaluative continuum, the mediator, by virtue of his or her expertise, assumes that the parties want guidance in reaching an appropriate settlement.

To understand the problem-definition continuum—from narrow to broad—you need to know that there is often more than one interest underlying the issues in conflict. A narrow interpretation would look at how to settle the matter quickly and in a way that most closely approximates the results if the matter went to court. However, in addition to settlement, a broad approach would also consider the personal, business, or community interests that might underlie the dispute. The following scenario and discussion should help you understand this continuum.

SCENARIO: An Unhappy Customer

A customer has launched a civil suit against a garage owner in a small, rural town in Nova Scotia. The customer has been going to this garage because of its convenience to his place of work, and because, for the last 15 years, the work has been quite acceptable. Now, however, he thinks that the work done on his car by a new employee was lacking, causing him to be in a car accident soon after picking the car up from the garage. The work done on the car involved installing four new winter tires. After leaving the shop, the car owner set out for Halifax, a distance of about 200 kilometres. About one hour into the trip, the car started to swerve out of control and, with great effort, the driver was able to bring the car to a stop, but not before running through a guard rail and into a deep culvert. The front and side of the car were badly damaged, and the owner received minor injuries. The police determined that the accident had likely been caused by the wheel nuts not having been put on tightly, causing the wheel to come loose.

The angry car owner has sued the garage owner for the cost of repairs to the car in the amount of $4,500. He would like to avoid an insurance claim because it would increase his premiums. The car owner also wants an apology from the garage owner for causing him trauma and inconvenience, and some reassurance that the owner will be more attentive in the future to whom he hires to work in the shop.

The garage owner prides himself on good workmanship and stands by his solid reputation in the community. He does not accept that his shop should bear the full cost of the repairs, because the body of the car was not in good condition in the first place. He is concerned as much about losing his good reputation as about the lawsuit itself.

To illustrate Riskin's continuum (and putting aside insurance issues), assume that the customer and the garage owner have agreed to mediation.

If a narrow form of mediation were undertaken to resolve this dispute, the goal would be to settle the financial issues as expediently as possible, based on the legal merits of each side's case. In other words, the goal would be to determine how much, if any, the garage owner would pay the customer. This decision would be based on the legal rights of the parties and negotiations would take place in the "shadow of the law."

If the negotiations were to broaden, to include business and personal interests, we might imagine the discussions drawing out the garage owner's interest in continuing to do business with this customer and to maintain his good reputation, so as to not lose other customers. As for the customer, we would likely discover that he does not want to use another garage, given that it is far from his work, making it very inconvenient. In addition to the fact that the work on the car has been satisfactory for the past 15 years, he still has confidence in the competency of the owner, but not with some of the staff. This mediation would include discussions about individual business and personal interests and link them to the issues of financial settlement. As the scope broadens, community interests could also become a part of the discussions. In a small town, a long-standing, family-owned business may disappear if required to pay a substantive settlement. Jobs are at stake if the garage closes, and neighbours could become polarized as they are forced to take sides on the issue. As the discussion broadens, the issue of payment becomes linked to personal, business, and community interests, thus becoming less central to the overall negotiations.

Figure 4.3 highlights differences among the transformative, problem-solving, evaluative, and facilitative approaches to mediation.

Social Norm Approach

Waldman noticed that mediation practices have distinguishing features, based on the amount of attention the mediator pays to social norms. Her examination of differences in mediator approaches led her to conclude that most mediation models share common assumptions, follow similar procedural routes, and employ many of the same techniques. Some mediators assume that the goal of mediation is to make parties aware of the social norms applicable to their dispute. Others assume that their role is to persuade parties to accommodate the structure imposed by these norms. Still others see their role as creators of relevant norms.

This focus on social norms led Waldman to identify three mediation types: norm-generating, norm-educating, and norm-advocating. Waldman is quick to point out that "all three models represent a valid

FIGURE 4.3 Contrasting Transformative, Problem-Solving, Evaluative, and Facilitative Approaches to Mediation

	Problem-solving approach	Transformative approach
Bush & Folger 1994	• individualist world view • disputes viewed as problems to be solved • focused on reaching agreement • mediators decide what case is about, drop issues that cannot be handled, with a directive style • conflict emerges from unmet and incompatible needs • solutions maximize joint satisfaction	• relational world view • disputes viewed as opportunity for moral growth and transformation • greater sense of own efficacy • two dimensions: 1. empowerment—strengthening of self to reflect, make choices, and act 2. recognition—ability to move beyond self to relate to others
	Evaluative approach	**Facilitative approach**
Riskin 1996	• urges parties to accept settlement • develops and proposes settlement • predicts court outcomes and impact of not settling • assesses strengths and weaknesses of legal claims and probes parties' interests	• helps parties evaluate proposals • helps parties develop proposals • asks about likely court outcomes • helps parties understand issues and interests • asks about strengths and weaknesses of legal claims and focuses discussion on underlying interests

mediative approach and that appropriate model selection depends upon the dispute context and the parties' expectations" (1996, p. 727). Let's look briefly at each of these three types of approaches.

Norm-Generating

Norm-generating mediators seek, above all else, to give maximum autonomy to the parties, leaving them total discretion over the content and outcome of the dispute. Agreements are formed from their personal norms and values, with relatively little attention being given to related legal or social norms. Parties are encouraged to share all relevant facts and consider all possible options, to "think outside the box" and not be restricted by predetermined legal or social norms. A norm-generating mediator is commonly found in community-based mediation and neighbourhood justice programs. Disputes are often between people who live in the same community and are over issues such as barking dogs, loud noise, roaming pets, or conflicting land use. In these cases, mediation can become a forum for improving communication patterns, preserving relationships, and finding ways to deal with future conflicts. It is not very often that there is much at stake for society at large in terms of the outcomes of these issues. This means that most disputes are private, between individuals, and can be resolved according to the parties' own standards.

Norm-Educating

Norm-educating mediators believe that knowledge of social norms is a precondition to autonomous decision making, and that mediators are responsible for ensuring that the parties are educated about legal entitlements and relevant financial, technical, or psychological data before they make any decisions. Once they have this information, it is up to the parties to decide whether, and how, to incorporate it into an agreement. Some mediators believe it is within their role to provide the requisite information; others believe that to do so would jeopardize their impartiality, and they encourage parties to seek outside experts for the information. The norm-educating model is frequently found in divorce and custody disputes, as well as in court-mandated and anti-discrimination cases. It is protective in nature, ensuring that the rights of systematically disadvantaged individuals are not neglected. That being said, the parties are free to take or leave this protection, and the mediator has no responsibility for enforcement.

Norm-Advocating

The norm-advocating mediator claims that some values are more important than a party's autonomy, so this mediator assumes responsibility for ensuring that these values are included in any agreements reached in the mediation. Helping parties search for mutually agreeable outcomes is secondary to ensuring that agreements do not violate societal principles. In fact, a mediator may withdraw from the mediation if he or she suspects a violation of social norms. Norm-advocating mediators are found in public policy, human rights, or environmental disputes where decisions could have an impact on generations to come. Here are a few examples of normative beliefs: non-renewable resources should be conserved; every person deserves equal treatment and opportunity under the law; and children should not suffer undue financial hardship because their parents' divorce. Hospital ethics, zoning regulations, and civil rights are other dispute areas where this type of mediation is likely to be found.

Social Norm Exercise

Revisit the conflict you thought about at the beginning of this chapter. Which of the three social norms discussed above (norm-generating, norm-educating, norm-advocating) is the most important to attend to in this conflict? Why?

Thinking about social norms is one way that people can select the type of mediator they think would be best suited to mediate a particular dispute.

RESTORATIVE JUSTICE APPROACH AND VICTIM–OFFENDER MEDIATION

Restorative justice is "a response to conflict that brings victims, wrongdoers and the community together to collectively repair harm that has been done in a manner that satisfies their conception of justice" (Law Commission of Canada, 1999, p. 25). There are many types of restorative justice programs. The most commonly found in North America are family group conferencing, sentencing circles, youth justice committees, and victim–offender mediation. Restorative justice programs are based on three principles: (1) crime is a violation of a relationship among victims, offenders, and the community; (2) restoration involves the victim, the offender, and community members; and (3) justice requires a consensus approach (pp. 29–30).

Canada's first restorative justice process, in a modern legal context, is believed to have taken place in 1974, when two young men from Elmira, Ontario, who had pleaded guilty to vandalizing 22 properties, were ordered by the judge to visit the homes of the victims, at the request of their probation officer. In chapter 10, we talk more about the theory of restorative justice and contrast it to retributive justice. For the purposes of this chapter, we focus on victim–offender mediation.

Victim–offender mediation involves a facilitated dialogue between an offender and a victim. In most instances, it takes place in cases where offenders have admitted committing a wrong that could be considered a crime, have accepted responsibility for it, and have expressed remorse. In less serious cases, especially in youth cases, the referral to mediation may be a diversion from the formal criminal justice system, either before or after a charge is laid. In other cases, the referral comes after a guilty plea or conviction and as a possible alternative or complement to sentencing.

Unlike other conflict situations, the offender's wrongdoing is not an issue in the mediation process—all participants have already agreed on that. The primary issue to be mediated is what is to be done to restore "right relations" among the offender, the victim, and the community. Mediation is considered successful to the extent that the offender hears and understands the victim's experience and feelings about the crime, he or she experiences genuine empathy and remorse, and the victim experiences the offender as a person with potential for transformation and growth.

Victim–offender mediation has given rise to another model of mediation called "humanistic mediation" (Umbreit, 2001). Humanistic mediation is based on beliefs in (1) the connectedness of all things and our common humanity; (2) the importance of the mediator/worker's presence and connectedness with the involved parties in facilitating effective conflict resolution; (3) the healing power of mediation; (4) the desire of most people to live peacefully; (5) the desire of most people to grow through life experiences; (6) the capacity of all people to draw upon inner reservoirs of strength to overcome adversity, to grow, and to help others in similar circumstances; and (7) the inherent dignity and self-determination that arise from embracing conflict directly (Umbreit, 2001, p. 4).

NARRATIVE APPROACH

Narrative mediation is an approach that encourages parties to tell their personal "conflict" story as a means of producing an "alternate" story that will lead them to a resolution of the dispute. It is based on social constructionist theory, which posits that people organize their experiences in story form as a way to make sense of their lives and relationships, and that "they act both out of and into these stories" (Winslade & Monk, 2000, p. 3). Narrative mediators do not seek one "factual" story; instead, they find it more useful to accept each person's story as a lived reality and then "seek out the points where the story might incorporate some different approaches" (p. 3). A key task of the mediator is to lessen the rigid and negative motivations that parties attribute to each other's actions. This is accomplished by building party trust in the mediator and the mediation process; developing conversations that externalize, as opposed to internalize, the conflict; mapping the effects of the problem on the person; deconstructing the dominant story lines; and developing shared meanings about the conflict and it's solutions. (For more information on social constructionist theory, see Burr, 1995, and Gergen, 1999.)

Important to narrative mediators is the belief that the parties' conflict stories are drawn from the cultural stories of the world around them. As a result, there are always multiple stories at play during a mediation session. Narrative mediation has three phases: engagement, deconstructing the conflict-saturated story, and constructing an alternate story (Winslade and Monk, 2000, p. 58). In the engagement phase, the mediator concentrates on establishing a relationship with the conflict parties by attending to the physical setting and the non-verbal behaviour displayed by all parties. Attention is also given to the roles that the mediator and the parties will take on as a result of the mediation. In the next stage, deconstructing the conflict-saturated story, the mediator works actively to separate the parties from their perceptions and understandings of the conflict by "undermining the certainties on which the conflict feeds, and inviting the parties to view the plot of the dispute from a different vantage point" (p. 72). The assumption is that elements of cooperation, points of agreement, and mutual respect have been left out of the conflict-saturated story, and deconstructing it can lead to creating an alternate story that includes these areas. The final stage of narrative mediation is to construct an alternate story. In this stage, the mediator is "occupied with crafting alternative, more preferred story lines with people who were previously captured by a conflict-saturated relationship" (p. 82). The development of a cooperative attitude may be more important than reaching an agreement.

INSIGHT APPROACH

Insight mediation, like other interest-based approaches, is a process of assisted negotiation where an impartial person facilitates the negotiation process while parties determine the outcome. What differentiates it from other approaches is that its goal is to help parties gain insight into the cares and concerns that underlie the conflict situation and that are affecting their lives and the lives of others. This insight enables them to reach consensual decisions that accommodate their needs. Similar to the transformative approach, insight is a self-empowering process that emphasizes self-determination and interconnectedness.

Insight mediation assumes a relational view of conflict, a view that sees relationship and interdependence as cornerstones of conflict. It has many of the same features as other models of mediation—a beginning, where the issues, parties, and positions are identified; a middle, where the needs and interests underlying parties' positions with respect to the issues are explored; and an end, where options to resolve the issues that meet parties' interests are generated, evaluated, and agreed upon. It is important to emphasize that in insight mediation these stages are fluid, not linear or static, and that parties often move between the stages throughout the mediation. The goal of helping parties achieve insight requires the mediator to focus attention on different factors than would be the case in narrative or transformative mediation. Furthermore, mediators practising this model place significant importance on the role of communication in resolving conflicts. Insight mediators need to have exceptional listening skills and they need to be able to discover both the broader and deeper nature of the conflict situation, as well as the relational elements. Krauss and Morsella tell us that "good communication cannot guarantee that conflict is ameliorated or resolved, but poor communication greatly increases the likelihood that conflict continues or is made worse" (2000, p. 143). Insight mediators use many of the same communication skills and mediation strategies as other mediators. Some of the more common ones include active listening, reframing, effective questioning, probing for interests, and generating options. (These skills are discussed in later chapters.)

Staying curious, non-judgmental, and transparent is emphasized in insight mediation. The aim is to help parties discover the causes, elements, emotions, and relational nature of the conflict situation in which they are involved. Mediators probe for insight into what the conflict situation "means" to each party. In other words, they try to discover what each party cares about and is concerned about, as a means of helping the parties find a mutually agreeable way to solve the conflict.

Insight mediation is not a "new" model, nor is it significantly different from other interest-based models of mediation in the procedures it follows. Perhaps it is more accurate to say that it is a "newly named" model that uses strategies that are either not well articulated or not present in other relational models of mediation. Most important to this model is helping the parties gain "insights" that help them shift the course of the conflict and create space for collective action. To fully understand this model of mediation, you first need to know what is meant by "insight."

The Theory of Insight

We all experience insights; however, few people examine how and why they occur. They seem simple, but actually are quite complex, involving experience, understanding, judgments, and decisions (Morelli & Morelli, 2002). Canadian philosopher Bernard Lonergan (1957) has made a helpful contribution toward understanding insight, and scholars have drawn upon his work to help us appreciate what is involved when we get insights into concerns, values, and ethical decision making. Lonergan's philosophy is not principally a set of ideas that can be learned from reading a book or listening to others; rather, it is a discovery process much like that of reflective practice, where we observe and come to understand ourselves in our day-to-day actions. (For more on Lonergan's philosophy, see Flanagan, 1997; Melchin, 1998; and Morelli & Morelli, 2002. For more on reflective practice, see Lang & Taylor, 2000, and Schon, 1987.)

Insights can shift the value placed on a particular position, and this, in turn, can cause the conflict dynamic to change. Insights are what some call the "magic" of mediation—that moment when something changes and the parties are freed from their positions to work jointly on meeting their mutual interests. Folger and Bush suggest that it is "the transformative effects of the process," and what makes mediation "most meaningful and successful" (1996, p. 264).

Psychologists agree that once an insight has occurred, a radically new understanding occurs, which often leads to a simple and permanent solution to the dissonance. Insight involves "the full human person (intellect plus emotions, attitudes, intuition, experience and culture) and displays some of our deepest values" (Murray, 1995, p. 4). It also involves "the sudden unexpected solution to the problem" (Sternberg & Davidson, 1995, p. 560). It is both the "aha" moment and it gives us the experience of being transformed. Before the insight, we cannot imagine the answer to the problem; after the insight, we can neither imagine, nor can we remember, our inability to understand it. It is experiential, as well as knowledge producing—we *feel* the change.

Insights do not just happen or come out of the blue. They occur in "ready" minds through a process of wondering, wanting to understand, and wanting to "catch on." Getting insights often results in moving to a different line of questioning. This happens when we hit dead ends, go round in circles, or get nowhere. Hence, we search for new clues by trying a different tack, asking a different type of question, and paying attention to a different set of data. Getting the insight that "we can't get there from here" is what causes us to shift from one line of questioning to another. Insights are a personal acts of understanding that come from responses to questioning, imagining, sensing, remembering, and feeling. They often yield direction and therefore action.

Direct, Inverse, and Reflective Insights

Mediators work hard to help parties achieve insights into their conflict relationship and into the dynamic of the conflict situation, including the issues, the people, and their feelings, as well as past, present, and future relations. Mediators also work to gain their own insight into these dynamics. This type of insight is what Lonergan refers to as a direct insight (Morelli & Morelli, 2002). To reduce blockages to parties getting direct insights on their own, mediators help parties look at the situation from different angles, or new vantage points; expand sources of information so that parties are able to problem-solve the "bigger picture"; and identify and reconsider links between what they are encountering and what they know. Insight mediators use deliberate strategies, such as linking and de-linking, to probe for insights. We examine linking and de-linking in chapter 5. We will now discuss two other kinds of insight: "inverse" and "reflective" insights (Morelli & Morelli, 2002).

Let's begin with the inverse insight. Inverse insights are more than new understandings and clarity. They actually lead us to change current lines of questioning because they no longer make sense. They shift lines of inquiry, thereby opening up new horizons of intelligibility and new lines of questioning. Inverse insights mobilize curiosity and change expected linkages. To help explain an inverse insight, we will use a scenario.

SCENARIO: A Change Is as Good as a Rest I

Danny is a long-time employee of the Library working in the Documents Section. Teresa, an employee for less than two years, has been given the task of "modernizing" the library, especially the Documents Section. At every turn, Teresa meets resistance and opposition to her ideas from Danny and his small group of co-workers. Totally frustrated and confused by their resistance, she seeks help from an in-house mediator to see if there is any way to change this dynamic. She needs the support of this group to consider the merits and drawbacks of the changes she is suggesting, and she will need their support if they are to be implemented. Teresa is fed up with Danny's resistance, because it appears to be calculated to personally undermine her. Teresa believes that bringing about change in a collaborative fashion is the most effective and efficient way to do her job.

Danny and his co-workers, on the other hand, find it extremely difficult to continually adapt to change. They are more comfortable with routine, which is why they chose to work in the Documents Section in the first place. They are slow to pick up the new ways of working, especially cataloguing by computer, and they are threatened by the possibility that they might lose their jobs if cataloging becomes computerized. Even if jobs are not lost, they worry that change will make their jobs less interesting and fulfilling. Teresa's presence is threatening because it seems to imply that the work they have been doing is no longer considered to be of value to management. Their attitude is, "If it ain't broke, why fix it?"

At first, this looks like a conflict about change—one party advocating change and the other resisting it. As the mediator talks with the parties, she gets an insight that the real issue is not about "change" itself, but about the speed at which the ideas are being presented to Danny and his co-workers. Too many ideas for changing how things are carried out in the Documents Section are coming all at once, and the message the group is hearing is that "nothing they were doing was good enough." Earlier, the mediator had heard Teresa say, "In her assessment, most of the procedures in the Documents Section are working well; there are only a few things that need some changing." Picking up on this discrepancy, the mediator is able to help the parties hear more clearly what they are telling each other. Eventually, the negotiations move to a discussion, not about *if* there will be change, but about *how* new ideas can be solicited from Danny and his co-workers, and then communicated back to them for consideration. This complete shift in the line of questioning results from an "inverse" insight.

"Reflective" insights involve judgment, which is how we determine whether, in fact, the insight that has been reached is correct. In Lonergan's terms, it is the "Is it so?" question that follows the "What is it?" question. For Lonergan, insights are determined to be correct when there are no further pertinent questions (Morelli & Morelli, 2002, p. 174). For insight mediators, it means that they ensure that the insights gained by one party are understood and confirmed to be true by the other.

CONTRASTING INSIGHT WITH TRANSFORMATIVE AND NARRATIVE MODELS OF MEDIATION

The goal of insight mediation is to help parties gain insights that will help shift the course of the conflict and create space for collective action. This involves probing the underlying concerns that are driving the conflict—to help disputants understand and acknowledge their own underlying interests and those of the other party. To do this work, mediators use a range of questioning and listening strategies, as well as put their curiosity to work. They develop hunches as to what concerns might lie behind statements, and they continually reframe and reflect disputants' words and ideas. Curiosity draws them to search for insights into what it is that people care about, what concerns them, what their values and feelings are, and what drives their conflict. More important, they are in search of strategies to help the disputants themselves get insights into what really matters to them, what really matters to the other person, and how these two might be pursued together. Thus, the mediator's primary role is one of learning and helping others to learn.

This goal differs from the transformative mediation model discussed earlier in this chapter. Recall that the overall goal of the transformative model is for parties to achieve empowerment and recognition. Conflict is understood as being transformed through the ongoing communicative interactions of the parties and the mediator (Della Noce, 2001a, p. 77). A transformative mediator takes a micro-focus, concentrating on the here and now, being attentive to the parties' interactions as a means of seeking clues that signal opportunities to foster empowerment and recognition. The transformative model is significantly less structured than insight mediation. The mediator's role is less about probing the conflict situation and more about providing opportunities for parties to make decisions at every turn and "recognizing opportunities for recognition in the parties' conversational cues and creating responses that support the development of empathy" (Della Noce, 2001b, p. 108). In the insight model, we spend more attention and time probing the issues, underlying interests, and concerns in the conflict. There is a more concerted effort to "get at the roots of the conflict." This is one of the most striking differences between insight and transformation. The reason, of course, is that, in the insight model, insights—both direct and inverse—into the underlying cares and concerns is where one finds the source of the shifts in the disputants' attitudes toward the other party. In the transformative model, the mediator does not look to this deeper understanding for a source of transformation in the dispute. This is where the two models differ most.

The insight model also differs from the narrative mediation model (Winslade & Monk, 2000). As previously discussed, this model's goal is to form a partnership with disputing parties to better understand the stories behind the conflict—and to co-produce their alternative preferred stories in order to provide a basis of mutual understanding and to find a way forward. Instead of probing deeply into the conflict "story," as is done in insight mediation, the narrative-model mediator works to co-construct a preferred non-conflict story by deconstructing parties' positions, interests, and expectations so that shared meanings and understandings are constructed. This narrative model of mediation is more directive than the insight model, in that the mediator takes responsibility for co-constructing the alternate story with the parties. He or she uses their knowledge of cultural norms and history to do so. Again, unlike the insight model of mediation, narrative mediation does not go in any depth into the problem story.

In insight mediation, the mediator attends to several different tasks throughout the mediation process. This is especially noticeable during the stage when the mediator seeks insights into interests.

While exploring the interests, a mediator first engages in a process of gathering data by probing for information on how each party views and experiences the conflict. This can be thought of as discovery at the level of the "presenting" problem. Here, the mediator is asking a set of "What is going on?" questions. After getting a sense of what is going on, the mediator seeks to discover how each party *feels* about the conflict situation. Probing for those feelings is a way of getting insights into the "underlying" problem. By staying curious, the mediator seeks to discover where the parties' feelings come from and how their present feelings are linked to past experiences and anticipated outcomes. This strategy is called "linking." Continuing to be curious and getting deeper insights, the mediator elicits each party's reactions to the other's cares and concerns—to discover how these might be threatening. The nature of the questioning now becomes "What are you hearing as being important to party X and how does that threaten what matters to you?" Now comes some harder work—finding out if the other party's interests must necessarily pose a threat to their own. Discovering that they need not interfere with the pursuit of his or her interests is what we call "de-linking." Oftentimes, de-linking becomes an inverse insight, because one person's views of the other no longer fit. De-linking opens space for parties to appreciate what each other cares about. Questions sound something like, "Is your objection more about issue Y than issue X itself?" Parties are free to care about what the other cares about because it is no longer seen as threatening to them. Being freed up to be concerned about what the other person cares about enables parties to move to *generating options to meet interests*. The transition to this stage often involves raising the question, "What would make it possible for each of you to get what you need?"

Figure 4.4 contrasts the goals, roles, and strategies of mediators, using the transformative, narrative, and insight models of mediation.

FIGURE 4.4 Three Models of Mediation: A Comparison

DEFINING MEDIATION

Insight

This assisted negotiation model uses an impartial person to facilitate the negotiation process, but the parties determine the outcome. The aim is to help parties gain insight into the cares and concerns that underlie the conflict and that are affecting the parties' lives and the lives of others. This insight enables them to reach consensual decisions that accommodate their needs. It is a self-empowering process that emphasizes self-determination and interconnectedness.

Narrative

This process assists people who are negatively constrained by the effects and limitations of conflictual stories to co-author stories of cooperation and mutual respect. The mediator's role is to co-author, with the parties, lived experiences that lie outside the conflict. The new story narratives create shared meaning and mutual understanding. Narrative mediation strives to diminish the influence of those dominant cultural narratives that restrain people's efforts to understand the other. It seeks to create a context where diverse cultural perspectives are accepted—and in some instances embraced—by people previously in conflict.

Transformative

This model enables people in conflict to develop a greater degree of both self-determination and responsiveness to others, while they explore solutions to specific issues. It has the potential to strengthen the disputants' capacity to analyze situations and make effective decisions—and to see and consider the perspective of others. It is a self-empowering process that emphasizes party decision making and a relational perspective.

VALUES AND UNDERLYING BELIEFS

Insight

- People are individual and interconnected; they have separate identities but live in relation to others.
- People are affected by and act on their values, culture, history, and views of the world.
- More than achieving individual gain, people seek to reach mutual understanding of their values and concerns.
- People have the capacity to make their own decisions and are better suited to find solutions to their conflicts than outsiders.
- If given a fair chance, people will try to improve a negative situation.
- Individuals have the inner resources to solve their own conflicts and are best placed to do so.
- Mediation has the potential to empower individuals to achieve greater "insights" into the cares, concerns, interests, and values that are at work in the conflict—both their own and those of the other parties—as well as insights into the relations that connect them. It can also open the door to institutional and structural change. In most cases, mediation is a better dispute resolution process than litigation or other adversarial processes.

(Continued on the next page.)

FIGURE 4.4 Continued

VALUES AND UNDERLYING BELIEFS (cont.)

Narrative

- Culture, as opposed to inner forces and individual needs, shapes and constructs people's positions and interests.
- Stories shape people's attitudes, beliefs, and identities.
- People are restrained by discourses from acting respectfully.
- There are multiple descriptions of problems.
- The person is not the problem; the problem is the problem.
- When cultural discourses produce conflict between people, the deconstruction of cultural clashes provides an opportunity for people to act with agency and resourcefulness.

Transformative

- People are individual and interconnected; they have separate identities but live in relation to others.
- Conflict is a crisis in human interaction. Parties in conflict are self-absorbed and experience relative uncertainty about their goals, strengths, and needs.
- The parties have what it takes to deal effectively with their own conflicts, and are best placed to decide when, whether, and how to do so.
- Mediators hold an optimistic view about the parties' competence, motives, and values.
- More than achieving individual gain, people seek moral growth represented by empowerment and recognition.
- Out of their deepening confusion about the conflict, the parties will find clarity and strength.
- People in conflict are generally self-absorbed, but have the potential and the desire to achieve a sense of others and their perspectives.
- Individuals have the strengths to deal effectively with their own conflicts and are best placed to decide when, whether, and how to do so.

OVERALL GOAL

Insight

To help parties gain insights that shift the course of the conflict and create spaces for collective action.

Narrative

To form a partnership with disputing parties to better understand the stories behind the conflict and to co-produce their alternative, preferred stories as a basis of mutual understanding, to find a way forward.

Transformative

To support parties' desire for moral growth and development; to provide opportunity to act from *compassionate strength*; to assist parties to move from positions of relative weakness and uncertainty to strength—and from self-absorption to an ability to listen and respond to another's perspective.

(Continued on the next page.)

FIGURE 4.4 Continued

MEDIATOR TASKS

Insight

- Gathering data by probing for information on how each party views and experiences the conflict situation (discovery at the level of the presenting problem). The "What is going on?" question.
- Discovering how each party feels about the conflict situation. The "How do you feel about what is going on?" question.
- Probing for what each party's feelings are about (getting insights at the underlying problem level). The "Where do these feelings come from?" and "How are present feelings linked to past experiences and anticipated outcomes?" questions.
- Eliciting each party's reactions to the other's cares and concerns, and discovering how these might be threatening (deeper insights). The "What are you hearing as being important to X and how does that threaten what matters to you?" question.
- Seeking to "de-link" the perception that the other's cares and concerns must necessarily be a threat to their own (inverse insight), which opens space for parties to appreciate what the other cares about (I can care if it doesn't threaten me). The "Is your objection more about issue Y than issue X itself?" question.
- Inviting participants to suggest possible strategies for pursuing what is important to them together. The "What would make it possible for each of you to get what you need?" question.
- Eliciting parties' reactions to verify if proposed strategies meet both sets of cares and concerns. The "Will that suggestion meet your needs?" question.

Narrative

- Mediator establishes, with the parties, the interrelational and cyclical nature of conflict.
- Mediator invites historicizing the problem and storying its effects on the parties.
- Managing the relational position produced by conflictual interactions.
- Amassing exceptions and building preferred non-conflict stories.

Transformative

- A carefully constructed opening that describes mediation in terms of empowerment and recognition—setting the stage—one that invites parties to shape process as well as outcomes.
- Mediator follows the parties' lead while remaining proactive with regard to looking for opportunities to support empowerment and recognition.
- Mediator enacts a micro-focus, concentrating on the here and now, attentive to the parties' interactions, and seeking cues that signal opportunities to foster empowerment and recognition.

(Concluded on the next page.)

FIGURE 4.4 Concluded

KEY STRATEGIES

Insight

- Seeking direct insights brings about a sudden illumination and feeling of "aha" that transform parties through a personal act of understanding that comes from response to questioning, imagining, sensing, remembering, and feeling. Mediators seek direct insights by being curious about and listening for discrepancy, as well as how what one party cares about is linked to what threatens the other.
- Seeking inverse insights that lead to new lines of questioning, thereby opening up new horizons of intelligibility. Inverse insights shift lines of inquiry, mobilize curiosity, and change lines of expected linkages.
- Linking involves discovering how past histories and feelings are linked to current behaviours and attitudes, as well as to anticipated outcomes. De-linking involves finding out if what one person cares about must necessarily pose a threat to what is important to the other, and exposing incorrect links.
- De-linking incorrect links opens up space for curiosity, helps to keep interpersonal connections present, separates the parties as objects of conflict, and opens up circumstances for caring.

Narrative

- The use of curiosity, naive inquiry, and respectful persistence is employed by the mediator throughout the process.
- Externalizing conversations are employed to separate the problem from persons.
- Utilizing "relative influence questions" and mapping the effects of the problem.
- Deconstructing parties' positions, interests, and expectations to assist in the construction of shared meanings and understandings.
- Mediator uses a range of questions to co-construct the non-conflictual story.
- Unique outcome questions: "How is it that the conflict did not completely stop you from wanting to find your way through the present difficulties?"
- Unique account questions: "How have you been able to begin to understand X's point of view when you have suffered from so much distrust?"
- Redescribing questions: "What does your movement away from animosity say about your abilities to resolve a painful set of issues?"
- Using letter writing to document change.

Transformative

- Inviting reflection through the use of elicitive, open-ended questions.
- Inviting/encouraging the parties to hear, understand, and acknowledge the other person's perspectives—give recognition.
- Paraphrasing to assist parties in identifying a request for recognition or to acknowledge a request for empowerment.
- Asking clarifying questions, particularly with regard to opportunities for empowerment on topics, such as the parties' goals; their resources, strengths, skills, and knowledge; and how they might be used.
- Identify and clarify their options—both process and substance; decide what information they need and where and how to obtain that data.
- Supporting parties' expressions of emotions. Based on the belief that there is important information in those feelings.

Figure prepared by Cheryl Picard, Michael Lang, John Winslade, and Gerald Monk and presented at the 2003 Conference of the Association for Conflict Resolution. It is used here with permission.

Preferred Approach Exercise

Once again, revisit the conflict you selected at the beginning of this chapter. Based on what you have learned about the different approaches to mediation and the different types of mediators is there a model of mediation or type of mediator that you favour at this time? Think about how your choice is linked to your personal views about conflict and its resolution.

SUMMARY

This chapter presented a number of different ways to mediate that vary from pragmatic problem-solving processes to processes that influence individual and social transformation. The former view looks at conflict as a problem to be solved; the latter sees it as an opportunity for growth and empowerment. We discussed the evaluative and facilitative dichotomy of mediation styles. The difference between these two styles is that an evaluative mediator provides the direction needed for parties to reach settlement, while the role of a facilitative mediator is to help parties understand the problems they want to address. We also examined the social norm approach, as well as the restorative justice approach and victim–offender mediation. In the latter part of the chapter we described and contrasted the transformative, narrative, and insight mediation models, indicating that transformative mediators focus on the empowerment and recognition of parties in the dispute; narrative mediators focus on the creation of a shared alternate story to the problem-saturated story; while insight mediators focus on helping parties to gain insight into each other's cares and concerns, to reach consensual decision making that meets these needs. In the next chapter, we continue to take a more theoretical look at the art and science of mediation.

FURTHER READING

Bush, R.B., & Folger, J. (1994). *The promise of mediation*. San Francisco: Jossey-Bass.

Moore, C.W. (2003). *The mediation process: Practical strategies for resolving conflict* (3rd ed.). San Francisco: Jossey-Bass.

Picard, C.A. (2002). *Mediating interpersonal and small group conflict* (Rev. ed.). Ottawa: Golden Dog Press.

Winslade, J., & Monk, G. (2000). *Narrative mediation*. San Francisco: Jossey-Bass.

WEB SITES

The Institute for the Study of Conflict Transformation
http://www.transformativemediation.org/

> This institute was founded to promote the transformative approach, first articulated by Robert A. Baruch Bush and Joseph P. Folger in *The Promise of Mediation.*

Bernard Lonergan
http://www.lonergan.on.ca/

> This Web site contains many articles, research and conference reports, and other information relating to the work of Bernard Lonergan.

St. Stephen's House
http://www.ststephenshouse.com/

> This community centre in Toronto, Ontario offers services and training in mediation.

Carter Center
http://www.cartercenter.org/

> Based in Atlanta, Georgia, the Carter Center focuses on peace initiatives and conflict resolution.

CHAPTER FIVE

Seeing the Forest and the Trees: Mediation Artistry

> *You can only find truth with logic if you have already found truth without it.*
>
> *Gilbert Keith Chesterton*

> The mediation process is proceeding well. You are tracking the discussion, focused on the overarching issues as well as the moment-to-moment exchange of perspectives. You have a heightened awareness of your own place in the process and are mindful of the parties, the issues, and their interactions. Your attention is so intense that you are unaware of time passing. The conversation and your interventions are effortless, yet measured and purposeful. There is a sense of progress, without an effort to make something happen. You are engaged, pulled into the tasks of the mediation, but the work seems effortless and graceful. The process is elegant, flowing and productive. (Lang & Taylor, 2000, p. 3)

This is the mediator's dream—that the process flows effortlessly and effectively. The skills and integration needed to achieve this level of competency are the subject of this chapter. We will explore a holistic approach to managing and transforming conflict. We hope that considering its principles, values, practical significance, and impact will enable the reader to more fully experience the holistic approach that is the essence of the art and science of mediation.

The past 10 years have seen an unprecedented growth in the provision of mediation services. Mediation is regularly used and sanctioned by our courts in both family law and civil litigation. As well, mediation has become the dispute resolution option of choice among government departments and many businesses. The increased use of this process for resolving conflict offers evidence that something either inherent in or a product of mediation is appealing to a wide range of people.

Throughout this book, we discuss the process of mediation, as well as the skills and techniques required to conduct mediated processes. Yet, it is clearly not enough to paste together a few techniques to become a mediator. There is more to know about timing, "reading" the parties, being artful, and using creativity in the quest for excellent practice. The interrelationships between the skills, techniques, timing, intuition, creativity, experience, and knowledge—making an art of mediation—is part of the mediator's journey. This chapter looks more closely at what mediation offers and why it works, using a holistic approach that acknowledges its scientific nature (its parts), as well as its more artistic nature (the whole system).

WHY CHOOSE MEDIATION?

Since the beginnings of the alternative dispute resolution (ADR) movement in North America, mediation has been lauded as a more efficient and cost-effective alternative to the courts. It came into prominence in the late 1960s and early 1970s in the United States, largely as a response to public dissatisfaction with the justice system (Scimecca, 1991a), as well as from a desire for community self-reliance, social justice, and transformation (Picard, 2002, p. 9). Victim–offender reconciliation programs, family mediation, and community-based mediation centres emerged at around the same time in Canada. Canadian legal reform in the 1970s focused on alternatives to sentencing for young offenders that recognized adjudication was not addressing the root causes of crime. As well, those in the family law field sought more responsive and non-adversarial processes for divorcing couples with children. (For more history on the emergence of ADR in Canada, see Picard, 2002.) In the 1970s and early '80s, mediation processes were not well known, and few people outside of those working in the field would have been able to define it. Today, mediation can be found in our everyday vernacular, and it is rare to encounter people who have not heard of it or have not been touched by mediated processes in some form. What has led to this immense growth?

Mediation as a form of dispute resolution appeals to us on many levels, ideological and methodological. For us, as discussed later in this chapter, mediation rests on a relational world view, as opposed to an individualist perspective. This world view posits that

> the highest values of the social enterprise are these two: first, the fulfillment of the individual's capacity for moral development, for going beyond self-interest and being concerned with others; and second, the discovery of a common good beyond any private vision of the good, through the encounter between self and others in shared political discourse and action. (Bush, 1989, p. 14)

(A more detailed discussion of the relational world view can be found in chapter 4.)

There are also many good methodological reasons to adopt mediation for dispute resolution (outlined in chapter 2). Figure 5.1 reveals some of the many methodological differences between adjudication and mediation.

From the comparison in figure 5.1, it is easy to see why individuals, companies, and organizations might prefer to use mediation over other methods of dispute resolution, particularly adjudication, for many conflicts. Mediation usually ensures that the conflict won't exacerbate with time; its private nature enables parties to speak freely and without fear that honesty will cost them their public reputations; and its non-judgmental, non-adversarial, and non-blaming nature guarantees "face saving." Outcomes of this process benefit all parties involved—they are considered "win–win," because all parties' needs are considered and responded to in resolving the dispute. When agreements are arrived at through mediation, parties do tend to believe they are fair and cost-effective. (See Macfarlane, 1995; Bingham & Pitts, 2002; Tjersland, 1999; Burrell, Zirbel, & Allen, 2003.)

In many cases, mediation or negotiation is in fact the preferred choice, with a full 95 percent of all civil cases settling before they reach Superior Court. In very few cases does the suit actually proceed to court. Yet, the fundamental principles behind mediation are distinct from those of adjudication, and a great number of people expect a legal dispute resolution to follow the principles of adjudication (Macfarlane, 1995). The difference in approach and ideology are important to identify, particularly when a party is able to choose the process that best responds to his or her needs.

In addition to the process advantages of mediation noted above, parties who use mediation also report satisfaction with the quality of mediation. Aside from the clear benefits in efficiency and outcomes, mediation offers a number of other benefits to its users that are found in the beliefs and values inherent in mediation and the impact on those who go through the process. Reaching agreement is not necessarily the most important index of mediation success. Evaluation research indicates that between

FIGURE 5.1 Adjudication Versus Mediation

Adjudication	Mediation
Third party has authoritative decision-making power—the judge or panel makes the decisions	Third party has no authoritative decision-making power—the parties to the conflict make the decisions
Lawyers represent and speak for their clients, who are directly affected by the conflict	Parties to the conflict speak on their own behalf, even when counsel attends the mediation session
Only legal principles can be argued—the conflict must be expressed as a legal issue and effects of the conflict must be legally recognized	No constraint on subjects discussed—parties may bring all points they believe relevant to the dispute, including emotion
Once litigation is begun, it is mandatory that all parties attend	Voluntary process for all parties
Aggressively adversarial in nature—objective is to "beat" your opponent (win–lose)	Non-adversarial—objective is to promote understanding and outcomes that benefit all (win–win)
Fact-finding process employing the principle of falsifiability	Dialogic process where facts are not judged to be true or false
Public process that is recorded	As confidential as the parties desire, without need for any record
Decisions are rendered based on positions argued—conflict can be "settled," but the cause may be left unaddressed	Decisions are arrived at based on party interests unearthed during the process—conflict causes are addressed, as well as parties' needs
Relationship ending for the parties involved—focused on blame	Relationship preserving for parties involved—focused on mutual understanding and acceptance
Long delays getting to hearing	Quickly scheduled and completed
Expensive process	Relatively cost-effective
Very little educational value, given that parties do not participate directly	Great potential for discovery, because parties learn about one another, as well as creating a better means for future interactions
Focus on the objective, rational, and measurable effects of the conflict = *linear*	Equal focus on the subjective, emotional, and non-measurable effects of the conflict = *holistic*

92 and 97 percent of parties are satisfied with the opportunity to participate in a mediation (Bingham & Pitts, 2002, p. 141). Gaining new knowledge, clarifying issues, having concerns heard, and being responsible for outcomes were equally important factors in parties' satisfaction (Jones & Bodtker, 1998; Burrell, Zirbel, & Allen, 2003).

Mediation puts the responsibility and control for resolving disputes back into the hands of those most intimately affected by it—the parties to the conflict. This is considered the empowering nature of mediation, because it upholds the individual in conflict as the one who is best placed to know what she or he needs for conflict closure. Mediation holds that durable outcomes are based in processes that address the root causes of conflict, not merely the symptoms. Interest-based problem solving is the means by which conflict is resolved, not just managed. Mediation is also biased in favour of collaborative, rather than competitive, interaction between individuals, because it is premised on the world view that people are inherently striving to relate and connect to other people.

Resolving conflict is thus about re-establishing connections broken by the conflict. Given the opportunity, people will and do recognize and understand the other party, because

> the individual is an agent of reflection, challenged by some implicit common standard to enlarge himself by connecting to and serving others, and [that] society is an encouraging educator in that developmental process. (Bush, 1989, p. 14)

This world view is what makes mediation such an attractive option for dispute resolution. Indeed, many new mediators are drawn to the field for the values it reflects and inspires.

Unlike adjudication or other forms of conflict resolution that rely on the expertise of a third party to make decisions, mediation rests on the desire of parties to restore harmony to their relationships with others—and the subsequent capacity for humans to understand and empathize with others. Mediation can bring out the best in all of us. It works, in part, because it assumes that individuals are able to overcome selfishness in their relationships with the "other," and, as a result, a surprising number of people live up to these expectations.

Mediation Exercise

Think of a conflict in which you have been involved. Keeping in mind the differences between mediation and adjudication, think about which process you would prefer to use. Why? What is it about the nature of your conflict situation that lends itself to your choice? What is it about your own nature that lends itself to your choice?

WHAT MAKES MEDIATION EFFECTIVE?

It is not uncommon for an experienced mediator to say, "Trust the process" or "Let the magic of mediation work," to those who are training in the field. For a new mediator, these words are not at all reassuring, because they don't provide much guidance or insight into how mediation is successful. Those words, however, do illustrate the fact that mediation involves much more than simply meticulously following a recipe for success. While it is certainly possible to learn the science of mediation—the process stages, the communication techniques, and the skills required—a successful mediator needs more. This chapter is about the less concrete but more difficult component of mediation: the artistry. Mediation artistry can be found in the skillful employment of intuition, artfulness, empathy, connectedness, and creativity. Both the science and the art of mediation are prerequisites for successful practice.

The "Old" Scientific Method

The "old" scientific method relies on detailed analysis of that which can be known through our physical senses. We know what we can see, hear, smell, taste, and touch. If we take a machine as our example, this science asserts that by studying the parts of this machine, we can understand how it works. This interpretation of science assumes that we can take the machine apart and examine the workings of each component to learn how the whole machine works.

A further analogy can be found in the Western, scientific approach to medicine. A doctor observes symptoms (the parts), takes tests (verifies), analyzes the data, diagnoses the cause of the disease, and prescribes or performs the appropriate treatment. This approach is based on the premise that the root cause of the disease can be determined and resolved through the application of prescribed medicine or medical procedures. This is a linear, causal chain of inquiry.

A fundamental principle of Western scientific theory is that, with complete knowledge of a patient's condition and of current medical science, it is possible for a doctor to determine the optimal treatment. Although in practice there are many situations in which different medical "experts" may disagree on what it is, in theory there is one optimal treatment that may be objectively determined by proper application of prevailing medical knowledge, standards, and principles. However, by focusing on observable symptoms and scientifically determined facts, the medical diagnosis may be misleading. Consider, for example, a patient with an apparent wrist injury. The wrist problem experienced by the patient may be only one manifestation of a completely separate condition, such as a damaged disc in the patient's spine.

The "New" Science

Wheatley (1999, pp. 10–11) proposes that the new science focuses on holistic understanding, rather than an understanding of the parts. Systems are seen as a network of relationships, and knowledge is derived from understanding the relationships and their interconnectedness within the system. Taking the machine again as an example, the new science does not take the machine apart, but rather studies it in operation, trying to discover links and understand relationships between the component parts. This is a holistic approach to knowing, and it is nonlinear with unpredictable causal links.

If we return to our medical example of the patient with a wrist problem, an environmental doctor (holistic practitioner) might begin her intervention by seeking links between the wrist concerns and other symptoms. She would analyze the body's whole system of interaction—how the wrist is linked to other parts of the body, like the shoulder, the spine, the musculature. She might study the patient's hair follicles, eyes, or other systems for information about the wrist. The conclusion she arrives at may be that there is a stomach hernia (or a muscle tear) that is affecting the patient's posture. The poor posture is particularly evident when the patient works on the computer, and the spine misalignment has led to damage of the wrist tendon. Without a system (holistic) analysis, this doctor could have arrived at very different conclusions, possibly treating only a symptom instead of trying to eliminate its cause. Treatment in this instance involves strengthening the musculature around the spine and practising proper posture alignment when on the computer, as well as more conventional therapies designed to ease wrist pain.

The complete mediator combines the new and old scientific approaches to knowledge. This holistic approach requires that we continue to use analysis, but differently from before. To understand the causes of conflict, we need to understand its sources; however, more important, we need to understand how those sources interact or coexist with other elements of the conflict.

What Is a Holistic Approach to Mediation?

A holistic approach to dealing with conflict is based on a number of premises. First of all, holistic practitioners view conflict as a relational phenomenon. Conflict arises from and is manifested as a feature of the interactions and relations among two or more people or groups of people. Any attempt to explain, understand, or resolve conflict as an individual phenomenon will be incomplete. Conflict is a complex, multi-dimensional phenomenon. In a particular case, it is impossible to isolate or identify all "causes," manifestations, and effects of the conflict. How individuals respond to conflict and how people and groups interact in conflict situations are uniquely determined by historical, cultural, psychological, environmental, economic, social, political, and other factors that defy complete "old science" analysis.

Conflict is perceived as a phenomenon arising from the mind, heart, body, and spirit. People in a conflict experience it with and through their minds, their emotions, their physical sensations, and their souls. Likewise, people influence the conflict situation—and other involved people and groups—through ways of the mind, heart, body, and spirit. This inevitably means that logic and rational discussion are inadequate alone as ways to understand conflict, to describe it, and to deal with it (Benjamin, 1995a, pp. 143–144; Benjamin, 1995b, pp. 3–4; Fisher, 2000, p. 88). There are other non-scientific ways of discovering and of knowing important truths about people in conflict situations and relationships.

The more that parties and intervenors know about the people and their conflict situation and relationships, the greater their capacity for resolving or managing the conflict productively. An understanding of the connections and relationship—historical and contextual—between the parties will be most informative in the approach to mediation. The mediator must see the conflict and the parties through a systems lens. This involves observing and sensing the interconnections between the parties and the elements of the conflict.

The mediator should expect a process of inquiry and discovery that will be non-linear and unpredictable. Conflict conditions tend to cause people to think and behave in ways that may be contrary to their rational best interests, both individually and relationally. As Benjamin (1995b, p. 6) says, "virtually every conflict, whether a business or a family dispute, has subjective, nonrational aspects that must be addressed."

It is thus important to remember that, while an understanding of the parts is important, a holistic approach advises us to observe, feel, and understand the relationships. In addition to individual characteristics of conflict, the mediator must always consider how connections and relationships are affecting each party's willingness and ability to negotiate effectively. It is this understanding that can move a conflict from its destructive to its constructive nature. The mediator is simultaneously observing the individual (the part) in mediation at the same time that he is observing the entire relationship (the system). To practise holistically, the mediator must interact with the parties in conflict in both rational and non-rational ways. He often starts with logical, analytical frameworks and integrates what he knows intuitively into his reactions and responses. Figure 5.2 shows the assumptions about knowledge and how we know what we know under the old science and new science paradigms.

As we can see from figure 5.2, one of the key assumptions of a holistic approach to mediation is that the observer or "knower" can never stand completely outside whatever is being observed. Interestingly, this claim comes to us from theoretical physics, the heartland of the old scientific method—not from the social sciences. It was Einstein who taught us that there is no Archimedean point from which we can obtain a completely unbiased and objective view of reality. Our perceptions of reality are always influenced, knowingly or unknowingly, by a pre-existing framework of ideas, expectations, and beliefs about the way the world is ordered. We see and hear through filters. We may disregard or fail to perceive information that is incompatible with our pre-existing assumptions, or we may interpret it in a subjective, self-serving way.

Imagine an anthropologist doing field work among a tribal people who had never before had contact with modern society. The anthropologist is excited because he is able to observe the organization and rituals of a society that has developed over centuries, free of external social or technological influences. The anthropologist believes that the data obtained from this research will provide crucial information about how societies adapt to their natural environment and whether humans are naturally peaceful social actors, or whether we are aggressive by nature. However, by arriving on the island to do the field work, armed with notebooks, computers, recording equipment, cameras, food supplies, a tent, and a hundred other basic supplies, the anthropologist has already influ-

FIGURE 5.2 The "Old" and "New" Science: A Comparison

The "old" (traditional) scientific method	The "new" scientific method
Knowledge is based on observation and analysis. We can "know" through our physical senses.	Knowledge can be based on observation and analysis and the physical senses. But we can also "know" through experience and insight.
The observer stands outside the activity or phenomenon that is being observed—a "standpoint of objectivity."	The observer can never stand completely outside that which is being observed. There is always some interaction between the observer and what is being observed.
The observer (investigator) must take care not to influence or interact with the data or information being analyzed—the observer is passive and non-interactive with the thing that is being observed.	The observer ("knower") is actively engaged in the creation of knowledge. The observer is not just a passive observer of objective data, but consciously or unconsciously influences the selection and interpretation of information or data.
Conflict is a social phenomenon that can be objectively observed and analyzed.	Conflict is a form of social interaction that may be *experienced subjectively* by the participants in ways that are not always evident to an objective observer.
Conflict behaviour can also be observed and analyzed objectively.	It is not enough to rely on observation and analysis alone to understand conflict behaviour. We also have to rely on experience and insight to understand how the conflict is experienced subjectively by the participants.
The emphasis is on the search for objective knowledge—the "truth" about the conflict.	The emphasis is on gaining insight into the different ways in which the participants experience the conflict—the different "truths" about the conflict.
Observer neutrality is a crucial process value to prevent observer bias.	An interactive observer can never be strictly neutral, in the sense of having no influence on the data or information being observed. Instead, the observer strives to be conscious of his or her influence on the selection and interpretation of data, and to act in an ethically responsible manner.
That which can be objectively known through observation and analysis can also be modified in predictable ways through external intervention. The "purpose" of conflict intervention, therefore, is to treat or cure the conflict situation.	Because observation and analysis alone will not enable us to obtain the full truth about the conflict, any external intervention based on this assumption is likely to have unanticipated consequences. Intervention should therefore be directed at transforming or changing the parties' subjective experience of the conflict.

enced the very society he set out to study. It is no longer a society that has developed "with no contact with the outside world." The members of the tribal people are likely to behave in the anthropologist's presence in ways that differ, if only slightly, from the manner in which they would interact in his absence. The problem is that the anthropologist can never know this for sure. His very presence has altered the dynamics of the society he has come to observe. What he observes has therefore been affected by his presence.

As mediators, we recognize that the presence of a third party in a conflict situation is likely to alter the dynamics of the conflict and the relationships between the participants in the conflict. Indeed, this is the main purpose of the mediator's intervention. The mediator cannot impose a decision on the parties if they are unable to reach a negotiated agreement. Yet, the intervention of an impartial third party may assist the parties in altering their perceptions of the conflict, and in moving from an adversarial bargaining stance to a more collaborative approach. The focus of the mediator's intervention is thus to change the dynamics of the conflict relationship, to unblock obstacles to communication, to give the parties more insight into their own conflict, and to alter or transform the parties' subjective experience of the conflict they are engaged in. A mediator is *always* actively engaged in the communication process between the disputants, and in the creation of knowledge about the conflict. Mediation is a form of interactive engagement in a conflict relationship. The mediator can never be strictly neutral between the participants in the sense of being a passive observer. Instead, the mediator strives to act impartially with respect to the disputants, to build trust with all the participants, and to allow all the participants to tell their own stories or truths about the conflict.

Now, compare the interactive standpoint of a mediator with the neutral standpoint of a judge in a courtroom hearing. In the adversarial system, the judge is supposed to be a passive observer while the litigants introduce evidence and cross-examine one another's witnesses. Judicial neutrality requires that the judge not identify with or assist the litigants in their case presentations. A mediator's role, by contrast, is to assist both participants in presenting their case, so to speak, or in telling their stories. Moreover, in mediation the parties are not telling their stories to the mediator as such, even if it often appears this way, but to each other. In explaining their interests, cares, or fears, the parties may be talking to the mediator, but they are being heard by the other party. Indeed, as we will explore in later chapters, one of the key roles of a mediator is to act as a communication bridge between the parties.

This brings us to a second core element of a holistic approach to mediation that we wish to emphasize: the importance of incorporating the *subjective experiences* of the parties into any resolution to the conflict. A holistic approach to mediation is premised on the belief that there is always more than one truth about any conflict situation or relationship. To gain an understanding of the various truths about the conflict—as seen from the standpoint of the participants involved—mediators need to obtain information about the parties' subjective experience of the conflict—their perceptions, hopes, fears, emotions, values, beliefs, or expectations. Once again, we can contrast this holistic approach of mediation with the assumptions about the "truth" that underpin the litigation process, where the emphasis is placed on the objective facts of the conflict—what actually happened—rather than on the subjective experiences of the parties themselves.

A key objective in litigation is to determine the "truth" of the conflict. Anything that does not assist in determining the core truth is considered irrelevant to the proceedings. Most especially, the parties' subjective beliefs, emotions, interpretations, or experiences are dismissed. This is one of the main reasons why the parties are represented by lawyers in the litigation process. Lawyers can present the parties' arguments in a more objective, unemotional manner than the parties are likely to do. In addition to professional expertise and knowledge of the law, the capacity to be objective and unemotional about the facts of the case is highly prized in the legal profession.

For most mediators, however, the capacity to be responsive to the subjective, emotional needs of the disputants is as important as the capacity to manage the objective dimensions of the conflict. This is one reason that participants in mediation tend to express satisfaction with the process, even if it does not necessarily result in a negotiated agreement. All conflicts have both objective and subjective dimensions. Any proposed agreement that is not attentive to the subjective beliefs, values, and experiences of the participants is unlikely to be a lasting agreement. Indeed, much of a mediator's intervention is focused on adjusting the parties' subjective experience of their own conflict so as to help them move from an adversarial to a more collaborative approach to resolving the conflict.

MEDIATORS' WAYS OF KNOWING

A mediator derives knowledge through his or her analytical skills, as well as more creative ways of knowing. Intellectual ways of knowing are well developed in mediation education, research, and practice—through theories about human behaviour, communication, negotiation, and conflict. More emotional, physical, or intuitive ways of knowing have not received much discussion in this field. They are not easily trusted because they do not follow linear, "old" science methods of discovery. They are a part of the "new" science or the holistic understanding of conflict and human interaction.

LeBaron (2002) outlines four types of intelligence that are important to those working in conflict: emotional, somatic, intuitive-imaginative, and "connected" intelligence. Emotional fluency, the awareness and capacity to develop insights into one's own and other's emotions, enables the mediator to recognize, understand, and respond to emotion that is connected to the conflict. Emotional intelligence—what it means and how we may develop it—has been widely discussed since the publication in 1995 of Daniel Goleman's book of that name. An example of emotional fluency activated in mediation might be seen if one party begins to physically withdraw from the mediator and the other party, by moving back in her chair and breaking eye contact with them. The mediator is "emotionally fluent" if he recognizes that a deeper emotion, a feeling of isolation, is behind the withdrawal. The party does not articulate this verbally, but the mediator's "fluency" enables him to "hear" the sentiment as strongly as if it were spoken.

Somatic intelligence is the capacity to "read" and flow with the body's instincts, whether one party is physically withdrawing, reacting, or connecting. If we use our earlier example of a party withdrawing, the mediator is responding somatically if he moves his body closer to the party, offering a form of physical support and encouragement with his proximity and open, attending posture.

Using imagination and visualization—and guided by our intuitive senses—we are able to disconnect from old ways of seeing, to be able to consider new paths forward. If the mediator asks two co-workers in conflict to each picture a working relationship in the future, and both are able to visualize an effective partnership, describing what they will contribute and need to receive, they are using imagination and visualization to end their deadlock.

Metaphor is a key tool for getting to know—and for fully addressing—important conflict experiences. For example, imagine that we describe a mediation process as an expedition that starts in a desert, crosses rocky ground, moves into a thick jungle, and eventually emerges on wide, fertile fields. This metaphor speaks volumes about what people have experienced and achieved in this mediation. The use of metaphor and stories is covered more fully in chapter 8.

Connected ways of knowing are essential for seeing conflicts as part of relational systems. These connections emerge from the links we have with others and by acknowledging and understanding the influence of those ties that bind us to one another. Recognizing the importance of one another in carrying out their work, and being able to discuss each other's relative strengths in doing so, constitutes a type of connected knowing for our co-workers in the previous example.

Metaphor Exercise

Revisit that earlier conflict you have been involved in. Now, think of a metaphor or analogy that describes how you viewed that situation. Think creatively. Was it like a "pot boiling over," "walking on eggshells," "a cold Canadian winter"? How evocative—and successful—is your metaphor at describing what it felt like to be in the situation? What emotions does it evoke? How rich and full is the picture you have painted?

Like Benjamin (1995a, 1995b), LeBaron (2002) recognizes the need for resourcefulness and flexibility in mediation, acknowledging that mediators draw from knowledge sources in their actions, which complement the more traditional analytic ways of understanding. Some of these are outlined in chapters 8 and 9. Developing these other ways of knowing is critical to the mediator's effectiveness. We believe that creative tools are essential for fully knowing and expressing the human conflict experience. Indeed, all forms of artistic expression—music, painting, dance, and so on—are ways of expressing aspects of human experience that cannot be described with words.

As trainers in the field of mediation, we often speak of analytical skills, intuitive skills, and communication skills as the fundamentals for any practitioner. But how do you combine analytical and intuitive skill sets with the communication techniques? Below are some ideas about how to connect and integrate them into mediation contexts. (Additional suggestions for creative communication are offered in chapters 8 and 9.)

What Actually Happens in a Mediation To Make It Work?

Because we believe that the system (relationship) is in conflict, we must make changes within it. This is largely accomplished when the parties are able to shift their perspectives of one another and "reframe" the situation, establishing a different and shared understanding of events and needs.

The objective of changing parties' links and relationships is present in almost all models of mediation. In chapter 4, various models of mediation were described and discussed. Winslade and Monk (2000) direct the mediator to create, with the parties in conflict, an alternative contextual understanding of events and behaviours, embedding them in new narratives. Bush and Folger (1994) believe that the mediator's task is to assist the parties in enhancing their connectedness, first by understanding themselves better (empowerment), and subsequently by linking emotionally to the other through recognition. Bodtker and Jameson (1997) discuss the mediator's role in sharing his or her interpretation of events with the parties. They view reframing as a process of creating new and shared interpretations among the parties and the mediator. The insight mediator believes that parties' relationships are altered when new insights are developed about one another's beliefs, feelings, and behaviours. Relationship transformation occurs when one party's cares and concerns are "de-linked" from the other party's fears and threats through the process of gaining insights.

While there are many names for the process of shifting or creating new understandings of the links between parties, being strategic about this process is most critical for creating success in mediation—because the mediator is *not* the one who needs to open up his or her understanding of the conflict. Rather, it is the parties who need to become joint problem solvers, who need to collaborate in resolving their conflict. The key is to shift the parties' ways of knowing, as well as their ways of communicating, to help them find a more holistic approach to resolving their own conflicts. This shift, when it occurs, is what mediators are referring to when they speak of the "magic" of the process.

Where Does a Mediator Begin?

First, mediators must listen carefully to each party's story—to the connections and links one party has made with the other. Chapter 8 outlines *how* to listen. Here, we want to indicate what to listen for, and to discuss the importance of being strategic.

Although mediation is often described as non-directive, the mediator is far from inactive. A good mediator must be assertive and confident, using strong leadership skills to guide parties through the process. The mediator must be a strategist. Using her analytical skills, the mediator sifts through information received in the session, developing hypotheses about what she is hearing, and relying on intuitive knowledge about the parties and their relationships to one another. The mediator hypothesizes from knowledge gleaned from her theoretical understandings of conflict, communication, and negotiation, as well as social and psychological theories about human behaviour and interaction. Many of these theories have been alluded to elsewhere in this book. Other non-traditional forms of knowledge have been outlined earlier in this chapter.

How a mediator responds to a surprising statement, an unanticipated action, a moment of uncertainty, or a particular roadblock is determined through a process of *awareness*—then *reflection* and *hypothesizing*—before she undertakes any action or makes any statement. To an experienced mediator, this process is often so rapid that it is reflexive. For a new mediator, processing information tends to take more time. To illustrate this process in action, let's return to Teresa and Danny in chapter 4's scenario A Change Is as Good as a Rest.

SCENARIO: A Change Is as Good as a Rest II

Teresa: She moves her chair back a few inches and states, "You think that asking me to join your group at this late stage is going to solve my problem? Well, think again!" She then leans back in her chair and crosses her arms over her chest.

Mediator: *Awareness (observation)—What is happening in the moment?*

Teresa has physically moved out of our dialogue circle and is strongly rejecting the option suggested by Danny.

Reflection (analytical and intuitive)—Why is this happening?

She is withdrawing because we haven't understood her perspective on this, and she is becoming more frustrated at not being heard. This is evident in her physical withdrawal and the locking of her arms in front of her body. Moreover, she has broken eye contact with both Danny and me.

Hypothesizing—What response is required and why?

Based on what I know about human behaviour, communication, and interaction, I need to better understand her and why this option doesn't work for her. I also need to let her know that I have seen her frustration. Once she knows that I understand some of what she is experiencing, she may begin to trust me and will thus be more willing to provide information about what she needs to move forward.

Response—Acting on what is hypothesized

I move forward in my chair as though reaching out to Teresa. "You're feeling progressively more isolated here. It's clear we haven't understood what is really important to you. What's missing for you in Danny's suggestion?"

This example is a "micro-moment" in a mediation where the mediator is required to draw upon her various domains of knowledge of how people behave in conflict and why; theoretical understanding of how communication works and why. These domains include emotional fluency, to understand emotions and read actions, and somatic intelligence, which tells her body how to move empathetically. While the mediator is not likely to be able to tell us where all the knowledge came from for that particular intervention, she is probably able to tell us that she had an intuitive sense about what was needed.

When the process of awareness, reflection, hypothesizing, and responding takes place without pause in the mediator's actions, this is what is known as "artistry" in mediation. (See figure 5.3. For a discussion on artistry in professions, see Lang & Taylor, 2000.)

Strategizing should not be undertaken as one would follow a recipe, but rather as a situational response that takes the entire context into consideration. It requires that mediators observe the individuals in conflict at the same time that they are attentive to the relationships and interactions of those same individuals. Mediators are continually processing and reflecting upon the information they receive (verbally and non-verbally). Their actions are based on theoretical knowledge about human behaviour and interaction, as well as knowledge drawn

FIGURE 5.3 Artistry in Mediation

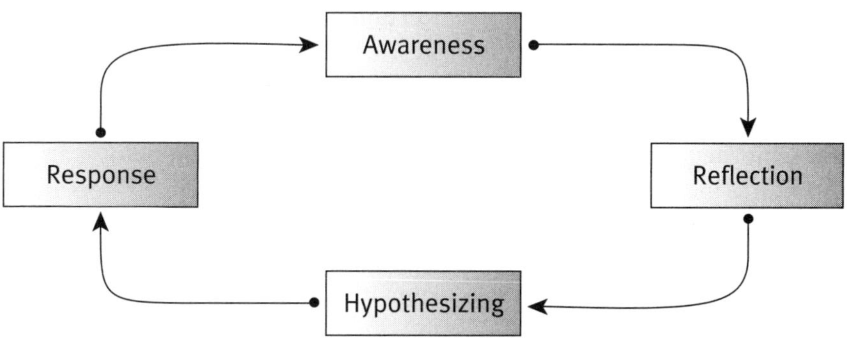

from more intuitive sources, such as somatic, imaginative, or connective intelligence, as outlined by LeBaron (2002).

Being strategic means that the mediator *intentionally* employs a skill or tactic because he or she is aware of its purpose and has learned that it will evoke a certain response. The mediator knows the skill or tactic is appropriate, based on theoretical knowledge, intuitive knowledge, or experience. Of course, not everything turns out as expected, and the unanticipated response may require a different strategy. Flexibility is important in strategic practice—if something is clearly not working, then do not persist with it. Try something else.

The point is that knowledge and skills are used with intent—sometimes consciously and other times not. "Knowing" what works can be derived from sources other than traditional, intellectual knowledge. It is not unusual for a skilled mediator to describe the source of particular interventions as coming from what he feels. There is no such thing as a "technically" good mediator—to become truly good at this work, mediators must use both their heads and their "hearts."

Influencing Parties' Ways of Understanding

Few mediators would deny the importance of mediation's potential to educate. The process of mediation itself is one of learning (Picard, 2003). The education includes the mediator, who is engaged in a process of discovery similar to that of the parties, who are also learning about themselves and the others involved in the conflict. When parties learn, the nature of the conflict invariably changes (p. 478).

From the very start of the mediation session, mediators are in a process of discovery and learning—they are working to gain insights into the nature of the conflict situation and the dynamic of the parties. They need these insights to listen for and hear discrepancies that might lead parties to new insights. Mediators seek insights by listening. They are curious. They wonder. They question underlying motives, concerns, and needs. They notice. They get hunches. They listen for discrepancy. They probe intent. They acknowledge and validate. They restate, to open new horizons and shift horizons. They search for ways that parties can save face and negotiate away from their positional "corner." Being curious promotes individual viewpoints coming together to create a "bigger picture." Listening for discrepancies leads to changing the angle from which the problem is being viewed. Making links between the past, present, and future leads to a reformulation of original positions.

Many different strategies can be used to create new ways of understanding relations and parties' needs. Here are four of them: (1) linking and de-linking, (2) connecting through ritual, (3) visualizing, and (4) doing thc unexpected.

Linking and De-Linking Strategies

Mediators know that parties often make assumptions about how the other person's values or intentions pose a threat to their interests. Feeling threatened is what causes people to hold strongly to their demands or positions. Clarifying mistaken assumptions about latent threats helps mediators de-escalate the conflict situation and paves the way for collaborative problem solving. To do this, a mediator must first discover what peoples' feelings are about—in other words, discover their interests—so that the values driving their actions become clearer. Often, parties are not fully aware of these values, nor are they aware of how they are affecting the conflict situation. Linking and de-linking strategies are designed to help the mediator uncover these.

Seeking to learn how what one cares about is linked to what threatens the other is not as difficult as it sounds. To do this, mediators often ask parties very direct questions. In the scenario A Change Is as Good as a Rest (presented in chapter 4), the mediator might ask Danny: "So what is the link between what's been happening between you and Teresa, some staff being laid off a few years ago, and the ideas that Teresa has been bringing forward?"

Mediators also listen carefully for discrepancies between what one party is saying and the other is hearing. One way to discover this is for a mediator to ask one party what he or she heard the other party say. Mediators also listen for information about how past histories may be linked to current feelings. They are curious to find out whether something similar has happened in the past and how that affects a party's attitude and behaviour in the present. They also want to learn how the past is linked to a party's current position on the issues in dispute. If we return to the scenario with Danny and Teresa, we might discover that Danny does not trust Teresa. This is because, in the past, when new people came into the organization with ideas for change, they appeared to be more concerned about looking good to their bosses and getting promoted than about making a difference in the working conditions of the front-line staff. Because Teresa is also new and responsible for upgrading systems, she was labelled as having the same motives. Teresa, on the other hand, strongly believes that collaborative approaches to organizational change are best and, when used, will produce the most efficient and effective change. She perceives Danny as being "old school"—his behaviour is getting in the way of change happening.

Mediators also ask consequential questions and listen very closely for how a party's position may be linked to anticipated outcomes. Returning to our scenario, Danny knows that, in the past, when change happened, people lost their jobs. He expects that Teresa's ideas for modernization will end up in job cuts or, at the very least, people being put into new positions that they will not like. The link here is that Teresa's ideas mean job loss for Danny; thus, what she cares about (being collaborative and instituting change) is a threat to Danny (fear of job loss and being seen as incompetent). As for Teresa, she thinks Danny is outdated because he will not collaborate on her ideas for change, which makes him a threat to her being able to do a good job. Figure 5.4 sets out how present behaviours are linked to past and future expectations. We also use these linkages to show the conflict between Danny and Teresa.

Why do one person's cares pose a threat to what is important to the other party? Threats usually get constructed because parties have been engaged in one-on-one negotiation and the style is largely one of advancing and defending their positions. The parties have not yet understood, or perhaps even identified, each other's interests. Once these interests are discovered, the parties start gaining insight into the reality of this link. If a link is not accurate, the job of the mediator becomes one of "de-linking."

De-linking distinguishes past experiences from present feelings—and from anticipated outcomes. It also "contextualizes" these three timeframes, by helping the parties *link* a past experience with a current feeling. This, in turn, creates the potential for a party to have an insight such as: "If my past experience is driving these feelings, then maybe the other person is not as much of a threat as I first thought." Or another insight might sound something like, "Maybe my guesses about what's going to happen next are all wrong." Ironically, this "link" (a direct insight) leads to a de-linking (inverse insight). De-linking opens up space for curiosity, helps to keep interpersonal connections present, separates the parties as "objects" of conflict, and, perhaps most important, opens up circumstances for caring.

In our scenario, Danny can only become interested in, or curious about, what is important to Teresa when he starts to feel that what is important to her might not be a threat to him. The same is true for Teresa. When she hears that Danny is not resisting the ideas she is proposing but the speed at which they are being presented, she and Danny

FIGURE 5.4 Possible Linkages

Past ● ——→	Present ←——	● Future
Experiences, feelings, background, culture, values, beliefs	Positions and demands, attitudes, behaviours, underlying interests, and feelings	Anticipated outcomes: "If I don't win, I lose"

Danny's Linkages

Past ● ——→	Present ←——	● Future
Organizational change resulted in job loss and displacement	Block Teresa's ideas; don't buy into the notion that "old" ways are inept; she is authoritative, not collaborative	Teresa's ideas will mean job loss; staff will be seen as incompetent

Teresa's Linkages

Past ● ——→	Present ←——	● Future
Collaborative approaches work best and, when used, produce the best outcomes	It is guys like Danny who keep an organization outdated and stuck. They make it impossible for me to collaborate and make the workplace better for staff and clients. Why is he so resistant to collaborating?	Change will make the organization better. If I can't get Danny to collaborate, the changes I am proposing will not be as good.

can begin to share ideas—about how to present ideas so that staff can understand, consider, and give her feedback before the next proposal is presented. Another de-link for Teresa comes when she discovers that Danny perceives the work she is doing to be authoritative, not collaborative, and they are able to discuss what collaboration will look like to Danny and his team. (Remember, being collaborative is important to Teresa.) In terms of Danny's de-links, once Danny understands that the ideas being presented by Teresa are not likely to result in job loss, and that the training required to implement some of the changes can be undertaken at a speed manageable by staff—and in a way that does not make them look incompetent—they are able to discuss how to get more input from Danny and his team.

De-linking and gaining insights is one way of developing new relationships and understandings among the parties in conflict. We have highlighted this strategy first, because the insight model of mediation is the foundation for this book. Yet, the insight mediator also uses more than traditional communication techniques and strategies to create different contexts for understanding. Some of the other creative means are addressed below; others are discussed in chapter 8.

Connecting Through Ritual

The sharing of rituals between opposing parties has been demonstrated to be effective in creating bridges. Practitioners involved in international disputes, such as the Israeli–Palestinian conflict and others, have noted the positive impact on both sides when they share meals and social time during lengthy negotiations. Strong advocacy roles are dropped during social rituals. Then, the parties can begin to learn about one another as husbands and wives, mothers and fathers, sisters and brothers, professionals, sports players, and other identities. In essence, they become "human" to one another and are less likely to see one another as "the faceless other." Connecting through rituals—whether meals, social events, religious or spiritual ceremonies—promotes relationship building, a prerequisite to seeking resolutions of mutual benefit.

Ritual is also about what is commonly done before, during, and at the end of the mediation—bringing symbolic meaning for the people involved. Ritual is a patterned set of actions through which we communicate meaning, build community, and remind people of the connections between each other. Some mediators describe the ritual of sharing food and drink to the disputants during the negotiations. Others start with a statement of wisdom, a prayer or blessing, a song, or gestures such as the shaking of hands, to communicate respect, cooperation, hope, or other important messages.

In Canada, the use of ritual is perhaps most pronounced in mediations involving First Nations people, where the absence of ritual would create a negative impact on the negotiation process. Their common and important rituals include the use of prayer before and/or after the session, a teaching by an elder, the smoking of sweet grass, and the use of a talking feather or stick to indicate whose turn it is to speak.

Winslade and Monk (2000) also talk about the importance of ritual, pointing out that, for many Maori in New Zealand, the absence of rituals for engagement (negotiation) would likely lead to the failure of the mediation. Our experience with working with immigrants from Africa and Asia has also taught us the importance of allowing story telling (no matter how long it takes) to be part of the mediation process. The setting of a protocol for the mediation session can also be seen as a ritual, to ensure respectful and safe discussions. So, too, what happens before the mediation—during the convening stage—can also be seen as ritualistic.

Visualizing

The positive effect of asking disputants to visualize a less conflictual scene or ideal future is also well documented. (See, for example, LeBaron, 2002, pp. 111–117.) Visualizing an image orients parties to work from that image—it becomes, in essence, their guiding light. The power of visualizing lies in its ability to shift perspectives and transform antagonistic parties into collaborating allies.

Imagine that the mediator asks the parties to describe the situation; she is likely to receive negative reports on the relationship and the other's actions. If, instead, she asks the parties to describe their ideal vision of the relationship—and then has them focus on how to get there—they are likely to shift into more productive dialogue, working from current strengths or advantages in the relationship to ways of enhancing those positive attributes.

Visualization and imagining do require a level of "readiness" on the part of those in conflict. While some mediators may begin their sessions requesting that the parties visualize the ideal future, others prefer to wait until the parties have had the opportunity to discuss past hurts and disappointments, and to resolve these as far as possible.

Doing the Unexpected

A mediator might ask the parties to draw their conflict, in the hope of eliciting more emotional, holistic, and creative ways of discussing the situation. Other mediators might ask parties to physically move, in order to "shake off" their rational perspective and tap into other sources of knowledge. Yet others might begin a mediation with music with the aim of establishing a peaceful environment or seeking a more emotional orientation to the session, by tapping into these resources early.

Mind, Heart, Body, and Spirit

Mediators must use all of their capacities in a session—the communication skills that they've been taught through training, their own analytical capacities to process the information they are receiving, and their intuitive ways of understanding and acting. Often, introductory training workshops focus exclusively on the acquisition of communication skills, which is why new mediators often lack confidence in their ability to conduct mediations. There is very little "teaching" of what to do with information about how each party defines his or her connections to the other. If this is the crux of understanding for mediators and the key to why mediation works, it should be the area of greatest focus in training. Mediators need to learn how to tap into their resources and develop a capacity to work with metaphors, symbols, imagery, narratives, and rituals.

Successful mediators are keen listeners. They pay attention not just to the parties but to the various systems of knowledge that emanate from their analytical, emotional, somatic, and intuitive intelligence. Mediation requires attention from one's whole self—and conflict must be seen as a whole system requiring a transformation. This may not be reassuring to the new mediator who wonders how he or she will ever get there. Lang and Taylor (2000) describe the process of becoming a mediator as one of developing artistry. We begin as novices, move to apprentices, work as practitioners, and finally become artists. The process repeats itself in every mediation, for it is a circle that forms a system of learning. (See figure 5.5.)

FIGURE 5.5 The Dynamic Four-Stage Model of Professional Development

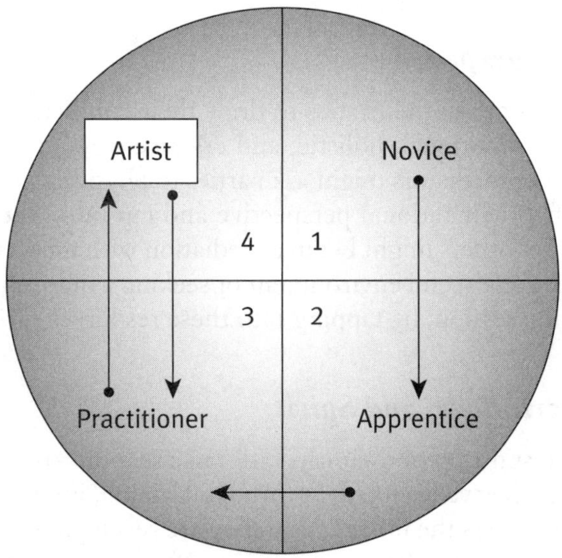

Novice: unaware, unskilled. *Apprentice*: somewhat aware, somewhat skilled. *Practitioner*: aware, skilled. *Artist*: heightened awareness, heightened skills.

Source: Lang & Taylor (2000, p. 12).

LeBaron (2002) urges us to develop our non-intellectual capacities so that we are better able to serve our mediation clients. Kydd (1996, p. 368) encourages us to return to the elemental sources of language—nature, family, love, and relations. He asks us to deepen our language, "exalt[ing] feeling, being and relation"; "green" our metaphors, using analogies that express relations that exist in nature—viewing the whole over the parts; and "culture" our language, adopting words of relation and feeling that come from other languages with richer and fuller understandings.

How Do We Know If Mediation Is Successful?

How should success be defined in mediation? Since the parties to the mediation are those who make the decisions, should success ultimately be defined by the parties themselves? Yet, the mediator also needs some template to determine whether he or she is meeting key objectives in practice. These are important questions for mediators and mediation evaluators to ask. In fact, success is often defined differently, depending on whom you ask (the parties, the mediator, parties' counsel) and which model of mediation is employed.

Some parties might define success in terms of how much they "win"—relative to the other party at the outset of a mediation. A party's counsel might define success in terms of how much more his or her party receives than what they could have got out of adjudication. Success here can be defined as relative material gain. Other parties come to mediation desiring to preserve their relationships—and so more collaborative outcomes will likely measure their success.

Different models of mediation will have different measures for success. Transformative mediators will likely consider their mediation a success if the parties leave the session feeling empowered, having demonstrated recognition. Mediators who use a narrative approach will call their sessions successful if an alternate narrative is created for the parties' understanding of their conflict. Settlement-oriented mediators deem a mediation successful if it ends in an agreement. Insight mediators will probably determine that a mediation is successful if the parties gain new insights and, thus, new perspectives on the situation and one another. This list could go on—there are as many definitions of success as there are types of mediators.

Based on the premise that mediation success is, at core, about transforming perspectives on relationships, measuring success requires that we seek information about any shifts in the understanding of the relationship, events, and actions that have shaped the new perspective. Few formal evaluations of mediation programs have undertaken to measure success. Perhaps the closest that some have come is in asking parties in conflict if they feel their relationship has been improved as a result of the mediation. This is an important question; however, explaining how the change in relationship occurred might be difficult for participants, particularly if the mediator engaged in a holistic approach to mediation, employing tactics to gain knowledge through non-traditional means.

A holistic approach to mediation can be healing, forward-looking, and educational for the parties and the mediator. It takes time to develop the artistry that this approach requires, and a new mediator does need to heed the "old" science while he or she is learning. If the mediator is truly connected to the parties, he or she will know whether the parties deem the mediation a success.

SUMMARY

There are both methodological and ideological reasons for selecting mediation as a dispute resolution process, yet its effectiveness is largely a result of its holistic approach to understanding conflict and helping parties to transform their relationship. A holistic approach is based on the "new science" method, which seeks knowledge through an understanding of relationships and interconnectedness of systems. Logic and rational discussion alone are not sufficient to understand the subjective experience of parties in conflict. Mediators still use "old" science methods of analysis and strategic planning, yet they rely equally on somatic, emotional, intuitive-imaginative, and "connected" knowledge to interpret and understand events and experiences. Mediators work to influence parties' ways of understanding, thus promoting relational change. This is done through the heart, mind, body, and spirit.

FURTHER READING

Lang, M., & Taylor, A. (2000). *The making of a mediator: Developing artistry in practice.* San Francisco: Jossey-Bass.

LeBaron, M. (2002). *Bridging troubled waters: Conflict resolution from the heart.* San Francisco: Jossey-Bass.

Wheatley, M.J. (1999). *Leadership and the new science.* San Francisco: Berrett-Koehler Publications.

CHAPTER SIX

Opting for a Guide: The Mediation Process

Mediation is the chicken soup of dispute resolution. It can't hurt, and it might just do some good.

Kent Stauffer, Director of Litigation, Chase Manhattan Bank

In this chapter, we examine more closely the interest-based approach to mediation. To this end, we consider a typical mediation of a two-party dispute, and examine what the mediator and the parties do at various stages throughout the mediation. In particular, we examine three key elements of the interest-based approach to mediation: the roles of the parties and their advisers, the role of the mediator, and the stages of the process. We then go into more detail about the stages of the insight model of mediation and end the chapter with a brief discussion on the role of advisers in mediation.

EXAMINING THE INTEREST-BASED APPROACH TO MEDIATION

Every mediation—indeed, every dispute resolution process—has a structure. Key elements of mediation include the participants, their roles, the conflict issues, and the process. To begin, we consider the principles of mediation, the goals of the mediator and the parties, and how these goals influence the process. One assumption that we make in our analysis is that the participants, including the mediator, are strategic in their approach. Strategic action is goal-directed action, so we assume that the participants have conscious goals relating to the outcome of the dispute, and that the actions they take in dealing with the situation are intended to help them achieve these goals. This does not mean that everything that a party says or does contributes to achieving his or her goals; far from it. Often what people in conflict say or do *prevents* them from achieving their goals, whether from irrational behaviour or bad strategy. Whether successful or not, mediation participants generally act purposefully—to achieve certain objectives.

Another assumption that we make is that the parties' dispute resolution goals are motivated by their personal values, needs, beliefs, and fears—in other words, their interests. Unfortunately, a person's goals may not always be the best thing in the long run. By way of illustration: a person who is primarily motivated to get revenge for a perceived injustice may be driven to pursue what proves to be a destructive course of action. In this case the person is driven by negative interests—getting revenge and punishing the perceived wrongdoer. As Rubin and Levinger (1995, pp. 18–20) say, in most conflicts, the parties have a mixture of competitive, cooperative, and individual motives, which can have destructive or constructive consequences. It is this mixture of motives that determines people's goals in mediation.

The goals of a mediator are influenced by the parties' goals. Having responsibility for facilitating the mediation, which is also goal-directed, mediators work to influence the parties' goals in a positive way. A mediator's goal is to increase cooperation and collaboration between the parties, while overcoming competitive and adversarial behaviours. The mediator's process goals are also influenced by the principles that govern his or her practice, and these are determined by their world views about conflict and its resolution. For example, many mediators adhere to the principle of self-determination, which says that the parties, not the mediator, should determine the outcome of mediation. Mediators may also act on a moral belief that people should live in harmony with each other.

To visualize the relationship among mediation, goals, and interests, see figure 6.1.

PRINCIPLES OF INTEREST-BASED APPROACHES TO MEDIATION

Many principles of mediation have been articulated in the literature. Some of these have been outlined for you in earlier chapters. Here, we have organized them into three categories: (1) process, (2) relational, and (3) outcome.

FIGURE 6.1 Influences on the Mediation Process

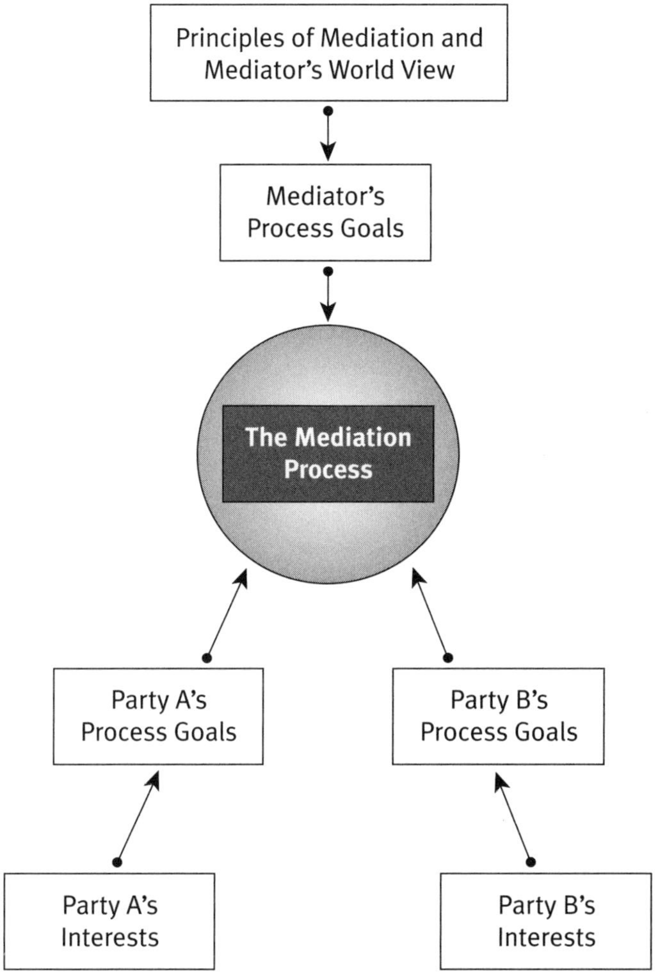

Process Principles

Interest-Based Process

The mediator will structure and implement a mediation process that meets the parties' collective needs and promotes their best interests. All process decisions, such as who attends, the roles of the participants, and the mediation guidelines, will be governed by what best suits the interests of all parties.

Process Integrity

How the parties and the mediator interact, their roles, and the nature and quality of their communications and behaviours will be consistent with what all participants have agreed. The participants commit to a certain type and quality of process—and their role and involvement in it. They do that during the pre-mediation process (covered in the next chapter). By mutual consent, any participant may modify that commitment at any time during the process. To the extent that what actually happens during the process and what participants actually say and do is consistent with their process commitment, there is a high degree of process integrity.

Process Efficiency

A primary responsibility of a mediator is to minimize the cost of a conflict and its resolution process—and, in particular, to minimize waste of time and expense.

Process Fairness

The mediator must ensure that the mediation process is fair to all parties. That will mean different things to different people. Indeed, the concept of "fair" has various philosophical and cultural formulations. One definition of process fairness is that (1) each party is able to fully express his or her perspective, concerns, needs, and interests so they are understood by all other participants; (2) each party's concerns are adequately explored, clarified, and addressed; and (3) the process for formulating a resolution is equally responsive to the legitimate interests of all parties. Whether a fair process will necessarily result in a fair outcome may be a matter for debate. Some say that the outcome of a fair process is, by definition, a fair outcome. (See further discussion of procedural justice in chapter 10.)

Participatory Process Determination

The parties decide the process guidelines and protocols—for example, how they will interact and communicate during the process, and the mediator's role in that. The mediator will facilitate the parties' discussion of different process options; however, all participants (including the mediator) will determine and agree on the guidelines and protocols that will govern their process and the roles that each of them will have in implementing them.

Relational Principles

Respectful and Mutually Beneficial Interaction

A good mediation process is one that is respectful, safe, and mutually beneficial for all parties. The mediator will develop and implement a mediation process that, as much as possible, promotes interaction that is respectful, constructive, and mutually beneficial among all parties.

Being Elicitive

This principle recognizes that people relate to and interact differently with others, especially in conflict situations. A number of factors determine how an individual will tend to think, feel, and act in a conflict situation, including culture, gender, age, education, physical setting, and context. The principle of elicitive process says that a mediator needs to explore these factors and elicit from the parties their individual and collective needs in relation to the process used to deal with the conflict. Using this elicitive approach, the mediator will develop, or help the parties develop, a process that will meet their needs, including who attends, the physical location and setting, and the nature and channels of communications.

Self-Motivated Collaboration

Genuine collaboration between parties in conflict occurs only when each party really understands what collaboration means and requires, and he or she truly wants to engage in a collaborative process. A party under the influence of a well-intentioned mediator may pay lip service to the collaborative approach. However, without true self-motivation, that party's actions and interaction with the "adversary" will probably belie his or her stated intentions.

Obstacles to Collaboration

People in conflict always have adversarial perceptions, emotions, assumptions, and beliefs that prevent them from engaging in constructive, collaborative interaction. Deliberate and strategic steps are required to enable disputants to overcome these and other obstacles to collaboration. Forces that are seemingly beyond the parties' control—and some of which are outside their awareness—cause them to act destructively. Chapters 3 and 9 deal at some length with these phenomena.

Outcome Principles

Self-Determination

The best outcome from mediation is one that is determined by the parties, not by the mediator. The mediator will structure and facilitate a mediation process that will enable the parties to do that—reach their own decisions about an outcome.

Right Relations

Good relationships are mutually and collectively beneficial. They promote and enable individual expression and self-actualization and, at the same time, create a collective synergy that produces a collaborative whole.

Collaborative Decision Making

The best outcome, both substantive and relationally, is achieved through a process of collaborative interaction whereby *all* parties participate in the *collective* decision-making process. The mediator will enable all parties to be full participants in a decision-making process for which "the whole is greater than the sum of the parts."

Principles of Mediation Exercise

Using the Car Repair Blues scenario from chapter 3, identify two or three main principles of mediation that would guide *you* as mediator in this case, then answer the following questions:

1. What are your principles, what do they mean to you, and what are their implications in this situation?
2. Why would these principles in this case be important for *you* as mediator?
3. How would you prioritize the principles you have identified for yourself? Is there one principle that you would say is paramount?
4. Can you imagine a circumstance in which one or more of your principles might conflict with each other? What effect, if any, would that have on the formulation of your principles?

GOALS OF THE INTEREST-BASED APPROACH TO MEDIATION

What is the goal of a particular mediation? Who determines it? What is a successful mediation? How do we define it? In chapter 2, we discussed the goals and impact of mediation; in chapter 4, we saw how different approaches set different goals for the mediator. In this chapter, we focus more specifically on the goals of the parties and the mediator. Although a party's goals may often overlap with those of the mediator, there are times when they conflict.

A mediator's goals might include the following:

- All issues are adequately explored and discussed, and the parties make the best decision possible with respect to each of these issues.
- Parties reach a point in their assisted negotiation process where they are able to interact in a mutually respectful and collaborative manner.
- Parties are empowered to resolve their dispute and they recognize how the situation affects the other party.
- Parties understand each other better, and blocked channels of communication are opened.
- Parties identify and understand all possible options for resolving the issues between them, including understanding how each option may satisfy the immediate and long-term interests of the parties, individually and collectively.
- Parties establish *right relations* in terms of future interactions/relations between them.
- Parties reach a "good" agreement, which settles all, or at least some, of the disputed issues.

Mediation goals are embedded in different approaches to mediation, and it is these goals that draw a mediator to adopt a particular approach. A party, when informed, can also seek a particular mediation approach. By way of illustration, the goals of insight, narrative, and transformative mediation are listed below.

Insight Mediation

This approach helps parties gain insights that shift the course of the conflict and create spaces for collective action.

Narrative Mediation

In this approach, the mediator forms a partnership with disputing parties, to better understand the stories behind the conflict, and to co-produce their alternative preferred stories as a basis of mutual understanding in order to find a way forward.

Transformative Mediation

In this approach, the mediator helps to support the parties' desire for moral growth and development, to give them an opportunity to act from *compassionate strength*, and to assist disputants to move from positions of relative weakness and uncertainty to strength—and from self-absorption to an ability to listen and respond to each other's perspective.

In the Car Repair Blues scenario described in chapter 3, or any other conflict for that matter, consider how a person's dispute resolution goal may be contrary to his or her long-term and best interests. One scenario that comes to mind is that unresolved "negative" emotions, taken too far, can drive people to action that ultimately takes a toll on their psyches, bank accounts, careers, or family relations.

Mediation Goals Exercise

Re-read the Car Repair Blues scenario from chapter 3. Then, reflecting back on a mediator's possible dispute resolution goals listed above, think about what Dale's goal(s) might be? How about Chris's goal(s)?

Imagine another version of the same scenario, if Dale and Chris were other people with different personalities or backgrounds. How might their goals change?

THE ROLE OF A MEDIATOR IN INTEREST-BASED APPROACHES

Mediators' roles vary, depending on their approach to mediation. For example, in insight mediation, as in narrative and transformative mediation, the role of the mediator is elicitive, facilitative, and enabling. In evaluative and problem-solving mediation, the mediator's role is more directive, pragmatic, and involved in ensuring a dispute is settled. Generally, mediators who use interest-based approaches try to engage in a mutually beneficial negotiation process, to enable parties to achieve what *they* determine is their best outcome. Following are some of the key roles of an interest-based mediator.

Establish and Manage the Process

The mediator takes the lead in establishing and implementing the mediation process. He or she, in collaboration with the parties, determines the elements of the process, including who should attend, the roles of participants and the mediator, and process and communication guidelines. The mediator does not simply impose a rigid, standardized process on the parties, but elicits the parties' opinions and input in establishing the process. This emerges from a consideration of the needs and abilities of the disputants, recognizing that the parties often rely on the mediator's experience and expertise. The mediator assists the parties in reaching a decision on how they will interact in the mediation. Ideally, this involves committing to respectful, collaborative interaction and seeking to fully understand the perspectives and interests of the other party. Parties agree to this because they genuinely believe it is in their best interests to do so, not because the mediator suggests it.

The mediator needs to assume and commit to the responsibility of ensuring process integrity. An essential element of this is the mediator's commitment to managing the process, to ensure that both parties' experience of the process will be what they "bargained for."

Assess Parties' Collaborating Knowledge and Skills

The mediator needs to ensure that the parties have a genuine willingness to collaborate. Disputants may have things to learn—and obstacles and "disabilities" to overcome—before the core mediation begins, if it is to succeed. In addition, the mediator must feel assured that the parties understand the principle of collaboration, why it is beneficial for them, and what they can achieve by such an approach.

Educate the Parties

The mediator may need to tutor, so that each party has the communication skills necessary for a collaborative interaction process. The mediator may also need to educate the parties on the nature and elements of collaborative interaction, their role and responsibilities, and what they can expect of the mediator. This may include helping them appreciate—and overcoming—some of the difficulties and challenges of collaborating. Each party needs to understand and accept that the other party has different perceptions, interpretations, behaviours, emotions, and goals that are legitimate. We tell parties that "understanding does not mean agreement." With that knowledge, both parties must be willing to try to understand the other party's perspectives, even though they may disagree with them. Finally, both parties must be willing, at some level, to work at overcoming their barriers to collaborating—and must want to try to find a resolution that will serve their own interests and those of the other parties. The mediator's objective is to help each party come to understand the advantages to them of collaborative interaction and negotiation—and a willingness to commit to such a process. This education—through modelling, direct instruction, or other means—starts in the convening stage and continues throughout the mediation.

Facilitate Communication and Collaboration—and Intervene Selectively

Even with a good understanding of, and commitment to, collaborative interaction, parties in conflict generally need a mediator to facilitate their conflict communication, their exploration of their conflict perceptions, emotions, and assumptions, and the discovery of their own key interests. The mediator actively intervenes to help both parties resolve or overcome their obstacles to collaborative interaction.

In fulfilling this role, the mediator needs to recognize that the barriers parties have will impact how they communicate and interact. These barriers will *always* affect each of them individually and relationally. Throughout the process, the mediator intervenes to ensure that the mediation process is indeed serving the parties' best interests.

Help Parties Generate Options To Optimize Negotiated Outcomes

If the goal of the mediation process is to help the parties reach the best possible negotiated outcome, the mediator often encourages the parties to brainstorm options. He or she helps the parties to realize their shared creative potential, which will enable them to achieve the optimal win–win outcome. Adversarial attitudes and approaches rarely produce this.

THE PARTIES' PERSPECTIVE

Mediation is simply assisted negotiation. The primary objective of an interest-based mediator is to enable the parties to engage in collaborative negotiation. In this process, disputants are encouraged to be respectful, open, and cooperative. However, think for a moment about two people in a dispute, who have never experienced mediation and know very little about it. What might they be thinking and feeling about the situation, and about each other? Let's return to our Car Repair Blues scenario and the two parties, Dale and Chris.

Before mediation, Dale might perceive Chris as a cheat and an arrogant chauvinist who would gladly gouge her for an extra $500. She feels anger and resentment and generally has a "negative attitude" toward him. Dale feels strongly that she has been victimized by Chris and that, as soon as the mediator gets the whole story, he will help her get her car back and resolve the dispute fairly.

On the other hand, we might find that Chris perceives Dale as a pushy, inconsiderate, "superior" person who expects him to drop whatever he's doing and jump when she calls. He may well believe that he bent over backward to provide Dale with fast, excellent service, and that he makes essential repairs at fair rates. Therefore, he is offended at Dale's attempt to get something for nothing, by twisting and manipulating the situation. Chris has agreed to mediation because he is certain that any fair-minded person will see Dale for the kind of person she is and will set her straight.

As in many conflict situations, Chris and Dale have strong *adversarial* perceptions, emotions, and assumptions toward each other—and these will obviously influence how they interact in mediation. As well, they apparently have very limited understanding, even misunderstanding, of mediation, the mediator's role, and their own role in the process. So, in the convening phase and in the early stages of the mediation, the mediator must address these adversarial attitudes, the parties' expectations of the mediator's role, and their own role in the mediation.

The mediator can help the parties move from an adversarial to a collaborative interaction, if each party understands what is required and takes individual responsibility to achieve that—but only if they both want to. The mediator *cannot* do that, only the parties can. Parties often need a lot of assistance from the mediator, but, no matter how much they rely on the mediator's skill, presence, and wisdom, they will successfully collaborate only by their own efforts, insights, and understanding.

This principle of self-motivated collaboration is fundamental to the role of a mediator. Genuine collaboration between parties in conflict occurs only when each party really understands what collaboration means and requires, and truly wants to engage in a collaborative process. However, in most conflict situations, such understanding and motivation will not, indeed cannot, be achieved at the start of the mediation process. Yes, the mediator explains the process and may try to persuade each party of the benefits of a collaborative approach, but this requires much more than a rational, analytical understanding. Mediators need to recognize that, if collaboration is to be achieved, party understanding and motivation must develop through the mediation process, as each party gains experience and insights of genuine collaborative interaction. In some cases, the mediator may have to "work wonders" if the parties are to fully engage and interact with each other as collaborative negotiators.

THE PROCESS USED IN INTEREST-BASED APPROACHES

Every mediation session has a structure and a style. Some may be "loose," spontaneous, and unstructured; others may be very structured, following a logical sequence of pre-patterned steps. Different models of mediation are used for different types of disputes. For example, the more therapeutic model of mediation often found in divorce mediation is different from that of "muscle mediation" used in international disputes. And mediation between neighbours or school children looks different from mediation between business partners, or between an insurance company and a person injured in a car accident.

Different models of interest-based mediation set out the various aspects of a mediator's involvement with the parties, both individually and jointly, from the time of initial contact until the completion of the mediation, including any followup. Most models include convening, possibly even before the mediator is contacted, and any activity by parties on their own, as in the case of parties doing individual preparation.

The mediation approach that we use and focus on most in this book is insight mediation, a form of interest-based mediation that is based on principled negotiation. Interest-based models of mediation are structured in stages that can range from as few as 3, found in narrative mediation (Winslade and Monk, 2000), to as many as 12 (Moore, 1996). More commonly we find 4 to 5 stages that tend to follow a pattern of storytelling, exploration of interests, and option generating. The fact that the stages can be different highlights a major advantage of mediation: its flexibility and diversity. Each stage in mediation has certain objectives—in other words, a strategic purpose. The mediator needs to know what types of activities and communications occur in each stage of the model she is using and why parties need to engage in these activities at this particular time. By way of illustration, if our goal is to have a beautiful garden that will delight the eye and calm the soul, one of our objectives will be to start with a deep garden bed of rich, fertile soil. We will have to invest hours of time and effort in digging out and carting away the useless rocks and dirt that are 4 inches below the surface, and bringing in many loads of "super soil," mushroom compost, and other smelly stuff that plants love. Our objective of having 18 to 24 inches of fertile, aerated, and well-drained organic material in the entire garden bed is a key requirement for achieving our goal of a beautiful garden. It is one of our strategic objectives.

While different models of interest-based mediation differ in the number of stages, as well as the roles and goals of the mediator, there is a general pattern of progression that each model follows—and each stage has certain objectives, a strategic purpose. To illustrate, before parties discuss possible options for resolving the issues, the mediator tries to get the disputants to reach a deeper understanding of the other party's interests in the issues. This is based on the fundamental principle that the more the parties know about their individual and collective interests, the greater will be their ability to generate a broad range of creative and mutually acceptable options. If the parties go directly to discussing options and negotiating their final agreement before they have explored their interests and gained a deeper understanding of each other, they will be confined to a narrower range of options. This may result in agreements that fail to last, or at best serve as a Band-Aid solution, rather than one that is more likely to be long term and stable. Furthermore, parties will fail to discover and appreciate potential benefits they could have realized from their negotiation.

Now, we look more closely at the mediator's goals in a specific, interest-based approach—the insight model of mediation—as well as the stages of the process.

GOALS OF AN INSIGHT MEDIATOR

The insight mediator's primary goal is to help parties gain insight into the cares and concerns that underlie the conflict situation and that are affecting their lives and the lives of others. This insight can enable the parties to reach consensual decisions that accommodate their needs. It is a self-empowering process that emphasizes self-determination and interconnectedness. In insight mediation, relationship and interdependence are seen as cornerstones of conflict resolution.

By helping the parties gain insights into their own and the other party's interests, the mediator can help shift the course of the conflict and create space for collective action. When one party articulates his or her interests, the other party has the opportunity to gain an insight—a discovery about why this is important to the other person—and begin to relate to this interest. One party doesn't suddenly make the other's interests and values paramount; he or she just begins to see how and why the other person finds these important. There is an empathy that arises because the interest expresses more than just an idiosyncratic desire of the other person. Rather, it evokes something broader and deeper that can be shared by the other person, who can appreciate that it is something worth caring about.

The underlying philosophy for this implies that interests are not simply individual—they are shared human experiences. This is what we mean by the holistic approach. We can discover deeper human values, and others can come to understand and appreciate those as worthwhile because they form part of a shared experience. Connected to this is the idea that we really should come to appreciate the interests of others and that this appreciation is a key to resolving conflicts.

Chapter 4, listed the beliefs that underlie the insight model. These can be condensed into two overarching tenets. First, people are both individual and interconnected; living in relation to others leads them to want to understand each other more than to achieve individual gain. Second, people do act on their values and interests; however, mediation has the potential to empower individuals to achieve greater "insights" into these values and interests—and these insights can change how people see and feel about things, which in turn can change the conflict dynamic. Insight mediation is thus a relational activity that takes a holistic approach to the practice of mediation.

STAGES OF THE INSIGHT MEDIATION MODEL

The insight model of mediation has five stages determined by the values, beliefs, and goals mentioned above. After pre-mediation, the stages are as follows: (1) establishing the process, (2) stating hopes and problems, (3) seeking insights into interests, (4) collaborating to meet interests, and (5) making decisions. (See figure 6.2.)

FIGURE 6.2 The Stages of Insight Mediation

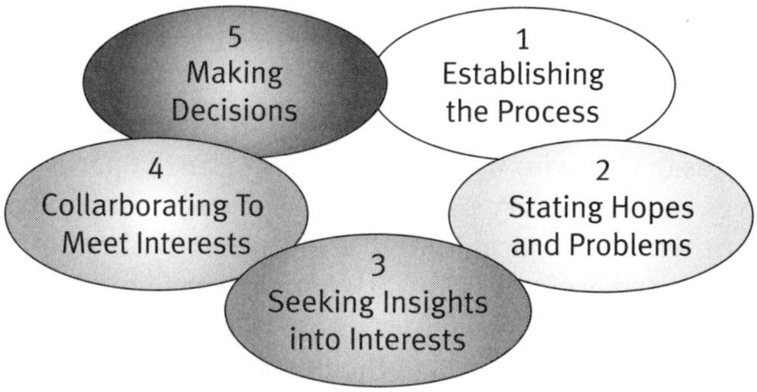

While there is a pattern of progression that these five stages follow, they are fluid, not linear or rigid. Often the parties' negotiations occur in such a way that the mediator does not complete a stage before moving to another, thus having to go back to complete the stage.

Before we explore the five stages of the insight model, what goes on before parties actually meet face to face? The next chapter examines the convening process in great detail, but here is a summary of what can be considered "pre-mediation" work.

Pre-Mediation

Before mediation takes place, all parties are informed of the various features of the process, and agreement is obtained to proceed. The issues discussed and agreed to beforehand usually include who will attend, confidentiality, impact on possible future proceedings, stages of the process and their objectives, communication and interaction guidelines, the roles of the mediator and the parties, as well as logistical information and requirements. Some mediators put this information into a written Consent To Mediate form, which is reviewed by the parties and signed at the first joint session. (A sample form is reproduced in appendix A.) In cases with complex substantive or legal issues, preparation means collecting and becoming familiar with relevant data.

For parties to make fully informed decisions, they usually need to be educated about the mediation process, their role, and the role of the mediator. Since imposing a set of rigid terms and conditions would be contrary to the principle of self-determination, the mediator (or convenor—the person coordinating the mediation) will elicit each party's opinions and input on various process decisions, ensuring that all parties understand and commit to a process that is in each of their best interests.

The final task of a mediator in pre-mediation is to determine how best to conduct the mediation. This question involves when and where to hold the mediation, what physical arrangements are needed to accommodate disabilities, the seating pattern to use, the use and shape of a table, and the need for and availability of private caucus rooms. It also includes considering who will participate, in terms of parties, their representatives, and secondary parties such as friends, constituents, or the media. Furthermore, consideration is given to whether co-mediation, or even panel mediation, would work better than single mediation.

Now, using the Car Repair Blues scenario to illustrate, we describe in some detail what happens through the five stages of the insight model of mediation.

Stage 1: Establishing the Process

It is essential in stage 1 that the mediator review all aspects of the mediation process, answer any questions, and get verbal confirmation of each party's understanding and commitment. This is done even when most, if not all, of the process issues were discussed and agreed to by the parties before the initial joint session. (A mediation can comprise several or many sessions.) Both parties need to know, with some degree of confidence, that the other party has the same understanding and commitment toward the process.

Included in the mediator's explanation of the process are issues of confidentiality, goals for the mediation, the role of the mediator and parties, protocol or guidelines to be followed, use of caucus, length of the session, confirmation of authority to settle, and how decisions will be formalized. Parties are reminded that they are in charge of outcomes and that the mediator has no decision-making authority.

Stage 1 gives the mediator a chance to establish a relationship with the parties and set a tone of warmth, trust, and competence. It also provides the first opportunity for the mediator to demonstrate his or her promise to listen and to respond to the concerns of the parties. Mediators who employ "alternative" strategies might begin this stage with a ritual—the smoking of sweet grass, an exercise to release physical tension, or other creative strategies.

Using the Car Repairs Blues scenario, a typical script for introducing the process might sound like this:

Hello, Dale and Chris. I am pleased you both came today, because I know it takes effort to talk face to face about issues you do not agree on, and that you feel strongly about. I want you to know that while mediation may not be easy, in my experience it is often useful and successful.

As you recall, I met with each of you separately to explain what would happen here today and to determine whether the issues that you disagree on are appropriate for mediation. We have determined that in fact they are. Let me begin by reviewing some of what we talked about:

- *My role is to help the two of you talk about your differences so that you gain insights into what is motivating you to feel the way you do—and that might help you to understand each other better. It is these insights that lead to collective action and finding ways to resolve conflict.*
- *I will not judge who is right or wrong, nor will I be telling you what you should do to change the situation. Whatever decisions are reached here today will come from the two of you. If you decide it would be useful to put these decisions in writing, we can talk about how best to do it.*
- *At any time you can ask to meet with me privately. I may also feel the need to talk with each of you privately, in a caucus, and will let you know if I do.*

Dale and Chris, do each of you understand and agree to these points? Do either of you have anything to add or change about my role in the mediation?

From my experience, there are ways of behaving in mediation that help it to work best.

- *The first is that you listen to each other and wait until the other is finished speaking before presenting your views. In particular, I am going to ask you to listen carefully for information that brings new meaning to the issues. This may not be easy, because you already know that you do not see things the same way. I have brought paper and pens so that you can note any points you want to comment on when it is your turn to talk.*
- *I am also going to ask you to be open and honest with each other and share whatever information is relevant and that might help you find ways to resolve this dispute.*
- *Finally, I would like you to focus on what this situation has been like for you, rather than attaching blame or accusing each other of being the problem. It is hard to listen when we feel judged and blamed.*
- *Is there anything that either of you would like to add to ensure a productive and safe discussion today?*

Although I have already discussed these points with each of you individually, I want to ensure that each of you is agreeable to these process guidelines, and also that you have a chance to add anything to improve the process. Chris? Dale? Are you each okay with what has been discussed thus far?

I want to assure you that what I hear today will remain confidential. I will not be discussing what I hear outside the room, nor am I required to report on what the two of you discuss. I am wondering what expectations the two of you have regarding limits, if any, to confidentiality?

I also want to find out if each of you has the authority to settle this dispute today. Dale or Chris, do you need to consult anyone before making final decisions on the issues between you?

We have scheduled three hours for this mediation. Are you both still prepared to be here for that long? I will keep track of the time and will let you know, a half hour or so before our time is up, so that you can decide if it is possible to complete the mediation today, or if you want to reschedule another session. I would also ask that you turn off any cellphones or pagers while you are here.

Do either of you have any questions or want to add anything? Are you both ready and willing to proceed with the mediation?

Thus ends stage 1. Of course, the mediator needs to deal with any additional points or questions raised by the parties. Many times, this requires negotiating differences of opinion about confidentiality. Then, the mediator moves to stage 2.

Stage 2: Stating Hopes and Problems

Stage 2 begins with the mediator's request for a brief opening statement from each side. In insight mediation, the opening statements consist of two parts: the problem each party has come to discuss and their hopes for the mediation. This gives each party a chance to tell the other party—and the mediator—what is important. Stating their "hopes" for the mediation is useful because it helps to establish a sense of good will early in the process. It often elicits positive, "hopeful" comments shared by the parties, thus encouraging them to participate. It also tends to shift the first set of statements—by the parties in joint session—away from positional demands and accusatory remarks.

The opening statement is intended to be brief, so the mediator does not probe for detailed information at this time. Instead, he or she assures both parties that they will have ample opportunity to describe the problem more fully as the mediation progresses. By not allowing one party to speak too long in the beginning, mediators reduce the risk of the non-speaking party feeling excluded—or wondering whether the mediator might have already sided with the other party. It also lessens the chance that the second speaker will feel defensive, before having a chance to present his or her views.

The mediator's request for an opening statement might go something like this:

Dale and Chris, I would like each of you to give me a brief statement about what it is that you have come to talk to each other about—and what you hope will happen as a result of this conversation. Please be assured that you will have ample time to go into the details of the situation as we proceed. At this point, I would very much like you to share some of your hopes for the mediation, along with a general sense of the problem needing to be discussed. Which one of you would like to begin?

Mediators often have to give parties time to think about the question of who should begin. If neither party offers, they find an impartial way to ask one party to start. A common practice is to begin with the person who first requested the mediation.

It is important for mediators to paraphrase immediately after each person's opening statement, as it is the first opportunity they have to demonstrate, in a joint session, that they are interested in what each party has to say. It models good listening and often helps the other party hear things in a new light.

During this stage, the mediator is trying to identify the main problem that has given rise to this dispute—the "presenting problem." After each party's opening statement, the mediator seeks to broaden the story line through comments such as,

It would be good to get some background to this situation and how it became a problem for the two of you.

Or

Dale, please tell me more about how you came to be at Chris's garage.

It may take a while to surface all the issues, especially in multi-issue disputes. At this stage, the mediator is trying to get a "snapshot" of the problem and the issues that need to be discussed in the mediation. The mediator is not yet probing for underlying motives or emotions; that happens during the next stage.

To conclude stage 2, the mediator summarizes the views of both parties and begins to "map a framework" for their discussions. Some models of mediation refer to this as an "issue statement," a statement of the overall problem to be negotiated. A summary or issue statement in this case might sound something like this:

Dale, a few days ago you left your car at Chris's garage for a tune-up because it was running rough. You needed your car, so you asked Chris to have it ready by the end of the day. Chris, you agreed to try and move things around to accommodate Dale's request to have her car fixed in one day. After inspecting the car, you found that the radiator was almost shot. You tried to reach Dale, and when you could not you went ahead and did the work. Dale, when you came to pick the car up you were shocked by the amount you were being charged, which angered you and you left without your car. It seems we need to talk more about the repairs to the car and the costs, how the situation has affected each of you, and how to deal with the car, which is still in the garage.

Stage 3: Seeking Insights into Interests

This stage is the heart of the mediation process. It is where insights are gained and confirmed as accurate—and the "magic" occurs. After identifying the problem in stage 2, the mediator attempts to "peel back the onion" to find what underlies the issues, what is at the core of the problem. It is quite common for parties to be reluctant to talk about the underlying problem, because it is private and risky. They may not even be fully aware of what lies underneath their positions.

Strategically, the mediator tries to broaden the discussion and uncover interests, asking open broadening questions such as:

What happened when you found the radiator faulty, Chris?

What made you decide to go ahead and replace it?

Dale, how did you feel when you saw how much you were being charged for the work on your car?

After broadening the "story," the mediator will explore more fully, asking deepening questions, which are generated directly from answers to the broadener questions. (Broadening and deepending questions are described in detail in chapter 8.) The mediator's objective is to help the parties gain insight into what is important to them about the issues, to hear and learn what is important to the other person, as well as what is motivating each of them, and why. The mediator then links each of these interests to the issues in dispute. For this stage, a mediator takes on the role of a *curious* guide embarking on a path of *discovery* with the parties, to help them gain *insights* into their separate as well as shared needs. These insights are what help parties collaborate on the construction of a plan to satisfactorily resolve their issues.

Quite simply, mediators seek insights by listening. They are curious. They wonder. They question underlying motives, concerns, needs. They notice. They get hunches. They listen for discrepancies. They probe intent. They acknowledge and validate. They paraphrase to open new horizons and shift horizons. They search for ways that parties can save face and negotiate away from their positional "corner." Being curious promotes individual viewpoints coming together to create a "bigger picture"; listening for discrepancies leads to changing the angle from which the problem is being viewed; and making links between the past, present, and future leads to a reformulation of original positions. The mediator then verifies, with the parties, that these insights are accurate. The discipline of collecting data, getting insights, and judging them to be correct constitutes, for Lonergan, the cognitional process (Morelli & Morelli, 2002, p. 162).

During stage 3, a mediator asks lots of questions to draw out interests. Interests are the motives underlying a person's demands. We call them CHEAP BFV questions, which you will recall (from chapter 1) stands for concerns, hopes, expectations, assumptions, priorities, beliefs, fears, and values. In this scenario, here are some CHEAP BFV questions the mediator might ask:

What are some of your concerns regarding the cost of repairs?

What did you hope Chris would do upon finding problems with the car?

What were your expectations of what you should do after finding problems with Dale's car?

It seems you made some assumptions about how the repairs were carried out. What were some of those assumptions, Dale?

Getting your car back without having to incur a large debt is a priority for you, isn't it, Dale? It might be helpful to tell us more about why that is.

What has been your biggest fear through all of this?

Chris, you talked about how you place a high value on quality work at your garage. How did this influence the actions you took with Dale's car?

An important strategy in the insight model is called "linking and de-linking." It helps mediators discover what the parties' feelings are about, what really matters to them, and why. This strategy is important because it helps to make sense of people's present behaviour. Our experience shows that parties often make assumptions about how the other's values pose a threat to their own. Clarifying mistaken assumptions can often de-escalate the conflict situation. Furthermore, by finding out what feelings are about, the values that are driving people's actions become clearer. Learning how one person's cares may be linked to what is threatening or concerning the other is often at the root of the conflict. Parties themselves may not be fully aware of this relationship and how it is affecting the conflict situation.

Finding how one party's cares are linked to what threatens the other is done intentionally. Insight mediators often ask parties this very question. Throughout the mediation, from beginning to end, they are listening carefully to each party's story—in particular, they are listening for discrepancies in what each of the parties is describing. They are listening for information on how past histories are linked to current feelings. Has something similar happened in the past and how is that affecting a party now? How is that event linked to his or her current position on the issues in dispute, and how is it linked to his or her behaviour in the conflict? They also listen for and ask about how present behaviours are linked to anticipated outcomes—and how parties' experiences are currently affecting their relationship with one another. Accomplishing this task may require the mediator to employ creative and intuitive knowledge and skills, as well as linear logic tools.

Once the parties and the mediator get insight into the interests and values that lie behind both parties' positions, the mediator attempts to discover whether what one party cares about is *necessarily* a threat to the other party's cares. If it is discovered that this is not necessarily true, the mediator works to "de-link" these connections. De-linking incorrect links is an inverse insight that results from the mediator listening for discrepancy and from his or her continued curiosity. It involves separating the parties as objects of conflict, identifying incorrect assumptions, and separating past experiences and anticipated outcomes from present feelings. This opens up space for parties to be curious and circumstances for them to care about each other.

Once each party's key issues have been identified and the interests behind them understood, the mediator works with the parties to prioritize these issues through the process of hypothesis generating, building, testing, and accepting or rejecting, which we discussed in the previous chapter. The mediator may do this by determining the level of importance of each issue for each party, or by identifying the most likely areas for movement at the time. Large concerns may be broken into smaller ones; negative concerns or perceptions may be reframed. If appropriate, the mediator may write the issues or interests, or both, on a flip chart, chalk board, or easel.

Another important strategy for mediators is to identify what both parties agree on and what they have in common. Often, parties have the perception that they do not agree on anything, making them feel less than hopeful about finding a collaborative solution. Effective mediators allow silence to exist. Other activities in this stage can include highlighting areas of progress, reframing indirect or negative interests, and working to achieve and maintain a climate of productive interaction. These tasks require the mediator to use effective communication skills, such as reflective listening, broadening and deepening questions, bridging, immediacy, normalizing, and confronting discrepancy. Mediators are also transparent about their intentions, and they share the responsibility for the mediation with the parties. They avoid premature assessments, act as an agent of reality in joint sessions and in caucus, help parties to focus on objective criteria, and continuously remind parties of their progress, emphasizing areas of agreement and common ground.

In chapter 4, we identified seven distinct tasks of a mediator seeking insights into interests. Here is a summary of these tasks, framed as questions:

1. What is going on?
2. How do parties feel about what is going on?
3. Where do these feelings come from?
4. How are parties' current feelings linked to culture, past experiences, feelings, and values, and how are they linked to anticipated outcomes?
5. What does one party hear as being important to the other, and how does that threaten what matters to him or her?
6. To what extent must one party's cares necessarily be linked to what threatens the other party?
7. What would make it possible for each party to get what he or she values?

After individual and mutual issues and interests have been identified, the mediator may form a goal statement as a way to make a transition from stage 3 to 4. In this scenario, the mediator's goal statement might be something like this:

> *Given that you both want to settle this today—so that you, Dale, have the use of your car, and Chris, you can get on with work at the garage—what might each of you do that will meet your need, Dale, for fair and reasonable payments for the work that was done, and your need, Chris, for recognition for your work and service and having a reputation for that in the community?*

Stage 4: Collaborating To Meet Interests

During this stage, the mediator continues to encourage the parties to negotiate by inviting them to think about additional options for agreement and closure. "Brainstorming" is often used to generate a larger range of options. Brainstorming invites parties to put creative energy into thinking of as many solutions as possible to solve the problem, no matter how far-fetched the ideas may seem. Parties are discouraged from judging or belittling the ideas, because doing so inhibits the generation of new ideas. It is easier to go back and eliminate unworkable ideas than create good ones.

After working to generate a number of suggestions, the mediator goes through each one separately so that the parties can evaluate the strengths, weaknesses, and feasibility of each option. The mediator will help the parties elaborate and develop their ideas, sometimes combining two or more ideas into an option that has features that appeal to each of them. Parties are asked to consider their best alternative to a negotiated agreement (BATNA). Parties and mediators often start with the most promising options, to see if they are indeed workable. During stage 4, the parties "operationalize" ideas for resolution. In this stage, the mediator may also periodically do a reality check, test assumptions, and encourage the parties by letting them know that there may be more than one "best" option.

After gaining insights into one another's experiences, parties may be able to readily agree on a course of action that meets their individual interests as well as their joint needs. In these instances, there is no need to go through a brainstorming process. Insight mediation enables this to occur by the very nature of insight. The "aha" that results from an insight is often accompanied by the answer to the problem. In mediation, this may well be the path forward for the parties.

In other cases, parties may have difficulty coming up with solutions. Here, mediators may tentatively offer suggestions, being careful that parties do not feel obligated in any way to accept these suggestions. The parties must feel free to reject the mediator's suggestions, without losing face or feeling threatened. A mediator might do this with phrases such as,

> *I'm wondering whether you might want to look at what others have done in similar situations.*

Or

> *Would it be worth considering what the pattern of compensation has been in other cases?*

An insight mediator will be careful not to come up with too many suggestions, for fear of undermining self-determination by the parties. Instead, mediators keep encouraging the parties for suggestions that are mutually acceptable and in which both of them can "win" some of what they want.

Stage 5: Making Decisions

After the parties are satisfied that they have found mutually agreeable options, the mediator's task is to ensure that there is no misunderstanding about what they have decided to do. Often, this means preparing a written Memorandum of Understanding (MOU), also called minutes of settlement (see appendix B). In some cultures, people find that insistence on a written contract is insulting—they interpret the request as a challenge to their honesty and integrity. The mediator needs to be sensitive to situations when written agreements may be unnecessary or even counterproductive.

During this stage, it is important that everyone is clear about what has been agreed to. Mediators generally write, in "lay" terms, specifying in as much detail as necessary, what each party is promising to do—the "who, what, where, how, and when" of their agreement. Generally, the terms will be set out in a series of separately numbered paragraphs, which specify what each of the parties has promised to do. The mediator should also ensure that there is some degree of reciprocity and balance to the terms of the agreement. Fisher and Ury (1981) say that a good agreement will be fair, wise, efficient, and stable.

Here are some of the various ways that mediation agreements may be drawn up:

1. The mediator will write out the terms, with input and direction from the parties, who then review and sign the agreement.
2. The parties draft their own agreement.
3. In cases where parties' lawyers are present, the lawyers may draft the agreement.
4. In some cases, it may be appropriate for the mediator or the parties to propose that the basic terms be sent to a lawyer (or lawyers) for drafting of the final agreement.
5. In some cases, it may be appropriate for parties to draft their separate versions of the agreement, which then can be circulated for input from others, with a final document being drafted to include all terms agreed to in the individual versions.

However it is done, it is crucial to recognize that the agreement belongs to the parties, and whatever method suits their needs and interests should be used. Even at this stage, flexibility and creativity continue to be important.

No matter what approach is used to finalizing stage 5 of the mediation, it is essential that the mediator and all parties have a clear, common understanding about the legal consequences and enforceability of any agreement or MOU that is prepared. There are three possibilities:

1. They intend the written document to be a legally enforceable contract.
2. They intend the written document to be a MOU that will be incorporated (by their lawyers or others) onto a legally binding contract, but that, until so incorporated, it is not to have legal consequences.
3. They intend the written document to be a MOU that will be a record of their understanding for purposes of future clarity, but without it being legally enforceable or having "legal" consequences.

When the final agreement is intended as the basis of a legal settlement, the mediator encourages the parties to get legal advice or assistance. The mediator also informs the parties that their lawyers may raise certain issues that will require further negotiation or, in some cases, may raise obstacles to final agreement.

One way to think of the decision-making stage is that it creates a "plan for the future" for the parties. So, a way to know if the plan is working needs to be included. Mediators ask what the parties will do if their agreement fails—return to mediation? seek other outside help? or pursue other adjudicative methods? If no agreement is reached, mediators generally suggest resources such as counselling, arbitration, or litigation to help them deal with the dispute.

To conclude this final stage, the mediator congratulates each party for their hard work to resolve the problem. Some mediators have rituals as part of the closing—handshaking, formal signing procedures, toasts, or other celebratory or culturally appropriate activities. The mediator often reminds and reassures the parties about confidentially, as well as any post-mediation activities that have been discussed, such as ratification of the memorandum of understanding, consultation with lawyers, or, in some cases, reporting to the court.

Post-Mediation

The work of the mediator does not always end after stage 5. In some circumstances, the mediator can be involved in the ratification of an agreement by external parties, such as boards of directors, or in circumstances where the parties in the negotiation are representing groups of people, or if the agreement is to be sanctioned by the court. In other situations, reports might need to be sent to referring parties or program directors, as in the case of community programs that use volunteer or private mediators. These reports generally indicate that the case has been resolved, or not, and are written in such a way that they do not breach confidentiality protocols agreed to in the mediation.

In co-mediation situations, the two mediators generally arrange to debrief. This analysis often takes place immediately following, or soon after, the mediation session. These discussions involve sharing individual experiences and perceptions about what happened, emotions that occurred and may still remain as a result of the interactions, self- and peer perceptions of strengths and weaknesses as mediators, and thoughts about how to improve their work as mediators in the future. Where there is only one mediator, some practitioners have mentors with whom they can discuss the events and emotions of the mediation, to further their learning, reflective practice, and development of artistry as mediators.

In some circumstances, mediators may be involved in monitoring the agreement and supervising its implementation; have responsibility for steering it through to the making of a consent order by the court; or be involved in the holding of funds or documents until the agreement has been completed (Boulle & Kelly, 1998, p. 124).

Many mediators simply find it considerate and respectful to contact the parties after a reasonable period of time, to see how things are going as a result of the mediation.

There is one other aspect about the process of mediation that needs discussion. It involves the participation in mediation of advisers, lawyers, and other advocates. Nowadays, their presence is more commonplace—as a result of mandated mediation programs and other quasi-judicial mediated disputes. Not surprisingly, this changes the dynamic of the mediation and brings about a particular set of considerations and challenges.

PARTICIPATION OF PARTIES' ADVISERS IN MEDIATION

Advisers to parties in mediation may be lawyers, union representatives, accountants, staff relations advisers, professional agents, or other experts in the substantive areas under dispute. Usually, these advisers have been trained and are experienced in adversarial approaches to dispute resolution, but may have little training in collaborative processes like mediation. This raises particular challenges for them. While most of the discussion in this section will be about the role of lawyers in counselling their clients in mediation, much of what is covered also applies to other types of advisers.

Certainly there is no reason, in principle, why participating lawyers should undermine the mediation and prevent it from being a collaborative process. Indeed, participation of lawyers who understand and are skilled at principled negotiation may significantly enhance the collaborative process and contribute to the success of mediation. In some cases, a lawyer who understands the potential benefits of collaborative negotiation—and knows how to pursue such an approach assertively and effectively—may enable his or her client to pursue collaborative interaction, particularly in a case where, without such assistance, the client would be unable to do so.

In some disputes, a party's lawyer may encourage or cause the party to have an adversarial mindset and pursue an adversarial approach. Why? Below are various reasons why that may happen, even in situations where the lawyer is skilled at principled negotiation:

- The lawyer and the client may believe that the opposing party and his or her lawyer or representative will be aggressive or will use adversarial tactics such as intimidation or stonewalling.
- The lawyer may be concerned that if the client openly reveals his or her wishes, preferences, and intentions, the other party may use that to advantage in negotiation.
- The lawyer may be concerned that if the client provides all the evidence and information he or she has of the situation, the opposing party (and lawyer) may acquire a tactical advantage by being able to find other evidence, information, or arguments to refute it.
- The lawyer may believe that the other party and lawyer are deceitful and manipulative, that they will appear to collaborate, but will simply lead them and the mediator "down the garden path."
- There has been so much animosity and "bad blood" between the parties that, even if their intellect tells them to collaborate, their hearts will say "no."

Mediators need to recognize the psychological, relational, and systemic reasons why lawyers or other advisers may be inclined not to engage in collaborative interaction.

THE ROLE OF LAWYERS IN MEDIATION

One role that lawyers play is to inform and educate their clients about the timely and effective use of mediation. This should be done at an early stage of the lawyer's involvement in the dispute. In Ontario, rule 2.02(3) of the *Rules of Professional Conduct* of the Law Society of Upper Canada states, "The lawyer shall consider the use of alternative dispute resolution (ADR) for every dispute, and, if appropriate, the lawyer shall inform the client of ADR options and, if so instructed, take steps to pursue those options."

To meet this professional responsibility, lawyers must be knowledgeable about the possible merits of using mediation—and understand how mediation can be used effectively in their clients' circumstances. That includes knowing how to achieve maximum success from a mediation, while at the same time ensuring that their clients' legal rights are protected.

Counsel must also provide legal advice to their clients throughout the mediation and in relation to any mediated agreements or settlements. Lawyers also help their clients select a mediator. Some factors to be considered are the mediator's orientation, objectives, and style; training and experience; ability to be impartial; gender, cultural background or ethnicity; and fees and availability of the mediator.

One of the more difficult role changes for lawyers may be allowing parties to speak for themselves and participate fully in the mediation process. In some cases, this may mean the lawyers take a "back seat" in the joint session, and provide their input and advice in caucus. While some mediators may discuss the lawyers' role during the convening process and at the beginning of the mediation, legal counsel must understand and respect the importance of allowing their clients to be the primary "voice" in the mediation and the primary decision maker. Being successful in the adversarial legal process generally means achieving the best possible legal result, which in large measure is determined by the lawyer as the legal expert. In the interest-based mediation process, in contrast, being successful means achieving an outcome that satisfies the client's interests—personal, social, and emotional, as well as professional, vocational, and economic. In other words, the scope for successful outcomes in the interest-based process is much broader than in the legal, rights-based process. Lawyers must recognize this fundamental difference and ensure that their clients are given ample opportunity and support to fully engage in mediation in a way that will satisfy their interests as much as possible. For many lawyers, this requires them to transfer significant control and responsibility for the process to their clients.

SKILLS AND COMPETENCIES AS A MEDIATION ADVISER

To help achieve their clients' best interests, lawyers need to understand what mediation is, the different approaches that can be taken, and the different types of mediators (discussed in chapter 4). Lawyers will also need to help their clients decide whether mediation is a suitable process for their clients' dispute. (This is discussed in the next chapter.)

As with various legal processes, lawyers play a pivotal role in helping their clients prepare for mediation. This includes advising them of the strengths and weaknesses of their legal case and that of the other party. The lawyer should be familiar with the mediator and the mediator's approach to mediation. To prepare their client to fully and properly engage in the mediation process, lawyers need to

- clarify the issues and identify the client's interests and emotions that underlie his or her position;
- identify the range of possible options to meet the client's interests;
- consider and analyze what the other party's positions, interests, and meaningful outcomes are likely to be;
- discuss the types of strategies and behaviours that might be expected from the other party or lawyer—and how they might respond to that constructively;
- gather and organize information, and prepare documents or summaries to be used at the mediation;
- clarify issues of confidentiality, the use of agreements to mediate, and written agreements, and ensure that communications within the mediation may occur "without prejudice" to the client's legal rights and position;
- formulate and analyze the client's BATNA (see chapter 3), including the strengths, weaknesses, costs, and risks of proceeding with legal action for *both* parties;
- deal with logistics, including location, timing, who attends, and other matters determined during the convening process; and
- advise the client about options other than court or mediation that could be used to resolve the dispute, such as arbitration, mediation-arbitration, or, in some cases, fact finding or investigation.

A basic goal of collaborative processes is to create value. As explained by Lax and Sebenius (1986, pp. 29–41) and by Mnookin, Peppet, and Tulumello (2000, pp. 11–43), in most negotiating situations there is a fundamental tension between creating and claiming, presented as the Negotiator's Dilemma (see chapter 3). In cases in which parties have formulated their positions in terms of their legal claims and rights, the Negotiator's Dilemma is ever-present. The traditional legal approach, in which lawyers are trained and well practised, is the adversarial method. To the extent that parties and their lawyers pursue the adversarial method, they will forcefully advocate their claims, argue the merits of their position, minimize any contrary views, and undermine the positions and opinions of the "opposition." Clearly, such an approach will elicit claiming and defensive strategies from the other side and will stifle any potential for collaborative interaction.

This, then, is the challenge for the lawyer who wants to provide effective legal representation and, at the same time, serve the client's best interests. This is what we call the "Lawyer's Dilemma." To meet this challenge, the lawyer needs to develop an approach that assertively presents the client's legal position in an articulate and clear way, while simultaneously enabling the client to pursue an effective, principled negotiation approach through the mediation process. To succeed, the lawyer will need to know how to apply the elements of principled negotiation in the mediation process, and what the roles of the parties, lawyers, and mediator will be in such a process. The lawyer will need to have a sufficient understanding of those roles and expectations so that the participants, especially the lawyers and mediator are complementing each other and not working at cross-purposes.

In some cases, a party and his or her lawyer may anticipate that the other party and/or the other lawyer may be aggressive, intimidating, or abusive. In a case where a party client may feel threatened or overpowered by the other party, the lawyer should give particular thought and care to what he or she can do to ensure that the client can participate in mediation safely and securely—and in a way that serves the client's best interests.

SUMMARY

This chapter has provided an overall understanding of the interest-based approach to mediation, with particular detail given to the five stages of the insight model of mediation. By working through this chapter, you should understand not only what happens in a typical two-party dispute throughout these five stages, but also why an insight mediator would proceed in that way. By understanding the goals of this approach to mediation—and how they illuminate and inspire the mediator's involvement with the parties—you will appreciate what is meant by a strategic approach to conflict resolution.

FURTHER READING

Boulle, L., & Kelly, K.J. (1998). *Mediation: Principles, process, practice.* Toronto: Butterworths.

Cloke, K.K. (2001). *Mediating dangerously: The frontiers of conflict resolution.* San Francisco: Jossey-Bass.

Moore, C.W. (2003). *The mediation process: Practical strategies for resolving conflict* (3rd ed.). San Francisco: Jossey-Bass.

Picard, C.A. (2002). *Mediating interpersonal and small group conflict* (2nd ed.). Ottawa: Golden Dog Press.

CHAPTER SEVEN

Deciding On and Preparing the Path: Convening a Mediation

And since you know you cannot see yourself so well as by reflection,
I, your glass, will modestly discover to yourself, that of yourself
which you yet know not of.

William Shakespeare, Julius Caesar

In this chapter, we examine general suitability for mediation through an understanding of convening and the screening process. We set out the basic elements for convening a mediation, including convening objectives and goals, a framework for conducting convening interviews, and assessment criteria for pursuing mediation.

WHAT IS CONVENING?

Convening is the process by which an impartial person, the convenor, assists parties to determine how and when mediation may be used to help resolve their conflict issues. The convenor also helps parties to become ready, willing, and able to use mediation. The convenor accomplishes this by speaking to all parties involved in the conflict in order to understand the conflict issues; deciding, with the parties, whether mediation is both suitable and preferred; informing parties of the expectations and goals of mediated processes; obtaining their agreement to proceed; and preparing and coaching them for the process. Some of these elements can be covered during pre-mediation, which begins once all parties agree to mediation and before the actual session commences.

Mediation is not a panacea. In some cases, it may not even be appropriate; for example, where the issues are not negotiable, such as some human rights violations; when the power differential between disputants is too great for uninhibited conversation; or in those cases where there is no stake in resolving the issues for one or both parties. This latter situation is common where one party plans to remove himself or herself from the conflictual relationship.

Mediation advocates support an assessment to determine whether mediation is suitable or not—and this is a primary aim of convening. (Later in this chapter, we talk about some of the issues to consider when determining suitability for mediation, and we encourage you to look back to chapter 2 to review some of the limitations of interest-based processes.)

Convening consists of three components. It begins with the "first contact"—when someone connected to the situation, either a party or a referral agent, gets in touch with the convenor to explore whether or not mediation is suitable for the conflict. At this stage, the convenor does not usually open a file until a commitment is made to continue. The second component is the "intake and assessment." During this phase, the convenor begins to collect information about the conflict, as well as provide the party or parties with information about mediation, its principles, and the expectations of participants. The convenor and parties then assess whether mediation is appropriate and determine what other information or research may be required by the parties before they proceed. At this point, a case file is opened. The final component of convening is "case development and pre-mediation." In this phase, the convenor or the case mediator works to prepare the parties for mediation, by coaching their communication and asking consequential or reality-testing questions.

The intake phase consists of recording names and contact information for the parties, as well as outlining the basic issues in conflict. A convenor listens carefully and actively, summarizes information, and asks pertinent and often difficult questions. He or she is engaged in a process not unlike the actual mediation, exploring the interests, insights, anticipated consequences, and the degree of understanding of each party. The convenor must be a skilled communicator with well-developed mediation skills and techniques.

The convenor may also take on the role of mediator, should the parties go forward with mediation. This commonly occurs in private practice, where there is only one person performing convening and mediation activities—as well as in some programs staffed by a single mediator, such as a program manager. There are both benefits and drawbacks with such a model. The advantages are that the convenor has already developed a relationship of trust with all parties, he or she has gained a solid understanding of the issues in advance, and the parties' communication and negotiating styles are well known. All of these factors contribute to the effectiveness of the mediation. In fact, we have noted that many parties prefer to use the convenor as their mediator, since they have already established a mutual rapport. This is particularly true in cases involving people from cultural groups in which mediations are conducted by practitioners who are well known to the disputants.

The greatest disadvantage of convenors becoming the mediators can be that they believe they know all there is to know about the conflict dynamic. Then, if the parties bring new information to the session, the mediators do not "hear" it, because they are "stuck on" the information acquired during the convening process. The convenor, as mediator in this case, subsequently becomes less curious. Convenors may plan an entire strategy for the mediation based on misleading or incomplete information.

In mediation programs that employ case development officers to conduct convening activities, the mediator is usually distinct from the convenor. St. Stephen's Conflict Resolution Services in Toronto, Winnipeg Mediation Services, and many community-based mediation programs use volunteer mediators to facilitate mediation sessions, and paid case development officers to conduct the convening process. Some federal government departments with in-house mediation services, such as Canada Revenue Agency, the Department of Justice, and the Department of National Defence, may use coordinators or directors to perform intake and convening tasks, while staff or external mediators conduct the actual sessions.

A modified convening process can be undertaken by people in human resources, those in the labour relations field, on union executives, from equity and human rights advisory groups, and in supervisory positions. This modified process includes learning about the conflict situation and ascertaining, at least at a superficial level, which dispute resolution options would best address the situation. While most of these referral agents are not likely to be as skilled in mediation as full-time convenors, they should be able to make preliminary determinations about whether mediation is a good option, by following some of the same stages of information gathering outlined later in this chapter.

When convening is not performed by the mediator, the mediator ought to conduct a pre-mediation session with the parties. This includes introducing oneself to the parties, getting a brief overview of the issues, assisting the parties to prepare for mediation, and determining whether the process is suitable. The mediator should speak with the parties before the first session. At the very least, a telephone conversation prior to mediation is a must for developing a relationship, building trust and legitimacy, and being comfortable with the issues and suitability of the process. An exception to this is found in family mediation practice, where the intake and assessment process sometimes begins in a joint session. The mediator explores issues and discusses the potential of mediation with both parties, with the intention of arriving at a decision to proceed. The mediator would likely schedule another session, if the parties decide to continue, although the parties might also agree to begin the mediation then and there.

Convening requires a good deal of knowledge about the limits of mediation, as well as its potential. The following scenario could be a typical neighbourhood conflict, and it illustrates the complexity of helping people choose the best possible process for their situation.

SCENARIO: Not in My Backyard

Jack Morgan is a professor of law at the University of Wisdom. He lives in Yogaville, next door to the Osmans, a recently immigrated Somali family of seven. Jack's wife, Janna, runs her own catering business in an upscale neighbourhood. Mrs. Osman is a single parent of six children, ranging in age from 4 to 16. She lost her husband and eldest child in the war in Somalia—in fact, her fear of losing other family members to the war brought her to Canada. (She also has a cousin who lives close by with his family.)

Recently, Jack Morgan and Mrs. Osman have stopped speaking to one another. Last week, Jack ran out into his backyard when he saw Mrs. Osman's son, Karim, 16, starting to chop down the beautiful old maple tree that grows in the Osman's yard, but extends its branches into the Morgan's yard. Jack began yelling at Karim that he was desecrating a heritage tree and that he had better stop, or Jack would call the municipality and the police. Karim was stunned—he did not know, nor did his mother, that he could be told what to do on his own property! Karim began arguing with and swearing at Jack. Jack nearly hit him.

The tree does extend into the Morgan's yard and forms quite a lovely shaded area for the summer garden parties that the Morgans like to have. Jack believes that it will destroy the ambience of his backyard; moreover, he doesn't want to see such a beautiful tree destroyed.

For the Osmans, who had no idea it could get so cold in winter, the tree could provide weeks of firewood to heat their home more effectively than it is currently, with electricity. On his own initiative, Karim thought that he would help his mother and family out by making firewood.

Jack Morgan has approached Community Mediation Services (CMS), a four-year-old organization devoted to resolving neighbourhood disputes in Yogaville, to settle the conflict with Mrs. Osman over the cutting down of this old maple tree. CMS has been funded by the municipality, and it offers a free service to residents in the community. CMS has agreed to mediate this dispute and has appointed Ruth Callaghan, a strong volunteer mediator who has been with CMS for its entire existence. Ruth is now retired, but she worked for many years for a municipal court judge. It's not unusual to find volunteers like Ruth at CMS, where many white-collar professionals seeking career changes check out whether mediation might be a new path to follow. Ruth would eventually like to mediate in the court-mandated program in Yogaville. She has also just taken a two-day course in diversity and believes that she will be sensitive to the cultural needs of Mrs. Osman.

1. Would you recommend that this case go to mediation? Why or why not?
2. What, if any, would your concerns be about this case?
3. What, if any, additional information do you need before proceeding further?

The Osman-Morgan case demonstrates how complicated a decision about going to mediation can be. Here are just three of the many questions that arise in this case.

What are the legal parameters for cutting down maple trees on private property?

While this information is useful and probably necessary to both parties' perspectives, the conflict is not likely resolved by answering the question. The convenor will need to know more about the relationship between the neighbours, other misunderstandings in the past, and, perhaps, the role of culture and ethnicity.

How imbalanced is power in this particular situation?

Certainly, Jack Morgan has an advantage over the Osmans. As a law professor, he would be familiar with the legal parameters of the case, and quite knowledgeable about rights and entitlements. Mrs. Osman and her family, as newcomers to Canada, will likely not have such extensive knowledge of these laws. Moreover, the fact that the Osmans will be speaking English as a second language might also place them at a disadvantage. A skilled mediator or co-mediation team would be aware of socio-economic, linguistic, and other power inequities that could affect the balance in mediation. A cultural interpreter might also help the process along.

Who should mediate this particular case?

While there is no doubt Ruth Callaghan, the volunteer mediator with CMS, has a certain type of experience, it is not certain that she would be the best candidate. First impressions lead us to think that she would hold the same values as the Morgans, and have shared similar experiences with them. It would be important to consider using a mediator who has also had similar experiences as the Osmans. Perhaps a co-mediation team, with balanced values and experiences that are more representative of everyone's, would be the best alternative.

Here are some other questions to consider in the convening stage: What do the Osmans—and Morgans—really think is causing this conflict? Before this conflict arose, what was the relationship between the families? If they had the opportunity to replay the conflict, what would they have done differently? How has this conflict affected them? For the Morgans, what is most important for the Osmans to understand? For the Osmans, what is most important for the Morgans to understand? What kind of relationship would they like to have with their neighbours? What would they need to get there? What options do they have available to them to resolve this conflict? What process is most likely to assist them in reaching their goals? What kind of mediation and mediators would be most helpful? How comfortable would the Morgans and Osmans be in mediation? What accommodations, if any, would they be seeking? Are there negotiable issues to mediate?

This list of questions to address before this case proceeds to mediation is by no means exhaustive; however, it does provide a taste of the convenor's work and the importance of collecting necessary information. Convening a mediation is a time-consuming and complex undertaking. Let's now look more closely at the actual process of convening.

THE CONVENING PROCESS

By and large, convening, like mediation, is a responsive process. This means that the convenor takes cues from the parties during the conversation. Some people need to speak about their situation before they can really listen to a convenor. In these instances, the convenor first listens actively, to build trust and demonstrate understanding. Other people may not begin to speak about their conflict until they have clear information about the mediation process. Here, the convenor responds by providing an overview of mediation goals, roles, and processes. Written or visual materials—brochures, information sheets, flyers, or videos of mock mediations—can also be very helpful. Convening requires strong intuitive skills since the convenor tries to "read" the needs of the parties first. Although our framework for convening is outlined in a systematic way, the convenor, like the mediator, seldom works in a linear fashion through these stages.

Support in Conflict Exercise

Think about a conflict situation in which you have been involved recently. If you spoke with someone about it and found him or her supportive and helpful, list the reasons you found that person supportive.

If you weren't able to speak with anyone helpful about the situation, what would have made someone supportive to you? What actions and behaviours would not have been helpful?

Now that you understand *what* convening is, let us discuss *why* convening is undertaken. First and foremost, convening helps the parties begin to think and speak differently about the situation. To achieve this, the convenor has a number of tasks to perform, including building trust, having parties reflect on the situation, determining suitability for mediation, ensuring the parties are making an informed choice, and preparing them for mediation. Let's look at each of these five tasks more closely.

Trust Building

Early in the convening process, the convenor works to develop a rapport with the parties, gaining their trust and confidence. Doing so encourages frank discussion and full disclosure, enabling the convenor to extract the information necessary to understand the situation and determine whether mediation is suitable.

Reflection

One of the convenor's main tasks is to assist the parties to reflect on the situation, consider their motivations, the conflict's effects, their needs, and their options for resolving the conflict. This encourages a fuller understanding of the conflict for everyone involved, increasing the parties' capacity to make decisions about what they need.

Mediation Suitability

An important task for both the convenor and the parties is to determine whether or not mediation is appropriate and likely to be helpful. The convenor and parties can then judge whether to proceed with mediation.

Informed Choice

The parties must know what processes—ranging from no action to litigation—are available and which are likely to work best. Only then can the convenor be sure that the parties are choosing a process knowingly and will thus be committed to it. The convenor's overriding objective is to assist parties in making an informed process decision that is best responsive to their needs.

Preparation

If the disputants choose mediation, the convenor begins coaching the parties by helping them think about what their interests are, how to express themselves, how to test the realism of their alternatives, and to think about their overall hopes for the session. Convenors sometimes give parties materials to read or activities to complete. All of this ensures the best possible orientation to and preparation for mediation, maximizing the potential for success from the parties' perspectives.

Whether parties opt for mediation or decide to pursue another process, they still benefit from going through convening. We have heard many people say, "You have made me think about things differently. No one ever asked me those kinds of questions."

HOW CONVENING VARIES IN DIFFERENT SITUATIONS

The process of convening will be different with different types of conflict. The first difference will be whether the convenor also acts as the mediator, should the case go forward. As already indicated, divorcing couples who seek mediation in order to divide family property or decide child custody arrangements may go through a different process. In these situations, a mediator in private practice is usually selected by both parties, sometimes with the assistance of their legal counsel. A preliminary telephone conversation with both parties, to arrange a joint meeting time, begins the process. During the joint meeting, the mediator outlines the process of mediation, learns what some of the issues for discussion are likely to be and assesses whether mediation is suitable.

Court-connected mediation usually follows a similar process. The mediator, a private practitioner recommended by the parties' lawyers, begins convening with phone calls to the disputants or their lawyers.

Public policy, multi-party, and environmental disputes, such as in the Sonata Development scenario given in chapter 2, also tend to use private practitioners as mediators. The mediator takes on the convening role here, but with a different twist. In the Sonata Development scenario, you may remember that a suburban community and home developer were in conflict. It would be far too time consuming to interview each and every member of the community before a mediation. In this case, convening would likely take place either with one or a few representatives of the community and one or a few representatives of Haven Homes, the developer. Some convenors might meet with the entire community in a town-hall session, in order to understand all the concerns and to help the group develop consensus on its needs. In addition, the representative for the city government would be interviewed during a convening process.

Most community-based mediation and neighbourhood justice programs have separate mediators and convenors. Staff, often the program directors or case developers, undertake convening, while volunteer mediators are used for the mediation sessions themselves. The use of volunteers to mediate disputes is also often found in victim–offender and other restorative justice programs.

Increasing numbers of organizations and large businesses have in-house mediation services, and employees in dispute meet with the mediation program coordinator or director for a convening process. The coordinator may or may not mediate the case, if it proceeds to mediation. Workplaces without in-house services retain private mediators to conduct both convening and mediation sessions.

Convening does need to address certain issues, whether it takes place in a joint session, by a mediator or a convenor, over the telephone or in person. Below, we outline how a convening process is undertaken and provide a model for convening.

A FRAMEWORK FOR CONVENING

Three stages are outlined in this framework, or model, for convening. Although each convenor develops a particular style, at some point, each of these stages needs to be addressed—and some convenors might well revisit some stages several times during the process. This process can extend anywhere from one meeting or telephone conversation to several meetings with each party, before mediation begins. Remember that some parties may opt for other processes, once they understand the principles of mediation.

This framework is usually followed when the issues are interpersonal and the group is not large. Public policy and multi-stakeholder disputes, by virtue of the numbers involved, are not conducive to individual interviews with everyone, as indicated above. In these cases, spokespersons are often interviewed. It is still important that expectations about the process be clear in these situations, so the convenor does need to contact representatives of the various stakeholder groups to discuss the mediation and everyone's roles within it.

The convening framework is shown in figure 7.1. Stage 1, First Contact, is when the convenor or mediator comes to know about the conflict. In stage 2, Individual Interviews and Assessment, the convenor, either in person or by phone, contacts all those involved to elicit information about the situation, parties' needs, and the viability of mediation. The convenor will educate each party about mediation and make an assessment about whether mediation is suitable and, with the parties, determines what steps should be followed in stage three, Decision Making and Planning. During this stage, the convenor, in collaboration with the parties, plans for the mediation process, including coaching the parties, determining a suitable venue and any accommodation required, as well as selecting the mediator.

Stage 1: First Contact

People come to mediation for many reasons. Public policy disputes; environmental conflicts; divorce, separation, custody and access issues; collective bargaining and union grievances; and disputes requiring a mandatory mediation process are some of the types of cases where parties might initiate contact with a convenor. Even in these situations, however, legal counsel is often the first to propose that a mediator be employed. When parties contact a mediation service directly, they have often already tried other dispute resolution processes and found them wanting.

FIGURE 7.1 The Three Stages of Convening

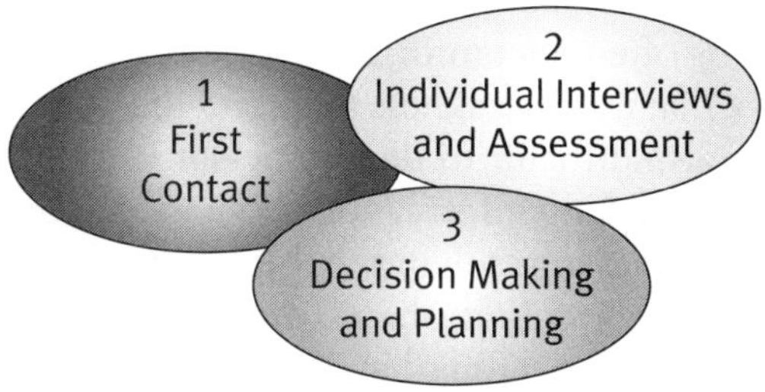

In workplaces, contact is usually initiated by a third party—someone who knows one or both parties, yet is not directly involved in the conflict (such as a supervisor, union representative, lawyer, elder, co-worker, friend, or representative of another dispute resolution office). Examples of third parties in workplaces include members from the ombuds office, a union, human resources, a human rights or employment equity office, as well as supervisors in the parties' unit. This person is considered to be the referral agent and is most likely "checking out" the viability of mediation in this particular situation. The referral agent usually seeks information about mediation, specifically for the conflict and regarding his or her role in such a process. A supervisor may be frustrated by trying to figure out how to deal with two employees who cannot get along, and she may contact mediation services. In a situation where harassment is alleged and a formal complaint process is not chosen, a human rights adviser might recommend mediation. These are the most common referring agents for mediation services offered within organizations. When mediation services are provided to an organization by external mediators on a contractual basis, the referral most frequently comes from a human resources department.

For victim–offender reconciliation programs, a spiritual adviser, lawyer, or someone within the corrections system, such as the police department, the Crown attorney's office, or the probation service, refers the offender to the process. In many instances, community-based disputes arrive at mediation services through the recommendation of social service or health departments, or housing offices.

Lawyers are required to inform clients about the possibility of mediation in many dispute situations, and may contact a service themselves to explore its suitability. The heavy reliance on referrals to mediation necessitates that private-practice mediators and mediation programs within organizations develop strong relationships with referral agents. We discuss how mediators locate work in the last chapter of the book.

One of the parties involved in the conflict may also contact a convenor, to explore whether mediation might be constructive in his or her situation. The party is often uncomfortable initiating contact, because he or she may believe that it is a weakness to not be able to resolve conflicts on one's own. It is also difficult to discuss personal issues with a stranger. The party is likely seeking information about mediation, and looking for assistance and support in resolving the situation. This approach occurs most frequently in community-based mediation programs or in some conflict resolution services found in workplaces.

Less commonly, all the parties involved in the conflict approach a convenor. In this instance, parties have already agreed that mediation can help them solve their conflict. Public policy and environmental disputes might use this approach. In addition, this may be the means through which divorcing spouses arrive at mediation. For the convenor, this situation is ideal, because the parties themselves have an understanding of mediation and have selected it as the first option to resolve their conflict.

Another way that disputes come to mediation is through the convenor. From time to time, the convenor might hear about a conflict situation and seek to contact either the parties involved or a referral agent, to offer the services of mediation. These situations are known as "cold contacts"—where the convenor enters a conflict situation without any invitation. The nature of these conflicts is usually public, possibly with some media attention, and the convenor just ensures that those who can resolve this conflict have an awareness of mediation. Using the Sonata Development scenario, the convenor might contact both the community organization's chairperson and the president of the housing developer. In situations like this, convenors must act with a great deal of sensitivity and compassion, to discourage defensiveness.

In all cases of first contact, the convenor's first duty is to put the party at ease through skilled listening and empathy. When meeting with the disputants, the convenor needs to collect information about confidentiality; what the information needs are of a superior, union representative, or others who have been or should be informed; and what additional information about rights or entitlements or other dispute resolution options the party needs to seek before proceeding. There may also be some discussion of how the party's concerns about mediation might be addressed; about the consequences of not addressing the conflict or addressing the conflict through another process; and about who, if anyone, the parties would like present in a mediated process for support, expertise, or comfort. Usually, the convenor also discusses with the party the best way to approach the others involved.

Stage 2: Individual Interviews and Assessment

This stage is the core of convening. Here, the convenor and parties in conflict gather and sift through information, determining whether mediation is a good way to resolve the conflict.

Some mediators believe this stage to be unnecessary, proceeding with intake information only. These mediators are most often found in private practice, where they would perform convening functions themselves. It is their belief that individual meetings could lead to mediator bias, as the information could likely orient the mediator to think through the issues in advance and perhaps come up with a plan for the mediation. However, this information could change or be expressed quite differently in a mediation session. Informal discussions with colleagues working in family mediation have revealed that some mediators actively choose to not know anything about the issues before they begin the mediation. This is due, in part, to the different nature of the family mediation process, where the first meeting is with both spouses. This meeting can be seen as an orientation, with the mediator giving parties process information, receiving questions, and conducting some of the same activities found in what we've called the convening process.

Preparation is essential. Individual meetings help the convenor gain a general understanding of the issues; the parties' needs, particularly with respect to support, accommodation, or adaptations in mediation; the appropriateness of mediation; as well as strengths and characteristics required of mediators. Without individual meetings, key information can go missing.

When contact has been initiated through a referral agent or with a party leaving a phone message, the convenor should get in touch as soon as possible, ideally within 24 hours. Delays can diminish the chances of success in mediation. People tend to contact mediation services late in the course of conflict, and this tendency is further exaggerated when organizations request the services of an external mediator. Often, a mediator in private practice will receive a request for services when a dispute has already been dealt with by the organization's human resources department, unions have become involved, or perhaps an adversarial process (such as a grievance, a harassment complaint or even a legal suit) has commenced. The longer a situation festers, the greater the likelihood is that people will entrench their positions, lash out at the other party, escalate the conflict, and harden their stance toward adversarial options (Folger, Poole, & Stutman, 1993, pp. 10–11).

Not in My Backyard Exercise

Think about the Not in My Backyard scenario, provided at the beginning of this chapter. Imagine that you have been asked to conduct the convening. In order to assess and decide whether mediation would be suitable, what information do you think you need from the Osmans and the Morgans?

Individual interviews can take place in person or by phone. The average time spent, when convening, is about an hour or so for each person. However, interviews can take 12 hours per person or group.

In our experience, it is best to conduct convening face to face. When convening is done over the phone, the convenor is more likely to miss subtle cues and opportunities for trust building from the parties. There are other factors that encourage in-person interviews. If one of the parties is elderly, has a disability, or is from a minority cultural group, in-person interviews will make communication clearer for both the party and the convenor. If there is a language barrier, it is much more beneficial to meet in person and use an interpreter, if necessary. If the case involves some complicated issues, it is strongly encouraged to meet in person to ensure fuller understanding. If the party is not free to speak over the phone, given the lack of privacy in his or her environment, a face-to-face interview enables a free flow of information. In addition, if the party is particularly anxious about the conflict and about resolving it, the convenor can provide more support in person.

Exchanging information can be time consuming and complex. Given the importance of building rapport and legitimacy throughout this stage, individual interviews tend not to be linear. Thus, convenors need to be flexible and responsive if they are to understand the conflict from the party's perspective—and help him or her decide how to proceed. To understand the complexity of this stage of convening, we have organized this stage into five tasks.

Task 1: Setting a Comfortable Climate

Early in an interview, the convenor is building trust and rapport, encouraging the party to talk about the situation and reflect on it. Umbreit (1995) underscores the importance of relationship building in individual interviews. Satir (1988) also emphasizes authentic human connection as essential to change processes.

He or she begins by introducing himself or herself and explaining the meeting's purpose and how mediation services came to be involved. The convenor then informs the party of the meeting's purpose and parameters, as well as any limitations on confidentiality (see Boulle & Kelly, 1998, pp. 300–314). If the contact is by phone, the convenor determines whether it is a good time to talk, clarifying that he or she would like to meet in person. Finally, the convenor outlines an agenda for the conversation. In the Not in My Backyard scenario, the convenor might follow this script:

> *Hello, Mrs. Osman. My name is … and I am calling from the Yogaville Mediation Centre. Jack Morgan has contacted me regarding the situation he and your family are involved in, and he is hoping that you will consider mediation to resolve it. I would like to hear your perspective on events, find out what your concerns are, and what you would like to see happen in this situation. You might find it useful to hear what we do at the Mediation Centre and how we might be able to assist you. I also want to let you know that what you say here is confidential. Please let me know if now is a good time for you to speak. … Great. So, how would you like to proceed?*

Task 2: Exploring the Conflict

Listening intently and with empathy is critical in this phase of the interview. The convenor must make connections with the party by demonstrating understanding and acknowledging emotional impacts. To do this, the convenor should adopt an open and attending posture, using reflective listening skills (see chapter 8) and tone of voice to convey respect and openness. The convenor should be recording facts, issues, interests, relations, and goals identified by the party during the interview. Here are examples of what the questions might sound like, gathered under topics and using the Not in My Backyard scenario.

What is the conflict about?

> *How did this situation between you and the Morgans come about?*
>
> *When did things start going wrong between the two of you?*
>
> *How long has this situation been bothering you?*

What are the party's interests?

> *What were you hoping to gain by cutting down the tree?*
>
> *What concerns you about Jack Morgan's reaction?*

What was so important about the tree?

How were you expecting him to react?

Who is involved in the conflict?

Who would need to participate in a discussion about events?

Who else has strong opinions about these issues?

What has been the impact on those close to you?

Is it an interpersonal or group dispute?

How has your family been affected by the conflict?

How have other families in the neighbourhood been affected?

What is the problem to be resolved?

So, how can your families coexist peacefully? It also sounds as though you would like the Morgans to understand how difficult this winter's been for you.

What was the relationship like before the conflict, and what is it like now?

How did the two of you get along before this happened?

What kind of relationship did you previously have with the Morgans?

What is your relationship like now?

Task 3: Coaching and Motivating the Party

During this phase, the convenor's role is to help the party see the conflict in a different light, consider the implications of a variety of outcomes, assist the party to focus on his or her real concerns, and find the best possible way to address those. Here, the convenor is listening for anxieties and fears, as well as misperceptions about mediation.

How might mediation help the situation?

How do you see mediation making things worse?

Because the experience may have produced strong emotions, the convenor may need to assist the party in communicating feelings, so that they can be more readily heard and understood during mediation. The convenor helps the party to frame these emotions in a more constructive way. This is often accomplished through "owning" one's feelings, rather than projecting them on the other.

What has the experience been like for you?

How has it made you feel?

How do you think Jack Morgan will react if he hears you say that? How could you express it differently?

The party should also be encouraged to focus on his or her interests and to speak from needs, not demands. As well, he or she needs to develop an awareness of previous communication patterns and clarify what kind of relationship would be ideal in the future.

How do you need to relate to one another in order to be good neighbours?

What is important to you in your relationship with your neighbours?

The convenor needs to ask the party to reflect on how best to resolve the conflict—and ask about the best possible, worst possible, and most likely outcomes if the conflict is left unaddressed, addressed through a rights-based process, or addressed through mediation. Fisher and Ury refer to these as BATNAs (best alternatives to negotiated agreements) and WATNAs (worst alternatives to negotiated agreements). They assert that a mediated solution should provide no less than a BATNA; otherwise, there is little incentive for a party to participate (1981, pp. 104–109). To review BATNAs, see chapter 3.

What do you think is likely to happen if you don't address the issue?

What is the worst thing that could happen if you and the Morgans come together in mediation to try to talk about this?

What is likely to happen if you take this to court?

Finally, the convenor should acknowledge the positive step taken by the party to engage in the present conversation. It is not easy to speak with a stranger about a situation that we do not believe we have handled well. Doing so often makes us feel inadequate and vulnerable. The convenor should recognize and reward risk-taking behaviour, which will need to be cultivated further if the case goes to mediation.

You are showing a strong commitment to resolve this issue today.

You are demonstrating just how important it is for you to fix this relationship.

You have really taken a big step forward in coming here today, and I know it wasn't easy for you.

Task 4: Educating the Parties About Mediation

The convenor needs to ensure that the party has enough information about his or her options, enabling the party to make the best informed decision about how to proceed. During this stage, the convenor describes mediation, detailing what will happen during the process and the roles of the parties and the mediator. The convenor then discusses confidentiality and its constraints, and invites questions about the process from the party.

> *Mediation is a process that will enable your family and the Morgans to hear about events from one another's perspectives; to have the opportunity to talk about what the situation has been like; to have the Morgan family gain insights into your experience while you gain insights into theirs; and to all come up with practical ways to live together in the future. A mediator will assist you in this conversation, by asking questions, listening intently, and guiding you toward a resolution that you choose to meet your needs.*
>
> *The mediator has no obligation to report to anyone and will keep confidential anything she hears in mediation. Only your two families need to know what happens.*

In the Not in My Backyard scenario, the community-based mediation service has no reporting requirements, particularly because the referral came from one of the parties. In other situations, as discussed earlier in the chapter, there may be a need to get back to the referral agent, and there may be some limits to confidentiality. The mediator must be upfront about this with all concerned. Also, the convenor may share how mediation has been helpful in similar situations—and will certainly check out and respond to the party's fears and anxieties about the process.

> *You're worried that Jack Morgan will dominate or overpower the discussion. ... Let me tell you how that will be addressed in mediation.*
>
> *What other things concern you about going to mediation?*
>
> *Do you have any other questions about the process?*

At this stage, the convenor will determine whether the party needs to bring a representative or someone to offer support or assistance to the mediation. There are certainly cases where supporters and lawyers are present: workplace conflicts involving legal or policy grievances, human rights complaints, unlawful dismissal, and many litigation claims. The convenor should speak with lawyers and other representatives in advance of the mediation, to clarify the role they will take in the session and to plan for their participation, if required. (The role of lawyers in mediation was discussed at the end of the previous chapter.)

Lawyers, representatives, and support persons can exacerbate conflict if they adopt an adversarial approach in mediation. The convenor needs to discuss mediation goals and process with them in advance, understanding what each "side" hopes to achieve. Most lawyers are very helpful when they have a clear understanding of the mediator's role. They usually wish to help their clients achieve goals that go beyond the upholding of rights and entitlements, such as maintaining relationships and other intangible needs that cannot be met through an adversarial process. The same is true of other advocates, supporters, and representatives.

The convenor must also determine whether the party requires information from advocacy or other process experts and, if possible, refer the party to other agencies to collect that information. The convenor needs to record his or her own information needs during this discussion, especially in cases with complex substantive or legal issues. Moore (1996, pp. 116–117) also suggests that data be collected from direct observation and site visits, and from secondary sources such as financial records, government and annual reports, minutes of meetings, newspaper articles, and any research on the issue. An organization's policies relevant to the issues and any correspondence between the disputants may also be needed. A convenor may also need to know about collective agreements in a unionized workplace; policies on human rights complaints, harassment, and abuse of power; the documentation needs from referring agencies; mediation agreement forms; and agreement to mediate forms.

The mediator, rather than the convenor, might handle some of these issues, if there is a distinction between the person who convenes and the person who mediates. Mediators often prepare parties and their advocates for mediation.

Task 5: Determining Suitability for Mediation

Before completing stage 2 of convening, three important sets of questions need addressing in ascertaining suitability for mediation:

1. Can you ensure the safety of all participants, including the mediator?
2. Are the parties able to negotiate freely, ably, and in good faith?
3. Is there an invisible party, not present at the table, who could be adversely affected by the outcome of the mediation? Is this a public or private dispute? Are there systemic problems that are better addressed in other forums?

The first question is about security. If any party's security cannot be assured throughout the process, or if a mediator cannot maintain a safe and non-threatening environment, or even when the mediator's own safety could be compromised, the process should not go ahead. Cases involving a risk of violence, or any situation in which one party has concerns about safety, or cannot speak openly without fear of reprisals or intimidation, are not suitable for mediation and should usually be pursued in another forum, such as litigation.

Some accommodations can mitigate some of the safety concerns, such as "shuttle" mediation, where the parties do not meet face to face, and staggered arrival and departure times. In addition, the party who feels particularly threatened can be invited to bring along a support person. These strategies are often employed with divorcing couples in situations where one party has felt threatened by the other, and in cases of workplace harassment.

The second question is about the parties' motivation and competencies. Although not usually a trained psychologist, the convenor must explore the capacity of parties to participate in mediation. Some parties are too emotionally invested in a dispute to hear the other party's perspective at all. Other parties may not have the competencies to negotiate, because of an inability to express or understand emotions, interests, or consequences (Crawford, Dabney, Filner, & Maida, 2003). In other situations, the imbalance of power may not enable one party to freely negotiate, fearing the consequences of "talking back" to a boss or spouse. Also, a party may not have authority to settle. Finally, a party may not see that there is anything to gain from going through mediation. If these obstacles cannot be overcome, mediation is not recommended.

Sometimes, to accommodate those who are not ready or able to go through mediation, the convenor can delay the process. A "cooling-off" period or personal counselling might help a party prepare for a session. In these instances, a convenor may give "homework" to the parties to help them develop skills for mediation. When a party doesn't appear to have any stake in resolving the situation, a convenor might encourage him or her to see the conflict differently and to recognize his or her role in the situation. If the party will not participate in good faith, a successful process has little chance. In all cases, the convenor needs to ensure that people with the proper authority to make decisions are present or available.

Both convenors and mediators tend to focus on what they can do to encourage parties to participate in a mediation. This can often be accomplished by having a support or advocate person attend with the party, coaching the party to communicate effectively, and assisting the party to develop the competencies needed to negotiate effectively.

The third question asks whether the dispute between the parties is a private or public dispute. A common criticism levelled at mediation is that it privatizes public disputes (Goundry, Peters, Currie, & Equity Matters Consulting, 1998). Conflicts of a systemic or structural nature should not be addressed only through mediation. Where the protection of rights (granted through collective agreements, employment law, the *Canadian Charter of Rights and Freedoms*, or other legislation/policy) is the issue of contention, a rights-based process can sometimes respond better to party concerns. People cannot be asked to negotiate away rights in mediation. At other times, a case involving collective interests (for example, a harassment-free workplace) should not be diverted to mediation alone, particularly if the application of existing policy requires that an alternative process be undertaken.

This does not mean that cases should not go to mediation when there are both interpersonal and structural elements to a conflict. Consider a situation where a female soldier feels discriminated against by her superior. The collective interest might be to address a poisoned work environment because gender equity does not appear to be present. Responding to the collective interest may require training of all staff, the implementation or application of a policy on human rights, or even disciplinary action against an employee who does not follow organizational policy. However, the female soldier may still wish to work in that particular unit. Her individual interest is in improving her relationship with her supervisor. In this case, it is possible to address both needs, if the convenor works closely with other dispute resolution advisers in the organization to address different aspects of the conflict. Organizations should, as a matter of policy, adopt integrated systems that include rights-, power-, and interest-based processes for responding to organizational conflicts. Systemic problems cannot usually be addressed through interpersonal approaches.

Stage 3: Decision Making and Planning

The disputants alone cannot voluntarily decide to go forward with mediation. The convenor must also agree that mediation is the best option. Mediation is not a panacea, the convenor must feel sure that participation in mediation will not harm parties. In workplace disputes, when the convenor is a fellow employee, he or she has to consider both the well-being of individuals and his or her responsibility to improve the institution.

This provides strong incentive for a responsible and extensive screening process. In all cases, criteria for assessing the suitability of mediation should always be applied.

If the convenor has determined that mediation is suitable, he or she still needs to help the parties to decide whether mediation is the best process for resolving their conflict. Many people need to be encouraged to try mediation; resistance to the process is common. Much of that resistance comes from preconceived notions about what is likely to happen in mediation. For example, some people think that mediation is a "touchie-feelie" process, where they will be expected to express emotions and to hear the emotions of the other party. Others believe that mediation is not a serious process designed to resolve disputes. There are also those who cannot imagine that speaking with the other party could be helpful, given the amount of animosity between them. The convenor devotes a good deal of time to addressing these misconceptions and educating parties about mediation.

If a party needs time before making a decision about mediation, the convenor usually sets a date and often takes responsibility for follow up, because she or he knows how easy it is for a party to procrastinate. Most people just hope the problem will go away, although few actually believe that it will.

If the parties decide to go ahead with mediation, the convenor has a number of items to discuss. First, if the convenor is in private practice, he or she needs to talk about fees. Fee structures range broadly, depending on the area of practice, the educational background of the mediator, and sliding scales. Most mediators charge between $100 and $300 per hour, or they might charge by the day or half-day (Picard, 2000). If parties themselves are paying for the services, the cost is usually split evenly between the two. If an organization is paying for the mediator, the discussion of fees usually occurs early on, when the organization first contacts the service.

Second, the convenor introduces a Consent To Mediate form, if he or she uses one (see appendix A). This is usually a one- or two-page document that outlines the principles of mediation, the role of the mediator, the parties' roles, and clauses protecting the mediator from being called as a witness to a formal dispute resolution process, in the event that the mediation is not successful. It is common practice for parties to take away this form, so they can reflect upon the information and share it with their significant others. It is then brought back to be signed at the beginning of the first joint mediated session.

Although the convenor has likely already spoken with all those involved in the situation, there are times when he or she still needs to contact others. In these cases, the convenor discusses the options for contacting other parties, as well as the role of the referring party, if there is one. This can happen in a number of ways, as was outlined earlier in the chapter. Most convenors solicit advice about how to best approach them and what will be said.

> *I will contact Mrs. Osman this week, telling her what we agreed upon—that you came to see me to explore whether mediation would be helpful in the situation your two families face, and that I would like to speak with her in order to see whether she too thinks mediation has potential.*

When a case has been referred by someone not directly involved in the dispute (such as a supervisor, lawyer, or union representative), how that person will be contacted is discussed. Many convenors have standard processes for handling referred cases. This issue is critical when the referral comes from an office that requires written confirmation about case outcomes. For example, a human rights adviser may refer a complainant to mediation and require written correspondence to prove that the case has been closed. Courts with mandatory mediation programs also require correspondence indicating that the case has been settled. If the referral agent does require additional information about the mediation process or wishes to be privy to mediation documents, this is discussed or negotiated with the parties in advance of mediation.

In referred situations, when the first party contacted does not wish to proceed with mediation or the convenor does not believe mediation is appropriate, the convenor is obliged to inform the referring party. In these circumstances, the convenor needs to respect confidentiality. A convenor would never say, "A mediation will not be going ahead because Jack didn't want to." This statement could be used against Jack in future proceedings, which a convenor would not wish to influence.

When the parties determine that the referral agent should be involved or advised, it is often the parties' responsibility to relay the request. At the behest of the parties, a convenor can take on the task of informing the referral agent of further steps—or request that she or he be present. When a conflict is referred, the convenor respects confidentiality. Upon conclusion of the mediation, he or she may be asked to report back to the person making the referral, informing them of the outcome, without divulging details about any agreement reached, unless this is a legal requirement. The parties themselves or the mediator can also report back to the referring agent.

Convenors often send parties off with "homework," to help them prepare for mediation. This homework might be a series of questions to ponder; the collection of research on their situation (learning policies, collecting cases of precedent, understanding their best and worst options if this case is pursued in a different dispute resolution process); or the honing of communication skills needed in the mediation.

Finally, the convenor and parties should determine a reasonable time for getting back to each other, if they wish to proceed with mediation. If mediation is to happen, the convenor next needs to determine who should mediate the case.

MEDIATOR SELECTION

Having facilitated the information gathering and assessment stages, the convenor gets a sense of which skills and strengths are required of a mediator and which characteristics the mediator should possess. These characteristics might have to do with gender, age, language, ethnicity, and status, to name a few. The convenor also gets a sense of how the process will need to be adapted to accommodate the parties' needs. These might involve co-mediation, support, interpreters, or separate sessions with each party. Because of this knowledge, the convenor plays an important role in making recommendations as to who should mediate the case. If the convenor is the mediator, she needs to reflect on her own capacity to take on the mediation. Does her model of mediation work for the parties? Can she act impartially? Does she need, and then have, substantive knowledge of the issues to be mediated? Would she be more effective with a co-mediator?

How much knowledge does a mediator need about the substantive issues in dispute—and the context in which the conflict takes place? To mediate divorce settlements, mediators do need to know family law. Custody and access issues are usually mediated by someone with experience and knowledge in child development and family systems. Workplace mediators are required to have an understanding of the workplace culture and systems, as well as knowledge about workplace policies, collective agreements, labour laws, and any other relevant legislation that could have an impact on the issues in contention. For complex disputes in contract law, construction, business, environment, and public policy, a mediator with knowledge and experience of the area is likely to follow discussions more effectively. For mediators with substantive knowledge and experience, the caveat is that they not impose their own judgments about the issues, particularly if the parties are not seeking an evaluative process.

Returning to the Not in My Backyard scenario, it is clear that the mediator should have an understanding or experience of being in a new culture, sensitivity to differences in communication across cultures, and possess enough charismatic power to balance some of Jack Morgan's. Parties of one ethnic group don't necessarily require a mediator of the same ethnicity. However, "peer" mediators may be essential when particular issues in conflict centre on cultural norms and traditions. In other situations, parties might consider the dispute too personal to be witnessed by a member of their peer group. Perhaps a co-mediation team or a cultural interpreter would help to provide better understanding of the different cultural positions.

Should the convenor become the mediator? To have a mediator distinct from the convenor is typically not an option in many private practices. However, it is a possibility for internally funded conflict resolution services or community-based programs. In private practice, mediators usually refer their cases to other mediators, if they realize they are not the best person in this role. It *is* appropriate for a convenor to mediate when she has developed a strong rapport with the parties in conflict and believes that she can mediate impartially. It may not be best if the convenor has spent a good deal of time with one of the disputants and not the other.

After considering all these issues, the convenor needs to select a mediator who meets the requirements and with whom the parties are comfortable. The convenor may also conclude that the situation might best be resolved through co-mediation, using two mediators rather than just one.

CO-MEDIATION

As a mode for dispute resolution, co-mediation is a popular and effective means of apprenticing less experienced mediators; balancing the mediators' characteristics with those of the parties to maximize perceptions of impartiality and understanding; as well as ensuring that the mediators are sufficiently knowledgeable about complex legal, psychological, economic, or environmental matters. Whatever the rationale, Love and Stulberg (1996, p. 180) emphasize that "for co-mediation to be effective, the mediators must match themselves with compatible partners and must make a plan for effective teamwork, or they will lose the potential benefits." Here are some of the advantages and methods of co-mediation.

Mediation can be intense—physically, intellectually, and emotionally draining—so, having another mediator working alongside can lighten the load. It is also easier to listen and observe when temporarily freed from the mediator role. The co-mediators can then reflect the gender, ethnic, or other attributes of the parties. Seeing someone who "looks the same as you" often helps parties feel at ease. Co-mediation can provide invaluable training for inexperienced mediators, demonstrate cooperative teamwork in action, and provide mediators with the opportunity to debrief and obtain peer review and feedback on their skills (Picard, 2002).

Co-mediation is not quite as simple as having another mediator in the room. It requires forethought, experience, and compatibility to maximize potential and minimize harm. First and foremost, co-mediators need to have a similar vision of their role and a congruent style of mediation. Having different understandings of fundamental goals is likely to result in the mediators working against one other. Furthermore, they should complement each other's strengths and weaknesses and know how to support each other. Preparation is key. How will the responsibilities be divided, especially in stage 1? We think it is best for co-mediators to share what needs to be communicated to the parties, and to do it in a natural and balanced way. Having both mediators speak early in the session allows each of them to obtain voice legitimacy, and it models cooperation and teamwork. It is also a good idea to decide, in advance, who will begin the session, who will record notes on the whiteboard or flip chart, who will write the agreement, and so forth. Determining how a caucus will be handled is another issue. We generally think that both mediators should talk to each party together, rather than conduct caucuses simultaneously, to ensure a similar understanding of issues and interests. Ideally, co-mediators will have some way of knowing when one would like the other to take the lead, especially when one is unsure of how to deal with the situation at hand or where to go next. Being able to do this in a natural manner and at appropriate times is important. A co-mediator should avoid interrupting a conversation and taking it in a different direction, when the other is following a hunch and doing some deepening work. Co-mediators don't need equal air time. Flexibility, cooperation, and teamwork are necessary.

Co-mediation provides an excellent opportunity for the co-mediators to analyze and reflect on conflict dynamics during breaks in the mediation process. A good team will use this time to modify and improve their strategies for the mediation. Having the opportunity to debrief together is one of the special advantages of co-mediation. Being able to analyze the strengths and weaknesses of the mediation and learn from each other is helpful, for both less experienced and senior mediators. Debriefing can improve your teamwork and provide the opportunity for peer review and reflective practice.

On the matter of seating, we suggest that co-mediators be able to see one another easily, so that they can "read" the other's non-verbal and pickup signals—for example, that it is a good time to become more active and take over the lead. We also suggest that the parties sit across from each other. In particular situations, other seating arrangements may be more appropriate. Love and Stulberg (1996, p. 183) say that having the mediators sitting beside each other can help to unify the focus of the conversation, and "contributes to balancing and harmonizing the room." Once again, the point is to be thoughtful and intentional about how best to convene the mediation session.

Intentionality in terms of set up would also include choice of venue. Usually, this would be a private neutral location that has sufficient space to caucus, equipped with paper and pens, a flip chart or whiteboard, water, and tissues. Based on the convenor's assessment, rooms may be set up formally, with a board table and upright chairs, or more informally, with a low coffee table and more informal seating. The first joint session should be scheduled as soon as possible after the convening has been completed.

Finally, we want to talk briefly about followup. Although the convenor doesn't usually monitor adherence to agreements or provide ongoing support to parties after mediation, there is often a need for some followup. This role is more commonly filled by mediators.

FOLLOWUP

Sometimes the parties request a subsequent mediation but want some time to evaluate their progress between mediations. At other times, a mediation agreement is seen as the end of the conflict. In either case, a "check-in" can be valuable. This can be informal, with the convenor or mediator contacting all parties several weeks after the session, to inquire about the situation and checking on the parties' satisfaction with their mediation. It is also possible to use a more formal followup questionnaire to determine party satisfaction and agreement longevity. Whatever means is chosen, there should be some methods in place to evaluate the mediation service.

It is also not uncommon for a referring agency, such as a human rights office or human resources department, to request a copy of any final agreement. Forwarding agreements can be compulsory when the case is part of a mandatory mediation or court-referred program, such as the civil court mandatory mediation programs in Ontario and other provinces.

Other followup is necessary when the referral agent's approval is required to implement an agreement, such as in a situation where two employees negotiate flexible work hours. Their supervisor, who may have referred their conflict to mediation, will need to be consulted before a final agreement can be reached. To facilitate this, the referral agent can be involved in the mediation, contacted by phone before the parties sign an agreement, or, in instances where pre-approval was not necessary, informed after the mediation is completed.

SUMMARY

Convening is not easy work, neither for the convenor nor for the parties in conflict. Yet, if the process outlined in this chapter is followed, parties can be transformed by going through a convening session. In a safe and trusting environment, their perspectives are challenged by the convenor, who attempts to open up possibilities of interpretation that will be followed through in the mediation. Like a mediator, a convenor needs to prepare for his or her work, devoting maximum energy and attention to the tasks at hand. Convening, like mediation, can be a magical process conducted by an artful guide, leaving the parties with new insights.

Convening a mediation demands full use of one's senses and skills. The process is composed of stages similar to those of mediation, and the communication skills employed are precisely those needed by mediators. The convenor must follow the lead of the parties, flow and bend with the process, and, at the same time, ask the questions required to elicit the information needed to assess mediation's suitability and put together a coherent understanding of the issues, interests, and goals of the parties. The convenor should not feel pressured to have every case go through mediation. If the situation is better addressed through other avenues, the convenor should encourage this. His or her role is only to assist the parties in making an informed and appropriate choice about what path to follow. The importance of this is paramount.

FURTHER READING

Groundry, S., Peters, Y., Currie, R., & Equity Matters Consulting. (1998). *Family mediation in Canada: Implications for women's equality*. Ottawa: Status of Women Canada.

Moore, C.W. (2003). *The mediation process: Practical strategies for resolving conflict* (3rd ed.). San Francisco: Jossey-Bass.

Picard, C.A. (2002). *Mediating interpersonal and small group conflict*. Ottawa: Golden Dog Press.

Umbreit, M. (1995). *Mediating interpersonal conflicts: A pathway to peace*. West Concord, MN: CPI Publishing.

WEB SITES

Department of National Defence/Canadian Forces—Conflict Management Program: http://www.forces.gc.ca/hr/engraph/about_cmp_e.asp.

St. Stephen's Conflict Resolution Services: http://www.ststephenshouse.com/.

Winnipeg Mediation Services: http://www.mediationserviceswpg.ca/.

CHAPTER EIGHT

Packing Your Toolkit: Communication Skills

An understanding attitude doesn't presume to know a person's thoughts and feelings. Instead, it is an openness to listen and discover.

Michael Nichols, The Lost Art of Listening

This chapter introduces mediation communication principles and techniques. We begin with the process of communication and the importance of non-verbal communication, then we examine how communication is socially constructed, culturally rooted, and a relational process. We consider four paradigms (different ways of understanding) of communication, and we consider some responses that inhibit communication. In the last half of the chapter, we discuss a variety of communication skills: the facilitator's listening and questioning skills; some connecting skills and assertive conflict communications that are essential for managing conflict; and, finally, an introduction to creative, artful communication.

Good communication is both an art and a science. The science focuses on understanding why certain communication patterns tend to evoke certain responses. The art of communication involves becoming proficient at producing shared meaning. Communication happens in a variety of ways: direct and indirect, explicit and implicit, verbal and non-verbal, rational and intuitive. With different personalities, cultures, education, and life experiences, we all communicate differently, so there is infinite potential for miscommunication and misunderstanding. However, there is unlimited scope for each of us to develop our potential for being skilled and artful communicators—with many different people in many different situations.

People spend about three-quarters of their waking moments communicating with others (Katz & Lawyer, 1994, p. 16). This suggests that we cannot *not communicate*. Our smiles, frowns, stances, and silences reveal our thoughts and feelings.

Although we constantly receive messages, correct interpretation is not easy, because the listener "can't possibly know what is in the sender's private world of meaning" (Gordon, 1977, p. 51). It is also because communication is culturally rooted in norms, symbols, and rules. The following scenario (adapted from Gudykunst, 1991) highlights this point.

SCENARIO: Unintended Meaning

A businessperson from Canada is negotiating a contract in an Arab culture. During the meeting, the Canadian crosses his legs in such a way that the soles of his shoes are pointed in the direction of the Arab. While the Canadian attaches no meaning to this action, the Arab interprets it as an insult and acts accordingly—showing the sole of the foot to another person is intended to be insolent. Even though the message received was not intended, it nonetheless created a negative reaction.

In individualist cultures, such as those found in mainstream Western societies, messages are primarily conveyed through spoken language. The more open, direct, and clear people are in sending a message, the more likely they are to be considered good communicators. Messages that are not muddled by contextual factors are highly valued—the less room for misinterpretation, the better. This style is called "low-context" communication (Gudykunst, 1991). However, in more collectivist cultures (in Africa, Asia, and Latin America, for example), direct, open communication is thought to be disrespectful, causing the receiver of the message to lose face and feel hurt. In these cultures the message is encoded within the context of the discussions. Context might involve where one meets, what is worn or what is served, as well as a person's non-verbal expression, body gestures, or other behaviours. Communication is indirect; a relatively small part of the real message is communicated verbally.

This next scenario (adapted from Gudykunst, 1991) exemplifies "high-context" communication, where very little of the message is transmitted verbally.

SCENARIO: High-Context Communications

An Indonesian man wants to marry an upper-class woman. To do this, he must send his mother to visit the woman's mother to get permission for the marriage. During the visit of the mothers, the woman's mother serves the man's mother tea and bananas. Since tea is never served with bananas, that signals that the answer about the marriage is "no." In this way, the woman's mother does not have to insult the man's mother by openly saying "no." The objects speak for her.

Cultural diversity brings many benefits to our lives, including new perspectives, attitudes, values, and creativity. For these advantages to flourish, we must be open to new ideas and understand that people communicate differently, depending on culture, status, age, gender, and a host of other factors. Language need not be a barrier. It is our lack of knowledge about the norms and rules guiding communication that often gets in the way of having productive conversations.

The essence of mediation is in communication, and communication is a relational activity: it involves at least two people who are in a relationship of interdependence. Conflict is socially created, with a historical context that affects meaning and behaviour. Conflicts can be managed through communication. In fact, communication is believed to be the *sine qua non* of conflict (Folger & Jones, 1994, p. ix).

The entry of a mediator (or other third party such as an arbitrator, lawyer, advocate, or other intervenor) changes the conflict dynamic. Third parties become part of the conflict relationship; their presence influences the nature of the interaction; and they, like the parties, become changed as a result of their involvement. Folger and Jones (1994, p. 37) say that "mediators are not third parties who act on others without being acted upon, yet most of our theory implicitly or explicitly confirms this view." The very nature of human interaction means that we cannot be part of an interaction without shaping, moving, directing, and being affected by it. This is why the concept of "mediator as neutral" no longer makes sense.

THE COMMUNICATION PROCESS

The exchange of thoughts and feelings to convey meaning can occur verbally or non-verbally. Verbal exchange includes words, voice tone, and tempo. Non-verbal communication is expressed through facial expression, body posture, and gestures. Surprisingly, words alone comprise only 7 percent of what is communicated. Body movement and facial expression account for 55 percent, and the remaining 38 percent comes through voice tone, volume, pitch, and rhythm (McKay, Davis, & Fanning, 1983, p. 59).

All messages have two components: content and emotion. To understand a message fully, we must uncover both its emotional and its factual content. Words alone can mislead. Stone, Patton, and Heen (1999, p. 1) expand on this by suggesting that "no matter what the subject, our thoughts and feelings fall into the same three categories or 'conversations.'" These conversations are (1) the What Happened? Conversation, (2) the Feelings Conversation, and (3) the Identity Conversation.

In communications about conflict, the What Happened? Conversation refers to the disputants' struggle to get to the "truth" about what happened. In conflict—as in many life experiences—there is no one truth; instead, truth is in the eye of the beholder. This means that, in mediation, the focus is not on who is right (as in rights-based processes and adjudication) but on ensuring that all "truths" are identified and understood.

The Feelings Conversation is about emotional messages. Sometimes a person's internal Feelings Conversation is loud and clear; at other times, it may be muffled or even silenced. Retzinger and Scheff (2000, pp. 76–77) say that the suppression or denial of deep-rooted emotions like shame, hurt, and fear, when such emotions are "hidden from self and others," can be a leading cause of intractable conflict. Likewise, the emotional messages that people convey to each other, often non-verbally, are sometimes clear, sometimes confusing or misleading. When someone is crying, we conclude that they are hurt or sad. When someone is speaking loudly and behaving in an angry or agitated manner, we may have no idea of the feelings of insecurity or fear that may be motivating this. Understanding and responding to the parties' Feelings Conversations is essential to good conflict communication.

The Identity Conversation is about how we see ourselves in the conflict and how it affects our self-image and self-esteem. It is the conversation we have with ourselves about whether we are competent or not, good or bad, strong or weak, or even whether or not we are "special"—that is, worthy of love or high regard. When our sense of self is shaken by conflict, it affects our emotions, communications, and decisions in ways that may be difficult to understand and predict, even for us.

Feelings and Identity Conversations are often hidden, difficult to discern and respond to in direct, explicit ways. That is why mediators need to develop indirect, intuitive, and artful ways of discovering and communicating about these sources of conflict.

"People don't get down to the real problem until after they have first ventilated a feeling or some opening message" (Gordon, 1977, p. 50). By "opening message," Gordon is referring to statements such as "I knew I should have stayed home today" or "I'm not sure what I am even doing here, the situation is impossible!" Explosive statements like these are common in the opening stage of the mediation process. Communicating what is important—so that the other person really understands—is not easy, especially in situations of heightened emotion. There are a number of reasons why this is so difficult.

First, we hear through filters. Filters include factors such as our background and ethnicity, our life experience and worldviews, as well as our education, gender, and social class. We are usually unaware of filters, yet they play a major role in interpreting what someone says or means. Our personal filters allow us to generalize, distort, and delete information. Some sociologists claim that there is no *objective* reality or knowledge, that, in fact all reality is *subjective* or *interpretive*, due to cultural influences (Gergen, 1999; Burr, 1995). Lakoff and Johnson (1980, p. 159) also reject the long-standing theme, in Western culture, of objective or absolute truth. They believe "truth is always relative to a conceptual system that is defined in part by metaphors that have evolved in our culture over a long period or are imposed by people in power." Narrative mediation (see chapter 4) is based on this idea—that we generate individual stories to make sense of ourselves in the world and that we are influenced by the dominant stories of the society in which we live (Winslade & Monk, 2000). These stories create meaning for us, and they set the context for the messages we "hear." So, we often hear what we *expect* others to say, not what they *actually* said.

Second, "actions speak louder than words"—we "hear" as much with our eyes as with our ears. If someone tells us something but she doesn't look as if she means it, we do not believe her.

Third, non-verbal cues have different meanings in different cultures. Take eye contact, for example. For most Anglo-Saxons, direct and sustained eye contact sends the message that we are being truthful and honest. Social mores teach us to look a person in the eye if we want to be believed. However, for some of Canada's First Nations peoples, sustained and direct eye contact may be considered disrespectful or a sign of dishonesty or trickery.

Fourth, listening is a two-way process. As speakers, we become more effective when we show interest in listening to others. Covey's (1989) idiom comes to mind: "Listen first to understand before you speak to be understood." Nichols (1995, p. 64) says something similar: "Most people won't really listen or pay attention to your point of view until they become convinced that you've heard and appreciated theirs."

Fifth, misunderstanding can exist and we may not even know it. The fact that a speaker's intent and a listener's impression may never openly be disclosed causes this to happen.

Sixth, feelings are not easily shared. Also, disputants may not know what it is that they are feeling, or they may not have words to express these emotions. They also may not feel safe in talking about what really matters.

Seventh, listening is hard. Research suggests that our average listening efficiency is about 25 percent (Katz & Lawyer, 1994, p. 15). We may be distracted by what is going on around us, by our own internal strains and stresses, or we are too "busy" thinking about what we are going to say. As well, we can think much faster than we speak, so listeners have time to "tune out" information or "fill in" the story in ways that may not be relevant.

Eighth, listening is a skill that is not often taught—or learned—in school or everyday life. But good mediators must be good listeners. The majority of a mediator's time is spent listening, really listening, to the hopes and concerns of the individuals he or she is trying to help. It takes immense concentration, because the mediator must listen for both facts and feelings, ensure that the message heard is correct, and withhold judgment about what is said.

Communication Paradigms

Communication involves the transfer of information. That idea is common to most descriptions of the communication process. Krauss and Morsella (2000), however, suggest that there is more to it than that. To support their view, they set out the following four paradigms.

Encoding and Decoding Paradigm

In this paradigm, communication is seen as the transfer of information by means of codes. Selecting how you send a message to another person is called *encoding*. The person receiving the message (and extracting meaning from it) engages in a process of *decoding*. Another way of saying this is that the speaker engages in *expression*, which creates an *impression* with the listener—and the communication process is cyclical, involving the encoding (expression) and decoding (impression) of messages as depicted in figure 8.1. Reddy's "conduit metaphor" shows how our language to talk about language is structured. His metaphor equates ideas (or

FIGURE 8.1 Encoding and Decoding Paradigm

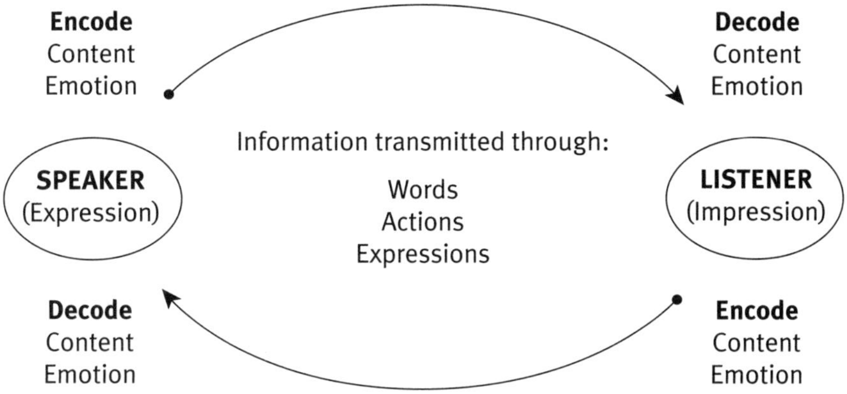

meanings) as objects, linguistic expressions as containers, and communication as sending. Thus the speaker puts ideas (objects) into words (containers) and sends them (along a conduit) to a hearer, who take the ideas/objects out of the words/containers (cited in Lakoff & Johnson, 1980, p. 10).

Remember that messages contain two parts: content and emotion (the facts and the feelings). When feelings are not heard or acknowledged, the speaker will increase the volume of that part of the message, because it is such an important element. In a real-life scenario, if a listener does not recognize or acknowledge the speaker's anger, the speaker becomes angrier. So the skill of reflecting feelings is important for mediators to acquire and practise.

The Intentionalist Paradigm

In this paradigm, "understanding consists of recognizing communicative intentions—not the words used, but rather what speakers intend those words to mean" (Krauss & Morsella 2000, p. 135). This should alert us to the danger of misconstruing the other person's intentions. It also points to a relationship between literal and intended messages. Misunderstanding of messages is common in conflict situations, because parties interpret messages consistent with their own beliefs. Ideal communication involves ensuring the intended message is the one actually received. This requires parties to express themselves intentionally—in ways that lead to the desired interpretation, and to try and see the world through the other's eyes. A mediator tries to help ensure that both these things take place.

Perspective-Taking Paradigm

This paradigm is based on the assumption that individuals perceive the world from differing viewpoints, and that interpretation of a message is influenced by the listener's beliefs. The more unlike two people are, the more difficult it is to understand the other's perspective accurately. To illustrate, many speakers assume that they share their listeners' beliefs and knowledge, which leads to incorrect assumptions about how much common ground exists between them. This paradigm requires that, when formulating a message, the sender keep the listener's perspective in mind. Two factors make this difficult. First, the other person's perspective is not always obvious. Second, there may be different and contradictory perspectives if more than two people are involved in the conflict. One example that Krauss and Morsella (2000, p. 139) use to illustrate this second point is that of a mayor who is negotiating a salary increase with the teacher's union, feeling it is necessary to "send a message" to other municipal unions that he is willing to run the risk of a strike.

Dialogic Paradigm

The dialogic perspective—opposing the idea that communication is a set of independent, albeit related activities—takes the view that communication is a relational, not an individualist, process. In other words, it takes two to have successful communication. Furthermore, meaning is socially constructed and can only be understood by taking into account the context and circumstances of the interaction. This paradigm takes listeners out of a passive role, requiring them to be responsive and active.

Kraus and Morsella use these four conceptualizations of communication to generate seven principles of communication.

1. Avoid communication channels with low signal-to-noise ratios; if that is impossible, restate the same idea in various forms.
2. When listening, try to understand the intended meaning of what your counterpart is saying.
3. When formulating a message, consider what the listener will take your words to mean.

4. When speaking, take your listener's perspective into account.
5. Be an active listener.
6. Focus initially on establishing conditions that allow effective communication to occur; the cooperation that communication requires, once established, may generalize to other contexts.
7. Pay attention to the form of the message.

While good communication cannot guarantee that conflict will be resolved, poor communication surely increases the likelihood that it will be made worse. Parties in conflict are often unable to engage in effective communication on their own because of strong feelings that they are right and the other is wrong. Thus, the other must be made to change their view, giving rise to the "attack–defend" pattern of communication. Through the interventions of mediators and other third parties, channels of blocked communication can be opened and effective communication restored.

Responses That Block Communication

Some ways of responding inhibit people from sharing their thoughts and feelings. These responses get in the way of building trust and rapport, and they create barriers to ongoing and deep conversation. Before discussing roadblocks to good communication, we would like you to think about what makes a good listener, by answering the following questions.

Good Listening Exercise

1. Who are the people you listen to most?
2. Who are the people you listen to least, or pretend to listen to?
3. What is it about the people in groups 1 and 2 that makes it easier or harder for you to listen?

Communication blockers are responses that result in a person feeling judged, blamed, considered incompetent, or not listened to. The message received, whether intended or not, is that the person is in the wrong and should change his or her behaviour or not feel as he or she does. Not feeling accepted for who we are leaves us less willing to disclose our real needs and feelings. Instead, it increases our defensiveness and resistance to new ideas. Blockers close off communication or, at best, keep it at the "presenting problem" level, preventing the exploration of the more important underlying issues. If you recall, we discussed the difference between a presenting and underlying problem in chapter 1: the underlying problem is what motivates us to see the issue as a problem. These motives are often linked to human needs, values, fears, expectations, and beliefs.

Most times, it is not our intent to "cool" conversation; instead, our responses are often unconscious habits that have been learned over time, without awareness of their effect. For communication to work well, Cornelius and Faire (1989, p. 41) tell us that we must

- respect an individual's right to her opinion by not manipulating her into seeing it our way,
- regard the person as our equal by not dominating her, and
- value her decisions by not undermining her.

The more common communication blockers can be organized into three broad categories (below). No doubt you will find it obvious why some of the responses might block communication. Others, however, may be less obvious because they frequently are accompanied by good intentions.

Being Judgmental

Criticizing, moralizing, diagnosing, disagreeing, and analyzing all fall into the judging category. When people feel judged, their common reaction is to defend themselves, which, in turn, makes them more aggressive and less cooperative. Criticizing focuses on the negative aspects of the situation—or the other party. It induces guilt and lowers self-esteem. Moralizing involves backing our viewpoint with social, religious, or moral authority. Diagnosing and analyzing involve playing detective by probing for hidden agendas and motives, and that can threaten and undermine an individual's self-confidence. Disagreeing places the speaker in a superior position, leaving the listener feeling inferior and belittled.

Giving Advice

The category "giving advice" includes ordering, threatening, using too many "shoulds," and providing solutions. You might ask what is wrong with giving advice, especially when a person solicits it. Here are four things to consider. First, often the person asking for the advice has not had a chance to explore what really matters about the issue. As a result, the adviser can only comment on the presenting problem, not the underlying, more important problem. Second, giving advice sends the message that you believe the person unable to solve her own problems. Inviting her to talk through the problem with you—rather than telling her what to do—shows respect for, and confidence in, her ideas and feelings. Third, each of us is different, and what works for us may not work for another person. Fourth, when we give advice, ownership of the problem shifts from the person to us. If the advice does not work, we are likely to be blamed.

Minimizing

Name calling, reassuring, diverting, and praising to manipulate are all minimizing tactics. Having our ideas minimized through name calling and sarcasm invites negative reaction, often creating feelings of resentment and frustration. Reassuring a person by telling him that everything will be all right overlooks his feelings and suggests that he should not feel the way he does. Trying to smooth things over is not empathetic; it may also be overly optimistic. Using praise to entice a person do something that she does not want to do—or to change her behaviour—is manipulative. Even when the praise is sincere, it often is not heard. Diverting attention from the listener's problem to your message says that you are more important. Using logical arguments and focusing on the factual aspects of the situation tends to minimize the listener's emotions. This can be infuriating; it says that feelings are not important, and the listener should not have them.

The minimizing category of responses are perhaps the least obvious roadblocks, because they are frequently intended to be helpful and show empathy. Regardless of the speaker's intent, if the listener does not feel valued and respected, he or she is not likely to want to discuss what really matters to them.

Communication Blockers Exercise

Identify some communication blockers that you commonly use. (You probably use more than one.) For example, do you find yourself giving advice to your younger sibling before discovering the real problem as a way of trying to be helpful? Or, did you try to reassure a co-worker when he encountered a problem, thinking you were being supportive. Then again, you might have used logic to respond to your neighbour's fear of being alone after a recent break and enter in the neighbourhood, as a way of reassuring her. We encourage you to keep a tally sheet for a day or two of the communication blocks you use. Then answer the questions below.

1. How often did your responses block communication?
2. Which one did you use most often?
3. With whom did you use the block most?
4. When you responded this way, recall what you were feeling (impatient, bored, preoccupied, rushed, etc.).
5. Select one person whom you would most like to stop blocking, and identify how you would go about doing it.

The Skill of Reflective Listening

"Genuine listening means suspending memory, desire, and judgment—and, for a few moments at least, existing for the other person" (Nichols, 1995, p. 64).

Active listening or, as we call it, *reflective listening*—to accentuate that the listener is reflecting what she or he heard—was popularized by Thomas Gordon in his 1977 best-seller *Parent Effectiveness Training*. The success of his effectiveness training books and programs has been influential in teaching parents, teachers, administrators, as well as leaders in organizations of every type the skill of how to listen so that others will talk. This presentation of the skills of good listening is rooted in Gordon's ideas, which we have adapted as we gained experience. Some of what we describe here can also be found in Cheryl Picard's 2002 book, *Mediating Interpersonal and Small Group Conflict*.

The skill of reflective listening is used, to some extent, in all models of mediation, but it is not just for mediators. It is a life skill for anyone involved in or helping with conflict. It serves a number of purposes: to demonstrate interest, to help people feel understood, to ensure correct understanding, to let a speaker think about what he or she said, to encourage the speaker to explain further, to enable a person to express strong emotion, and to check out unintended meanings through nonverbal expression.

Reflective listening involves four steps:

1. gathering information,
2. processing and decoding the information,

3. interpreting what the speaker meant,
4. checking out that your interpretation of what was meant is correct. (It is this last step that makes communication reflective.)

Remember that reflective listening pays respectful attention to *both* the content *and* the emotion of a speaker's message. Proficiency involves the sub-skills of attending, paraphrasing, and identifying emotion.

Attending

Attending involves using non-verbal indicators and watching for congruence between what is said and what is expressed non-verbally. These indicators include actions such as leaning forward; making eye contact in an open, accepting, and non-judgmental manner; and using hand gestures and body posture to indicate interest.

Paraphrasing

Paraphrasing involves *restating* briefly, in our own words, the content or facts of what the speaker has said, and suspending judgment on what was said. To illustrate what paraphrasing sounds like, consider the scenario A Change Is as Good as a Rest, the dispute between Danny and Teresa depicted in chapter 4. Let us suppose the mediator asks Danny to describe what he needs to talk about in the mediation. This is his response:

> Danny: *Until Teresa started with us, everything was going fine. We had a good little group going. We had our nose to the wheel and did our work. Our organization has gone through a lot of change in the past five years and we've managed to get through it okay. Don't get me wrong, we aren't against improving things. Computers were introduced to the section recently, and that has worked out, except that a couple of people lost their jobs as a result. We were told that would happen, I guess. Then Teresa starts coming up with all these ideas of doing things differently again! Some of us got upset because it's not one idea she has, it's like 150 ideas! But we said okay, we'll give her ideas a try. The reality is that these ideas have really disrupted our lives, and to make matters worse she doesn't seem to be interested in the changes that, in our view, don't work. Sure, she talks to some of the others in the department, but they're afraid to speak out; I'm not. I've been around for 15 years. I know what I'm doing. These are tough times for all of us and we need to stick together. She can't just go about saying that everything we do here is wrong and that we have to change or perish. Some of us like it the way it is now. I've got 10 years left, and I don't want to die before I retire. There are just so many changes people can take at one time!*

The mediator checked out that she understood Danny accurately by restating, non-judgmentally, the content of what she heard.

> Mediator: *Over the last five years, you've seen lots of changes in your organization. The introduction of computers was one thing. This went okay, although some staff did lose their jobs. Recently, Teresa has approached your group with a number of new ideas, some of which you have given a try. However, they are disruptive, and you have not found Teresa to be open to hearing about ideas that are not working. While some of the staff are afraid to speak out about how they feel, you are not. You have worked here a long time and it is important to you to continue to have a good working environment, because you hope to work here until you retire.*

Danny will let the mediator know whether or not she heard his message correctly.

Identifying Emotion

Reflecting feelings involves listening for and naming what the other person is feeling, without appearing negative or judgmental. This skill often requires that we first figure out what the feelings are, since people do not readily share their emotions. Carrying on with the conversation above, Danny responds to the mediator's paraphrase by adding more information.

> Danny: *Well, change leads to people losing their jobs and people being hurt. Take Joe, for example. He is trying to do this new thing suggested by Teresa. But he doesn't know how to do it, and there is no time allotted for people to learn new stuff. Teresa is too busy coming up with ideas to help Joe out. It is embarrassing for him and makes us look incompetent.*

The mediator responds by *reflecting* back the emotion that has been exchanged through this new dialogue.

> Mediator: *It is clear, Danny, that you and others are feeling overwhelmed by the number of changes that are being suggested by Teresa. Not being able to do them has been embarrassing, especially for Joe, and many of you are concerned about possible job losses. Furthermore, it seems to you that she is saying nothing you do is right and this is hurtful.*

Once again, Danny will tell the mediator whether she has in fact correctly understood his message.

We can't emphasize this enough: reflective listening, like all skills, has to be learned and practised for it to be effective. It is a life skill that can be used by all of us in our everyday lives. Here are some tips for effective reflective listening:

- Do not agree or disagree with was has been said.
- Do not take sides.
- Respond to non-verbal clues.
- Concentrate on what is being said by avoiding distractions.
- Show understanding through non-verbal gestures such as appropriate eye contact, tone of voice, nodding of the head, and hand gestures.
- Be sure to *restate* the content (facts) and *reflect* emotion (feelings).
- Be brief and to the point.
- Try putting yourself in the other person's shoes, to get a sense of what they might be experiencing.
- Avoid interrupting, finishing sentences, or offering suggestions.
- Do not bring up similar problems or feelings from your experience.

Reflective listening skills are not unique to mediators. Human resource professionals, business people, counsellors, parents, teachers, and others who want to understand what an individual is truly saying use these skills. When first learning to use reflective listening, it may feel insincere and somewhat artificial. To reduce this feeling, keep the following in mind:

- Focus on key points rather than trying to get all the details.
- Use your own words—parroting is not appreciated.
- Avoid using lead-ins such as: "So, if I am hearing you correctly …" or, "If I understand what you are saying …" or, "What I think you are saying is … ." They are cumbersome and not a natural way of speaking.
- Avoid sounding too tentative and unsure. Don't worry, the person will correct you if you are wrong and will appreciate that you are trying to understand them. Good listeners demonstrate close attention.
- Be transparent and honest. If you don't understand, say so—and ask for clarification.

Reflective Listening "Tools"

When learning to reflectively (actively) listen, it is helpful to think metaphorically that you have a "job to do." To do the job effectively and efficiently, you need a number of different "tools." Each of these tools is designed for use in specific circumstances, to achieve a particular outcome. As with any tool, knowing when and how to use it takes knowledge and considerable practice.

Here are six tools for reflective listening.

Encourage the Conversation

This tool communicates interest in what the speaker is saying, and is used to encourage the person to continue talking. It involves the use of both verbal and non-verbal messages.

Gesturing for the person to continue speaking, moving forward in your seat to show you are listening intently, making eye contact, and nodding your head all demonstrate interest. So do short statements, such as "Please go on," or, "Say more about that." More pointed statements, such as "I am happy to listen while you talk," "I am interested in hearing more about the changes," and "Talking about our fears often lessens them," provide assurance that you are willing to listen.

Clarify Your Confusion

This is an important tool, because when you are no longer able to follow the story, it is hard to continue listening. Use this tool to reduce confusion, not gather more information, even though asking for clarification may result in the speaker elaborating further.

A clarifying intervention might sound something like one of these examples:

> *Teresa, I don't understand the acronyms you are using. It would help me if you would explain what is meant by "NLHRS."*

> *Danny, you keep mentioning your little group. Who is it that you are referring to when you speak of this group?*

Restate the Facts

This tool is used to check that you have correctly heard the "content" of the speaker's message. All messages contain *content* and *emotion*, and restating is how to confirm that your understanding of the basic ideas and facts is correct. It also shows that you are listening. If you have not heard correctly, the speaker is able to correct that misunderstanding. Do not be afraid if you get the message wrong or leave out important parts. Speakers will let you know if you missed something important, and they will appreciate that you are trying to understand them.

Use your own words when restating. Here is an example of what a restating statement might sound like:

One of the things you've mentioned, Danny, is that the group takes exception to the lack of discussion with Teresa about the ideas she has that do not work.

Reflect the Feelings

Reflecting is the tool used to check out the emotional part of the speaker's message. It requires the listener (you) to use "feeling" words when you confirm your impression of how the person is feeling, based on what he or she said. Sometimes we are fortunate and speakers will tell us, in words, how they are feeling. More commonly, feelings are hidden and we have to guess at them. Furthermore, we can never know exactly what a person is experiencing because we cannot get inside of them. A person's body posture, tone of voice, and facial expression are often good clues to their feelings. An example of a reflecting statement would be: "Not being asked for your opinion is frustrating for you and for the group, leaving all of you feeling undervalued."

Many people first learning to mediate find it difficult to find the right feeling word, so here are some of the more common words that reflect both negative and positive feelings.

annoyed	excited	miserable	shocked
anxious	excluded	neglected	slighted
appreciated	frightened	nervous	stressed
apprehensive	frustrated	offended	supported
betrayed	glad	ostracized	surprised
cared for	happy	pained	trapped
comfortable	helpless	perplexed	troubled
concerned	humiliated	powerless	undecided
confident	hurt	provoked	undervalued
depressed	impatient	puzzled	uneasy
disappointed	irritated	rejected	unnerved
displeased	insulted	sad	unsure
eager	let down	satisfied	upset
embarrassed	manipulated	secure	worried

Summarize the Major Ideas

Summarizing involves restating a group of understandings or perceptions that have been expressed. You can use this tool to review progress, link important ideas, and establish a basis for ongoing discussion. It is also a useful tool when the conversation seems to be going in circles and you want to refocus on key issues. Here is an example of a summarizing statement, again using Danny's and Teresa's conflict.

> Mediator: *Danny, you and your co-workers are worried about how to implement the changes that Teresa is suggesting, especially since no time has been allotted for retraining. You have not told her about your concerns because you are not sure how tight she is with management, so you feel vulnerable by letting her know that you are not able to use the new computer system. Teresa, you indicated that learning to use the new system could be done in less than a day. In fact, you could provide this training yourself, and there would be no need for management to be involved. You have not offered to do this before because no one has let you know that they need help. Let's talk more about training.*

Validate the Effort

Validating is an important and often underused listening tool. It involves acknowledging the efforts of the speaker and showing appreciation for her actions. Here is one way the mediator might validate Teresa:

> Mediator: *Teresa, you clearly wanted to jump in when Danny was talking, and I asked you to hang on until he was finished. I appreciate that you allowed him to finish his point. It is not always easy to refrain from interrupting a person when you have a different point of view. Please tell us what you wanted to say.*

Asking Productive Questions

Since the mediator is there to help parties discover the underlying issues and get insights into the root of the conflict, he or she must be able to ask useful, productive, and sometimes difficult questions. Questions designed to elicit insights are non-judgmental and do not put parties on the defensive. Rather, they assist parties to articulate their values and concerns. Parties trying to negotiate on their own also need to be able to ask open, non-accusatory questions. Cloke (2001) wants mediators to refrain from taking the easy route to a quick compromise. For him, the central task is to help the parties create choices for themselves—and this means exploring what sometimes might be dangerous terrain, to help parties get to the heart of the matter. Learning how to ask deeply honest questions designed to elicit values and concerns with empathy and in a safe environment is what we believe collaborative problem solving and mediation is all about.

Mediators use questions to gather information, understand experiences, learn about perspectives, explore issues, discover interests, develop options, and find solutions. The types of questions asked reflect how a mediator understands the goal of mediation and his or her role in it. They shape relations within the mediation and they set the tone. A skilled mediator asks questions that are both purposeful and strategic; a less experienced mediator has a tendency to ask questions that are either too broad and unfocused or too narrow and limiting. As a result, answers tend to be vague and noncommittal, making the job of the mediator harder. As with listening, asking effective questions is a skill that takes considerable practice.

Types of Questions

Basically, there are two types of questions: open and closed. Closed questions yield "yes" or "no" answers. They are useful when we want an individual to affirm or deny a statement. These questions are often used in a courtroom context. But they are not useful when we are trying to discuss something or gather new information. Here are a few examples of closed-ended questions:

Will it be okay if Danny seeks you out over coffee breaks to discuss his ideas?

Will you give Teresa feedback on her ideas, if she approaches you directly instead of at staff meetings?

Open-ended questions are elicitive. They invite a person to go beyond what is already known. They generally start with "what," "when," "where," "who," "how," and, to a lesser extent, "why." Asking "why" too often causes people to feel judged and become defensive because the emphasis is on them rather than on the issue. Open-ended questions (or probing questions, as they are also called) elicit information by encouraging a speaker to provide new information, to expand further on something he or she said, and to go more deeply into issues and concerns. Here are some examples of very broad open questions:

What else can you tell me about the situation?

Who else is part of the group?

When were you hoping this would happen?

Where did you plan to take the training?

How would you prefer that Teresa present new ideas?

Why is this issue so important to you?

Open questions can be used for various purposes. Ten of these purposes are listed below along with an example of what each question might sound like.

1. Clarify: *What do you mean when you say that she is pushy?*
2. Explain: *What makes you think that he should replace the missing computer?*
3. Challenge: *What will happen if the two of you are not able to settle this matter here today?*
4. Brainstorm: *What are all the possibilities that you can think of to solve this problem?*
5. Identify interests: *What do you fear will happen if she is given access to the files?*
6. Fact-find: *How long will it take for you to be able to offer the training?*
7. Seek opinion: *What do you think about the idea of meeting during breaks to discuss the group's views?*
8. Test consequences: *How do you think he will react to hearing about this decision?*
9. Problem-solve: *How have you tried to resolve this problem, and what is preventing you from resolving it now?*
10. Empower: *Think back to a time when someone told you that they appreciated your assistance to help work through a tough situation? What did you learn about your capacities through their appreciation, and how might these capacities help you now?*

Broadening and Deepening Questions

Another way of thinking about questioning is whether you want to *broaden* your knowledge about the situation or *deepen* your understanding of what was said. Broadening questions are "curious" questions designed to expand the information each party has about the situation. They tend to be general and indirect. "What is the problem?" "What brought you here today?" "What is the background to this incident?" Broadening questions are often fact-finding in nature, seeking information about what may have helped give rise to the conflict situation.

Deepening questions go more deeply into information already known. They arise out of answers to broadly based questions. They help to peel back the onion, metaphorically speaking. Here is a short dialogue that starts with a broad question followed by deepening questions, to help you see the difference.

> Broadening question: *What is it that you want to talk about here today, Teresa?*
>
> Response: *I want to get this problem with Danny settled once and for all! I've had it with him and his little group!*
>
> Deepening question: *What is it about Danny's behaviour that is causing you to feel so annoyed and frustrated?*
>
> Response: *Well, I keep asking him to tell me if he has problems with my ideas, before we go into meetings, but he never does. Instead, at staff meetings, when I bring forward my ideas for improving the Documents Section, he just says, "No, that would never work here." Then he refuses to discuss why. It is so maddening—and embarrassing at times.*
>
> Deepening question: *Danny's behaviour is clearly a problem for you. How is it that you find it embarrassing?*
>
> Response: *Well, isn't it obvious? I am trying to do a good job by coming up with suggestions that respond to what the staff have been telling me is not working. Danny's constant blocking of my ideas must leave the staff thinking I am either not listening to their concerns or that I don't care. Both of these are so untrue!*

Having obtained insight into Teresa's difficulty with Danny, the mediator now tries to expand her understanding by asking a broadening question.

> Broadening question: *Clearly, you want to be seen as doing a good job and this means having the opportunity to present your ideas at staff meetings. How do the others at your meetings respond when Danny rejects your ideas without explanation?*

Remember, the way a question is worded—and the tone in which it is sent—will greatly affect the answer obtained, along with the willingness of a party to continue the discussion. You need to stay "curious" and avoid judging or problem solving. You know there is no single truth. Your goal is to seek insight into the meaning of the conflict situation for each of the parties involved.

Different models of mediation ask specific types of questions to further the process goals. Insight mediators ask broadening and deepening questions to gain insight. Transformative mediators ask elicitive questions to empower parties. Narrative mediators ask specific types of questions to construct an alternate story to the problem-saturated story. Let's look more closely at these questions, as outlined by Winslade and Monk (2000, pp. 87–89).

Types of Questions Used by Narrative Mediators

The first type of question is the *unique outcome question*. It is designed "to invite people to identify actions and intentions that stand apart from the problem story." The example they give is, "Why did hurt feelings and blame not stop you from cancelling this meeting?" Their second type is the *unique account question*, which "asks a person to make sense of an event that is an exception to the conflict story it represents"—a contrast that may not have already occurred to the party. Their examples are, "How do you explain that you were able to be more in charge of blame, humiliation, hurt feelings, or injustice than you initially thought?" and "What do you think it means that you are agreeing about that issue?" Their third type of question is the *unique redescription question*. This invites people to reflect on themselves and on their relations with the other party, to develop a fuller articulation of who they would like to be. For example, "What does this tell you about yourself that you would not otherwise have known?" The *unique possibility question* is the fourth type of question. It moves the focus toward the future and "encourages people to speculate about the implication of what has been talked about in the mediation and to project it forward." The example they use is, "Given your present understanding and your desire to heal the wounding effects of blame, what might be your next step?" The final type of question they present is the *unique circulation question*. This is designed to "anchor the newly developing more-preferred story through the provision of an audience, as stories are not always the property of those at the center of a dispute." Here are two of their examples: "Who will be most likely to support the continuation of these developments?" and "If your children were witness to these discussions, who would be most excited about this change in direction?" In their book *Narrative Mediation*, Winslade and Monk give many examples of each of these questions and go into much fuller descriptions.

Connecting Skills

Some communication responses can be thought of as "connecting skills"—they purposefully link what a mediator has heard or seen with a related question or statement. We discuss three of these responses: bridging, immediacy, and confronting discrepancy.

Bridging

Bridging requires the mediator to first check out the meaning of the speaker's statement by paraphrasing what she heard, followed immediately by a deepening question designed to lead the speaker to further explore the interests, intent, or assumptions behind the statement. Earlier in this chapter, the mediator paraphrased Danny's statement. Here's an excerpt, followed by a bridging statement, to show what it would sound like.

> Mediator: ... *Recently, Teresa has approached your group with a number of new ideas, some of which you have given a try. However, they are disruptive, and you have not found Teresa to be open to hearing about ideas that are not working. ... You have worked here a long time and it is important to you to continue to have a good working environment, as you hope to work here until you retire.*
>
> Bridge: *It may help the two of you understand each other better if you would give an example of how Teresa's ideas have been disruptive to the staff and to you, Danny. It would also be helpful if you could tell Teresa why the staff believe she is not open to hearing about ideas they believe will not work.*

Here's one more example of bridging to illustrate this communication skill. The mediator uses a reflecting statement to let Danny know that she heard the emotion behind his statement. Only this time she follows with a bridge that is in the form of a deepening question.

> Mediator: *It is clear, Danny, that you and others are feeling overwhelmed by the number of changes that are being suggested by Teresa. Not being able to do them has been embarrassing, especially for Joe, and many of you are concerned about possible job losses. Furthermore, it seems to you that she is saying nothing you do is right and this is hurtful.*
>
> Bridge: *Where is the concern about job loss by the staff coming from, Danny?*

A bridging statement or question can also be used to return to information that was discussed previously, or take the conversation in a new direction. To illustrate:

> Mediator: *Danny, earlier you mentioned that in the past the department had done some downsizing. When did this take place and how did it come about?*

Immediacy

The second connecting skill that we highlight is immediacy. Mediators use this response to deal with what is happening "in the moment." Focusing on the here and now requires the mediator to interrupt the general direction of the conversation and attend to strong verbal or non-verbal messages. It is used to keep emotions from escalating, by attending to them as they emerge. Immediacy takes both proficiency and courage. Proficiency is needed when we are being highly attentive to what is going on between one party and the other, between one or both parties, and within the process itself. The mediator needs courage to share his or her feelings and thoughts directly and respectfully. The following two examples of immediacy interventions by the mediator illustrate this skill.

> Mediator: *Teresa, when Danny just told you why he and the staff are concerned about job loss, you shook your head and crossed your arms, which looked to me like an expression of exasperation. What was that all about?*
>
> Mediator: *Danny, when I look at you right now, you appear to be both discouraged and defeated. Perhaps you are wondering if there is any point in continuing with these discussions. It would be very helpful if you could tell us what you wanted to happen that has not—and why you are feeling so hopeless.*

Confronting Discrepancy

This connecting skill has three elements: observing, describing, and questioning. Mediators use it to point to discrepancies in words or actions, as well as to point out discrepancies between a person's goals and his or her actions toward achieving them.

Mediators use this communication response sparingly and with sensitivity—parties can hear it as judgmental, even when that was not intended. Tone of voice is critical when using this skill and should reflect curiosity rather than blame. Here is an example of this skill.

> Mediator: *Danny, you told us a few times now that you want to know what Teresa's job really is, yet every time she tries to explain her job, you respond in a dismissive manner, saying that if she was telling the truth she would not behave as she does. It is hard for Teresa to explain her job when she is cut off and criticized. Could you restate what you have heard her say, thus far, about her job—and why you find it so hard to believe her? Then, Teresa, perhaps you would add what else you would like Danny to understand about your job and your motives.*

Externalizing the Conversation

One communication skill used primarily by narrative mediators is called *externalizing the conversation*. This skill relates to one of Fisher and Ury's (1981) principles of negotiation: separate the people from the problem. Using this skill, a mediator often talks about the conflict as if it were a third party. Winslade and Monk (2000, pp. 144–145) report that this way of speaking opens up possibilities for new ways of thinking and, importantly, avoids parties feeling blamed. Here are some of the examples they give:

- How did this argument catch the two of you in its clutches?
- How does what happened invite you to feel?
- To what extent is blame stopping you from resolving your differences?
- What did the argument make you think about the other person?
- The conflict has made you feel a very strong emotion like hatred. How did it manage to take over your feelings in such a strong way?
- What has been the effect of the rent arrears on you?

Personification allows mediators to "make sense of phenomena in the world in human terms—terms we can understand on the basis of our own motivations, goals, actions, and characteristics" (Lakoff & Johnson, 1980, p. 34). Viewing conflict in human terms provides explanatory power that often leads to action. This is why mediators "focus on the problem, not the person," "externalize the conversation," and use "metaphors" to help parties define their everyday realities.

Non-Blaming and Non-Defensive Responses

For some, the difference between aggressive communication and assertive communication is not clear; however, understanding this distinction is critical in achieving effective interest-based conflict communication. Fisher and Ury (1991) make clear distinctions between what they call hard bargaining and principled negotiation, and between soft bargaining and principled negotiation. A hard bargainer engaged in strong positional negotiation will typically use aggressive communication that may attack, accuse, or intimidate the other party. Aggressive communication tends to elicit adversarial behaviour and adversarial relations between the parties. In contrast, a so-called soft bargainer will typically use passive communication to avoid confrontation. As Fisher and Ury (1991, pp. 12–13) point out, principled negotiation is neither "hard" nor "soft."

For successful principled or interest-based negotiation, a person needs to engage in assertive communication, whereby the person clearly communicates his or her experiences, feelings, and needs related to the conflict interaction. Effective, assertive communication tends to elicit collaborative behaviour and collaborative relations between the parties.

The aim of assertive communication is twofold: first, for us to say how we feel in a way that is non-accusatory, or to teach the parties to do this; and second, to break the communication pattern of "attack and defend" that is prevalent when parties feel defensive. As mediators, we might use these skills when we see that parties are wrongly judged or attacked and we need to stop this behaviour from continuing.

Non-Blaming Statements

As a form of communicating assertively, non-blaming statements are commonly known as "I" messages. They are contrasted with "you" messages, which blame, accuse, threaten, and cause people to feel guilty and respond defensively. "I" messages tell another person how you feel, what you want when you feel that way, and why you feel that way. Mediators use this communication tool in two ways: to let a party know the effect of his or her behaviour on the mediator, and to educate parties on how to improve their pattern of communication.

Basically, "I" messages have three parts, which can be expressed in any order.

- *"I feel …"* (a statement of your feeling(s) using a feeling word);
- *"when …"* (an objective description of the problem behaviour or situation);
- *"because …"* (an explanation of the effect of the behaviour or situation on you).

Don't be fooled. The formula may look easy enough, but in our experience is difficult, because it is so easy to send unintended, disguised "you" messages. Avoid saying, "When *you* do this … ." To illustrate a non-blaming "I" statement, let's assume that the mediator is speaking, but that Danny starts to speak before the mediator has finished. The mediator intervenes and says:

> *Danny, a couple of times now, you have started to speak before I finished. When that happens, I feel cut off and, frankly, somewhat annoyed, so that I have difficulty listening to what you have to say after that.*

"I" statements are not intended to be "polite" or soft or passive. They need to be clear and appropriately assertive.

Non-Defensive Responses

The aim of a non-defensive response is to neutralize a verbal attack and break the cycle of "attack and defend." To do this, the person receiving the attack asks for clarification, instead of defending his or her position. Asking for clarification involves using an open-ended, inquiring question, such as "What have I done to annoy you?" or, "What is it about my attitude that makes you so angry?" Non-defensive responses, intentionally, do not give the combative party any further dialogue with which to attack the speaker. They also try to avoid putting the aggressor on the defensive. Like non-blaming statements, the non-defensive response is a skill that takes practice. It also takes patience—often a series of questions is needed before the speaker de-escalates enough to engage in constructive conversation about the problem. Tone of voice and expression are critical to your success with this skill.

Fisher and Ury (1991, p. 108) refer to this type of response as "negotiation jujitsu"—a way to counteract one party's adversarial statements or actions:

> If the other side announces a firm position, you may be tempted to criticize and reject it. If they criticize your proposal, you may be tempted to defend it and dig yourself in. If they attack you, you may be tempted to defend yourself and counterattack. In short, if they push you hard, you will tend to push back. Yet if you do, you will end up playing the positional bargaining game. Rejecting their position only locks them in. Defending your proposal only locks you in. And defending yourself sidetracks the negotiation into a clash of personalities. You will find yourself in a vicious cycle of attack and defense, and you will waste a lot of time and energy in useless pushing and pulling.
>
> If pushing back does not work, what does? How can you prevent the cycle of action and reaction? Do not push back. When they assert their position, do not reject them. When they attack your ideas, don't defend them. When they attack you, don't counterattack. Break the vicious cycle by refusing to react. Instead of pushing back, sidestep their attack and deflect it against the problem. As in the Oriental martial arts of judo and jujitsu, avoid pitting your strength against theirs directly; instead, use your skill to step aside and turn their strength to your ends. Rather than resisting their force, channel it into exploring interests, inventing options for mutual gain, and searching for independent standards.

To illustrate this communication skill, let's suppose that Teresa says to Danny: "Frankly, Danny, I have had just about as much of your dismissive and disgruntled attitude as I can take! You belong with a one-man crew, not here!"

Danny wants to understand Teresa's frustration, so he responds non-defensively by asking, "Teresa, what am I doing that seems so dismissive to you?"

However, Teresa is not so easily deflated and she retorts, "It doesn't matter what I say or do, you trash every idea I bring forward at our meetings."

This time, the mediator intervenes with a non-defensive response: "Teresa, you are clearly upset. What is it that Danny does that seems so unreasonable and dismissive of your ideas?"

Teresa hears that both Danny and the mediator are interested in her frustration, so she begins to offer more useful information: "Well, for one thing, I brought new proposals to the last two staff meetings. Even before I explained the details, Danny said, 'It is too soon for the team to consider new changes.' He doesn't even know what my ideas are before he starts rejecting them. It is just not fair or professional."

As a final point, some words and phrases tend to inflame, no matter how well intended their meaning. Phrases such as "I know how you feel" are presumptuous. We are all separate beings and our individuality should be respected; we can never truly know how another feels. A better way of expressing empathy might be, "I can understand how you might be feeling about this." People speak from their own experience, so the words we used should describe, not judge. Also, avoid global statements such as "You always" and "You never"—they are dismissive and cause people to feel defensive.

THE CREATIVE COMMUNICATOR

To this point, we have taken a fairly traditional approach in looking at communication processes, strategies, and skills. In her wonderful book *Bridging Troubled Waters* (2002), LeBaron reminds us that conflict resolution work needs to come from the heart. This means that, as mediators, we need to be flexible and creative and operate "outside the box." We need to be authentic, imaginative, and aware. We need to remember that conflict is a relational activity and that helping others to resolve conflict requires us to have an open mind to diverse ways of knowing. LeBaron says this well: "It asks us to notice not only issues and relationships that befall each other but the deeper levels of symbol and meaning that fuel the collisions" (p. 181).

To encourage you to explore your creative mind and heart, here are some artful communication tools—the use of metaphor, storytelling, and other creative methods.

The Use of Metaphor

LeBaron (2002) depicts metaphors as windows into our worlds; Lakoff and Johnson (1980) link metaphors to how people organize and give meaning to events in their lives; Hocker and Wilmot (1995) use metaphors as tools for analysis in conflict intervention. All of these authors are reminding us that we can learn much about peoples' lived experience by listening for, or asking for, images that connote how parties position themselves in relation to others. Metaphorical concepts that are culturally and experientially created govern everyday functioning, down to the most mundane details (Lakoff & Johnson, 1980, p. 3).

In her article "Symbol in Mediation," Fisher (2000, p. 88) says:

> There appears to be a groundswell of sentiment that "rational discussion and logic are not sufficient to effect the changes in perspective required by disputing parties for conflicts to be settled" [Benjamin, 1995a, p. 3]. The emotional and spiritual dimensions of every conflict escape rational expression. When eloquence deserts us or words seem inadequate, we need a more universal language. "When we use words it's more difficult to dip into your soul. With symbol there's something that goes on at an entirely different level," says mediator Nancy Good Sider (interview, Nov. 20, 1997).

In this quotation, the term "words" means attempting to describe an experience in a rational or scientific way, and "symbol" refers to ritual, visual art, metaphor, and story.

When people use metaphors and other comparisons and images, they often make explicit their assumptions, judgments, and views about the world. Metaphors manifest cultural differences and perceptions, and they tell us much about one's approach to conflict. Proverbs, like metaphors, provide a window into how different cultures define and respond to conflict. Lederach (1995, p. 78) points out that "this is especially true in societies with oral traditions where drawing on wisdom and oratory skills is both a revered art and a conflict resolution tool." Besides mediation, metaphors are also used as process design tools in conflict dialogues by groups such as Common Ground, Public Conversations Project, and the Institute for Multitrack Diplomacy. This dialogue includes naming and sharing metaphors, unpacking their dimensions, comparing them, generating inclusive metaphors, and designing a process that invites participation (LeBaron, 2002, p. 216).

When coupled with visualization techniques, metaphors can be extremely powerful in assisting the parties to shift their perspectives. Imagine being asked to describe your ideal workplace in a metaphor. It would likely lead to a rich description of your future ideal, and it could also lighten the mood—you would probably laugh as you try to explain how your metaphor works practically. Metaphors can be effectively employed in cross-cultural conflicts, where linear logic models of knowing often fall short.

Fisher (2000, pp. 88–89) makes another very interesting observation about how parties in conflict may use metaphor:

> Metaphor presents the most profound opportunity for an "I" message available. Searching for their own metaphor encourages people to own their feelings, values, and assumptions in a conflict rather than focus solely on the shortcomings of their opponent. They may connect with previously unrecognized desired outcomes or needs, which refocus their approach in the mediation.

Metaphor Exercise

Sit back, close your eyes, and think for a moment about common metaphors that you have heard in relation to conflict. Jot these metaphors down on a piece of paper. Reflect on the amount of information you learn about a person's experiences and viewpoints from these short phrases.

To further explore how much information is contained in a metaphor, look at some of the phrases, below, that people link to conflict. For each, consider the speaker's values, feelings, expectations, and relationships, as well as experiences, judgments, and assumptions.

Shape up or ship out

We are embroiled in a battle

She has a real short fuse

We are now clearly at war

Put a lid on it

She blew up at me

Time is money

Let's cross that bridge when we come to it

Your behaviour is indefensible

I need to let off some steam

We must attack or be attacked

Our office is like a war zone

I keep getting caught in the cross-fire

Negotiating with her is an uphill battle

He did an end run on me

They dropped a real bombshell

I'm at the end of my rope

You hit the nail on the head

Let's bat around some ideas

Scratch my back and I'll scratch yours

Talking to him is like talking to a brick wall

I think the odds are in my favour on this one

Better half a loaf than no loaf at all

I can't dig any deeper into my pocket

Kill your enemies with kindness

He certainly knows how to push my buttons

When we asked mediators what metaphors they would use to describe their work, they responded in various and sometimes surprising ways: peacemaker, conduit, bridge builder, guide, assistant, marathon runner, yogi, trickster, firefighter, orchestra conductor, cabinet maker, chef, interior designer, meandering river, referee.

LeBaron (2002, p. 187) finds metaphors useful because they "invite us into imaginative conversation" and because they "offer shorthand ways to enter other worlds of meaning, bridging difficult conflict and deeply divided communities." She also reminds us of the danger of interpreting the meaning of the metaphor incorrectly. It is always wise to check out the meaning of messages by restating and reflecting. Remember that metaphors are culturally, socially, and gender-based.

The Use of Stories

LeBaron (2002, p. 223) suggests five reasons why third parties (mediators) might want to use stories as part of their conflict resolution work. She says they can (1) engage our attention, (2) stimulate empathy, (3) provide contextual information, (4) convey messages indirectly to save face and preserve harmony, and (5) engage us in deep listening. Stories convey more than just facts; they also contain important information about cultural norms, personal motivations, and expectations. They build connection, invite us to listen with our minds and our hearts, and engage our imaginations. Stories are often used to provide clues for change and ways to break down resistance. The brainstorming process in mediation provides a concrete example of how mediators use stories. In this stage, disputants are asked to visualize then share scenarios for positive change. These stories can form the basis for more detailed discussion of possible options and final solutions.

Lederach (1995, p. 82) also advocates the use of stories in conflict resolution work. He says if we can get past linking stories to playtime, "it propels us toward the view that stories create a holistic approach to thinking and understanding in which people are invited to mingle with the characters as a device of interacting with their own realities." Therapists have long known the value of using stories and fables in their work with children and families.

As discussed in chapter 4, narrative mediators deliberately work to engage parties in the co-creation of an alternative story (to the problem story) as the means of helping parties resolve their differences. Narrative mediators pay particular attention to cultural and historical stories, as they believe them to be windows to both understanding the dispute and resolving it. As a side note, Cobb and Rifkin (1991) point out that the order in which a person is asked to tell his or her story in mediation is significant, and that he or she is doing more than just taking one's turn. Using social constructionist theory and based on the analysis of over 30 videotaped mediation sessions, these authors tell us that it is the first person's story that gets played out in the actual mediation. That story becomes the primary narrative; the second party's story becomes the subplot. Several authors emphasize the importance of creating an alternate story that re-positions the parties in more positive ways.

Other Creative Methods

Effective mediation requires creativity and flexibility. In fact, LeBaron sees creativity as a core competency for a mediator (2002, p. 205). Being creative allows us to do something different from the way others do it or the way "it has always been done." Here are some other creative tools: ask parties to draw their conflict on paper; ask children to act out their conflict; ask disputants to use imagery, visualizing, free association, and mimetics to describe difficult events; and, of course, use metaphors, fables, and stories—to learn from the past and highlight emotion and experience.

SUMMARY

In this chapter, we have introduced some of the essential communication skills and tools that a mediator needs in her or his toolkit. But first, one needs a sound understanding of basic principles of communication and conflict behaviour, which we have tried to provide in this chapter and elsewhere in the book. As with any skill, one starts with brainwork—analysis and understanding—and, over time, moves beyond that to fluency, to using these skills and tools in a more holistic and organic way. These skills are life skills, not ones to be used only when we put on our "conflict resolver hats." We all have the ability to become artful communicators in our own way, provided that we can overcome our own self-imposed limits.

FURTHER READING

Gudykunst, W.B. (1991). *Bridging differences: Effective intergroup communication*. Newbury Park, CA: Sage.

LeBaron, M. (2002). *Bridging troubled waters: Conflict resolution from the heart*. San Francisco: Jossey-Bass.

Nichols, M. (1995). *The lost art of listening*. New York: Gilford Press.

Picard, C.A. (2002). *Mediating interpersonal and small group conflict.* Ottawa: Golden Dog Press.

Winslade, J., & Monk. G. (2000). *Narrative mediation: A new approach to conflict resolution*. San Francisco: Jossey-Bass.

CHAPTER NINE

Bridging Differences: Managing the Interaction

Relationships are all there is. Everything in the universe only exists because it is in relationship to everything else. Nothing exists in isolation.

Margaret Wheatley

Most conflicts have potential for beneficial, collaborative interaction between parties, as well as factors that prevent or limit that potential from being achieved. Given that a primary goal of the mediator is to help people collaborate, knowing about the factors that influence conflict behaviour and strategies that can help people manage these behaviours is important for both the mediator and the parties involved in the conflict.

In the first part of this chapter, we examine psychological, relational, and systemic factors that influence conflict behaviour. In the second half, we present some intervention strategies that mediators use to manage the conflict interaction and help parties engage in more collaborative behaviour. These strategies are used in combination with the communication skills discussed in the previous chapter.

FACTORS THAT INFLUENCE COLLABORATION

As depicted in figure 9.1, there are positive and negative influences that affect the degree of collaboration in a given conflict situation. Positive influences include goodwill, trust, and respect between the parties. Negotiation skills and confidence are also significant. Likewise, many factors

FIGURE 9.1 Factors For and Against Collaboration

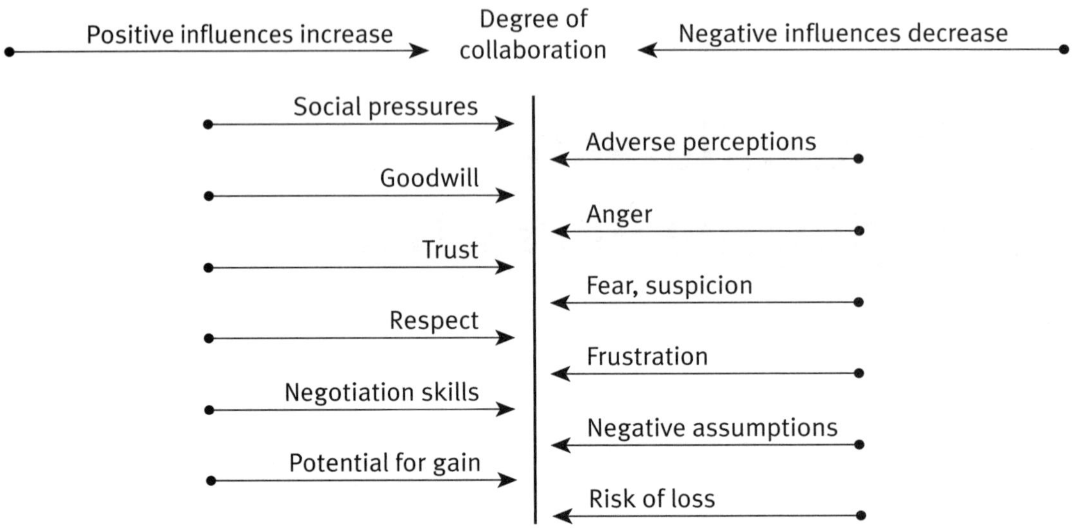

inhibit collaboration. Negative influences that escalate conflict include adverse perceptions one party has of the other, emotions such as anger, fear, or frustration, and negative assumptions.

Without intervention or management, fears, frustrations, and negative assumptions may increase as the conflict unfolds, causing the interaction to become more adversarial and, possibly, destructive. Negative influences can overpower the goodwill, respect, and human connection that might otherwise result in productive interaction. Mediator interventions that reduce negative forces will allow the positive forces to take effect and increase the degree of collaboration.

Collaborative interaction will not be achieved by having people suppress or ignore their adversarial emotions, perceptions, and inclinations. Nor will it be achieved by asking or trying to persuade people in conflict to be civil or "nice" to each other. It will definitely not be achieved by a mediator simply establishing a process with ground rules that require people to be civil and respectful, although such a process, if consistently applied, can certainly help. What is essential is that mediators recognize the negative influences. If they are ignored, they will wreak havoc. If they are addressed, the parties will have an opportunity to deal with them beneficially.

It is important to distinguish when an emotion is being destructive and when an emotion is being protective. All emotions, including fear, suspicion, mistrust, and anger, will at times play an important role in our safety and well-being. Indeed, an important element of emotional intelligence is knowing when to heed a well-placed emotion and when to "turn off" one that is misplaced or overactive. According to the principles of self-determination and empowerment, people should decide for themselves how they will deal with their own emotions. It is not a mediator's role to make such decisions, nor, for that matter, any decisions for others. But with effective mediator intervention, disputants can respond to their emotions positively and make decisions that are truly in their best interests.

Psychological Factors

Fisher and Ury (1991) teach us that an essential element of the interest-based approach to negotiation is to "separate the people from the problem." This means that, before disputants can negotiate collaboratively, they need to discuss and resolve their conflict perceptions, emotions, and assumptions. Resolving these does not mean that they will agree on them—there are some things they will never agree on. However, they can reach a level of understanding that allows them to sufficiently separate their personal differences from the conflict problem. It also means that each person's cares and intentions become less of a threat to the other, thus increasing their ability to interact collaboratively.

Perceptions are what a person observes and remembers. In a particular conflict, perceptions usually include the other party's aggressive and blaming actions and words. Although some perceptions are subconscious, most are consciously remembered. Therefore, unless an individual is particularly confused or evasive, we can generally know a person's perceptions by asking about them. However, our perceptions *always* involve some degree of selection and interpretation—our brains cannot register and retain every detail of an event. Regardless of how accurate people's perceptions are, they will have contributed to and become an essential element of the conflict. In order for a mediator to understand the parties and to help them understand themselves and each other, some discussion of their perceptions is necessary.

To really understand a dispute, mediators must also explore each party's emotions. In conflicts, some emotions are readily apparent, while others may be suppressed or denied. Fear, disappointment, frustration, or irritation are commonly displayed. Other emotions, such as anxiety, embarrassment, jealousy, or resentment may be beneath the surface, and the individual may be only vaguely aware of them—and these emotions may or may not be apparent to others. Some emotions, however, such as fear or shame may be completely buried or denied. Retzinger and Scheff (2000) theorize that intractable conflict and alienation are caused by suppressed shame that is hidden from both the self and others.

In conflict situations, emotions and perceptions are inseparable. Our perceptions and observations of someone will influence what we feel toward them, and our feelings, in turn, will influence how we see them. Adverse emotions beget adverse perceptions and vice versa. People in conflict tend to see the worst in each other, and that fuels—and is fuelled by—the fears and suspicions that usually arise in conflict situations. Cobb (1994) describes this as the construction of narratives that confirm our role as the "victim" and the other's as the "villain."

A psychological reaction that occurs in most conflict situations is the "fight or flight response" (Benson, 1975; Goleman, 1995). A *perceived* threat to our safety or well-being stimulates the release of chemicals that enabled our early ancestors to respond to danger. Today, for people in conflict, the fight or flight response tends to suppress rational thought and good sense, exaggerate fears, increase aggression, and reduce our capacity to relate constructively to the threat.

In a conflict, a person's perceptions and emotions inevitably lead to, and are influenced by, assumptions they make about the situation and the other parties. Assumptions are often derived from past experiences, cultural norms, personal values and attitudes, as well as anticipated outcomes. Under stress, people may not be fully aware or mindful of the assumptions they make. Sometimes those assumptions are based on misperceptions or miscommunications, and distorted or incomplete information can cause them to take an unreasonable or counter-productive stance—one that is unlikely to be in their best interests. Mnookin, Peppet and Tulumello (2000) identify the following specific psychological barriers to rational, collaborative negotiation.

Partisan Perceptions

People see the world subjectively and construct their own reality based on the sensory data they have selected and retained in their memory and their interpretation of events. All of that is influenced by their self-interests—in particular, their identity interests.

Judgmental Overconfidence

People often place unwarranted confidence in their own predictions about future events.

Loss Aversion

Decision makers tend to attach greater weight to prospective losses than to prospective gains—the fear of "losing" (or of the other party winning or "beating them") will outweigh their confidence and motivation to pursue collaborative gains.

Endowment Effects

People usually put a higher value on something they own, because it is theirs, than they would if the same item belonged to someone else.

Reactive Devaluation

A party often devalues a proposal received from someone perceived as an adversary, even if the identical offer is acceptable when suggested by a neutral party or ally.

Psychological Factors Exercise

In the Car Repair Blues scenario in chapter 3, review the dialogue between Dale and the mediator, and consider the following questions:

1. What are Dale's emotions and perceptions toward Chris?
2. What are her assumptions?
3. Which of the specific psychological influences identified by Mnookin, Peppet, and Tulumello (2000) might be present with Dale vis-à-vis Chris?
4. What might that mean in the context of this scenario?
5. How might these factors influence Chris's and Dale's interaction with each other?

When you finish identifying Dale's psychological factors, do the same for Chris.

Now consider the following discussion between the mediator and Chris during the convening phase.

Mediator: *Chris, you've told me basically what happened the day that this disagreement arose between you and Dale. What was your impression of Dale that day?*

Chris: *She came in that morning without an appointment, expecting me to drop everything and work on her car right away. She seemed pushy, almost rude. But, I figured she was in a hurry and really needed her car back as soon as possible. So I decided to give her the benefit of the doubt. I decided I would do whatever I could to get her car back to her the same day.*

Mediator: *Why was that important to you?*

Chris: *I've had this garage for 18 years. I have always done everything I can to provide excellent customer service. I have built up a loyal clientele by giving people what they need for a fair price. I really go out of my way to do that.*

Mediator: *So, what happened?*

Chris: *When I inspected her car, I found that her radiator was almost shot. It was clear to me that it had to be replaced, if not right away, then very soon. If I could get her a good rebuilt radiator and put it in right away, in my opinion, she would be much better off than waiting and having to come back in a month or two, be without her car for one or two days or more, and perhaps have to pay a lot more. In fact, I was able to locate a good rebuilt radiator for $250, instead of the $300 or even $350 I have to pay sometimes. Even though I didn't have her express authorization, I went ahead, confident that it was what she would want me to do.*

Mediator: *So, how did you feel when she came in and refused to pay your bill?*

Chris: *I was steamed—especially when she made that crack about my place being a "licence to print money." She might as well have called me a crook! I bend over backward to do everything she needs right away, and what do I get in return? She expects me to do all that for next to nothing, and slaps me with insults at the same time. Forget it!*

Identifying and verbalizing assumptions is essential in resolving interpersonal conflict and separating the people from the problem. It is often the implicit assumptions people make about what others are thinking or intending that are most problematic. For example, Chris may have assumed that Dale believed he had done unnecessary work on her car, or that he had deliberately overcharged or "gouged" her. Likewise, Dale probably assumed that Chris thought she knew nothing about cars, that she would be incapable of deciding what work should be done, and that her thoughts on that could be safely ignored.

Review the excerpts from the Car Repair Blues scenario in chapter 3 and immediately above. To what extent did the mediator's interventions surface and resolve the negative assumptions of both parties? It is very important to appreciate how often mistaken or exaggerated assumptions are a source of conflict and what a mediator can achieve by surfacing them.

Relational Factors

You may recall from chapter 5 that a holistic approach to understanding conflict requires that we understand the disputants' relationship. This means that we need to be aware of how particular behaviours affect the parties' relations. As discussed in chapter 3, claiming tactics by one will tend to cause similar behaviour from the other party, escalating the conflict (Lax & Sebenius, 1986). Typical claiming tactics include bluffing, exaggerating, distorting, discounting, bottom-lining, attacking the other person or his or her position, actions, or beliefs, and stonewalling or threatening.

In mediation, each party observes and reacts to the other party's actions and communications, including body language. Obviously, explicit insults or threats by one party will cause a negative reaction, escalating the conflict. Even subtle or unintentional actions—a slight frown, rolling the eyes, a look of impatience or irritation—may be interpreted in a way that aggravates feelings of mistrust, suspicion, or resentment. The mediator needs to be attentive to both the verbal and non-verbal emotions communicated, at times intervening to address what may seem fairly minor displays.

It is essential to understand that a mediator's intervention to address conflict emotion or adversarial behaviour is not for the benefit of only one of the parties—either the party displaying the emotion or the party who is on the receiving end of the emotion. Rather, such interventions are *always* for the benefit of *both* parties. The aim of the mediator's intervention is to address a conflict emotion or behaviour, which, if not addressed, will likely cause relations between the parties to worsen, to the detriment of both. As long as the mediator is centred and clear in his or her own mind about this relational purpose of the intervention, the mediator will be able to intervene in a way that is experienced by both parties as impartial. Although the intervention is directed at one party, it can be done in a way that ensures that both parties realize it is intended to improve their interaction and is for their mutual benefit.

In addition to observing parties' interactions, the mediator should continue to seek knowledge of the history and development of their relationship, including hopes for the future. Understanding of a relational system comes through intuitive and physical insights, as well as direct observation. Non-traditional and holistic ways of understanding human relations were explored in chapter 5.

Systemic Factors

Everyone lives within the context of numerous systems—the legal system, their church, workplace, family, community. Systems offer a framework for understanding, as well as a lens through which actions can be interpreted. Any conflict between two or more people in the same organization exists within the organization's hierarchies, rules, policies, and culture. Some organizations, for example, advance individual employee rights; in other organizations, individual rights are downplayed and even suppressed for the good of the organization. Some organizations have a history of adversarial relations between management and unions, whereas others are much more cooperative.

Mediators might also look beyond the organization, to the industry or profession of which it is a part. Standards and protocols within a given industry or profession can significantly influence a conflict. Our social, political, economic, health care, and educational institutions are all systems within which we live and interact.

To a greater or lesser extent, the legal system influences nearly all disputes within our society. The legal system in all North American courts (with the exception of Quebec) is the English model—the "adversarial system." In all court cases, each party is expected to present the strongest case possible, in support of their position, through evidence and arguments, including evidence and arguments to undermine the "opposition's" case. Usually, all of this is done by their lawyers, who are trained in this adversarial method, and whose success is measured by its standards. Parties attempting to resolve a legal dispute through non-adjudicatory processes, such as mediation, are influenced by the legal system's adversarial method. Even in cases where legal action has not been commenced, its pervading influence is often felt. For example, when a husband and wife go through a separation and divorce, they generally frame the property and financial issues between them in terms of their perceived legal rights and obligations. They each ask: "What am I entitled to?" The legal system's traditional adversarial paradigm is a challenge for any mediator seeking to use a holistic, relational approach.

Insurance Claim Exercise

While driving alone, Nick was stopped at a downtown intersection when he was rear-ended by a van driven by Graham, who was in the middle of an important cellphone conversation. Nick developed neck pain, headaches, lower back pain, and other symptoms of a substantial whiplash. Nick consulted lawyer Frank Buck, who sent a letter to Graham's insurance company, claiming compensation for his client's injuries, including ongoing loss of income as a piano tuner. Jessica, the insurance company's adjuster, responded to Frank's letter and they entered into discussions to try to negotiate a settlement of Nick's claim.

1. Consider, in specific terms, how the legal system will probably influence the parties' interaction in this case, directly or indirectly, even before a lawsuit is issued.
2. Consider, in particular, how the negotiation and Nick's decision making may be affected by Frank's involvement.
3. How would that be different if Nick was handling his claim alone with Jessica?
4. What other systemic influences might be present in this case?

Assume that, in their initial discussions, Frank and Jessica don't settle but agree to wait for a few months to see how Nick progresses. Six months later, Nick is complaining of serious headaches, lower back pain, and substantial right arm dysfunction. Unbeknownst to Nick and Frank, the insurance company's investigator made a video of Nick bowling and getting lumber at a building supply store.

5. How might that affect the negotiation interactions between Frank and Jessica?

Group Dynamics

Social psychologists have developed many theories of group behaviour. Four theories of group behaviour and interaction that apply to conflict are (1) group features and processes, (2) in-group/out-group attitudes and behaviours, (3) conformity and groupthink, and (4) collective behaviour and deindividuation. Let's look briefly at each.

Group Features and Processes

How people behave in groups and factors affecting group relations are important considerations in many conflict situations. We look at five of these group features.

GROUP BELIEFS AND VALUES

Members of groups hold many of the same beliefs, values, ideologies, and worldviews. For example, an employee group or union may have unfulfilled "social justice" beliefs and values and see itself as "second-class citizens" or "underdogs" in relation to management or the "ruling class."

DIFFERENTIATION WITHIN THE GROUP

Members within a group also have some degree of differentiation. For example, members may have different functional roles. The group may need to have someone as treasurer, someone else as secretary, and so on. Groups have "task leaders" or "relational leaders," or both. A task leader is a group member who has greater experience or ability at key group tasks and has authority over the group in relation to these tasks. A "relational leader" is someone whose personality or social skills make him or her well suited to dealing with intra-group relations. Every group also has a "pecking order." Some members, especially group leaders, are "high-status" members of the group, while others are "low-status" members.

GROUP NORMS AND REGULATION

Every group has norms, which are shared beliefs about what behaviours and practices are acceptable or not within the group. These norms serve to regulate the activities and relations of the group. Some norms may be explicit rules or practices, while others may be implicit.

GROUP DECISION MAKING, LEADERSHIP, AND POWER

Some groups are "vertical" or hierarchical, with autocratic or command-and-control leadership and decision making. Other groups are more horizontal, participatory, and democratic, with all group members having significant input into and influence over group decisions and actions.

GROUP POLARIZATION

Group polarization occurs when the attitudes or beliefs of some members within the group deviate from that of other members or from the group's "position." In some cases, polarization around a serious issue may lead to *factions* within a group and significant intra-group conflict.

In-Group/Out-Group Attitudes and Behaviours

According to social psychologists Alcock, Carment, and Sadava (1998) and Patton and Downs (2003), various cognitive processes affect intra-group relations and intergroup relations. Here, we discuss four.

Social Identity Theory

People tend to identify and associate themselves with—and their self-esteem is enhanced by—the positive attributes of the groups to which they belong.

In-Group/Out-Group Bias

People favour their own group members over out-group members. This is known as "in-group favouritism." To some extent this arises from *partisan perceptions*, whereby a person tends to recognize the positive and affirming aspects of their own group and be more aware of any "negative," competing, or threatening aspects of an out-group. As well, people naturally get along and relate more readily to people in similar circumstances, rather than people with whom they have less in common.

Inter-Group Bias

Inter-group bias is the perception that members of the in-group are "better" than members of the out-group in terms of their abilities or moral attributes. In a conflict and over time, people come to genuinely believe that their own intentions and actions are good and those of the out-group are bad. Without much evidence, they may readily interpret the out-group and its members as being malevolent, underhanded, or deceitful. Negative stereotyping that occurs with social differentiation is often a significant factor in inter-group bias or devaluation of out-group members.

Out-Group Homogeneity

People tend to see all members of an out-group as being more or less the same. For example, members of lower social status groups often believe that rich people are selfish, dishonest, and deceitful opportunists.

Conformity and Groupthink

Every group requires some degree of conformity from its members. Group well-being and functioning requires that its members accept and adhere to group beliefs, values, and decisions. However, excessive conformity can be counterproductive. When individual concerns and different, potentially beneficial ideas are suppressed, this phenomenon is called "groupthink" (Janis, 1982; Alcock, Carment & Sadava, 1998, pp. 163–164).

When individual members suppress their beliefs, preferences, concerns, or ideas because they differ from the consensus or majority view of the group, groupthink is at work. It happens when a group and its members strive to avoid or minimize conflict within the group. Groupthink often occurs unintentionally, without the conflict avoiders being fully aware that they are suppressing their own different views to "go along" with the group. Here are four causes of groupthink.

DEVALUATION OF DIVERSE VIEWPOINTS AND CRITICAL THINKING

Members give excessive deference to the views and proposals of group leaders. Disagreements and opposing ideas are considered disruptive and counterproductive. There is no belief or practice that airing different ideas and opinions can help produce a better decision.

GROUP PRESSURE

A group norm seems to be that non-conforming members "rock the boat" or are a threat to the well-being and good functioning of the group. Disagreeing is equated with disloyalty.

THE GROUP IS "PERFECT" OR "ALWAYS RIGHT"

If the group is arrogant or overconfident, it may be unable to recognize potential concerns, weaknesses, or risks in its demands or position. To do so would be taken as an admission that the group, and its leader, are imperfect and susceptible to error.

CONTRARY VIEWS ARE CONSIDERED UNIQUE

Individuals who disagree with a group's position sometimes keep silent, believing that everyone else agrees with the group position or "party line." When a number of members keep silent, the group may reach an apparent consensus, even though the majority disagrees.

Collective Behaviour and Deindividuation

Deindividuation is an important element of group behaviour for conflict management purposes (Alcock, Carment & Sadava, 1998, pp. 394–398). An extreme example of this phenomenon is the collective behaviour of a crowd or mob. In this situation, a person experiences deindividuation as a loss of self-awareness, a lowered sense of individual responsibility, abandonment of normal restraints and inhibitions, and reduced concern about how one's actions may be judged by others (Perry, 1998). So-called mobbing or bullying is a particular form of workplace collective behaviour that was first identified and described in 1984 by Swedish psychologist Heinz Leymann (Leymann, 1997). Group psychology or groupthink, along with a complex array of social-organizational dynamics, begins to play its part in situations where extreme behaviour develops.

STRATEGIES AND TECHNIQUES FOR TRANSFORMING NEGATIVE EMOTION AND CONFLICT-ESCALATING BEHAVIOURS

As we discussed earlier, conflict behaviour includes the display of strong emotion and adversarial communication. It is often spontaneous and unplanned, stemming from patterns of behaviour that have historical roots. There are times, however, when it is intentional or strategic, as in the case of threats or deliberate intimidation.

To deal effectively with a person's conflict behaviour, a mediator needs to establish a relationship of trust. Indeed, in many cases, it is the person's personal connection with the mediator that helps shift that person's attitude from one that is adversarial to one that is more collaborative. When the mediator develops such a connection with both parties, the mediator becomes a bridge or channel between the parties. Whatever the mediator achieves with one party gets "transmitted" to the other. In mediating the conflict between Dale and Chris, the mediator's understanding, validation, empathy, and respect for Dale helps Chris to experience the same toward Dale, in some measure. By seeking and eliciting what is positive and good in each party, the mediator enables the disputants to connect those qualities with each other. When the mediator helps to reduce the negative forces that decrease collaboration, the positive forces that are already present will tend to move parties toward increased collaboration.

Mediators use a number of strategies and techniques to respond to and transform negative influences in conflict situations. In particular, we will be examining the following interventions:

- Educating
- Acknowledging
- Affirming
- Normalizing
- Asking for suggestions
- Inviting expression
- Exploring consequences
- Naming conflict perceptions, assumptions, and behaviours
- Inviting response
- Reframing
- Unexpected interventions.

We also discuss the use of *caucus*, a process in which the mediator meets privately with each party. In addition to the specific techniques outlined in this chapter, a number of the communications skills and techniques discussed in chapter 8 will be used to manage strong emotion and conflict behaviour. In particular, we refer the reader to "Connecting Skills," "Non-Blaming Statements," "Non-Defensive Responses," and "The Creative Communicator." Let's look now at some of the other ways mediators intervene to facilitate collaboration between parties.

Educating

Educating a party for collaborative interaction begins with the first contact between the mediator and the party, likely in the pre-mediation phase. For example, a mediator will often discuss the benefits of mutually respectful communication and help the party to gain a genuine appreciation of how this is in his or her best interests. Then, during the mediation process, if a party becomes overly disruptive, the mediator can refer to those earlier discussions and help the party become aware of how such behaviour is contrary to his or her own interests. In this way, the mediator is not educating through "telling" the party what to do; rather, he or she is assisting the party to develop awareness and make decisions based on that awareness. Such a conversation, before mediation, might sound as follows:

> Mediator: *Sam, what kind of communication do you hope to have with Terry in the mediation? How do you hope she will speak to you? What do you hope that Terry will feel toward you during the mediation?*

During the mediation:

> Mediator: *Sam, I really don't know if such allegations by you against Terry are going to foster the open communication and mutual understanding that you both want to create. How else might you express to Terry your feelings and experience of the situation?*

In addition to pointing out communication patterns, mediators can educate the parties about their non-verbal interactions, including gestures and tone of voice, which might be negatively influencing their abilities to resolve their conflict.

Acknowledging

Listening for and verbally acknowledging peoples' negative feelings is an essential first step to helping them move beyond these feelings. Letting a party know that you recognize the emotion, and are not judging it, is a very powerful acknowledgment of his or her experience. Such acknowledgment helps parties to move beyond those strong feelings, once they have been recognized and accepted. It can also help the other person better understand that person's experience of the conflict. The following examples use the skill of *reflecting* (discussed in chapter 8) to point out strong feelings.

Mediator: *John, you are clearly angry and frustrated over what has been happening between you and Martha over the past few months.*

Mediator: *You are upset, and that tells me that this issue is important to you.*

Mediator: *So Dale, you were surprised, even shocked, when Chris presented his bill for $750, and you reacted strongly to that.*

Mediator: *You have had considerable difficulty whenever you've tried to discuss this situation with Farah.*

Affirming

Acknowledging and affirming parties' efforts, ideas, or intentions may achieve a great deal in helping them resolve their conflict. Positive feedback has a tendency to "open up" possibilities in a mediation session. When a party's actions or intentions are appreciated, she or he often becomes more generous in the mediation. This can result in a party accepting the other's good intentions, considering an option that she or he might otherwise have dismissed, or owning up to a moment when his or her intentions were not so honourable—all of which provide opportunities for positive or constructive discussion.

Mediator: *Dale, when you went back the next day to speak to Chris, even though it didn't go well and tempers flared, it certainly sounds like your intentions were good. You wanted to discuss the situation and try to sort things out. Indeed, in choosing mediation, you both have shown that you want to try to do that.*

Normalizing

Mediators are often able to recognize when the emotions, perceptions, and behaviours that parties are experiencing are "normal" for people in similar situations. Saying this can help a person accept difficult or negative feelings and behaviours, enabling them to deal with them more constructively. Normalizing can also help to humanize the parties' experience of each other and thereby help them to move forward.

Mediator: *In my experience, it is quite common for this kind of thing to happen when people have been feuding for a long time.*

Mediator: *It's pretty normal to feel that way when the well-being of your own child is involved.*

Mediator: *It is certainly understandable that someone in your situation would feel (or act) that way.*

Mediator: *In my experience, people in difficult conflict situations such as yours often feel frustrated and discouraged at this stage.*

Mediator: *Dale, I know you are anxious to jump in and say how you see the situation. People in mediation often feel and act that way when they have to sit and listen to the other person tell their story, especially when they disagree with it. I want you to know that you will have ample opportunity in a few minutes to say everything you need to say. For now, I would encourage you to take this opportunity, difficult as it may be, to really listen and understand Chris's view of the situation. Okay?*

Asking for Suggestions

Having identified counterproductive behaviour, it is often useful for the mediator to ask one or both parties for suggestions of how they might behave or interact more productively, rather than advising them what to do. This is part of the education process. Mediators often ask the parties for suggestions on how to proceed when things seem blocked or resistance is strong. This gives the parties an opportunity to take responsibility for their own actions and for their mediation process. When done well, it can be empowering.

Mediator: *You have been arguing and criticizing each other for a couple of minutes. This has happened a few times during the mediation, and I don't think it's accomplishing very much. I'm wondering if either of you has any suggestions for how to deal with this in a more productive way?*

Mediator: *It seems to me that this discussion is going around in circles. What do you need to address to break this cycle?*

Inviting Expression

Inviting a party to express his or her feelings about—or experience of—a difficult situation may sometimes be the key to enabling him or her to move forward. As a mediator, you should use this strategy only when a party is comfortable enough in the session to discuss his or her private thoughts and feelings. Again, this can be a very powerful experience for parties who feel that someone (the mediator) is connecting with them for the first time in the conflict situation.

> Mediator: *Chris, you seem upset about what Dale has been talking about. My impression is that this situation has been very difficult for you. It might help if you were to talk about your feelings and experience of the situation.*

Exploring Consequences

It is also helpful to invite one or both of the parties to consider the possible consequences of continuing a certain type of behaviour or interaction. Questions that invite the exploration of consequences can assist the mediator and the parties in refocusing the discussion more constructively.

> Mediator: *It's happened a few times now that when this issue comes up, you end up arguing over who was supposed to do what. I don't think either of you is achieving much by doing that. What do you think? Chris? Dale? Do you want to talk about the consequences of continuing to take that approach?*

> Mediator: *Dale, you have said that if Chris doesn't agree to what you have asked, you will speak to the Better Business Bureau. I wonder if you could say more about what really concerns you about this situation and what you would hope to achieve by speaking to the Better Business Bureau.*

Naming Conflict Perceptions, Assumptions, and Behaviour

Here the mediator's objective is to be openly curious about unspoken perceptions and assumptions that each party might have toward the other—and give each of them an opportunity to express them. The basic premise of this approach is that unstated negative perceptions and assumptions often fuel aggressive feelings, attitudes, and behaviours. If they remain unstated, they continue to adversely influence the discussion's dynamics. However, when such perceptions and assumptions are honestly expressed and "named," then everyone can better understand this source of aggression and deal with it.

> Nathalie: *It's been this way for a long time. He comes in and hangs around. I can feel him leering at me. He gives me the creeps.*

> Mediator: *Nathalie, from what you've said, it sounds like you believe that Pierre has been having conscious sexual thoughts or fantasies toward you.*

> Nathalie: *Yes, I certainly do!*

For such an intervention to succeed, the mediator must first establish an environment in the mediation that will allow these perceptions and assumptions to be discussed safely. In the above example, this would mean that

- Nathalie's assumption may be expressed without her being criticized or attacked for being "ridiculous" or "crazy"; and
- Pierre, in hearing this, is able to appreciate that this is her honest belief and how she has been experiencing their interaction, regardless of what his thoughts and intentions actually have been. Pierre is able to hear this without feeling and reacting in an excessively defensive way.

Provided that it is done appropriately and in a way that respects the interests of both parties, an intervention where the mediator names a party's perception or assumption can be helpful for both parties. By ensuring that perceptions and assumptions are openly acknowledged and, if appropriate, normalized, the parties will be able to resolve or move beyond them. This strategy often leads to discovering that prevalent assumptions are false and thus can be de-linked from the conflict interaction.

In addition to naming assumptions and perceptions, it can be helpful to describe in specific, concrete terms the conflict behaviour of each party and its effects on the other—to help each party understand the other's perceptions. Getting these underlying issues out, on the table, gives parties the full information they need to consider how they will deal with their conflict constructively.

Inviting a Response

A powerful strategy for the mediator is to invite one party to respond to what the other party has been saying. However, this is a potentially high-risk intervention that should be used only when parties have moved, to some extent, beyond their adversarial attitudes and behaviours. To invite a person who is feeling hostile or defensive to respond to another is to invite escalation of the conflict. Therefore, this tactic should be used only when the mediator has good reason to believe that the party invited to respond will do so constructively.

> Mediator: *Pierre, you've heard what Nathalie has said about her experience when you have been in her presence over the last while. What would you like to say to Nathalie about that?*

Another variation of this strategy is to invite a party to restate what he or she just heard the other party say. This ensures that what one party is saying has been accurately heard by the other, and demonstrates that he or she has been listening. If what has been heard is not accurate, it can be corrected. This strategy can be perceived as a paternalistic or condescending approach, so the mediator should have a strong rapport with the parties before attempting it.

Reframing

Reframing is a process used to convert an interaction from adversarial to collaborative. We call reframing a "process" because it usually takes two or more steps to achieve. Reframing may take different forms and be used in different ways in many different situations. Picard (2002, p. 83) puts it this way:

> Reframing is the process of changing how a person defines or conceptualizes a particular situation or event. In resolving conflicts, it is important to remember that our perception and emotional response to a particular event is based on the frame of reference within which it is viewed. It is possible to change the meaning of an event by changing this frame of reference. If this happens, our attitude and our response to the situation can also change.

Reframing can be used to shift positions to interests, statements to issues, or negative orientations to more positive ones. Let's look at an example:

> Jose: *I'm fed up with Shana's constant whining. She complains about everything, no matter what we do.*

Instead of focusing on the blaming, the mediator focuses on Jose's experience of Shana, his feelings, and his perceptions of her.

> Mediator: *Jose, it seems that your interactions with Shana have been frustrating for you for some time.*

The mediator has acknowledged Jose's feelings. In making this statement about Jose's experience interacting with Shana, the mediator has shifted the focus away from Shana's "negative" behaviour, which Jose has characterized as "whining." In attending to the speaker, Jose, and his feelings and experience, the mediator essentially prompts him to say more about his experience, which provides more information and insight for the mediator to work with.

> Jose: *Darn right. No matter what I say or what I try to do, she's unhappy with it.*
>
> Mediator: *Sounds like you want to find a way to interact constructively with Shana on an ongoing basis. What do you think?*
>
> Jose: *Yes, that would certainly make my life better.*

The mediator has completed the reframing process. At the beginning, the focus was Shana's behaviour—her "whining" and complaining. After the reframing, the discussion has been redirected to focus on problems in the interaction between Jose and Shana, which, for all we know, both may be contributing to. Jose is ready and willing to discuss his interactions and communications with Shana in a future-focused, remedial way. This is a very positive step. Jose is willing to consider and address their "interaction" as the problem, which is something that can be constructively addressed by both parties in the mediation. As long as each person sees the other as the problem, there is little prospect for progress.

Reframing is one of the more difficult tools for the mediator. The process requires the mediator to find and open the right door so that parties can move from a negative frame of mind to a more positive, constructive or, even creative attitude. The intervention usually requires a number of steps, with appropriate timing or pacing from step to step. Let's dissect a typical reframing process and analyze the component steps:

1. Focus on the speaker's experience, perceptions, emotions, and needs.
2. Be open and curious.
3. Respond empathically to the speaker.
4. Acknowledge the speaker's perceptions, concerns, and emotions.
5. Ask for the speaker's confirmation.
6. Verbalize the speaker's key interest.
7. Frame the speaker's interest in such a way that satisfying it will be mutually beneficial for all parties.

Unexpected Interventions

Many of the techniques and strategies outlined above can be considered "scientific" interventions. By and large, they are based on communications and psychological theories. Yet, a whole other set of interventions do not follow a scientific logic. When mediators want to break or transform a destructive pattern of communication, they might ask parties to think differently about the issue, or tap into other parts of their knowledge. Mediators might strategically attempt to shift parties' perspectives from "left brain" logic into the more holistic "right brain." For example, a mediator might ask parties to think of metaphors that describe how they are experiencing that moment in the mediation. Metaphors, holistic descriptors, can elicit much more than simply asking someone what they are feeling. A metaphor can give the parties much more information, some of it less negative, to work with in the moment.

Mediators sometimes ask parties to physically move—to switch seats or to get up to stretch and walk around. The intent here is to change the somatic effects of the moment. Since people carry their emotions in their bodies, asking them to transform their physical state can release some of their tension.

Music or artwork can also help parties break destructive patterns. Some mediators ask parties to draw what they are experiencing or diagram the conflict situation as they see it. This tactic tends to release parties from the moment of tension, and most disputants end up laughing at the drawings, lightening the mood. Drawings and diagrams, as holistic expressions of experience, can help transform perspectives, if parties have become dogmatic about them. A word of caution: not all people appreciate being asked to create a piece of art. Many people are uncomfortable and less familiar with these forms of expression and may resist, particularly if they do not feel comfortable with the mediator. Using his or her intuitive skills, a mediator should recognize when the time is "ripe" for these sorts of interventions.

Caucusing

A "caucus" is a separate or private meeting that a mediator has with one party (or others, such as counsel who might be attending the mediation with the party) to discuss some matter in private. With such a variety of mediation models, there are many approaches to using a caucus. Some mediators hardly caucus at all; others spend more of the mediation in caucus than in joint sessions. With the insight model of mediation that we use, caucus is used sparingly and selectively, for a specific purpose. Generally, we believe that a mediator should avoid negotiating between the parties in caucus. In other words, they should avoid "shuttle diplomacy."

Reasons for Caucusing

In some situations, caucusing with a party may be in the best interests of all parties and the process. Here are six possibilities.

To Deal with Strong Emotion or "Difficult" Behaviour

Sometimes, there is an underlying source of conflict that a party has not revealed in joint session, and that is causing him or her to continue to exhibit adversarial or disruptive behaviour. A private caucus will allow the mediator to explore whatever may be causing such disruptive behaviour. A caucus discussion might sound like this:

> Mediator: *Jean, I can tell you're still very upset about the situation and seem very angry with Alex and his counsel. I thought you might like a chance to talk about it privately. If there is something specific that is bothering you, it could help to get it off your chest.*

To Bring Out Information or Interests

The mediator may believe that one of the parties is reluctant to communicate significant information or reveal his or her concerns or interests. A caucus may help to determine why.

To Educate or Empower the Parties

Generally, the mediator will have taken steps to educate and empower each party in joint session—to help them interact in a constructive, beneficial manner. However, if the mediator notices that a party is doing something on an ongoing basis that seems to be interfering with or undermining his or her ability to engage in productive negotiations, the mediator may choose to deal with that in caucus.

To Encourage or Re-energize a Party

If it becomes apparent in joint session that a party's enthusiasm or motivation for the process has declined, a private caucus discussion with the party may be helpful. It can give that party an opportunity to open up, express any difficulties or frustrations, let off steam, take a break, or otherwise do whatever is needed to refocus and re-energize and come back ready, mentally and emotionally, to continue with the process.

To Explore or Develop Possible Settlement Options

In some circumstances, some of the techniques for the resolution phase, outlined below, may work best in caucus. A party may be reluctant to respond positively to such mediator suggestions or interventions in the presence of the other party. If there is a significant risk that a party may react negatively or positionally to a particular mediator suggestion or intervention, the mediator may decide to try it out in caucus—to "run it up the flag pole"—where any negative reaction can be managed with less adverse fallout.

To Overcome Impasse

Reality checks, exploring BATNAs, or other techniques for overcoming impasse can be employed in caucus. In an impasse situation, a party may be reluctant to fully discuss his or her analysis or assessment of the situation in the presence of the other party for fear that it could put them at some disadvantage or expose them to some risk. Having this type of discussion in caucus allows parties to *save face*.

Guidelines for Caucusing

- Don't caucus too soon.
- Ensure that everyone understands that either party or the mediator may request a caucus.
- Ensure that everyone is clear on the rules of confidentiality for caucusing.
- Caucus for a specific reason, and tell the parties what that reason is.
- *Always* caucus with both sides. The mediator may have a different reason for caucusing with each party.
- Keep the caucus brief and to the point.
- After caucusing with both parties, return to joint session and summarize in general terms the results of the caucus, respecting caucus confidentiality, of course.

The overriding purpose for caucusing is that, by meeting privately with each party, the mediator may be able to positively influence the dynamic between the parties. If the parties' interaction has been adversarial and non-productive, the mediator hopes that by breaking the interaction with brief and purposeful caucus sessions, the dynamic will change and both parties will be able to re-engage with a different and hopefully more positive mindset.

Despite the potential benefits of caucusing, we urge mediators to not caucus prematurely. Private meetings can undermine the trust between the parties, and even their perception of the mediator. A party might wonder what the mediator is doing with the other party while she waits for their return. It is our experience that some mediators use caucus for interventions that could just as easily be undertaken in joint sessions. For example, if strong emotion is difficult for mediators, instead of "hiding" it away in a caucus, we suggest that mediators acknowledge it and work with it in joint session. This not only normalizes emotion in negotiations, but also ensures that important, albeit difficult, communication is taking place between the people who really matter—the parties themselves.

TECHNIQUES FOR THE RESOLUTION PHASE

During the later stages of mediation, when parties are in the resolution or "deal-making" phase, a mediator can expect some "claiming behaviour" or even impasse, which the following techniques are intended to address.

Flip Chart or Whiteboard

Using a flip chart or whiteboard to develop options or proposals can be a very powerful tool for integrating parties' ideas and proposals, to bring about collaboration. In a "two-sided" mediation, parties tend to have a competitive, "us versus them" mentality. The mediator represents the "third side" (Ury, 2000), whose role is to create an integrative place—a common ground—where both parties can go to find or develop a resolution that belongs to both of them. The mediator represents the "neutral space." However, even with the mediator, mediation discussions usually have parties facing each other across a table, emphasizing the two sides. When the mediator uses a flip chart or whiteboard, it can become a physical manifestation of the common ground where parties can collaborate rather than compete. When the mediator writes on the flip chart, parties face in the same direction and gain a sense of working together on a common problem.

Back to the Future

During the option-generating stage, parties should be focusing on the future—what they need to do now and tomorrow to resolve the issues. If a party continues to talk about the past, the problems suffered, and the other party's actions or failures, more work probably needs to be done to uncover interests. Another strategy for the mediator to try is to invite the parties to consider a ground rule that brings them "back to the future." This is a particularly useful strategy when parties are pressed for time and must settle their dispute. It is preferable for parties to take the time they need to get to this stage, but unlimited time is not always possible.

"In Principle"

A party may be reluctant to discuss an option suggested by the other, even though it may have potential benefit. Specific concerns or risks may lead one party to reject such an option. By asking parties if they will consider the idea "in principle," the mediator is asking them to acknowledge the potential merit of the idea and their willingness to discuss and develop it further. Such a statement might sound like this:

> *I know you have concerns about how this might work, and that a number of details would have to be worked out. I assure you that you will have the time to talk about that. For the moment, however, would you be willing to consider* in principle *the idea of reinstating your contractual relationship?*

"What Would It Take?"

Asking the parties what it would take for an option to work can also reveal new information that helps parties move forward in the resolution phase. A mediator might ask the following questions:

> *You seem to have reservations about that offer. What would it take to make it work for you?*
>
> *What would it take to make that proposal into something you could accept?*
>
> *What do you think it would take to make that proposal into something the other side could accept?*

Role Reversal

A variation on "what would it take" is to ask a party to put themselves in the other party's shoes.

> *If you were Alex, why do you think your proposal may not be acceptable?*
>
> *Put yourself in her shoes and imagine the arguments or objections you would have to this proposal. What options can you suggest for overcoming those?*

Trading on Differences

As explained by Lax and Sebenius (1986, pp. 92–106) and by Mnookin, Peppet, and Tulumello (2000, p. 14), the differences between the parties provide opportunities where value can be found or created to the mutual benefit of the parties. Trading on differences is central to most negotiation. Mnookin, Peppet, and Tulumello identify the following five types of differences.

Different Resources

Different resources can include goods, services, money, knowledge, knowhow, opportunities, natural resources, and land.

Different Relative Valuations

Each party values actions or resources differently. Think about the Fruit Exchange scenario from chapter 3. By creating an unusual trading scheme, everyone "wins."

Different Forecasts

Parties have different knowledge or beliefs about what the future will hold. Michelle may be confident that there will be high future demand for a particular product she has invented. Mario may feel less optimistic. Therefore, Michelle may be happy to agree that a substantial component of her compensation will be based on a percentage of "net" income, if Mario markets and sells the product.

Different Risk Preferences

Each party has a different capacity to take on risks, depending on its nature. For example, the insurance industry can bear risk much differently from an individual policyholder.

Different Time Preferences

One party may be more concerned with what happens in the short term; the other may only be concerned about the longer term. If one party is going to pay money to the other, often there are differences as to when it is ideal for that to happen. In some cases, the benefit to the payer in being able to pay the amount over an extended period of time may be substantially greater than the burden to the payee of waiting for full payment. In other cases, receiving cash sooner than later may be important to the payee, in which case the payee may be happy to receive a lower amount than he or she otherwise might be entitled to.

"What If?"

The mediator or either party may introduce a "what if" idea as a hypothetical option. This is a relatively non-threatening and non-forcing way of exploring an idea that may itself become a term of a settlement agreement, or may open the door to other settlement ideas. Any such idea may be introduced in an exploratory way, by asking about the consequences of a particular decision or action.

> *What if, during specified daylight hours, the railway did what Karim has suggested and carried out all of its shunting operations in one particular corner of the yard?*

Exploring the consequences of an action enables the parties to deal with, and potentially resolve, concerns that may have prevented one, or even both, of the parties from presenting it as a settlement option earlier.

Often accompanying "what if" ideas are suggestions that involve trial periods.

> *What if you tried Karim's idea of using one corner of the yard for shunting, strictly as a trial for two or three months, without any commitment to continue beyond that time? A few weeks before the end of the trial period, the two of you could confer to discuss what, if anything, would continue to happen after that time.*

"Some People"

There are times when it may be appropriate for the mediator to suggest an option or idea as something that "some people" in such circumstances have found to be useful.

> *In similar situations to yours, people have developed communication protocols that are instituted on a trial basis for one or two months. What do you think about exploring something similar?*

Assuming Ownership

A party may have an option to propose, but he or she believes there could be some disadvantage or risk in proposing the idea. Nonetheless, the party would like to know whether it might "fly" with the other party. The mediator may *assume ownership* of the idea and test the water by putting it forward as a "what if" to the other party. An option or idea generated by the mediator may avoid reactive devaluation by one party.

Reality Check

A "reality check" occurs when the mediator asks parties to examine their expectations, and helps them ensure that they are realistic. Cognitive factors, such as partisan perceptions, judgmental overconfidence, and endowment effects, often cause people in conflict to have unrealistic expectations. One important aspect of a reality check is to examine the consequences of not reaching agreement in mediation. This may involve a detailed consideration of the potential benefits, costs, and risks to a party of pursuing their best alternative course of action—that is, their BATNAs. A cost–benefit analysis of a party's BATNA can be done in caucus, in which case the mediator may walk through the exercise with each party separately.

In assisting parties in examining their BATNAs and expectations, the mediator does not need to be evaluative. He or she does not need to express an opinion about what would likely happen if parties pursued alternative courses of action. In helping them to do a reality check and carefully examine the potential benefits, costs, and risks of their alternative action, the mediator is helping parties form their own opinions and make their own fully informed choices. When done in a way that satisfies and promotes the principle of self-determination, the mediator is truly helping parties decide on a course of action that is in their best interests.

Reflect on Progress

To help the parties maintain a positive attitude and to encourage them to continue, mediators often summarize the progress they have made, especially process accomplishments such as entering into mediation, improved communication, cooperative interaction, and increased understanding. Any progress, no matter how small, is worth mentioning. When the going gets tough and people get discouraged, awareness of what they have achieved, and the time and effort they have invested to do that, may be the incentive they need to push forward to a successful conclusion.

Take a Break

During a break, pressures and emotions may ease off, enabling people to step back and get a broader perspective. They can then come back to the table, refreshed and renewed with the insight, energy, and creativity they need to bring the negotiation to a satisfactory conclusion.

SUMMARY

For various reasons, people in conflict may think, say, or do things that influence their conflict interaction adversely. Yet, we believe that there is the potential for positive, constructive negotiation between parties in all mediations. In fact, people need to connect with the other in conflict and strive to achieve this. The mediator's role is to assist in reconnecting the parties so that they can move through their conflict productively. You should now have a grasp of some of the key strategies and techniques a mediator needs to help people in conflict overcome the barriers that limit their dialogue and inhibit their reaching a resolution in their best interests. The mediator needs to be artful and strategic in his or her role as a conflict bridge. The rewards are great for the parties who overcome the inclination to disengage from or hurt the other, and instead pursue a path of understanding and insight. The mediator's role is to help them arrive there.

FURTHER READING

LeBaron, M. (2002). *Bridging troubled waters: Conflict resolution from the heart*. San Francisco: Jossey-Bass.

Mnookin, R., Peppet, S., & Tulumello, A. (2000). *Beyond winning: Negotiating to create value in deals and disputes*. Cambridge, MA: Belknap Press.

Stone, D., Patton, B., & Heen, S. (1999). *Difficult conversations*. New York: Penguin.

CHAPTER TEN

Turning Swords into Ploughshares: Mediation and Justice

> *Reconciliation should be accompanied by justice, otherwise it will not last. While we all hope for peace, it shouldn't be peace at any cost but peace based on principle, on justice.*
>
> *Corazon Cojuangca Aquino*

This chapter discusses the relationship between mediation and justice—and the different meanings we attach to the idea of justice. We also address the objectives and applications of restorative justice.

JUSTICE AS A DIMENSION OF CONFLICT

Why do we need to talk about justice as a separate topic in analyzing conflicts? Perhaps the best answer to this question is provided by Morton Deutsch (2000, p. 41). He observes that the perception of injustice, the feeling that something is just not fair, is often a precipitating factor in the development of many conflicts. By way of illustration, two children are fighting over an orange. When their mother comes to see what all the noise is about, one child says, "That's my orange. I want it back," and then bursts into tears when her brother takes it—the feelings of injustice provoking tears of frustration. In another instance, the deep-seated frustrations of people who feel they have been wrongly treated may eventually produce violent confrontation. Two nations may go to war over contested territory. An aboriginal group may set up a blockade to protest against non-native logging of lands traditionally occupied by them, leading to an armed confrontation.

Deutsch (2000, p. 52) further suggests that different issues of justice may arise at various stages in a conflict. First, the perception of injustice may be one of the sources of conflict. Second, the choice of process used to resolve the conflict must also be perceived as just by the parties, or they are unlikely to accept the outcome. Third, there may be a fundamental disagreement between the parties over what is meant by "just." For example, one party believes that justice requires that affirmative action programs should be put in place; the other party believes that all candidates should be treated equally regardless of race or gender or religious affiliation, without need for special programs. Finally, the need to allocate blame—what Deutsch refers to as "justifying as a negotiating technique"—may often be used as a trump card to differentiate between the claims or demands of one side to a conflict and those of another. One party may feel justified in blaming the other for the conflict, and thus demand that the wrongdoer should pay the full costs of the resolution (as the victorious nations did to Germany and its allies in the Paris Treaty negotiations following the First World War). In such cases, the demands of the victors may sow the seeds of future conflict. As Deutsch puts it, "[b]laming tends to be inflaming" (2000, p. 52).

In each of these instances, the perception of injustice can lead to escalating conflict. Deutsch observes that "[c]onflict can lead to changes that reduce the injustice; or it can increase injustice if it takes a destructive form" (2000, p. 41). As individuals interested in the field of conflict resolution, therefore, we should always be attentive to the significance that the parties' perceptions of injustice may have on the prospects for achieving a fair and lasting resolution to their conflict.

What Does "Justice" Mean?

We need to be aware that justice often means different things to different people, and also that justice may mean different things in different contexts. Rather than try to find a single definition, applicable to every kind of conflict, we will examine five different justice stories, each of which emphasizes a different aspect of justice.

Justice as Punishment: The Retributive Justice Story

In many ways this is the most powerful, and often the most destructive, justice story that we encounter in our efforts to resolve conflicts peacefully. Fundamentally, the retributive justice story is based on the claim that when people have acted wrongfully, they should suffer the consequences of their wrongful act. The retributive justice story reminds us of the biblical prescription of "an eye for an eye." The Law Commission of Canada (2003, p. 18) calls it the principle of just deserts. As Peachey (1989, p. 304) puts it, the primary focus of the retributive justice story is the demand that "the person responsible for creating the injustice suffer in a way that is commensurate with the way the victim has suffered." Only then will the victim have obtained justice. Justice is therefore equated with punishment; and punishment is understood as the coercive imposition of pain or suffering on the person responsible for the injustice. The punishment need not be imposed by the person suffering the injustice. Indeed, in our modern democratic society, we seek to explicitly prohibit victims of injustice from exacting vengeance for themselves, or "taking the law into their own hands." Instead, we confer the power to punish on a particular authority figure such as a judge, or a parent, or a teacher, and only after an appropriate inquiry to determine whether the punishment is justified (Peachey, 1989, p. 304).

In the retributive justice story, there is little concern with whether the wrongdoer consents to his or her punishment. Indeed, the retributive concept is based on the *coercive* imposition of suffering on the wrongdoer. Nor does the punishment require the agreement of the person who suffered the harm inflicted in the first place. In our criminal justice system, an individual who robs a store is considered to have committed a crime against the state, rather than against the person who owns the store. It is up to the state, therefore, to punish the wrongdoer, not the store owner. The store owner is considered to be a third party to the offence, a witness who may be called to give evidence in support of the Crown's case against the accused; but the store owner neither advises nor consents to the punishment handed down by the judge. Neither of the persons most directly concerned with the actions giving rise to the conflict is given any control over its outcome. All too frequently, therefore, there is a concern that retributive justice, at least as practised in our present criminal justice system, does not provide for any meaningful sense of participation, or of satisfaction, or closure on the part of either the victim or the offender (Christie, 1977; Zehr, 1990).

Justice as Restitution or Compensation: The Corrective Justice Story

Like the retributive justice story, the corrective justice story is concerned with correcting a past injustice. But while the goal of retributive justice is to punish the wrongdoer, the objective of the corrective justice story is to provide compensation or restitution to the person who has been injured through the wrongful actions of another (Llewellyn & Howse, 1998, pp. 29–30; Fletcher, 1996, pp. 87–93). Examples of the corrective justice story would be a civil claim for damages by a patient who has been wrongfully diagnosed and treated by a physician, or a complaint of wrongful dismissal by an employee. The main focus of the corrective justice story is to determine whether the defendant committed the legally blameworthy actions. Without proof of legal wrongdoing or fault on the part of the defendant, there is no justification for imposing any legal remedy. (In the law of negligence, this idea is expressed in the phrase "No liability without proof of fault.") The needs of the injured party for financial compensation, or reinstatement, or an apology from the wrongdoer, are always subordinate to the primary concern with establishing fault on the part of the alleged wrongdoer. Without sufficient proof of fault, there is no basis for compensating the plaintiff.

What this means in practice is that the most rational response on the part of a defendant who is accused of negligence or wrongful dismissal is never to admit any wrongdoing—and never to acknowledge any injury caused to the plaintiff. Otherwise, this might be considered an admission of liability on the part of the defendant. However, if the plaintiff is successful in proving his or her claim, the court will order the defendant to compensate the plaintiff for the injury suffered. Normally, this compensation will take the form of an award of financial damages, even in the case of a plaintiff who has been wrongfully dismissed. It is assumed that the financial award will fully compensate the injured plaintiff for the injury suffered. Yet, very little attention is paid to the future relationship between the parties. Nor is the defendant ever required to personally admit responsibility for the injury caused. From a corrective justice point of view, once the liability has been determined and any damages awarded have been paid, the legal injustice has been corrected, and the slate is wiped clean for the future.

In the course of a legal proceeding, such as a negligence lawsuit, the defendant often proposes an out-of-court settlement—an offer to pay a sum of money to the plaintiff in full satisfaction of all legal claims. Typically, a condition of any such settlement is that the defendant makes no admission of wrongdoing or liability toward the plaintiff. The effect of such an offer, if accepted by the plaintiff, is to bring the legal proceedings to an end, but without any admission of liability or finding of fault. This is why many critics of the out-of-court settlement process consider such settlement negotiations to be less than true justice (Fiss, 1984).

Justice as Fairness: The Distributive Justice Story

Unlike the previous two justice stories, which are both concerned with redressing the wrongs of the past, distributive justice is equally concerned with prevention of future injustice. Issues of distributive justice pervade all levels of social life, from the most intimate interpersonal relationships to the most complex international disputes. Distributive justice issues arise whenever decisions have to be made about the allocation of scarce resources. Such resources can be economic and tangible, like the size of a pay agreement to be negotiated between management and a union, or the division of territory between two competing states; or they may involve less tangible but equally contested resources, such as access to elected office, to a promotion, to research funds, or to recognition as the discoverer of a new process for smelting metal or protecting crops from certain diseases. In any situation in which there is not enough of the available resource to satisfy every claimant's wants or needs, questions of distributive justice have to be decided.

The distributive justice story is concerned, above all, with the normative criteria or standards that are used in the allocation decision. Under what circumstances will an allocation decision be perceived as fair or just, even by those claimants who do not receive all that they demand? For instance, in the example of the two children fighting over the orange, on what basis should the orange be divided between them; and who should decide this critical question? The disputants may themselves agree on the distributive justice principles that will determine the outcome of the dispute, or they may rely on a third party to assist them in making the distributive decision. If a third party is involved in the distributive process, that party may have an authoritative decision-making role, such as arbitrator, judge, or parent. Alternatively, the third party may act as a mediator or conciliator whose role is to assist the parties in making their own distributive choice, but with no decision-making authority to impose a decision, even if the parties fail to agree.

Distributive justice theorists such as Deutsch (2000) have identified three broad principles often used in making distributive decisions: the equality principle, the equity principle, and the need principle.

The equality principle is based on the assumption that a fair outcome requires that all claimants should be treated equally or, as Deutsch puts it (2000, p. 42), that all members of a group of claimants should be entitled to equal benefits. For instance, in the example of the two children fighting over an orange, dividing the orange into two equal halves and giving one half to each child would be consistent with this principle.

Likewise, in a dispute over the allocation of family property between two divorcing spouses, the equality principle would normally result in both ex-spouses being entitled to an equal share of the assets accumulated during the marriage.

Equity as a distributive justice principle is based on the premise that people should receive benefits in accordance with their efforts or contribution (Deutsch, 2000, p. 42; Peachey, 1989, p. 302). For example, if Jennifer had saved her orange from lunch, while Paul had already eaten his and then tried to take the orange from Jennifer, a decision to divide the orange equally might result in an unfair outcome from Jennifer's point of view. (Of course, if Jennifer voluntarily agrees to share her orange with Paul, there is no inequity in distribution because she consents to the equal division.) If two people both assert their rights to a gold mining claim, the principle of equity worked out by the courts in the days of the gold-rush mining camps was that the first miner to stake the claim should be entitled to the claim. This was to deter claim jumping. But if the first miner failed to work the claim within a reasonable period after registering his claim, the claim was regarded as abandoned, and therefore open to the first comer to exploit (McCurdy, 1976).

Application of the equity principle often involves differentiating between the claims of the various claimants in a way that the equality principle seeks to avoid. It may be impossible to divide the contested resource equally between all claimants. For example, if 10 qualified candidates apply for an advertised job, it would clearly be impracticable for the organization to appoint all 10 candidates to the job and try to divide it between them (each occupying the position for one month in a year, with one-tenth of the pay and benefits attached to the position, and two months' vacation). The organization therefore seeks to appoint the best qualified candidate. In accordance with the equity principle, the job should be awarded to the candidate who appears best qualified for the job, based on the selection criteria identified by the organization.

Recruiting Policy Exercise

Consider this situation and answer the questions below.

A public sector employer, such as a police department, has a policy of recruiting women and members of visible minority groups in response to a perceived need to diversify the police force and improve police–community relations. An unsuccessful candidate asserts that he should be entitled to admission to the police academy on the basis that his qualifications are better than those of some female and visible minority candidates who have been admitted.

1. What would happen if a candidate who was rejected by the police department as insufficiently qualified claims that he has been unjustly discriminated against on the basis of race or gender?
2. What sorts of justice arguments are likely to be made by the various participants in this situation?
3. How should such distributive conflicts be resolved?
4. What if the distributive issue is not access to a job within an organization, but access to an artificial heart, for which the demand is far greater than the available supply?

The need principle—a third approach to resolving distributive conflicts—differs from both the equality principle and the equity principle. According to Deutsch (2000, p. 42), the need principle prescribes that those who need more of a benefit should obtain more than those who need it less. The application of the need principle is often seen in informal domestic conflicts. Imagine that there is only one orange in the bowl when Paul picks it up. Jennifer immediately cries, "That's my orange. I was saving it because I need it for my school health project tomorrow. You can have an apple." To which Paul replies, "I don't want an apple. I am going to eat the orange. If you needed it, you should have put it somewhere out of sight." Jennifer then grabs for the orange before Paul starts to eat it. Mom comes into the room to see what all the fuss is about.

How should this distributive conflict be resolved? Should Paul have to give up the orange because Jennifer needs it more? Or is Paul's claim, based on the "first come, first served" or equity principle, just as strong as Jennifer's? Note that the conflict cannot be resolved by reference to the equality principle, because Jennifer needs the orange for her school health project and there are no more oranges in the house.

This simple example illustrates that many distributive justice conflicts involve more than just a struggle over the size of the shares that each claimant will obtain in the disputed resource. More significantly, it asks which justice principle should be used in making the allocation decision. One of the roles of a third party in a distributive conflict is to assist the parties in reaching a determination about the distributive criteria (or justice principles) that should be used in making the allocation decision. If the parties cannot agree on the distributive criteria, or if no authoritative process for determining the distributive justice principles to be relied upon is available (such as an arbitrator's decision or an adjudicator's ruling), then the lack of agreement over the distributive justice principles to be applied is likely to be a major factor in prolonging the dispute.

Salary Negotiation Exercise

Read the situation and answer the questions that follow.

Employees demand catchup wages from their employer to compensate them for voluntary wage sacrifices made at a time when the employer was in financial difficulties. Management insists that the 2.5 percent offered is fair and reasonable and consistent with other wage settlements reached by other employers. The union demands some financial recognition from management for the financial sacrifices made by the employees in the past, especially now that the company is profitable again. Management responds that paying more than its competitors would put the company back into financial difficulties.

1. Should the dispute over wages be settled by reference to the equality principle (equality with other wage settlements in the industry), or the equity principle (recognition of the employees' voluntary efforts in helping the company survive the downturn)?
2. Is it possible to negotiate a wage settlement that involves a tradeoff between these two distributive justice principles?
3. How would the need principle apply in their negotiation?

Distributive Justice and the Problem of Power Imbalances

Before we leave the distributive justice story, you need to be aware that application of the need principle raises questions about how far the parties themselves should be encouraged to resolve their distributive conflicts through private negotiations, rather than through the intervention of an authoritative third party. In the situation involving the two children, suppose that Paul asks Jennifer, "What will you give me not to eat this orange?" How far should we leave this question to the children themselves? The distributive justice problem that arises from this situation is that Jennifer's greater need for the orange may place her in an unequal bargaining position vis-à-vis Paul. How far is it "just" for Paul to make bargaining demands from Jennifer that are not based on the value of the orange but on his awareness of her need for it? Is it fair or just if he asks for her to pay him for the orange? if he demands that she help with all his math homework?

Similar fairness concerns arise in other conflict situations where there appears to be an imbalance of bargaining power. Take, for example, a dispute over the division of financial assets and custody in a divorce context. The statutory rules governing division of financial assets on divorce are based on the equality principle—that both spouses are entitled to an equal share in the value of all family assets accumulated during the marriage. However, provincial family law legislation also permits the parties to contract out of the statutory provisions and reach their own negotiated agreement. (See, for example, part IV of Ontario's *Family Law Act*. Other provinces have broadly similar statutory frameworks. See also Payne & Payne, 2001.)

SCENARIO: Separating Spouses

During their marriage Russell has been a stay-at-home dad, while Hilary has been working as a lawyer. When they divorce, Hilary refuses to pay Russell half the value of the family assets that she feels she has accumulated through her own hard work; and she threatens to fight Russell for custody of their pre-school-age daughter, Tiffany, unless he accepts what she terms a "reasonable" settlement of one-quarter of the value of the assets. As a stay-at-home dad, Russell does not have the financial resources to engage in a lengthy legal battle with Hilary. And he is also concerned that a hostile custody fight would be very distressing to Tiffany, and make it harder for Tiffany to adjust to the divorce. After considerable heart searching, Russell agrees to Hilary's terms and accepts the house and one-quarter of the other assets, together with no claim to financial support in the future from Hilary.

On its face, this appears to be a consensual agreement between Hilary and Russell to settle all their financial affairs following the divorce. While it may be consensual, is it fair? Viewed from Russell's perspective, Hilary exploited her awareness of his unequal bargaining position to obtain preferential terms, which she would not otherwise have been entitled to under the equality principle (the principle governing division of family assets under most provincial legislation). From Hilary's point of view, there has been no exploitation of a power imbalance. She has legitimately asserted her claim to a larger share of the family assets based on the equity principle. In addition, she asserts that if Russell voluntarily agrees to the arrangement, then there can be no question of injustice.

Part of the difficulty in trying to resolve a complex distributive justice question, such as this one, is that there is no single distributive justice principle or standard by which we can evaluate the fairness of the result. Instead, we have at least three competing distributive justice principles to take into account. Under the legislation governing distribution of family assets on divorce, the equality principle trumps Hilary's equity principle. If Russell rejects Hilary's offer and goes to court instead, it is likely that the court would award him half the value of the assets instead of the one-quarter share that Hilary is offering. At the same time, most courts encourage divorcing parties to work out their own financial and custody arrangements after divorce, subject to the need to obtain formal judicial approval in the case of decisions involving children. So, from this point of view, the principle of self-determination, or voluntary consent, may override some inequality in distribution, provided that the parties have first obtained independent legal advice about their rights, and there is no evidence of undue pressure or coercion in reaching an agreement.

The problem is, what constitutes undue pressure? In legal terms, there is nothing to prevent Hilary from going to court to challenge Russell for custody of Tiffany. Does this amount to undue pressure? And Hilary can afford the costs of litigation far more than Russell. Does this amount to undue pressure? Regardless of the outcome of any future litigation, if Russell challenges the terms of the financial settlement he reached with Hilary, Russell's perception of injustice is likely to result in future conflict between the parties. To reiterate a point made earlier, the stability of a negotiated outcome to any conflict is greatly affected by the perception of injustice on the part of any of the signatories to the agreement.

In the context of a family mediation, a mediator may adopt a number of strategies to try to balance the power between the parties. Perhaps most important is to inform the parties of the importance of consulting with an independent legal adviser before reaching any final agreement.

The purpose of informing parties about independent legal advice is to ensure that each party is fully informed about his or her legal rights and entitlements before entering into any mediated agreement that may affect or otherwise alter those rights. The objective is for the parties to make as informed a decision as possible, on the assumption that the more informed the decision, the more likely it is to be a stable decision that both parties consider fair and just.

The presence or absence of independent legal advice is also likely to be a factor in a court's decision about whether to set aside the terms of a separation agreement (or other domestic contract) that appears to differ substantially from the parties' statutory rights if there were no agreement. In addressing these kinds of questions, the courts are inevitably involved in a trade-off between competing justice principles of fairness and certainty. (For a discussion of the factors that courts will take into account in deciding whether to reopen a domestic contract that has been entered into under part IV of Ontario's *Family Law Act*, see the recent Supreme Court of Canada decision in *Miglin v. Miglin*.)

Mining Claim Exercise

Consider this situation and answer the questions below.

Charlie and Mackenzie are two prospectors panning for gold. They agree to share costs and camp together. But when supplies run low, Mackenzie agrees to take the mule back over the pass and get some more supplies from town. Charlie continues prospecting and strikes gold on a small stream over the divide from where he and Mackenzie had been prospecting before. By the time Mackenzie returns with the supplies, Charlie has staked out the claim in his own name.

1. What kinds of distributive justice arguments can be made about the share that Mackenzie should have in the mine?
2. What distributive justive arguments can be made by Charlie about his claim to the mine?
3. Can you imagine any circumstances in which any other claimant could make a distributive justice argument based on greater need? For example:
   a. What if the province wants to expropriate the land for a railway right-of-way?
   b. What if Mackenzie is killed by a grizzly bear while he is packing the supplies back to camp? Can his heirs claim a share in the mine?

Justice as Process: The Procedural Justice Story

The three justice stories that we have considered so far have been primarily concerned with justice in substantive outcomes to any conflict. As Fletcher (1996, p. 81) comments, they speak to the result, rather than to the process by which the result was achieved. Yet most would agree that we cannot arrive at a just outcome unless we use a fair process. So, fairness in the process by which we arrive at the outcome—what scholars refer to as procedural justice—should be just as significant as fairness in the result.

Most authorities agree that the procedural justice story addresses two main justice concerns. The first is the substantive justice concern that if the process by which a conflict is resolved is fair, there is a far greater chance that the outcome is likely to be fair. Conversely, if the process is not fair, there is a greater chance that the result will be unfair or unjust. Essentially, this is an empirical claim that a just process is likely to result in a just outcome, while a biased process is likely to reach a biased outcome. This is one of the reasons why, as conflict theorists, we need to be concerned about questions of bias and impartiality in mediation.

The second main justice concern that the procedural justice story addresses has to do with the perceived legitimacy of the decision-making process. If the process by which the dispute is resolved is seen to be fair, there is a greater likelihood that all parties will accept the legitimacy of the result, even if the outcome does not satisfy all their needs or interests.

SCENARIO: The Boxing Match

Percival and Oscar are engaged in a 10-round boxing match, with the winner being awarded the championship belt. In round 2, Percival succeeds in knocking down Oscar. The referee counts to 8 before Oscar is able to stand up and continue the fight. Then in round 7, the tables are turned. This time, with Percival ahead on points, it is Oscar who knocks down Percival, who is unable to rise from the canvas before the referee can count to 10. Oscar is declared the winner of the match, even though Percival believes he could have continued and eventually won the fight.

What grounds might Percival have for challenging the ruling?

In this scenario, we can see two of the necessary elements of any system of procedural justice. The first is that each party to the conflict should have an equal opportunity to participate in the process, and to respond to the other party. Of course, the form of participation varies with the type of process. In a boxing match, each party participates by throwing punches at the other. In a formal adversarial court hearing, the disputants are represented by their lawyers. In a mediation process, participation is more informal and less adversarial than in a courtroom hearing. Yet, as we have seen, process integrity is an important value in mediation; it requires the mediator to reach a clear understanding with the parties over such matters as confidentiality, the goals of the process, the ground rules for participation, discovering whether the parties have authority to settle, and spelling out the legal consequences of any agreement reached.

The second requirement of a fair process is that the rules must be applied impartially to all disputants. Imagine what would happen if, after the boxing match, Percival alleges that the referee's decision was unfair. His claim is that in round 2, when he knocked down Oscar, the referee counted deliberately slowly, thereby giving Oscar the chance to recover and continue the fight. But in round 7, when Percival was knocked down by Oscar, the referee reached the count of 10 too quickly, thus depriving him of the chance to continue with the match, even though he was ahead on points at the time. If Percival's complaint could be proven, then it appears that the referee awarded the championship belt to the wrong boxer. If the league responsible for organizing the match, and under whose rules the match was convened, fails to address Percival's complaint seriously, then Percival may well challenge the integrity of the league's decision-making process, possibly by commencing a legal action against both the referee and the league. Far from settling the question as to which boxer should hold the title, the perception of bias on the part of the referee and the failure of the league to properly investigate the allegation calls into question the legitimacy of the entire league, not just the outcome of this particular match.

Now, reconsider our example of the two children fighting over the orange. Imagine that when Mom enters the room, both children claim that the orange is theirs, and the other is seeking to wrongfully take it. Both seek Mom's support for their claim to the orange. Remember that there is only one orange, and both children claim exclusive rights to it. No matter what the outcome is, one or other (possibly both?) of the children is likely to be disappointed.

In these circumstances it is important for all parties concerned that the third party intervene fairly. And there are various forms of intervention possible at this point. The mother may act as an authoritative third party who makes the final decision over which child is entitled to the orange, or what shares each should have. Or she may act more as a mediator or conciliator, by listening to the children and encouraging them to resolve the conflict peaceably by themselves. Whichever form the mother selects, she should appear fair and impartial, and not overly influenced by either side.

In this situation, if the mother listens to Jennifer without giving Paul a chance to explain his side of the story, Paul is likely to feel aggrieved about the process used. Moreover, his sense of grievance is now likely to be directed at his mother, rather than just over the outcome. Instead of helping to resolve the dispute, the mother's intervention may escalate the conflict and create a new source of anger. Consequently, there is a risk that the original source of the conflict will become submerged in a wider sense of injustice—that may affect the whole network of relationships within the family. Once again, any perception of injustice in the process used to resolve the dispute can often have ramifications that go beyond the outcome of the conflict itself.

Justice as Reconciliation: The Restorative Justice Story

The final story to consider in examining the many meanings of justice is the idea of justice as reconciliation—the restorative justice story. Much of the emphasis within the restorative justice story challenges the idea of justice as retribution or punishment (Zehr, 1990: Bianchi, 1994; Van Ness & Strong, 1997; Sharpe, 1998). As you will remember, the retributive justice story derives from the notion of equivalency—and from the biblical story of an eye for an eye—the idea that justice demands the infliction of an equivalent amount of pain and suffering on the offender as the offender has inflicted on the victim (Peachey, 1989, p. 304).

Retributive justice advocates make the assumption that the community's interest in upholding the law—and the victim's need for vengeance or retribution—will be satisfied by the action of punishing the wrongdoer. In this mode of justice, the primary responsibility for addressing the needs of the victim and the interests of the community is placed in the hands of the state. According to the retributive justice story, a crime committed against an individual, a group, or a company, is considered to have been committed against the state (Zehr, 1990, p. 81). The state, therefore, has a monopoly on the right to punish those found guilty, provided that the state's actions in prosecuting and sentencing the offender are carried out in accordance with the requirements of procedural justice.

For many restorative justice theorists, however, some of the basic premises underpinning the retributive justice story are far more problematic than the story allows us to see. Every story has a narrative that shapes the way we view the world. We become so familiar with the narrative that we can no longer see much of what the narrative leaves out. What the retributive justice narrative leaves out—what is sometimes difficult for us to see—is that the offender's wrongful actions are not just committed against the state. An act of violence, or even the robbing of a store, also involves a violation of interpersonal relationships. In significant ways, the harm done is also felt by the victim, by the community, and even by the offender. These harms cannot be repaired by the act of punishment alone. Punishing an offender may serve some justice needs, but it leaves other justice needs unattended to. These needs often remain invisible and unmet, hidden by the dominant narrative structure of the retributive justice story.

Chief among these hidden or unmet justice needs is the need to repair the harm done to the victim. Victims of crime do not just experience a material loss of money or goods or the physical trauma resulting from an act of violence. The victim's psychological loss—loss of trust, feelings of insecurity, a sense that something has been taken—may be very difficult to regain. The retributive justice story carries the assumption that the victim's primary justice need is to see the offender punished. To this end, the criminal justice system now allows victims a limited opportunity to speak about the impact of the offender's actions, prior to sentencing.

Another of the victim's losses is any sense of control over, or even participation in, the process that leads to the arrest, charging, prosecution, and conviction of the offender. The victim may be called as a witness and may be allowed or invited to present an impact statement before the judge hands down a sentence; otherwise, the victim has little say, or voice, in the process by which "justice" is meted out. Unless the victim is a witness, he or she is not even allowed a formal place in the courtroom, but has to sit in the public gallery with other spectators. If participation and party self-determination are important normative values in conflict resolution, then the retributive justice story, in defining crime as an offence against the state—and not against the victim—effectively robs the victim of the power to participate in the trial process in any meaningful way (Christie, 1977).

Recently, however, many provinces have enacted legislation designed to provide victims of crime with counselling and information about the court process (see Law Commission of Canada, 2003, pp. 22–24). But such victims' rights legislation still does not address the more fundamental issue that the offence is defined as a crime against the state, not against the victim.

Another unmet justice need for many victims is to have the offender acknowledge the harm inflicted on them. Here again, the retributive justice story tends to erase this unmet need from our collective consciousness. If the offender's wrongful action is viewed as a crime against society's laws, then it follows that society's public interest in justice should be given priority over the private needs of the victim. Once again, it is assumed that the victim's need for acknowledgment of the harm done will be assuaged if and when the offender is found guilty—and the subsequent public sentencing ritual symbolizes society's denunciation of the wrongful act and its disapprobation of the wrongdoer.

But what if these public and private justice needs are not identical? As mediation theorists and practitioners, we should be aware of the importance of attending to the needs of all the participants in a conflict situation. If we leave any of the participants' needs unattended to, conflict theory suggests that that party is likely to feel unsatisfied—with the conflict still unresolved, at least for them. In the operation of our criminal justice system, this is exactly what happens to many victims; they experience the justice system as alienating, even when the offender is convicted and sentenced (Zehr, 1990, pp. 30–32).

Moreover, as Zehr observes, this experience often remains the same, even when the offender pleads guilty to the offence charged. The problem, according to Zehr (1990, p. 67), is that in entering a plea of guilty, offenders are not really acknowledging responsibility for the harm done to their victims, but only following the advice of their lawyers, who may have reached a plea bargain arrangement with the Crown to admit to a lesser charge in return for a reduced sentence or the dropping of more serious charges. Such an arrangement says volumes about the institutional demands of the system, to process as many offenders as possible in the shortest possible time. It says little about satisfying the human justice needs of the victim, or the offender, or the community as a whole.

This is why commentators such as Zehr (1990), Braithwaite (1989), and the Church Council on Justice and Corrections (1996) have advocated the introduction of more "restorative" justice practices such as victim–offender mediation (Umbreit, 1994), sentencing circles (Stuart, 1996, 1997), and family and community group conferencing (Hudson, Morris, Maxwell, & Galaway, 1996; Galaway & Hudson, 1996), to redress some of the human justice needs that are left out of the retributive justice story. The dominant concern that animates the advocates of the restorative justice story is reconciliation—"making right" the harm done to shattered relationships, to social trust, and to traumatized victims and offenders alike, whose lives have equally been damaged by the experience of crime, and who need to be restored to some sense of completeness again as participants in the community.

As Llewellyn and Howse (1998, p. 1) remind us, the restorative justice story is not a new story, but one that is foundational to many of our central ideas about law and justice. Like the practice of mediation itself, the themes of restoring social relationships, of reconciliation, and of reintegrating offenders into the community have been elements of a restorative ideal of justice that crosses different cultures and different historical times. Like mediation again, the practice of restorative justice can take many different forms. There is no uniform model, nor any preferred time-frame. Mediating a dialogue between victim and offender, after an offender has been sentenced and is serving time in prison, can be as meaningful and "restorative" to both parties as entering into a pre-trial mediation process that might have resulted in the case being diverted from the criminal courts. Victim–offender mediation is not intended to be a substitute for punishment; nor is participating in a sentencing circle designed as a substitute for the judge's decision on sentencing after trial (Stuart, 1996). Restorative justice is not just about lessening the sentence served by the offender, or making restitution in financial or other terms to the victim, although these may both be elements of a restorative justice process. Rather, the goal is to address the human needs of those most affected by the crime—to recognition, to reconciliation, and to social connectedness—needs that are largely invisible or absent from the retributive justice story. Figure 10.1 compares restorative justice with retributive justice.

In his work on reintegrative shaming and restorative justice, Braithwaite (1989, pp. 133–134) compares restorative justice approaches to shaming offenders with a family model of discipline, in which the objective is to teach the offending child to respect the rules governing family behaviour. With this in mind and to explore some of the differences between these two stories of justice, let's return to the room with Jennifer and Paul arguing over who should have the right to the orange. Suddenly a cry rings out, which brings Mom running into the room. Paul is crying, and Jennifer (who is three years older than Paul and much bigger) is standing over him holding the orange. "What is going on?" demands Mom. Paul sobs that Jennifer hit him, and then shows his mother the bruise.

"Is this true, Jennifer?" demands her mother. Jennifer, who is very angry, starts to explain about why she needs the orange for her school health project. Her mother cuts off her explanation and demands to know, "Did you hit Paul?"

"Yes, but ..." explains Jennifer.

"No buts," says her mother. "Go up to your room now and stay there till supper time. You are grounded young lady!"

"But it's not fair," cries Jennifer on her way upstairs.

FIGURE 10.1 Restorative Justice and Retributive Justice Stories Compared

Retributive Justice Story	Restorative Justice Story
Crime is defined as a breach of society's laws.	Crime is defined as a violation of relationships or a breach of trust.
The objective of the process is to establish the offender's guilt.	The objective of the process is to repair harm to the victim or the community.
The process is adversarial and dictated by professionals.	The process is non-adversarial and encourages dialogue between the participants.
The victim has a limited right to participate in the process.	The victim can initiate the process.
The process encourages the offender to deny guilt.	The process encourages the offender to accept responsibility for the harm caused.
The state has a monopoly over the punishment of the offender.	The participants have more control over the outcome of the process.
Balance is restored by inflicting an equivalent amount of pain on the offender.	Balance is restored by repairing the harm done to the victim and the community.
Shaming is designed to stigmatize the offender.	Shaming is intended to promote reintegration of the offender.

"What did you say?" asks Mom, ominously.

"I said it's not fair," replies her daughter. "He took my orange when he knew I wanted it for my project."

"You are three years older than he is," replies her mother. "You know the rules. We do not hit in this house. If I hear one more word out of you, you will be grounded for a month. As it is, think yourself very lucky that I'm being this easy on you."

In what ways has Jennifer's act of hitting Paul altered the dynamics of the conflict? Perhaps the most significant change is in the way in which the conflict is defined. The focus of the mother's intervention is no longer to address the distributive justice question of who should be entitled to the orange. Nor is the focus primarily on the procedural justice concern of ensuring that both children have an equal opportunity to assert their claim (although there are clearly procedural justice concerns in Jennifer's claim that her mother is not being fair). Instead, this time the mother's intervention is solely concerned with the question whether Jennifer hit Paul. Every time Jennifer tries to explain what happened, her mother dismisses this as irrelevant. The only question to be investigated is whether Jennifer hit Paul. When Jennifer admits that she did so, she must be punished because she has knowingly violated a fundamental household rule. She has committed a crime, and crime demands punishment. In short, this is no longer a distributive justice conflict over the division of an orange; instead, it has become a retributive justice conflict over the consequences of Jennifer's violation of the household rule against hitting.

Second, consider the way in which Paul's role in the conflict dynamic has changed. The original dispute has now paled into insignificance beside the issue of Jennifer's punishment for hitting Paul. Oddly, this act has the effect of reducing the role that Paul is likely to play in the resolution of the conflict. In this scenario, Paul is now cast as the victim of Jennifer's action and as a witness whose testimony will be important in determining whether Jennifer should be punished or not. But Paul himself is no longer a central character in the drama. Although Jennifer's action was directed at Paul, it is not Paul who determines what Jennifer's punishment should be, or even whether she should be punished. That is her mother's prerogative. She is the chief authority figure responsible for enforcing and upholding the household laws. (Whether Jennifer would want Paul to have a say in her punishment is another question.)

The third major shift in the dynamics of this conflict involves the role of the mother. As an authority figure, she intervenes because she has a direct interest in the conflict, which quickly becomes redefined as a conflict between mother and daughter, rather than between brother and sister. We do not know if the mother would have been as quick to redefine the conflict if it had been Paul who had hit Jennifer, or if both children had been pulling each other's hair and yelling. In the latter case, probably both children would have been sent to their rooms. In the former case, the answer may depend on whether Paul is treated in the same way as Jennifer. One of Jennifer's complaints against her mother's punishment may have been her concern that Paul is never punished when he hits Jennifer. If it is only Jennifer who is ever punished for breaking this household rule, from Jennifer's point of view, her mother's intervention would be seen as one-sided and unfair.

We can now summarize some of the main elements in this retributive justice story.

- One, the conflict is now defined in terms of fault and wrongdoing, rather than in terms of needs—and the language of needs has all but disappeared.
- Two, the mode of participation in the conflict by all three parties has now changed. The primary parties to the conflict are now seen as Jennifer and her mother. Paul is reduced to watching from the sidelines.
- Three, there is a major imbalance of power in the relationship between the two primary disputing parties (Jennifer and her mother). In this relationship, the mother acts as an authority figure, with power to punish or impose consequences on Jennifer for her transgressions of household rules. Jennifer's rights as a participant in the conflict are correspondingly reduced.
- Four, the potential outcomes of the conflict are now dependent on proof of Jennifer's guilt or wrongdoing, not on the needs of the parties. Indeed, we do not even know what became of the orange.

Now let us consider how this story might be told from a restorative justice standpoint. First, Jennifer's action in hitting Paul would not be defined as an act of law-breaking, but rather as a breach of trust, or as a violation of relationships (Zehr, 1990, p. 181; Sargent, 2002, p. 213). This shift in defining Jennifer's actions does not take away from her responsibility for hitting Paul. Her wrongful behaviour remains at the centre of the story. But now we are able to pay more attention to the consequences of her actions in terms of the nature of the harm that has been done, rather than what punishment should be meted out.

What relationships have been breached by her wrongful act? What relationships need to be made right? One is the obvious need to repair her relationship with Paul. Jennifer violated this relationship by hitting him. From a restorative justice perspective, this relationship can only be put right by Jennifer acknowledging the wrongfulness of her actions in violating the relationship and apologizing to Paul, or by making some form of actual or symbolic restitution. In one sense, this sounds like the corrective justice story that we considered earlier. But in that story, there is no requirement that the wrongdoer acknowledge any responsibility to the victim, or even apologize for the harm caused. Provided that compensation is paid to the victim, the future relationship between the parties to the dispute is considered irrelevant. Instead, the slate is wiped clean, and the story assumes that the two parties just go their separate ways. But in the relationship between Paul and Jennifer they cannot do that.

They are members of a family, and the nature and quality of their relationship is likely to lead to future conflict. The unmended relationship—between wrongdoer and victim—is likely to have consequences, as any family member knows.

Other relationships also need to be addressed. Jennifer's act of hitting Paul also affects her mother, and the mother's relationship with both children. Unless Jennifer acknowledges the wrongfulness of her behaviour to her mother, her mother will probably feel compelled to impose some punishment or discipline on Jennifer. After all, the mother is expected to act as the authority figure within the family. If there are rules against hitting, it is the mother's duty to try to ensure that they are complied with by all family members. This may be why the mother sends Jennifer to her room, rather than strike her.

At the same time, Jennifer needs to understand why she is being punished, or why her mother expects her to apologize to Paul. The primary purpose of the punishment, and of the apology, is to ensure that all members of the family, Paul as well as Jennifer, respect the household rule against hitting, which, in turn, is designed to promote peaceful problem solving and conflict resolution. If Jennifer feels that the punishment is unjust, or that her mother refused to listen to her side of the story, the punishment will probably do little to increase Jennifer's respect for the rule or peaceful conflict resolution. In fact, it will probably do just the opposite. The message that Jennifer will receive, if she experiences her mother's punishment as unfair, is that, in the end, it is only power that counts. Presumably, we want children to obey rules, not out of fear, but out of a sense of self-respect and respect for each other in the community.

How might these multiple relationship interests—between Paul, Jennifer, and their mother—be translated into a restorative justice practice? Instead of sending Jennifer to her room, the mother might encourage Jennifer to apologize to Paul, and to create a process in which the two children could try to reach a reconciliation, and work out an acceptable resolution to their conflict, under the watchful eye of their mother. In doing so, the mother would not surrender her position as an authority figure. But she could delegate some of her authority to Jennifer and Paul, and empower them to reach their own resolution to their conflict. The mother might also encourage discussion about determining what should be the consequences of Jennifer's wrongful act of breaking the family rules by hitting Paul.

It is relatively easy to see how this restorative justice story can be applied to the relationships within a close-knit family. But it is more difficult to see how the restorative justice story applies in the larger community, where crime often occurs between strangers. Imagine, for example, that a store owner is robbed by two youths holding a knife or a gun. In this situation, are there any pre-existing relationships to repair? Is there any need for the state to justify its actions in punishing lawbreakers who steal other people's property and threaten violence to them?

For restorative justice theorists such as Zehr and Braithwaite, it is precisely in these kinds of situations that we need to apply the principles of restorative justice. Zehr (1990, p. 181) observes that even where the store owner and the person robbing the store were not known to one another, the very act of robbing the store creates a relationship between them—based on the harm inflicted on the victim—a relationship that needs to be made right. Likewise, the act of robbing the store has an impact on the community and its members' sense of safety and trust, affecting relations within the community generally. Moreover, the state's actions in punishing the offender also create a relationship between state and offender, a relationship that also needs to be made right, by making it possible for the offender to be reintegrated into the society, rather than permanently alienated from the community.

Braithwaite (1989) has developed these ideas even further in his work on reintegrative shaming. Shaming works best, according to Braithwaite, when it is used positively, to encourage offenders to make recompense for the harm they have caused, and thereby show themselves to be worthy of being included once more in the community. One of the key elements of reintegrative shaming is to separate the offence from the offender, to condemn the offence without condemning the offender, and thereby provide offenders with the possibility of acknowledging the wrongfulness of their actions and repairing the harm they have done. The opposite result tends to happen when we use shaming negatively. We stigmatize the offender in the hope that, by doing so, the offender will be deterred from ever wanting to offend again. Stigmatization works by identifying the offender with the offence, so that the offender can never be free of the stigma associated with the commission of the offence. We define offenders by reference to what they have done in the past, not by what they are capable of doing in the future. But stigmatization comes at a price. According to Braithwaite, the offender—the stigmatized "other"—may symbolically reject the legitimacy of the authority by which he is condemned, and thereafter take on a self-imposed identity as an opponent of authority, with little or no respect for the law.

In our example of the children and the orange, negative shaming translates into a concern that Jennifer might challenge the legitimacy of the punishment imposed by her mother, thereby compelling the mother to apply an even stiffer punishment, and making Jennifer even more of an outcast or rebel in her own family.

The danger is that by using shaming negatively—to stigmatize offenders who have violated our laws—we are likely to increase the possibility of future social conflict, not to reduce it (Braithwaite, 1989). This dynamic occurs in our own example. The conflict escalates when Jennifer tries to have her "voice" heard, and her mother hears this as a challenge to her own authority. In circumstances like this, the conflict is likely to escalate even further. The power imbalance between mother and daughter only makes a mutually respectful resolution even less likely, if the outcome is determined by the mother's superior power, rather than by any consideration for Jennifer's rights—or her need to be heard. A restorative justice approach strives to right this balance, and to address not only the rights but also the needs of all the participants in the conflict situation. These include not only Paul and Jennifer, but also the mother, who has a need to maintain good relationships with both of her children.

In this respect, the restorative justice story provides a very different way of responding to the competing justice needs that are raised by the wrongful act of robbing a store or of breaking the household rule against hitting. As we have seen, the retributive justice story presumes that the victim's needs and society's needs are satisfied by punishing the offender. The offender's needs for recognition and understanding are ignored. Provided that the punishment is equivalent to the severity of the offence, the interests of justice have been served. However, the restorative justice story is not so concerned with the *quantity of punishment* imposed on the offender, but with the *quality of justice* owed to victim, offender, and community alike (Zehr, 1990).

Can it work? Can we envisage a future in which the principles of restorative justice and reintegrative shaming replace our need to punish those who have knowingly violated society's laws? In some respects, this question is unanswerable. We cannot know unless we try. But we do know that our collective vision of social justice is not unchangeable. We do make reforms to our social institutions in the name of social justice. We no longer rely on the death penalty to punish those convicted of murder or treason. We no longer believe that confining inmates within penal institutions—with no opportunities for education or communication with the outside world—is the best way to build social connectedness. We no longer accept, without question, that the best way to teach children math or to internalize our social values is by threatening them with the strap or the cane. Perhaps the only thing we can say with any certainty is that two wrongs do not make a right. In the end, the restorative justice story that we see at work—within many victim–offender mediation programs, family group conferencing initiatives, and circle sentencing as an alternative to traditional retributive justice sentencing practices in the criminal justice system—is based on the simple idea that the violation of social relationships caused by an act of wrongdoing or injustice creates many different kinds of justice needs that cannot all be met by punishment alone.

CAN MEDIATION DELIVER JUSTICE?

In this chapter we have talked about different conceptions of justice as "stories." We have seen that these different stories have implications for the institutional arrangements that we rely on for resolving conflict. It is evident that both retributive justice and corrective justice are almost invariably associated with the courts. With their emphasis on fact finding, proof of fault, and the imposition of coercive sanctions, the courts provide a preferred option for those disputants whose primary conflict goals are vindication or retribution (Peachey, 1989, p. 307; Currie, 2003). Where the primary focus of the conflict is a distributive issue—as with our example of Jennifer and Paul and the orange—the process choice available to the disputants for resolving their conflict is much wider. They can range across the whole dispute resolution spectrum, from interest-based processes like mediation or negotiation to rights-based processes like adjudication, or even to power-based processes like majority vote. Mediation, with its emphasis on party self-determination and collaborative decision making, often provides a very effective and flexible interest-based process for resolving distributive disputes, whether between two parties or multiple parties.

Note that the three distributive justice principles we considered earlier in this chapter can be applied in negotiation, mediation, arbitration, or adjudication. There is no privileged dispute resolution process in which the "correct" distributive justice principle to use can be easily determined. Courts often have as much trouble as parties deciding which distributive justice principle should be applied in any given conflict situation. For example, in child custody disputes, each parent might propose competing post-divorce arrangements, each claiming it would be in the best interests of the child. Indeed, in situations where agreement is possible, a strong argument can be made that parties should be encouraged to settle distributive conflicts through negotiation or mediation, rather than use public institutions like the courts (Mnookin & Kornhauser, 1979).

With respect to the procedural justice story, we have identified some general principles applicable to most forms of the dispute resolution process. But as the proverb says, "the devil is in the details." What this means is that the process rules that may be appropriate for an adversarial fact-finding process in the courts may not be suitable for a non-adversarial, interest-based process such as mediation. So, be wary of judging the procedural adequacy of mediation by reference to the procedural standards developed for use in the courts. Also be wary of judging the outcomes produced by mediation by reference to the legal remedies provided by the courts. Both of these concerns have been raised by legal critics of mediation, who tend to assume that reliance on mediation to address rights-based conflicts will result in lesser justice for the participants (Shaffer, 1988; Grillo, 1991; Bailey, 1989). To critique mediation for lacking the procedural safeguards of the courtroom is to disregard the process differences between interest-based and rights-based approaches to resolving conflict. Moreover, this concern about the procedural deficiencies of settlement-based processes like mediation or negotiation also tends to assume that most legal disputes should be resolved through rights-based processes like litigation, regardless of the costs and delays involved—and regardless of the wishes or needs of the parties (Fiss, 1984).

As we have seen, concerns about the effects of power imbalances in negotiation are very real, and may have an impact on the outcome of the negotiation process. But it is not self-evident that the courts are the best forum for counteracting the effects of such power-imbalances. Indeed, given the costs and delays inherent in the court system, it is arguable that a party wishing to exploit a significant resource advantage may have more opportunities for doing so in the court system than in the more informal context of negotiation or mediation (Galanter, 1975).

Power imbalances based on inequalities of information between the disputants can often be addressed by the mediator recommending that all parties obtain independent legal advice before entering mediation, and before signing off on any agreement reached during mediation. This also helps ensure that all parties have a full understanding of the potential legal effects of any agreement reached through mediation, including how the agreement may affect their future relationship. Finally, obtaining information about their legal rights and entitlements may also help to improve the BATNA of a weaker disputant, which, in turn, is likely to improve the fairness and stability of any agreement reached in mediation

(Fisher and Ury, 1991, pp. 97–106). To use the language of principled negotiation, shared knowledge of the parties' respective legal entitlements, if an agreement is not reached, may provide the parties with objective criteria to rely on in crafting their own negotiated settlement to the conflict.

Finally, we consider the role of mediation in the restorative justice story. As we have seen, the principles of restorative justice practices can be used in judicial sentencing decisions, in pre-trial victim–offender mediation, in community or family conferencing, or in aboriginal sentencing circles (Law Commission of Canada, 2003). Yet mediation still holds a special place within the restorative justice story. In Canada, the use of a community-based victim–offender mediation process in Elmira, Ontario in 1974 is widely credited as a defining moment in the development of a restorative justice approach. It put the needs of those touched by the crime at the centre of the process, rather than the institutional needs of the state (Zehr, 1990, p. 158; Church Council on Justice and Corrections, 1996, p. 39; Wright and Galaway, 1989, pp. 14–24). This should come as no surprise, since the normative values of self-determination, social connectedness, and collaborative decision making—explored in our discussion of mediation throughout this book—are clearly related to many of the social values underpinning the restorative justice story. Therefore, in looking at the spectrum of dispute resolution processes (examined in chapter 2), provided it is done in an appropriate and beneficial way, mediation comes closest to the ideal of responding to the human justice needs identified by the restorative justice story. Bush (1989) goes so far as to say that genuine transformative mediation serves the public interest and promotes social justice more so than adjudication or the legal system, whereas settlement-type mediation, as is typically found in civil court-connected mediation, does not.

SUMMARY

In this chapter, we addressed the ever-challenging issue of how and to what extent mediation may achieve justice. As we have seen, justice can mean many different things to different people, in different contexts, and at different levels. This question will probably be debated forever. We believe that such social debate is healthy, even essential, to democratic systems of governance, especially if it is pursued in an integrative manner that respects and seeks to learn from *all* perspectives, especially those we may not agree with.

FURTHER READING

Braithwaite, J. (1989). *Crime, shame and reintegration*. Cambridge, UK: Cambridge University Press.

Law Commission of Canada. (2003). *Transforming relationships through participatory justice*. Ottawa: Law Commission of Canada.

Umbreit, M. (1994). *Victim meets offender: The impact of restorative justice and mediation*. Monsey, NY: Criminal Justice Press.

Wright, M., & Galaway, B. (Eds.). (1989). *Mediation and criminal justice: Victims, offenders, and community*. London: Sage Publications.

Zehr, H. (1990). *Changing lenses*. Scottdale, PA: Herald Press.

CHAPTER ELEVEN

Taking the Unknown Path: Mediation as a Profession

What you intend in your thoughts with passion, you will act upon and ultimately create.

Wayne Dyer

In this final chapter, we focus on the profession of mediation. We begin with an overview of the current trends and challenges faced by practitioners in this emerging field. Our overview often raises questions, because we want to open doors of inquiry. We also address some commonly asked questions about education and training, certification and ethics, mediator liability, and establishing a mediation practice. The chapter closes with our view of what the future holds for mediation.

TRENDS AND CHALLENGES

There is no doubt that mediation has come into the mainstream. Only a decade ago, many people would have been puzzled when mediators described what they did. Today, most people have heard of mediation, and many work for organizations that use these services. Mediation is now accessed through community conflict resolution programs, workplace mediation programs, tribunals, government and court-mandated programs, and public policy consultations.

Advances in mediation can be found in a variety of research publications, and scholar-practitioners have begun to ground their practices in theory. One of the most influential to emerge was Robert Baruch Bush and Joseph Folger's *The Promise of Mediation* (1994), in which they articulated the transformation story, which theorized their practice of emphasizing moral development in mediation. John Winslade and Gerald Monk, with *Narrative Mediation* (2000), followed suit with a theoretical model of mediation based on the creation of new narratives out of the conflict-laden stories parties brought to the table. In this book, we describe the insight model and use its theoretical foundations to inform our practice.

Not only has new scholarship emerged about models of practice, but more sophisticated analyses of what mediators do, why they do it, and new applications for it have become prominent. Both LeBaron (2002) and Cloke (2001) discuss the role of non-traditional knowledge sources in mediation practices. Ury (2000) views our roles in conflict as multi-faceted and rich, urging us to shift toward compassion and cooperation at the global level. Lederach (1997) examines the role of peace building and conflict resolution in deeply divided societies. These authors, among many, provide a rich source of new information about mediation.

Evaluation of Mediation

Although much scholarship is moving us closer to understanding what we do when we mediate and why we do it, relatively few studies examine the extent to which mediation processes are effective at achieving their stated goals. *Evaluation* of mediation processes—and their longer-term or social consequences—is an ongoing and important challenge. Most research has focused on client satisfaction. This is not surprising, given that much of the evaluation undertaken assesses the effectiveness of mediation programs that are part of court-mandated or institutional programs (see, for example, Macfarlane, 1995, and Bingham & Pitts, 2002). Since these programs were established largely to respond to delays in the justice or regulatory system, researchers are most interested in whether clients receive timely service, how that affects the dispute, the effects of the process on their satisfaction levels, and the outcomes.

Evaluating mediation is made more difficult because most mediators believe that the qualitative difference between mediation and more formal dispute resolution mechanisms lies in the *process* and not, necessarily, the *outcomes*. Chapter 10 focused a good deal of attention on the philosophical underpinnings of restorative justice versus retributive justice practices. Capturing and measuring philosophical differences is not an easy task—it is much simpler to compare outcomes rather than processes. A further problem arises when contrasting formal court proceedings with the process of mediation, since measuring process benefits is a more subtle undertaking—often it is like comparing apples and oranges. These evaluations, which rely on client self-disclosure and self-assessment, are nonetheless useful in understanding client reactions to mediated processes.

We think the profession as a whole needs to take a closer look at mediation's goals and objectives—and begin to measure to what extent they are being achieved. As you now know, not all mediation programs, and certainly not all mediators, have the same objectives. Community mediation programs seek to transform social relations in their neighbourhoods, whereas commercial mediators are often more interested in ensuring that their clients arrive at settlements that they can live with. For mediators and mediation programs that have still other goals—moral growth, transformation through insights, or empowering those on the margins—it is critical that they evaluate what they are achieving. Furthermore, the field needs to learn more about the expectations of the parties themselves. Are parties able to achieve their objectives through mediated processes? Do their objectives change as they work through the process? Are they empowered and transformed? Data derived from qualitative research—and the documentation of different modes of mediation—is critical to the continued improvement of the field. We already know from one study (Welsh, 2001) that one of the key principles of mediation, self-determination, can no longer be taken for granted, and that it needs to be protected if mediation is to continue to be qualitatively different from the dispute resolution process found in the courts.

A closely related issue is how the public, government, institutional, and corporate "consumers" of mediation services view the goals and objectives of mediation and mediation programs. In recent years, a challenge, particularly from the non-profit, community-based mediation sector, has been the relatively low public and government support for such programs. This support is unlikely to increase without readily demonstrable economic and social benefits. In Canada, *some* government funding is required to establish and sustain these programs, to achieve the longer term "macro" or social benefits they can produce. To the extent that such mediation programs can be shown to produce long-term social and economic benefits, the weight of public opinion and political support will decide whether, and to what extent, they deserve short-term funding. A key factor will be the role of the media in helping to shape public opinion.

Diversification of Mediation

Another trend in mediation is its *diversification*. Mediation has many applications, a number of which we have already discussed. Some examples are:

- insurance claims;
- land-use planning and development;
- trade and commerce;
- separation and divorce;
- organizational and workplace conflicts;
- civilian interaction with police;
- schoolyard squabbles;
- contractual disputes;
- human rights complaints;
- immigration and refugee issues;
- environmental assessments;
- banking and real estate disputes;
- community and neighbourhood issues;
- criminal and civil cases—and even civil war.

Mediation can also be an integral part of organizational and institutional conflict management systems. New applications are emerging all the time. Wherever conflict or the potential for conflict exists, mediation is becoming a preferred option for dealing with it.

Related to this is the trend toward institutionalization of mediation. It is encouraging to see that public and private organizations are increasingly adopting informal processes that include mediation to resolve disputes internally. Staff relations conflicts, organizational restructuring, and grievances are now being addressed through mediation in workplaces. Improving staff morale, as well as building effective teams and team consensus, are just two of the reasons for the increased use of interest-based, dialogic processes for resolving conflict. In November 2003, the Canadian Parliament passed Bill C-25, the *Public Service Modernization Act*. Among other things, this Act requires that mediation services be provided for labour relations and that informal conflict management systems be established in every federal department. (See the Treasury Board's Web site, listed at the end of this chapter.) Many public sector organizations, such as the Royal Canadian Mounted Police, the Department of Justice, the Canada Revenue Agency, the Department of National Defence/Canadian Forces, and Public Works and Government Services have established integrated conflict management systems (Lynch, 1997). No doubt this trend will continue.

A major concern raised by institutionalization is the fear that mediation has been adopted simply because it is more cost-effective than litigation. Efficiency arguments alone fail to capture the most compelling reasons for choosing mediation over other dispute resolution options. Mediation is not merely a procedural matter; it extends to relationships, new interpretations of needs, and future orientations and behaviours toward conflict. There are concerns that the rationale and motivations behind establishing mediation systems could preclude realizing the full potential of mediation.

Information technology has recently opened up new fields, with mediation sessions now taking place via e-mail, instant messaging, chat rooms, and video conferencing. Some of the advantages of using online dispute resolution (ODR) include its low cost—people do not have to travel to participate; reduction of time-zone differences; and its speed and availability. For some, ODR is less confrontational. On the other hand, communicating about contentious and emotional subjects, without being face to face with the other person, can be difficult. In the absence of facial expressions and body language, online or telephone communication can even cause the conflict to escalate. However, as technology develops, innovators will no doubt find new ways to deal with these challenges. ODR will be an ongoing area of development, and a potential market niche for some mediators.

As the field of mediation has broadened, so has it deepened. In Canada, our rich multicultural context has influenced some of the practices of mediation. Many newcomers have brought their traditions of using social network mediators (Moore, 1996, pp. 44–52) to community and neighbourhood disputes. International diplomacy, which influences parties with both "the carrot and the stick" techniques, has affected the form that mediation takes in trade and human rights tribunals. Canada's First Nations employed forms of community justice and sentencing circles well before mediation came into the mainstream. The legal profession has also placed its stamp on the process, as varied applications have brought mediation into the justice system.

All these influences have enriched the field. Educational institutions now label the type of mediation training they supply, such as the Institute for the Study of Conflict Transformation, which promotes Bush and Folger's transformative mediation. Professional conferences offer workshops on narrative practice, human rights mediations, workplace conflict resolution, and myriad other models of practice particular to a context or ideology.

What is not yet clear in this diversity is how often consumers of mediation are making knowledgeable and informed choices about which type of mediation they would prefer to use. The model that is often used is the more evaluative or "content expert" mediation. Civil and family conflicts, more than any other types of conflict, are often a mandatory process, and thus likely to capture a greater share of the mediation services market. Picard and Saunders (2002, pp. 235–236) worry that,

> given the increasing involvement of the state in mediation through mandated schemes attached to the courts, and the strong presence of lawyers within these schemes, both as practitioners and as consumers (via their clients), ... control of the field [is in danger of] falling into the hands of the legal profession.

Even before this, Picard (1994) was concerned by evidence indicating that counsel to the parties in civil disputes were favouring mediators who were lawyers and, in fact, sought them out over any other kind of mediator.

All this suggests that the legal model for mediation, generally a settlement-driven and often an evaluative process, is becoming dominant in the field. Community forms of mediation, which are always voluntary, risk being marginalized with the direction that practice is taking. Few people in conflict, if given the option, value the volunteer community mediator as highly as they value the professional mediator. Different cultural forms of mediation are rarely used outside their cultural contexts, regardless of whether these forms have something to offer. Many practitioners fear that the richness and diversity of practices could be lost as mediation use becomes increasingly institutionalized.

Some mediators say that having different types of mediation is a good thing—using the settlement approach for "legal" disputes, and transformative or holistic approaches, including insight mediation, for "relational" conflicts. With this market-driven view, observers could say that if a settlement, problem-solving approach is what people want and expect in legal or other contexts, then that is what should be used. As Mayer discusses (2000, pp. 195–198), clients often want a settlement approach, and their expectations of what the mediator will do and the mediator's process goals and intentions may be at odds. If mediators fail to deliver what clients want, mediation will not be used at all. Better that some settlement form of mediation be used than none at all. On the other hand, those with a transformative perspective could say that mediation's potential for individual, relational, and social growth will never be realized with a market-driven approach. A practitioner with this view could say that the settlement approach should not be used at all, because it simply maintains the status quo and extinguishes any transformative potential inherent in the conflict situation. Indeed, Bush (1989) says that if the mediation used in court-connected programs is simply pragmatic, settlement-type mediation, and is not in some way transformative, better that mediation not be used at all as a component of the civil justice system.

Yet, we believe that more integrated, holistic, and inclusive views of mediation are beginning to surface, bringing together shared commonalities, and at the same time recognizing multiple goals and a multiplicity of practices (Picard, 2004). We have tried to reveal these tendencies in this book, by giving attention to both the art and the science of mediation, by valuing other models of practice while teaching about our own, and by calling upon the field to ensure that broad standards of practice for mediators are set. This leads us to a discussion of a third trend—the *regulation* of mediation.

Regulation of Mediation

Mediation practice contains a complex set of interrelated and sometimes contradictory goals. On the one hand, it has the potential to generate inexpensive, efficient, and speedy settlements. On the other, it offers a forum where individuals have more opportunity to tell their stories, and more creative space to invent solutions (LeBaron, 1994). Those mediation advocates who call for certification seek the legitimacy and recognition accorded to other professionals, fearing that if practitioners do not set their own standards, less informed bureaucrats and policy makers will try to do it for them. Those on the other side of the debate fear that inappropriate barriers for entry to the field will be created and broad dissemination of peace-making skills hampered. Picard (1994, p. 155) believes that "the fear of creating a monopoly lies at the heart of the credentials debate." She speculates that only mediators who deal with legal, corporate, public policy, and international disputes will become legitimized through certification, while those who work in community-based and volunteer programs will be marginalized. In turn, non-adversarial dispute settlement options will become available only to the elite and wealthy, the very situation mediation sets out to change. While the debate goes on, the reality is that professional organizations and government departments have gone ahead and set standards of practice. Although, for the most part, they are advisory, not mandatory, they do set the bar for what professional mediators need to know and do to practise.

Some researchers (Kolb, 1994; Moore, 1996) have examined the areas of education, training, skills, and experience to consider what may contribute to mediator competency. Others (for example, Honeyman, 1990) have gone further, by proposing minimum standards for developing a "professional" status for the field of mediation. Even current job postings for mediators have established minimum criteria for applicants. Yet, there is no consensus on whether standards are advisable or achievable (Picard, 1994; Waldman, 1996).

Even when there is agreement on the idea of minimum standards, considerable debate continues about the criteria. Given the variety of mediation models, only some of which we have discussed, there is no agreement in the field on generic standards of practice, let alone the qualifications ensuring that mediators meet these standards. Since what constitutes success in mediation is contested, how can we possibly set generic standards for achieving diverse goals and objectives? Moreover, depending upon whether regulation is input- or output-oriented, the criteria would be quite distinct (Reeve, 1998). Output regulation would rest on quality standards for services, such as client satisfaction with the process and outcomes, and satisfaction with the mediator's comportment. Input regulation would refer to the qualifications required for a mediator to gain certification. Inputs would need to include certain levels of education, experience, training, and skills. Reeve identifies another regulatory form in licensing, where mediators pledge to adhere to and uphold a set of ethical standards. Family Mediation Canada, the Association of Conflict Resolution, and the Canadian Bar Association have gone this route, adding minimum qualifications to their set of minimum ethical standards (see appendix C). Licensing bodies then perform "policing" functions to ensure that members comply with the standards. Much of the current discussion about regulation concerns both input and output elements.

In the future, regulation, if deemed necessary, could take two forms—standards could be set by the government, or the practice of mediation could become self-regulating, similar to the medical and legal professions. Again, given the diversity of the field, no single area of practice is likely to be able to set standards for all mediation applications, since standards will vary depending on the context in which mediation is practised. A mediator for a divorcing couple who want to sort out custody arrangements will need competencies that are quite distinct from a mediator who is facilitating a healing circle within an aboriginal community or one who is mediating a construction dispute.

To some extent, consumers do help to maintain quality control in the field, because ineffective mediators are unlikely to receive work, especially when clients are paying for the service. Reputations are important, and good mediators are recommended by former clients, mediation service coordinators, and other mediators. In fact, new mediators often have a tough time breaking into the field—they do not possess the experience needed to develop a reputation. And it is risky to rely only on word of mouth and previous success at mediation, given the subjective nature of success in the differing contexts of the field.

Government licensing raises several problems. There is little agreement or knowledge about what qualifications produce effective mediators. In light of this, standards that are determined from one perspective could eliminate competent mediators from practising. Given the evolving nature of mediation, setting standards today could inadvertently "freeze" dynamic practice and eliminate innovation in the field. The new areas of practice and types of mediation that we have seen emerge over the past decade or so might not have been developed if rigid practice standards had been in place. Finally, there is a concern that, as a result of licensing, one particular group could dominate the field.

The group that seems best placed to dominate the field is composed of lawyers. The recent institutionalization of mediation within the legal field has produced a specialized field of ADR lawyering. Law schools now have significant mediation programs. Picard and Saunders (2002, p. 235) state that "the danger ahead for the regulation of mediation is not only that these groups will occupy and colonize the practice (or at least its profitable sectors), but also that they will do the same on the regulatory front." This would be a great loss to the transformative or communitarian goals of mediation, which have not been found in court-mandated or tribunal types of mediation. Court-mandated mediation is also one of the few areas where the process is mandatory, making the consumer a captive client. These clients are developing knowledge and experience of only one form of mediation practice. Picard and Saunders see that future standards of mediation are being set by legal and state professionals, to the detriment of practitioners whose practices have broader social goals.

A more holistic view of regulation, through the setting of standards of practice, comes out of the work done by commissions and working groups composed of Canadians and Americans involved in the Association for Conflict Resolution (ACR, formerly Society of Professionals in Dispute Resolution [SPIDR]). ACR continues to recognize the diversity of practice and, rather than calling for a uniform set of mediation principles—the one-size-fits-all model—ACR has determined that it is best to allow its sectors to identify standards that reflect the diversity of the work and of the parties involved.

Mediator Selection Exercise

Think of a conflict that may require the services of a mediator.

1. What questions would you ask of a mediator to ensure that he or she had the qualifications to intervene in this particular dispute?
2. Do you think you would be able to determine who is or is not a good mediator for this conflict, based on your questions?
3. If yes, explain why, and if not, why not?

Critiques of Mediation

Equally important to understanding the risks of institutionalization are the *critiques of mediation*. Here is a brief review of some of the authors and the issues they brought to our attention. Some of the early critiques came from those who argue against mediation in any case, asserting that it exerts covert state control (Abel, 1982), and that alternative dispute resolution has transformed disputes over facts and legal rights into conflicts over feelings and relationships (Merry, 1990; Nader, 1988; Harrington, 1985). According to these critics, the private nature of mediation, its lack of procedural rules, and the fact that most mediators are representative of the most privileged classes, result in mediated agreements that uphold the status quo of unequal social relations. Scimecca (1991a) believes that ADR, as a movement, has lost sight of its original purpose—to provide social justice, particularly to the poor. Furthermore, many practitioners have been heard to lament, "Pretty soon, we will need a new 'alternative' to alternative dispute resolution."

Some criticisms of mediation relate to its process deficiencies, which may result in harm or unfairness to the parties. A more fundamental criticism is that the transformative goal of mediation is a false promise. Retributive justice advocates, in particular, make this claim against proponents and practitioners of restorative justice, saying that restorative approaches are soft on crime and undermine the deterrence, peace and order, and social security goals of the criminal justice system. In effect, they believe and say that the transformative promise of restorative justice is a false one. Retributive justice advocates point to cases where criminals have got off with a "slap on the wrist," only to offend again. And, they are right; that has happened and will happen again. Restorative justice proponents say that social healing and transformation takes time, perhaps a long time. Society needs to trust the process—the social transformation process that a restorative justice approach will bring about. It may take a decade or a century; it may take forever. However, we all need to believe that we are going in the right direction.

As mediation processes continue to be applied in new arenas of conflict, the question of how and to what extent these processes serve justice will always be there. This is particularly true in post-conflict societies that are trying to come to terms with past injustice and oppression. Martha Minow, in *Between Vengeance and Forgiveness* (1998), eloquently articulates the tension between restorative, reparative, and retributive practices of justice in her overview of how societies attempt to heal after large-scale atrocities and tragedies, such as those that occurred in Rwanda and the former Yugoslavia. Reviewing the various options—trials, truth and reconciliation commissions, and reparations—she concludes by encouraging us to not be silent about these issues.

The same issues arise closer to home. Canada's First Nations are in the process of developing processes to promote healing and justice for the abuses suffered in residential schools. The federal government has proposed using mediation and alternative dispute resolution to provide a balance of healing and justice. Indian Residential Schools Resolution Canada, a newly created agency, is mandated to address past abuses and offer some form of redress. Its Web site is listed at the end of this chapter. Increasingly, healing processes that attempt to balance justice imperatives are being used for issues that warrant them, such as environmental mediation. However, these methods are not without critics, for many of the same reasons discussed previously, including the fear that entitlements, rights, and even social progress may be traded off.

Notwithstanding these important concerns, there is reason for optimism. Many of those who manage programs in mediation are believers in its ideals and transformative potential. Perhaps they have received training from outside institutions that promote relationship-enhancing mediation, or they might have been private practice mediators who have been convinced to join an institution in the hopes of shaping its programs in a meaningful way. Even if the leaders of institutions adopt mediation for the sole purpose of lowering costs, unintended good consequences can happen. Parties are able to preserve or enhance relationships through this process and, in most models of mediation, parties do gain some insights into themselves and the parties with whom they are in conflict.

The information we present next will be of interest to would-be mediators, as well as to people currently involved in mediation, mediation programs and systems, and those considering referring others to mediation. It could also be of value to anyone wanting to know more about the field in general.

EDUCATION AND TRAINING

Mediation practitioners have no single set of legal or national educational requirements. Training programs vary greatly, and, unlike other professions, the discipline has no governing body mandated to establish and enforce minimum training qualifications. To complicate things, there is no proof of a correlation between education or training and successful mediation.

The "standards" that identify educational requirements exist only as recommended guidelines, which are non-enforceable. For the most part, professional mediation associations set these guidelines, and these differ depending upon the context in which mediation is being used. We have included the standards set by three bodies—Family Mediation Canada, and the Association for Conflict Resolution, and the ADR Section of the Canadian Bar Association (see appendix C). Looking at the standards set by these three organizations, we see more commonality of standards—confidentiality, impartiality, informed consent, and self-determination—than divergence.

For would-be mediators seeking to enter the field, we suggest you ask yourself: Why do I want to be a mediator? What education, training and, experience do I already have that will lend itself to this type of work? What type of conflicts am I interested in mediating—family, workplace, commercial, community, environmental, public policy? With some sense of what you want, you will be better able to determine the educational or training resources that best suit *your* needs. Most people who currently work in private practice as full-time mediators in Canada have a professional degree in areas such as law, social work, business, education, or management, to support their more specialized training in mediation.

What Specialized Training Do Mediators Need?

Mediators need to acquire theoretical knowledge as well as the skills and techniques needed to intervene in a wide array of conflict situations and with diverse groups of people. They also need to develop a personal style that is rooted in their world views and cultural orientations. What's more, we believe, as do Lang and Taylor (2000), that mediators need to be aware of their core philosophy of human interaction, to sustain them through the difficulties they will inevitably face.

The beliefs, knowledge, and skills—both the science and the art—are developed through studies, coached practice, and ongoing interaction with others. It is a lifelong learning process of questioning, experimenting, discovering, and refining. As with any profession, some learning will be through practical, on-the-job experience; other aspects come from books, lectures, group discussions, peer review, and other classroom or workshop activities.

Typically, introductory mediation training programs cover basic conflict resolution, negotiation and mediation theory, communication skills, collaborative conflict resolution strategies, and principles of reflective practice. In addition to training in the science of mediation, mediators should also develop non-traditional skills. Introductory mediation rarely addresses this area, although advanced training courses are increasingly recognizing the importance of intuitive, somatic, and experiential knowledge. Training modules that address these topics can usually be found in courses that address emotional intelligence, creativity, and intuitive development. Mediators will be guaranteed to find at least a handful of workshops in this area if they attend a mediation conference. "Using Metaphors in Mediation," "Martial Arts and Mediation—The Yin and the Yang," and "Tapping into Your Creativity in Mediation" are just a few titles of workshops offered at recent mediation conferences.

As a minimum requirement, many institutionalized professional programs suggest 40 hours of training—after training in such disciplines as law, social work, education, or business management. Given the requirements of other recognized professions, the 40-hour (or 5-day) training standard seems far from sufficient to realize the larger social and more holistic visions of mediation. Consider, for example, how much training someone who is learning to play a sport or a musical instrument typically receives. In Canada, a youngster who aspires to play hockey at a high or even a professional level will participate in literally thousands of hours of training and coaching sessions over a period of 10 or 15 years. To reach their full potential, mediators should consider basic or introductory training as only the beginning of their journey to becoming competent practitioners.

Regardless of where mediators take their training, courses of study should cover three broad areas: (1) the process skills for analyzing, approaching, and resolving disputes; (2) the social and conflict theories embedded in these processes; and (3) the tools for becoming a reflective practitioner.

Where Do Mediators Get Training?

University and College Programs

Only a few universities in Canada offer degree programs in conflict resolution. Interestingly, there are more graduate-level than undergraduate programs. This is probably because individuals coming into the field tend to be mid- to upper-career professionals looking for a new career path, planning what they will do after they retire from their current positions, or have been assigned responsibilities that involve conflict resolution work. Many already have undergraduate degrees, have taken professional development courses, and now want to support their skills-based training in conflict resolution with a theoretical foundation. For the most part, these programs specialize in particular areas. For example, the master's program at the University of Victoria focuses on public policy dispute resolution, while the one at Royal Roads deals with peace and security, as well as group conflict. The Osgoode Hall Law School program in dispute resolution centres on ADR in legal matters, while a new master's program at Saint Paul's University in Ottawa will focus on international, ethnocultural, and religious conflicts.

At the undergraduate level, two of the more established programs are at Menno Simons University in Winnipeg and Conrad Grebel College in Guelph, Ontario. Although there are few degree programs, most if not all universities offer conflict resolution and mediation courses in a range of disciplines, including sociology, psychology, political science, international relations, law, and social work. Individuals can often enroll as special students, if they are not interested in embarking on a full program. Most law schools offer courses and opportunities to specialize in ADR. The University of British Columbia's Law School, for example, offers dispute resolution as a specialty.

Some Canadian universities offer certificate rather than full degree programs. For example, Carleton University in Ottawa offers an academic, for-credit, certificate program at the graduate level. Various universities, including Queen's, Dalhousie, Toronto, York, Mount St. Vincent, McMaster, Prince Edward Island, and Sherbrooke, offer non-credit certificate programs from their continuing education departments. College programs include those offered through the Justice Institute of British

Columbia, Laurentian University, Mount Royal, and Humber College. Certificate programs require students to take multiple courses and, in some cases, participate in a practicum or pass a skills assessment to graduate.

To find out more about university-based programs, explore some of the Web sites listed at the end of this chapter, particularly those for Campus Mediation Resources, Conflict Resolution Network Canada, and the Mediation and Information Resource Centre. These three Web sites list a host of graduate, undergraduate, college, and private programs offering courses in conflict resolution and mediation. You will also find information related to such topics as distance learning, research papers and reports, and textbook acquisition.

Professional Development Programs

Until recently, professional development courses provided most of the formal training in mediation. Many courses span 40 hours and primarily focus on the acquisition of skills. As mediation practice has increased, private sector courses—offered by for-profit or non-profit charitable organizations—have begun to flourish. Increasing numbers of students want some form of certification in a designated area, even though certification in this way only means that the student has completed a particular program of study in a particular organization. Some of these courses or programs provide some form of skills- and knowledge-based evaluation; others only provide certificates of attendance, without any assessment component. Individuals can find out about training courses in their area by consulting the home pages of Family Mediation Canada, Conflict Resolution Network Canada, and ADR Canada. The URLs for these and other organizations can be found in the Web sites listed at the end of this chapter.

In-House Training Programs and Other Short Courses

Organizations wanting to build a culture that includes collaborative problem solving are beginning to offer their staff short courses in conflict resolution and mediation. These courses are useful in educating staff members about conflict resolution and how to access in-house mediation services and other resources for dealing with conflicts. They are also designed to provide employees with the management tools to deal with conflict when it first surfaces. These types of courses are generally not designed to train people to mediate.

Half- or full-day courses are often offered at professional conferences. Focused on specialized topics or issues, these workshops are led by individuals who practice in the field.

Mentoring Programs

Learning happens through experience; training alone is rarely sufficient. Students preparing to go into practice on their own still need—and want—some mentoring and developmental assistance after their training program. Our experience with community-based mediation programs that use volunteers bears this out. The number of volunteer applicants far exceeds the positions available.

As with other social and mental health professions, would-be mediators commonly search for mentoring and co-mediation opportunities to develop their skills. Unfortunately, mentoring is largely a hit-and-miss opportunity in Canada, because there are few mediators who offer this service, with few guidelines for mentoring if they do. Students who have attended our classes find the lack of mentoring opportunities frustrating and confusing. The reality is that it takes time to mentor properly and, because few practitioners mediate full time, the opportunities are rare. We suggest that you find someone you'd like to work with and negotiate a mentoring relationship. We further suggest that you find parties who want mediation. In return, your mentor might agree to coach you through the mediation or, better still, work as a co-mediator, and debrief you after. In this situation, the fees generally go to the mentor as payment for his or her time. In this way, you, the new mediator, take responsibility for getting the business, and you gain experience and some one-on-one training in a real situation, while the mentor earns some income—a "win–win" arrangement.

New mediators often ask if they can observe a mediation. The answer is usually "no." In many cases, parties do not like to be "observed," and having observers may detract from the process. Instead, we sometimes offer to co-mediate with inexperienced mediators, as a way of giving them needed experience. Needless to say, we ensure that the person is capable of participating as a co-mediator. The parties' needs come first, and no party should ever leave mediation worse off than when he or she came in, especially due to a lack of mediator competence. Once new mediators find someone they would like to learn from, they should create a mentoring plan, which should include learning goals and objectives, proposed role and responsibilities, expectations, time frames, and fees. People should not expect experienced mediators to mentor for free.

Given the scarcity of established mediators willing to mentor someone new, coupled with a market that values reputation and experience, new mediators have few options to get themselves experienced enough for practice. This problem is not likely to go away any time soon. The field needs to find ways to address ongoing learning for would-be practitioners.

CERTIFICATION AND ETHICS

Although there is no centralized governing body for mediators, some universities, training institutes, and organizations with mediation programs certify mediators. People who are certified usually have basic levels of mediator aptitude and competence, an understanding of a body of principles and ethical guidelines, and a commitment to a code of conduct.

Certification standards define requirements for training, experience, education, skills, and abilities to meet a minimum level of competence. They provide consumers with some level of assurance that these requirements have been met.

Certification Standards in Canada

The acceptance and institutionalization of mediation has expanded rapidly over the past few years with a proliferation of court-connected, government, and community mediation programs. Most of these programs have certification requirements based on certain minimum qualification standards—for training, experience and subject matter, and process knowledge. For example, mediators with the Canadian Human Rights Commission, in addition to mediation training and experience, are required to have some level of knowledge and experience with human rights issues and cases.

Whether provincial governments in Canada will ever legislate requirements for general mediator licensing or certification, or whether they should, remains an open question. In the United States, some states "license" mediators, while others "register" or "certify" them through institutionalized certification programs. However, in Canada, the marketplace is, to some extent, establishing such standards—and no doubt will continue to do so in the future.

To illustrate some current ethical and practice expectations, the following are included as appendix C:

- standards of practice for family mediators set by Family Mediation Canada (FMC);

- mediation training standards approved by the Association for Conflict Resolution (ACR) Family Section;
- ACR's Model Standards of Practice for Family and Divorce Mediation;
- ACR's Ethical Standards of Professional Responsibility for all other conflict resolution professionals; and
- the Model Code of Conduct of the Ontario ADR Section of the Canadian Bar Association.

Even if a mediator's practice area does not require certification, we advocate following these standards; they reflect the collective knowledge, expertise, and efforts of many individuals and groups working in the field of mediation. Following these standards demonstrates a desire to be accountable and to hold a high level of practice.

Ethical Issues and Challenges

A number of ethical challenges face mediators. Here, we talk about just four: confidentially, impartiality, the impact on parties not at the table, and coercion.

Confidentiality

All guidelines set out a confidentiality standard for mediation. Such a standard is considered critical to the dispute resolution process, reflecting the belief that it promotes a party's trust in the process and a willingness to share information—and mediators are required to advise parties of circumstances when confidentiality would not be protected. Maintaining confidentiality is considered one of the most important ethical requirements of mediators.

An ethical issue around confidentially arises when mediators hear information about child abuse or neglect, or about actual or planned criminal activity. The law requires the reporting of child abuse. Only priests and lawyers—and only in some circumstances—can be exempted. So, most mediators include a clause in their agreements, disclosing the limits of confidentiality, and/or mention it at the start of a mediation session.

Impartiality

Another accepted standard is impartiality. This requires mediators to be free from favouritism and bias in their actions, to be committed to serving all parties equally. Mediators should remove themselves from mediation when they do not believe they can act impartially, or if they are in a real or perceived conflict of interest. They must also disclose any prior professional or personal relationship with all parties.

Impartiality presents an ethical challenge when family mediations expose profound sadness, bad treatment, and the impact on children when marriages end. Mediators must recognize their own personal biases and guard against influencing the mediation process in favour of one party. They must also recognize that parties can suspect bias in the mediator, for reasons generated by class, race, gender, culture, or professional stereotyping, even where there is no bias. In addition, mediators must also protect against bias if they have strong views about the issues being mediated. They are ethically obligated not to socialize with parties, adopt a different mode of addressing each party, or converse with one party without the other party being informed.

Ethical dilemmas can emerge in small communities, where everyone knows everyone—and when mediators are chosen because they are known and respected by the parties.

Parties Not at the Table

An ethical question arises for mediators when decisions are being made that will affect parties not at the table. Here are two examples. First, how are the interests of the children of divorcing parents represented? Should mediators take this responsibility? If they do, are they not contravening the standard of impartiality? The second example has to do with parties affected by an agreement reached who may not even be born yet. Menin (2000, p. 285) tells us that "a mediator has a right and a responsibility to bring to the table issues or perspectives that may not have been identified or addressed by either party but that affect an absent party."

Mediators advocating for the public interest need to be concerned about impartiality. The ethical dilemma is how to advocate for "reasonable" agreements and still stay impartial. Some family mediators ensure the children have an advocate to speak on their behalf, and in cases where the children are old enough and it is appropriate, they are invited into the negotiations.

Coercion

Mediators should not coerce parties into recognizing the principles of self-determination and informed decision making. At the same time, mediators are expected to help parties achieve settlement of their differences. This leaves the mediator in a potential ethical dilemma that stems from a subjective interpretation of what is considered help and what is considered coercion.

Boulle and Kelly (1998, p. 258) identify a number of other ethical issues. These involve "obligations not to engage in misleading and deceptive conduct, not to prolong mediation sessions where no agreement is likely, to exercise restraints in publicity and advertising, and to advise parties about and comply with their fee arrangements." Boulle and Kelly go on to suggest—and we strongly agree—that many of these ethical issues and dilemmas should be included in a mediator's training.

MEDIATOR LIABILITY

There are three ways a mediator may be vulnerable to liability. The first is where parties believe they could have done substantially better elsewhere. The second is when parties feel aggrieved about the process itself. The third is when one or both of the parties believe they have reached an agreement, but later disagree on what the agreement was or whether agreement was reached at all. Not to minimize the importance of this issue, we are not aware of any lawsuit against a mediator in Canada.

Potential Liability

Boulle and Kelly (1998, p. 262) tell us that mediators can "potentially be liable if they breach the mediation contract between themselves and the parties." Contracts can be written or verbal and are commonly used in pre-mediation agreements, where the procedures and expectations of both the mediator and the parties are outlined. If mediators do not do what they said they would do, they may be held liable for expenses the parties incurred by participating in the mediation, as well as consequential losses. We can also imagine a breach of contract occurring around issues of confidentiality and conflict of interest. Another area of liability is related to substantive knowledge and expertise or the lack thereof; however, this may be difficult to prove, given the absence of recognized standards.

Other issues that make mediators vulnerable to lawsuits include the withholding of important information from one party, parties feeling they were coerced into accepting a proposal, communicating with a party secretly, deceiving parties about credentials, revealing confidential information, and withholding information about child abuse, criminal activity, or possible harm to others. A particularly vulnerable area for mediators is if they trespass into professional areas where they are not qualified to practise. In the United States and South Africa, mediators were successfully sued on the ground that their mediation practice involved them in the unauthorized practice of law (Boulle & Kelly, 1998, p. 267).

When one or more of the parties at mediation believe that they have reached an agreement, the mediator must ensure that all parties have a clear and common understanding about what they have agreed to and its legal implications. Failure to do that would certainly expose the mediator to a potential claim by one or both of the parties. For example, a party to a divorce dispute may believe that the parties have reached a final, legally binding agreement on the issue of disposition of certain items of property, such as their house or car. The other party may believe that they have reached a tentative understanding, but that nothing will be final and binding until their lawyers review all terms of their mediation "understanding" and prepare and finalize a legal, written agreement, often referred to as a separation agreement. Generally, a mediator is not responsible for preparing, and should not be expected to prepare, a legal separation agreement (although some mediators will do this).

Generally, private practice mediators purchase professional liability insurance coverage. Court-connected and other mediation programs often will require evidence of such coverage.

ESTABLISHING A MEDIATION PRACTICE

A person who finds mediation principles and methods appealing may become highly motivated to become a practitioner. Unfortunately, many who start on the mediation career path are quickly disappointed. There is insufficient demand for their services. Without an established professional or business connection, new mediators often struggle to find clients who are willing to pay for such services. Unlike traditional professions with an established market demand, a mediator who opens a storefront office will probably wait a long time for the phone to ring.

However, we believe that there are ever-increasing opportunities for committed and capable people to pursue careers in mediation and conflict resolution. In that regard, here are some questions to consider—and possible strategies to pursue.

How Do New Mediators Set Up a Private Practice?

There are different models for establishing a private practice in mediation. Some new mediators associate themselves, as consultants, with existing mediation or conflict management firms. The benefit here is that the firm's profile and reputation are already established, so the newcomer has less marketing to do and can rely on the good name of the firm. Working as a consultant to a firm usually requires that these individuals establish their own contacts and locate their own work, usually contributing between 10 and 30 percent of their earnings to the firm. The amount contributed depends on the level of support offered by the company. It is likely to increase if the firm provides a receptionist, secretarial and billing functions, an onsite mediation room, and materials to conduct training sessions. To the extent that the firm does the marketing or advertising or has goodwill that may benefit the consultant, the firm's percentage of revenue would again be somewhat higher. The less support offered by the company, the lower the percentage contributed.

Another way to establish a private practice is to set up an office, either at home or in commercial premises. For a new mediator, this can be financially risky—it takes time to build a reputation and a clientele in the mediation field. If an individual has adequate upfront financing, is highly motivated and flexible, has a large network, and enjoys marketing, this can be a good option. To keep costs down, many mediators in private practice begin working from home offices.

Where Do Mediators Work?

Generally, mediators work in private practice, as volunteers, or as salaried employees. Most private practice mediators work full time; however, most do more than mediation work. Both Picard (2000) and Kruk (1998) found that mediators only spend between one-quarter and one-third of their time mediating. Family and divorce mediators receive the most work. Picard's study (2000, p. 116) showed that most mediators tend to be self-employed, with less than 20 percent working full time, as salaried employees. This may be changing, since the Canadian federal government has recently begun to hire a large number of trained mediators. Typically, these mediators work in or through ADR centres that have been established to serve a particular government department, such as the Department of National Defence or an agency such as the Canada Revenue Agency.

A fairly large volunteer mediator sector works in the areas of community mediation, victim–offender mediation, and restorative justice programs. Although sustained by dedicated and highly motivated volunteers, these programs require substantial funding and public support—but government and institutional support and funding for such programs has declined in recent years. Sustainable support for the community-volunteer sector is an issue that needs to be addressed by various levels of government, institutions, corporations, and associations.

Who Are a Mediator's Clients?

One of the first decisions mediators need to make is whether they will practise as generalists or specialists. In Canada, many mediators are generalists, offering their services to a broad range of clients. Referral agencies may prefer this, because they do not have to take the time to consider whether this case is appropriate to refer. On the other hand, if a mediator is not known to have specific expertise, he or she often does not get on the short lists of important referral agencies. Another drawback to being a generalist is that the client group is less obvious. Specialists, on the other hand, know who their potential clients are, however few in number they may be.

New mediators should consider and clarify for themselves what areas of practice they may be suited for, by reason of aptitude, experience, personal preference, and professional credibility. In some areas, it is difficult, if not impossible, to be selected as a mediator without professional experience and credibility in the area. For example, without experience and some technical knowledge of engineering and construction, a person will not be selected as a mediator of a construction dispute—and, without the "language," should not want to take on that role in any event.

Substantial demand for lawyer mediators seems assured with mandatory mediation programs in the legal system. Increasing development of mediation programs in public and private institutions also has created, and will continue to create, opportunities for mediators hoping to work full time. For the first time we can remember, job postings for mediators appear on a regular basis.

Mandatory mediation has certainly created a steady need for mediation services, yet voluntary programs, such as those located within institutions and found in communities, have not seen the same growth in demand. The diversification of areas of practice and the multiplication of programs have resulted in a dramatic increase in the supply of mediators—and supply considerably outpaces demand. Organizational conflict management programs are being contacted by supervisors and employees; however, the most frequent service request is for advice and assistance, so that the company and the parties can handle the conflict on their own. Most of these programs comply, believing that, ultimately, getting people to manage conflict on their own is the greater goal of the field of mediation.

Informal discussions with colleagues who coordinate programs in workplaces, both public and private, reveal that mediation requests remain lower than requests for other services. Speculation about why this is the case leads us to conclude that people are, by and large, uncomfortable with conflict and that mediation is still not a familiar process. Many employees overtly ask if they can have a facilitated discussion with the other party, instead of a mediation. Varying levels of support from senior administrators also has an impact on the use of mediation. For example, if directors would not use mediation, how can they expect their staff to do so?

What Else Do Mediators Do?

Due to the shortage of mediation work and to the fact that mediation is stressful work, finding other paid activities, or at least changing the terrain of one's work, can be both lucrative and restorative. Some of these activities include facilitation, organizational conflict analysis and system design, conflict resolution and mediation training, guest lectures, fact finding, case assessment, coaching and mentoring, convening of difficult meetings, and providing neutral-party drafting of dispute resolution clauses. This list is not exhaustive. Applying conflict resolution and mediation training in creative and innovative ways is one of the challenges for new mediators.

Perhaps the most common activity is providing mediation and conflict management training. There is a demand for training in conflict resolution. As well, developing mediation skills, with their emphasis on interest-based analysis, deep listening and questioning, and opening up different interpretations of events, helps build people's communication skills—so they can manage conflict more constructively. People, however, are usually reluctant to pay significant amounts of money to develop life skills; most students of mediation are interested in using these skills in a professional way.

How Much Do Mediators Charge?

Pricing is an issue that new mediators must grapple with. If you charge too little, you may send the message that you are not as "good" as the rest. If you charge too much, you place yourself in a highly competitive market with others who, no doubt, have more experience and a more solid reputation, thus lessening your chances of obtaining work. To find the right balance, you need to be businesslike and pragmatic, as well as fair and honest. In some areas of practice, fee levels are hard to change. This is especially true for mediators who do business with governments.

In Canada, and elsewhere, the range of fees for practising mediators is quite broad. Picard's study (2000) found that the average fee for mediators in private practice was $130 per hour, with the range of fees varying from $20 to $300 per hour. A study of family mediators (Kruk, 1998) showed similar pricing scales. Not surprisingly, those who mediate in business and those with legal backgrounds charge more than mediators with social science backgrounds, "almost half of whom charge less than $100 to mediate" (Picard, 2000, p. 119)—and they also charge higher training fees, which range from $100 to $2,500 per day. The average training fee in this study was $1,000 per day, while the more commonly charged daily fee was $500. Given what we know about employment patterns in the general work force, it should not be surprising to learn that women usually charge less than men both to mediate and to train mediators. You know you are charging too little when your clients do not question your fees or, better still, when they say you should charge more. If you are charging too much, your potential client might hire someone else.

How Do Mediators Market Their Services?

Most mediators make use of the common vehicles for marketing—the Yellow Pages, brochures, business cards, flyers, information packages, and so on. Some mediators go to the additional expense of general and directed mailouts, advertising in community newspapers, or even radio or television advertising. Creating an effective, informative, and user-friendly Web site can be an excellent marketing tool and very helpful to potential clients.

For most mediators, an important marketing strategy is to identify potential referral sources. These might include law firms, insurance companies, businesses, social service agencies, human resource departments, accounting firms, not-for-profit and government agencies, neighbourhood centres, doctors' offices, and other places mediation services and expertise would be of benefit. It is useful to leave information packets, brochures, and business cards at these places.

Other ways to become known are to speak at professional business luncheons or meetings. Join service organizations such as the chamber of commerce, or volunteer at local charities or community groups. Become known in the community. Offer to give workshops at conferences or lectures at colleges or universities. Write articles for journals or professional association newsletters.

Professional mediation association rosters are perhaps one of the most effective, direct, and least costly forms of advertising as a mediator, as well as an efficient means of finding a mediator. Associations such as ACR, FMC, ADR Canada, the Network, and the Canadian Bar Association, among others, have lists of mediators that they provide to individuals and groups looking to hire a mediator. Many post the list of names on their Web sites and in their publications. The basic criteria for inclusion on these lists varies from group to group. Some charge a fee, others do not. Those people looking to hire a mediator should note that few, if any, of these groups evaluate the performance of the individuals on their lists. In addition to professional association lists, there are rosters that support the government's use of mediators for mandatory mediations. For example, British Columbia has the BC Mediation Roster Society; in Ontario, local mediation committees retain rosters of mediators for use in the Ministry of the Attorney General's mandatory mediation programs.

Some new mediators find it useful to identify the groups they belong to or with whom they are familiar and known, and then target clients whose background, interests, and work milieu are similar. For example, a former teacher might think of people in the education field as potential clientele, including teachers, parents, students, administrators, teachers' associations, boards of education, and so on. Someone actively involved in sports might consider different sports in their local area. They may direct their marketing efforts to teams, coaching and referee associations, those who host sporting events, and other sporting organizations and enthusiasts. These groups may recognize the person's name and expertise, perhaps not as a mediator, but as someone who would have substantive knowledge and understanding of the contextual area in which the conflict is taking place.

Marketing Exercise

For would-be mediators, brainstorm a list of all the groups you and other members of your family belong to. To get you started, think about your church groups, homeowners associations, your children's day care, sports, Cubs or Brownies or other groups they belong to, recreation groups, and professional groups. Once you have your list created, ask members of your family or friends if they can think of any others. Prioritize the list based on which groups might have the most need for your services. Add a contact name, address, and phone number to your list, and decide the best approach for contacting them—in person, by telephone, or by mail.

How Do Mediators Network?

Getting connected in the field after completing one's mediation training is very important. One of the best ways to network is to join one or more professional associations. Most associations are open to anyone who applies and pays the membership fee. Some associations have membership categories that require the member to meet certain criteria.

Many professional associations have local chapters where mediators can attend meetings, periodic training sessions, and guest lectures or events, which allow them to interact with other mediators and keep abreast of new developments in the field. Many of these associations also produce newsletters, hold conferences, have lending libraries and bookstores, and offer training programs to educate and inform members about current issues, practice, research, and theory advancements. Web sites have become the least costly and most efficient way to find out about mediation events and to locate mediators practising in your area. Web sites are a valuable resource to both the new and experienced mediator. At the end of this chapter we list some of them. The list is not comprehensive by any means, so we encourage you to use your Internet skills to find more.

What Professional Associations Can Mediators Join?

New mediators should consider the association most connected to their area of practice. For example, if they want to practise as a family mediator, they might consider Family Mediation Canada. If they are interested in commercial mediation, they might consider joining ADR Canada. To enhance networking opportunities, we suggest joining an association in the province or country in which they reside. In Canada, one of the most diverse membership associations is the Network for Conflict Resolution Canada. We suggest joining an association that provides information about what is happening in other parts of the world and in other dispute resolution contexts. The Association for Conflict Resolution (ACR), which we belong to, meets these criteria.

Another consideration is cost. Some professional associations are expensive to join. Many have very reasonable rates for students. This information is generally listed on the association's Web site.

How Do Mediators Select Which Conferences To Attend?

Consider first what you want to gain from attending. Are you interested in practice-related topics, or is research and academic developments? What do you want to learn more about? ACR and FMC hold annual conferences; the Network holds a conference every two years. The Canadian Bar Association's Alternative Dispute Resolution Section, the Association for Family and Conciliation Courts, the National Conference on Peacemaking and Conflict Resolution, the National Association for Community Mediation, and Victim Offender Mediation are other organizations that hold annual conferences.

Mediators should also contribute to the field, and one way to do this is to submit a proposal to speak at conferences about your work and experiences. Many conferences have beginner, intermediate, and advanced tracks for attendees to follow. Some, such as ACR, offer youth tracks. Not only do senior practitioners have information to offer to conference attendees; new mediators do as well. They can talk about what it is like to be new to the field, the lessons they are learning, the problems they face, and the resources they have found.

BECOMING A HOLISTIC MEDIATOR

In 1938, the American racehorse Seabiscuit became a huge athletic and popular success story, one that has now been told in Laura Hillenbrand's book *Seabiscuit: An American Legend* (2001), as well as in the movie *Seabiscuit*. As Hillenbrand said, Seabiscuit's "body, built low to the ground, had all the properties of a cinder block. … He was blunt, coarse, rectangular, stationary. … His stubby legs were a study in unsound construction, with squarish, asymmetrical 'baseball glove' knees that didn't quite straighten all the way, leaving him in a permanent semicrouch. Thanks to his unfortunate assembly, his walk was an odd, straddle-legged motion that was often mistaken for lameness. Asked to run, he would drop low over the track and fall into a comical version of what horsemen call an eggbeater gait, making a spastic sideways flailing motion with his left foreleg as he swung it forward, as if he were swatting at flies. … One observer compared his action to a duck waddle" (2001, pp. 33–34).

In the book's preface, Hillenbrand described the four central characters of this story as follows:

> The horse, a smallish, mud-coloured animal with forelegs that didn't straighten all the way, spent nearly two seasons floundering in the lowest ranks of racing, misunderstood and mishandled. His jockey, Red Pollard, was a tragic-faced young man who had been abandoned as a boy at a makeshift racetrack cut through a Montana hay field. He came to his partnership with Seabiscuit after years as a part-time prizefighter and failing jockey, lugging his saddle through myriad places, getting punched bloody in cow-town boxing rings, sleeping on stall floors. Seabiscuit's trainer, a mysterious, virtually mute mustang breaker named Tom Smith, was a refugee from the vanishing frontier, bearing with him generations of lost wisdom about the secrets of horses. Seabiscuit's owner, a broad, beaming former cavalryman named Charles Howard, had begun his career as a bicycle mechanic before parlaying 21 cents into an automotive empire. (2001, p. xvii)

One of the amazing things about Seabiscuit's story is that, in 1936, when everyone else figured him for a dud, horseman Tom Smith saw the greatness that burned within the heart and soul of this horse. How did Smith know that? As his trainer, how did Smith connect with Seabiscuit in a way that ultimately led to such outstanding success? What about the other characters in the story? Wealthy California industrialist Charles Howard knew people. He had faith in Tom Smith and jockey Red Pollard and without his faith and financing it would never have happened. Finally, jockey Red Pollard, the other half of this high-performing team, came back after an accident that smashed and crippled his body to be a vital partner in the ultimate success.

As mediators or conflict practitioners or trainers or conflict management developers, there is something for us to learn in the Seabiscuit story. Seabiscuit had "it" and Tom Smith knew it.

We believe there is an indefinable "it" that people need to mediate conflict at a deep and powerful level. In our experience, some people have what it takes to become a skilled holistic mediator, at least at the practitioner level (Lang & Taylor, 2000), and some people do not. Helping students to discover and develop their talents and overcome difficulties and limitations is only part of the responsibility of mediation educators and trainers. They also need to be frank about a student's limitations and their potential for competence. Sometimes the evidence seems clear, especially in cases of exceptional talent and obvious aptitude. In any field of endeavour, the great ones—Gretzky and Mozart—are easy to spot.

However, many people's talent is wrapped in inhibitions, doubts, fears, and confusion, and that takes time and experience to unpack. Becoming a mediator requires the art and science of discernment—of people discerning their own as well as others' talents, as well as the path to take to realize them.

What Does It Take?

Do I have it? Does he or she have it? Experienced mediators who assess would-be mediators should be honest and forthright. Encouraging or inviting someone down a vocational path on which they will experience frustration and failure does no one a service.

Remember, however, that any assessment is always done within a particular cultural paradigm. Determining whether a mediator's aptitude is good or bad will not always yield the same results from different viewpoints. Within our own "system of meaning" (LeBaron, 1997, p. 318), we can have *some* degree of confidence in both our own and others' assessments. Outside our system, the criteria—and perceptions—change.

It is generally agreed that performance-based standards are more useful than knowledge-based standards when assessing an individual's ability to mediate. Standards of practice, however, vary from context to context, and different mediation programs use different assessment tools. Because there is no common set of guidelines, mediators rely on self-assessment tools to refine their skills.

Self-assessment helps mediators, experientially and personally, answer two important questions: (1) What makes a good mediation? and (2) What makes mediation successful? Asking these and other relevant questions, thinking about the answers, and discussing them with others "provides mediators with the opportunity to clarify their intentions, to reflect on their choices of intervention, and to become aware of the consequences of their interventions" (Bronson, 2000, p. 173). Through self-assessment, mediators gain a deeper understanding of the mediation process and they advance their skills. We believe it needs to become standard practice for all mediators.

To guide the process of self-reflection, we direct you to the "Self-Assessment Tool for Mediators" developed by the Wisconsin Association of Mediators. (See the listing at the end of this chapter.) This assessment tool assists mediators who want to explore and integrate their skills, knowledge, self-awareness, and ethical behaviour to better serve participants. It lists five common elements of mediation: (1) knowing the process,

(2) managing the process, (3) analytical skills, (4) empathetic skills, and (5) building agreements.

What are some essential attributes of a good mediator? Our list includes being empathetic, non-judgmental, tolerant, fair-minded, flexible, creative, patient yet persistent, and optimistic, and having a healthy sense of humour. Maggiolo (1971) presents an interesting list of characteristics that mediators need:

- the patience of Job;
- the sincerity and bulldog characteristics of the English and the wit of the Irish;
- the physical endurance of a marathon runner;
- the broken-field dodging abilities of a halfback;
- the guile of Machiavelli;
- the personality-probing skills of a good psychiatrist;
- the confidence-retaining characteristics of a mute;
- the hide of a rhinoceros;
- the wisdom of Solomon;
- demonstrated integrity and impartiality;
- fundamental beliefs in human values and potential, tempered by the ability to assess personal weaknesses as well as strengths;
- the hard-nosed ability to analyze what is available in contrast to what might be desirable; and
- sufficient personal drive and ego, qualified by a willingness to be self-effacing.

What Is Reflective Practice?

Reflective practice is what moves mediators from mediocrity to artistry (Lang & Taylor, 2000). It is how mediators acquire confidence and competence, enabling them to be creative, flexible, and to think "outside the box," rather than mimic a prescribed set of actions within a particular framework. Becoming a competent mediator requires commitment and openness to learning from mistakes. It requires mediators to review their performances, with the aim of improving their ability to better serve those who call on them for help. They assess their actions and strategies, then enter into discussions with others about how they can enhance their performance.

Lang and Taylor (2000, p. 47) say that being reflective is essential to achieving competence and artistry. They say that

> the ability to learn from each experience; to refine, adjust and enhance one's skills; and to respond thoughtfully to the unique and surprising events in professional practice can be achieved through the consistent, thoughtful and intentional application of the methods and principles of reflective practice.

Lang and Taylor (2000, p. 123) list six characteristics of reflective practitioners.

1. engaging in a continual process of self-reflection;
2. relying on theory to guide and inform their practice;
3. using experimentation to test observations, perceptions and formulations of the experience, beliefs, and needs of their clients;
4. willing to see perspectives other than their own, to experience surprise;
5. being open to new information about their practices—as lifelong learners, they are open to new strategies and techniques; and
6. not seeing themselves as experts—acknowledging that both they and their clients have expertise to bring to bear on the conflict situation.

The concept of "reflecting in action" comes from the work of Schon (1987). It means that the mediator is able to carry on an internal conversation about the unexpected. Reflecting in action is based on the premise that professionals usually know more than they say about their actions, more than the theory they are using. In other words, intelligent practice in more than an application of knowledge—"know-how is *in* the action" (1987, p. 50). While we may think before acting, much of the spontaneous behaviour of a skillful practitioner comes from somewhere other than prior knowledge. Taking the time to reflect upon our actions can lead us to examine the tacit norms underlying a judgment, the theories implicit in patterns of behaviour, the feelings linked to courses of action, the roles being played out, and the contextual framing of a problem, to name some reflection-in-action objects.

What Does It Mean To Be an Advanced Practitioner?

To separate the novice, apprentice, and practitioner, Lang and Taylor (2000, p. 12) use the concept of developing artistry. Picard (2002, pp. 140–141) also says that being a skilled mediator involves the integration of skills, knowledge, and self-reflection. She sets out five hallmarks of advanced practitioners.

1. Knowledge and skills—as well as assessment, timing, intuition, empathy, judgment risk, patience, confidence, and the ability to assume the many roles of a mediator.
2. Critical mind—which means that they are able to distinguish their orientation from other mediation approaches; reflect on how a mediation could have been improved; assess the possible good and harm that can come out of a mediation; know when it is time to consult or bring in the experts; and know when it is time to terminate a mediation.
3. Flexible, creative, and inquisitive—which means that they are willing to change their style of mediating to accommodate parties needs and abilities; they use humour, metaphor, drama, drawing, language, sculpting, and other creative tools to help parties present their points of view, understand each other, and continue negotiating; and they stay curious and non-judgmental.
4. Reflective—which means that they recognize personal limits, biases, values, and world views; that they are in touch with and can manage their own emotions; and that they can "think outside the box."
5. Lifelong learner—which means they are familiar with developments in theory and research; they read books, academic journals, and professional newsletters; they frequently attend professional conferences, workshops, and courses; they are members of professional associations, and they network with other professionals in the field.

How Do Mediators Develop Themselves and the Field?

One of the most powerful ways for an individual to advance their skills is to observe themselves mediating. A simulated mediation can be videotaped. As part of the debriefing, it would be important to discuss the mediation with the role players, stopping at various points to get their reactions to the interventions. It would also be useful to identify the mediator's strengths and weakness and, if possible, compare them with other assessments. Less experienced mediators could learn much by asking a more senior mediator to debrief a video with them.

Another suggestion for advancing skills and giving back to the field is to volunteer to coach new mediators. Some communities have organized coaching groups for ongoing skill development. Volunteer to participate as a role player in practice sessions.

Achieving artistry as a mediator requires lifelong learning. It requires experience, reflection, and a continuous stream of new knowledge and insights.

To close this discussion on mediator development, we share some of our hopes. We hope that all experienced and would-be mediators alike will approach their practices with open, yet critical, minds. We hope they will be mindful in their work by drawing upon both theory and practice, and we hope they will obtain sufficient knowledge and confidence to be transparent, strategic, and intentional. Finally, we hope they will achieve artistry through competence, creativity, intuition, and resourcefulness.

INTO THE FUTURE

What does the future hold for mediation? To what extent will the "promise of mediation," which Bush and Folger (1994) held up for us 10 years ago, be achieved in our lifetime or our children's lifetime? Is Bush and Folger's vision of human progress and transformation a legitimate hope worth striving for or a pipe dream? This last question was also raised by Deborah Kolb (1994), in her book *When Talk Works: Profiles of Mediators*, as she talked about the "myth of mediation," in effect questioning whether some of mediation's ideals are achievable in the "real world."

Students in mediation programs learn that mediation is a much better way to deal with conflict and disputes than traditional methods. Yet, when they go into practice, they find that the opportunities for paid work are not all that abundant. This creates a perplexing and discouraging question: if mediation is truly a better way, why is there not a higher demand for it? As Kolb (1994) suggests, is the promise of mediation a myth that has led many down a garden path?

We are more optimistic. One reason the demand for mediation services has not developed quickly is economics. Who should pay for these services? In community-based mediation, some people expect the government to make these options available. In some jurisdictions it has, but almost always on a pilot basis, which results in a lack of ongoing core funding. Growth and development of programs and services is proportional to consumer knowledge and confidence in mediation. To the extent that individual clients and organizational leaders and managers see mediation primarily as a means of settling disputes quickly and at low cost, that is what they will expect and demand. To the extent that short-term, bottom-line thinking shapes this demand, there will be limited opportunity for realizing greater economic and social benefits that collaborative processes can provide.

Another reason for the slow growth of mediation is the politics of organizations, professions, institutions, and governments. In this context, "politics" is about status, power, and influence. This is a complex subject, beyond the scope of this book, but one point to consider is that people in positions of influence often fear that new approaches will undermine existing corporate, legal, or social structures, or take away resources. We encourage those in positions of influence to "think outside the box." To encourage political and corporate leaders to become integrative thinkers, mediation practitioners must themselves apply and model holistic mediation principles to the very issues and people who control the development of the field and the profession. All of us must "walk the talk"; the future expansion of mediation depends on it.

The resistance to, or lack of support for, mediation programs is particularly prevalent in the volunteer and non-profit sectors devoted to community-based and restorative justice conflict resolution programming. Sustainable levels of support will come only when these programs can be shown to produce long-term social and economic benefits. To demonstrate this, sufficient resources to evaluate the long-term relational benefits, rather than individualistic ones linked to short-term costs, need to be provided.

Equally important is the ongoing need to develop ways for determining which approach—among the many described in this book—is appropriate. As the art and science of mediation approaches continue to evolve, we envisage an increasing ability to achieve a blending of methods. In this way, the interests of diverse social groups and political perspectives may be served, reducing fears of being "soft" on crime, and increasing acceptance and support for restorative methods.

Collaboration is a means for creating value, real economic and social value, in all kinds of situations in which traditional adversarial methods tend to stifle it. Yet, though we know that traditional dispute resolution methods often produce unsatisfactory outcomes at high cost, the "promise" of mediation is not enough to shift economic or political decisions. It remains an "intangible creature." Like beautiful music or great food, it cannot be fully appreciated by reading or talking about it. It is only through the actual experience of a successful mediation that one comes to genuinely appreciate the value of the mediation approaches talked about in this book. As well, for most mediators, it takes much practice over a long time to achieve a high level of mediation competence or mastery. Hence, it is likely to take years for the relational and transformational value of mediation to be generally recognized in the marketplace.

Today and in the future, the field of mediation needs to continue developing a spectrum of methods—and practitioners who know when and how to use these methods effectively. This is essential to the profession's strength and vitality and its ongoing ability to contribute to peaceful and collaborative conflict resolution.

SUMMARY

In this chapter, we looked at some of the current issues and challenges facing the field of mediation, along with how we envision its future. Some of you may be left wondering about our use of the term "profession" of mediation. How can mediation be a profession when there is no consensus on how to define it? The goals, principles, methods, and values of mediation defy scientific determination and we think of the profession of mediation in a more artistic or metaphoric sense. We have argued that the field of mediation is healthier because of the diverse and conflicting views on these fundamental points, and that attempts to standardize the field are likely to be counterproductive. Indeed, our hope is that mediators and peacemakers around the world reflect a diverse community of individuals committed to dealing with human conflict at all levels in a healthy, life-enhancing way.

Despite the difficulty in mastering the diversity of this field, we wholeheartedly believe that mediators as dispute resolution intervenors offer advantages distinct from any other processes. Some of the advantages of using mediation are methodological, while others are philosophical. Because we see ourselves as interconnected actors, a process such as mediation can reconnect us to one another, making the whole greater than the sum of its parts. Our connectedness enables us to create value where we might not have seen it as an individual. It encourages creativity and "thinking outside the box." We also learn and grow through relationships, particularly those that are not so easy to maintain. Mediation provides the opportunity for us to become better people through more profound and meaningful relationships with others.

Training and learning about mediation also offer great benefits. Students frequently tell us that they have been transformed through their education in mediation. They begin to see the world and their place in it in a very different light. People are no longer bystanders to conflict, nor do they see themselves as objects to which conflict happens; rather, they become confident actors who can work toward meaningful social change, person by person or institution by institution.

We believe that it is this potential of mediation that has led to its immense growth and diversification. In addition to mediation processes in workplaces, family and neighbourhood conflicts, public policy and planning, commercial disputes, and criminal justice applications, we anticipate that mediation, as its value becomes more commonly known, will be applied in an even wider range of contexts. Despite the current push to professionalize mediators, we see a future of even more diverse practices. Research and theory will need to soon catch up to all this activity. We will need to monitor and evaluate our mediation systems, processes, and interventions in a more systematic way to ensure that the roots of our practice remain embedded in social justice ideals.

We encourage you to explore the field further—whether that be through additional reading, training, or the use of mediation in your next dispute. We look forward to the new insights you will bring to mediation and we wish you a long and fruitful journey.

FURTHER READING

Boulle, L., & Kelly, K. (1998). *Mediation: Principles, process, practice.* Toronto: Butterworths.

Katsh, E., & Rifkin, J. (2001). *Online dispute resolution: Resolving conflicts in cyberspace*. San Francisco: Jossey-Bass.

Lang, M., & Taylor, A. (2000). *The making of a mediator*. San Francisco: Jossey-Bass.

Noble, C., Dizgun, L., & Emond, P. (1998). *Mediation advocacy: Effective client representation in mediation proceedings*. Toronto: Emond Montgomery.

WEB SITES

Information Resources

Campus Mediation Resources: http://www.mtds.wayne.edu/campus.htm

Conflict Resolution Network Canada: http://www.crnetwork.ca/

Educators for Social Responsibility: http://www.esrnational.org/

Mediation and Information Resource Centre: http://www.onlinemediators.com/

Marketing Monday: http://www.golden-media.com/

Department of National Defence/Canadian Forces' Conflict Management Program: http://www.forces.gc.ca/

Indian Residential Schools Resolution Canada: http://www.irsr-rqpi.gc.ca/

Treasury Board (for information on Bill C-25, the *Public Service Modernization Act*, 2003): http://www.tbs-sct.gc.ca/mhrm-mgrh/index_e.asp

Professional Associations

Association for Conflict Resolution: http://www.acresolution.org/

Association for Family and Conciliation Courts (AFCC): http://www.afccnet.org/

ADR Institute of Canada: http://www.adrcanada.ca/

Family Mediation Canada: http://www.fmc.ca/

National Association for Community Mediation: http://www.nafcm.org/

National Conference on Peacemaking and Conflict Resolution: http://www.apeacemaker.net/

Victim Offender Mediation Association: http://www.voma.org/

Wisconsin Association of Mediators: http://www.wamediators.org/

Educational Institutions

Carleton University: http://www.carleton.ca/law/conflict/

Conrad Grebel Peace and Conflict Studies: http://www.grebel.uwaterloo.ca/pacs/

Justice Institute of BC: http://www.jibc.bc.ca/

Menno Simons: http://www.uwinnipeg.ca/~msc/

Royal Roads: http://www.royalroads.ca/

Osgoode Hall Law School: http://www.law.yorku.ca/pdp/

University of Victoria: http://www.uvcs.uvic.ca/

University of British Columbia: http://www.mediator-roster.bc.ca/

APPENDIX A

Consent To Mediate

This *Consent To Mediate* is being made between the mediator, `Cheryl Picard`, and each of the parties involved in the conflict situation, `Chris Somerville` and `Dale Rochon`.

The signing of this consent form between the parties and the mediator expresses the intent of the parties to make a serious attempt to the resolve the dispute between them, and describes the process that the parties and mediator will follow.

As mediator:

1. I will act as an impartial facilitator. My role is to assist each of you to discuss the issues in disagreement so that you may gain insight into the needs and concerns that underlie these issues, and so that you may be able to resolve these issues in a manner that is satisfactory to both of you.
2. I will not make decisions nor impose my views.
3. I may decide to meet privately with each of you, to improve the chances of resolution. It is understood that you may request to caucus with me at any time.
4. I agree to keep all information shared during the mediation process confidential except in accordance with the law, or, for research or educational purposes on an anonymous basis.

As parties in this dispute,

1. We agree to engage in open, honest communication and share all relevant information.
2. We come with authority to reach an agreement or will have a rapid means of obtaining the requisite authorization.
3. During the course of the mediation, we agree to take no new steps in any legal action concerning the same issues of this mediation.

4. If we wish to terminate the mediation before its completion, we agree to make this known in sufficient time that it can be discussed before leaving.
5. We agree not to call you as a witness in any subsequent legal or administrative proceedings, compel you to produce any notes or records from the mediation, or sue you personally.

If, as mediator, I determine that it is not possible to resolve the issues through mediation, I may suggest the process be terminated and discuss with you the reasons why. In the event that decisions are reached as to how to resolve this conflict situation, and if you would like, this information can be written in a *Memorandum of Understanding*, with copies made available to each of you.

The mediation will be held at `Carleton University, Room D490, Loeb Building`, on `May 31, 2004`, beginning at `9:00 a.m.`, and going until `1:00 p.m.` It is understood that additional mediation sessions may be required to resolve this dispute and that the decision to engage in further sessions will be discussed and agreed to before closing the process.

I, ___Cheryl Picard___, consent to act as mediator in accordance with the foregoing agreement.

We, ___Chris Somerville___ and ___Dale Rochon___ have read, understood, and agree to the above terms of mediation.

APPENDIX B

Memorandum of Understanding (MOU)

Having successfully concluded a mediation of the issues between them, Chris Somerville and Dale Rochon agree as follows:

1. Dale will pay Chris $500.00 in five (5) monthly installments of $100.00 each starting June 1 and ending October 1, 2004, in full satisfaction of Invoice No. 5400819 dated May 3, 2004. This amount represents the actual costs of all parts replaced and one-half of the labour costs previously billed.
2. Chris will return Dale's automobile (1998 Chev) to her upon receipt of the first installment cheque. Chris confirms that the car is in good running order and that there is a 30-day warranty on all parts and repair work as described in the original invoice.
3. To encourage further patronage and show appreciation, Chris will give Dale a 25 percent discount (to a maximum of $100.00) on her next automobile service invoice at Chris's shop.
4. Dale recognizes that Chris is a conscientious mechanic who makes every effort to provide good value for the fees he charges. When the opportunity arises, Dale will readily recommend Chris and his automobile service centre to others.
5. Both parties acknowledge and agree that
   a. they fully understand the terms of this MOU,
   b. all terms are reasonable,
   c. they sign this MOU freely and without duress,
   d. they fully intend to abide by the points listed above, and
   e. in the event that either party is not satisfied with the completion of these terms, he or she agrees first to talk with the other party about their dissatisfaction, and if it cannot be resolved between them, they will return to mediation before any other recourse is taken.

Dale Rochon — *Chris Somerville*

Dale Rochon — Chris Somerville

Dated: May 31, 2004

APPENDIX C

Standards of Practice

FAMILY MEDIATION CANADA GUIDELINES FOR FMC FAMILY MEDIATORS

Family Mediation Canada is an interdisciplinary association of lawyers, social workers, human services, and health care professionals, working together to create a better way to provide cooperative conflict resolution relating in a range of family issues. FMC's practice guidelines and certification process was approved in 1996. Detailed information on these standards, steps in the certification process, and an application form are available on its Web site (http://www.fmc.ca/).

Family mediators generally deal with conflicts about pre-nuptial issues, the reorganization of the family after separation and divorce, the particulars of future parenting plans for children (including custody, access, and guardianship issues), financial support, property matters connected to separation or divorce, child protection matters, family business matters, and disputes within intact families about issues involving the division of responsibility for the care of elderly parents, parental conflict with or about children, family finances, estate matters, adoption, and educational matters. A family mediator is defined as an impartial third party who possesses expertise in non-adversarial conflict and dispute resolution processes and techniques. This professional assists in the management, control, and resolution of interpersonal conflicts. The following information is from FMC's standards of practice guide, available online at http://www.fmc.ca/pdf/standardsweb2003.pdf.

> Family mediators shall work with the participants to establish and maintain a mediation process that will:

1. Be client centered;
2. Facilitate the participants' involvement in the mediation while taking into consideration their respective:
   a) Abilities to negotiate … ;
   b) Abilities to make decisions in accordance with their own individual interests … ;
   c) Power to influence family decision-making;
   d) Psychological, emotional and economic states;
   e) Access to and understanding of relevant information; and
   f) Access to appropriate support services such as independent legal advice.
3. Ensure that the participants have adequate time to fully discuss, consider and resolve their disputes and conflicts;
4. [Ensure that families with histories of abuse or unmanageable power imbalances are assessed for appropriateness of mediation and are referred to other services if necessary];
5. Ensure that culturally appropriate forms of dispute resolution are included;
6. Ensure that the interests of all persons in the dispute or conflict are considered;
7. Ensure confidentiality of the process is discussed and maintained except when:
   a) the mediator suspects that a child is in need of protection; …
   c) the mediator determines that there is a need to inform a potential victim and the police about an imminent danger;
   d) there is a mutual agreement that the information may be released, as in an open mediation;
   e) the mediator must breach confidentiality in order to comply with a duty to disclose the whereabouts of a child in cases of abduction; …
8. Use language that is meaningful and appropriate to the participants;
9. Be fair to all participants;
10. Ensure that the special interests of children are recognized and considered by parents when they are making decisions about their children;
11. Assist participants to resolve family problems in a way that respects each family's interests, values, and rights to self-determination, while also respecting the interests and rights of others who may be affected;
12. Be sensitive to the participants' cultural perceptions, needs and understandings of fairness; …
16. Ensure that agreements reached in mediation reflect the range of options considered acceptable in law and if the participants wish to enter an agreement falling outside that acceptable in law, strongly

encourage the participants to obtain independent legal advice and reflect for a period of time before concluding any agreement; and

17. Attempt to ensure that no one suffers physical or emotional abuse as a result of participating in mediation.

ASSOCIATION FOR CONFLICT RESOLUTION (ACR) STANDARDS

ARC is a professional organization dedicated to enhancing the practice and public understanding of conflict resolution. Its mission is to promote peaceful effective conflict resolution. ACR represents and serves a diverse national and international audience that includes more than 7,000 mediators, arbitrators, facilitators, educators, and others involved in the field of conflict resolution and collaborative decision making. It hosts an annual conference, publishes a newsletter, and has chapter organizations and sector groups of special areas of interest.

The following standards were adopted by the Society for Professionals in Dispute Resolution (SPIDR) in 1986, and are currently being reviewed by the ACR Standards Committee. They are used to guide all non-family and divorce mediations. They are available online at http://www.acrnet.org/about/committees/ethics.htm.

General Responsibilities

Neutrals have a duty to the parties, to the professions, and to themselves. They should be honest and unbiased, act in good faith, be diligent, and not seek to advance their own interests at the expense of their parties'.

Neutrals must act fairly in dealing with the parties, have no personal interest in the terms of the settlement, show no bias towards individuals and institutions involved in the dispute, be reasonably available as requested by the parties, and be certain that the parties are informed of the process in which they are involved.

Responsibilities to the Parties

1. **Impartiality.** The neutral must maintain impartiality toward all parties. Impartiality means freedom from favoritism or bias either by word or by action, and a commitment to serve all parties as opposed to a single party.
2. **Informed Consent.** The neutral has an obligation to assure that all parties understand the nature of the process, the procedures, the particular role of the neutral, and the parties' relationship to the neutral.

3. **Confidentiality.** Maintaining confidentiality is critical to the dispute resolution process. Confidentiality encourages candor, a full exploration of the issues, and a neutral's acceptability. There may be some types of cases, however, in which confidentiality is not protected. In such cases, the neutral must advise the parties, when appropriate in the dispute resolution process, that the confidentiality of the proceedings cannot necessarily be maintained. Except in such instances, the neutral must resist all attempts to cause him or her to reveal any information outside the process. A commitment by the neutral to hold information in confidence within the process also must be honored.
4. **Conflict of Interest.** The neutral must refrain from entering or continuing in any dispute if he or she believes or perceives that participation as a neutral would be a clear conflict of interest and any circumstances that may reasonably raise a question as to the neutral's impartiality. The duty to disclose is a continuing obligation throughout the process.
5. **Promptness.** The neutral shall exert every reasonable effort to expedite the process.
6. **The Settlement and Its Consequences.** The dispute resolution process belongs to the parties. The neutral has no vested interest in the terms of a settlement, but must be satisfied that agreements in which he or she has participated will not impugn the integrity of the process. The neutral has a responsibility to see that the parties consider the terms of a settlement. If the neutral is concerned about the possible consequences of a proposed agreement, and the needs of the parties dictate, the neutral must inform the parties of that concern. In adhering to this standard, the neutral may find it advisable to educate the parties, to refer one or more parties for specialized advice, or to withdraw from the case. In no case, however, shall the neutral violate section 3, Confidentiality, of these standards.

Unrepresented Interests

The neutral must consider circumstances where interests are not represented in the process. The neutral has an obligation, where in his or her judgement the needs of parties dictate, to assure that such interests have been considered by the principal parties.

Use of Multiple Procedures

The use of more than one dispute resolution procedure by the same neutral involves additional responsibilities. Where the use of more than one procedure is initially contemplated, the neutral must take care at the outset to advise the parties of the nature of the procedures and the consequences of revealing information during any one procedure which the neutral may later use for decision making or share with another decision maker. Where the use of more than one procedure is contemplated after the initiation of the dispute resolution process, the neutral must explain the consequences and afford the parties an opportunity to select another neutral for the subsequent procedures. It is also incumbent upon the neutral to advise the parties of the transition from one dispute resolution process to another.

Background and Qualifications

A neutral should accept responsibility only in cases where the neutral has sufficient knowledge regarding the appropriate process and subject matter to be effective. A neutral has a responsibility to maintain and improve his or her professional skills.

Disclosure of Fees

It is the duty of the neutral to explain to the parties at the outset of the process the basis of compensation, fees, and charges, if any.

Support of the Profession

The experienced neutral should participate in the development of new practitioners in the field and engage in efforts to educate the public about the value and use of neutral dispute resolution procedures. The neutral should provide pro bono services, where appropriate.

Responsibilities of Neutrals Working on the Same Case

In the event that more than one neutral is involved in the resolution of a dispute, each has an obligation to inform the others regarding his or her entry in the case. Neutrals working with the same parties should maintain an open and professional relationship with each other.

Advertising and Solicitation

A neutral must be aware that some forms of advertising and solicitations are inappropriate and in some conflict resolution disciplines, such as labor arbitration, are impermissible. All advertising must honestly represent the services to be rendered. No claims of specific results or promises that imply favor of one side over another for the purpose of obtaining business should be made. No commissions, rebates, or other similar forms of remuneration should be given or received by a neutral for the referral of clients.

ACR STANDARDS OF PRACTICE FOR FAMILY MEDIATORS

The following standards are available online at http://www.acrnet.org/about/committees/ethics.htm.

The Standards incorporate much of the best of the previous standards, and update them to include topics such as domestic violence and child abuse. In addition, the Standards address the issue of the best interests of the children and how mediation can help parents to address them in divorce.

The Symposium, which developed the Standards, included representatives from Academy of Family Mediators (AFM), Association of Family Courts and Community Professionals (AFCC), American Bar Association (ABA) Family Section, and other national, state and regional organizations. The Standards represent a consensus of the best suggestions made over a period of two years in which the Symposium met to develop them.

The Standards had previously been adopted by the ABA Family Section and by AFCC, as well as several state mediation organizations. The adoption of these standards by ACR rounds out the trio of major national organizations whose members are family and divorce mediators.

The General Standards

STANDARD I: A family mediator shall recognize that mediation is based on the principle of self-determination by the participants.

STANDARD II: A family mediator shall be qualified by education and training to undertake the mediation.

STANDARD III: A family mediator shall facilitate the participants' understanding of what mediation is and assess their capacity to mediate before the participants reach an agreement to mediate.

STANDARD IV: A family mediator shall conduct the mediation process in an impartial manner. A family mediator shall disclose all actual and potential grounds of bias and conflicts of interest reasonably known to the mediator. The participants shall be free to retain the mediator by an informed, written waiver of the conflict of interest. However, if a bias or conflict of interest clearly impairs a mediator's impartiality, the mediator shall withdraw regardless of the express agreement of the participants.

STANDARD V: A family mediator shall fully disclose and explain the basis of any compensation, fees and charges to the participants.

STANDARD VI: A family mediator shall structure the mediation process so that the participants make decisions based on sufficient information and knowledge.

STANDARD VII: A family mediator shall maintain the confidentiality of all information acquired in the mediation process, unless the mediator is permitted or required to reveal the information by law or agreement of the participants.

STANDARD VIII: A family mediator shall assist participants in determining how to promote the best interests of children.

STANDARD IX: A family mediator shall recognize a family situation involving child abuse or neglect and take appropriate steps to shape the mediation process accordingly.

STANDARD X: A family mediator shall recognize a family situation involving domestic abuse and take appropriate steps to shape the mediation process accordingly.

STANDARD XI: A family mediator shall suspend or terminate the mediation process when the mediator reasonably believes that a participant is unable to effectively participate or for other compelling reason.

STANDARD XII: A family mediator shall be truthful in the advertisement and solicitation for mediation.

STANDARD XIII: A family mediator shall acquire and maintain professional competence in mediation.

ACR CRITERIA FOR TRAINING PROGRAMS APPROVED BY THE ACR FAMILY SECTION

The following criteria are available online at http://www.acrnet.org/referrals/trainers.htm.

The ACR Family Section has also approved the following standards for mediation training programs. These standards state that participants should be able to demonstrate the following knowledge and skills:

1. Ability to explain what mediation is (within the dispute resolution context) and what a mediator does;
2. Awareness of theories and current research and literature underlying conflict and its resolution, and their application to family mediation;

3. Ability to contract for mediation services;
4. Ability to screen for appropriateness of mediation, including knowledge and ability to screen for domestic violence and an awareness of appropriate responses when domestic violence or its potential has been identified;
5. Ability to assist the parties in surfacing and framing the topics to be discussed in mediation;
6. * Awareness of the consequences of separation/divorce for adults and children;
7. * Ability to work with the substantive information encountered in separation/divorce mediation;
8. Ability to build a working relationship and a constructive process with the parties;
9. Ability to facilitate communication between the parties by using specific skills (e.g., active listening, reframing);
10. * Ability to facilitate problem solving between the parties, especially in the areas of divorce including, but not limited to, parenting, support, division of assets/liabilities, insurance, tax filing, etc.;
11. Knowledge of conflict management skills;
12. Understanding concepts of mediator influence and neutrality;
13. Knowledge of standards of practice and how ethical issues are resolved;
14. Ability to recognize when the assistance of other professionals might be helpful to the mediation process and to facilitate this discussion with the parties; and
15. Awareness of what additional knowledge/skills/experience/supervision may be necessary for the successful practice of mediation and how to get it.

* *For 30-hour Family Mediation Programs, substitute appropriate content area(s).*

CANADIAN BAR ASSOCIATION, ONTARIO ADR SECTION MODEL CODE OF CONDUCT FOR MEDIATORS

The following code of conduct is available online at http://www.mnr.gov.on.ca/mnr/forests/adr%20program/conduct_mediator.pdf.

I. Objective for Model Code of Conduct for Mediators

The main objectives of this Model Code of Conduct for mediators are as follows:

(a) to provide guiding principles for mediators' conduct;
(b) to provide a means of protection for the public; and

(c) to promote confidence in mediation as a process for resolving disputes.

II. Definitions

In this Model Code of Conduct:

"mediation" means a process in which an impartial person, a mediator, helps disputing parties to try to reach a voluntary, mutually acceptable resolution of some or all of the issues of their dispute.

"mediator" means an impartial person whose role in mediation is to assist and encourage parties to a dispute:

- to communicate and negotiate in good faith with each other;
- to identify and convey their interests to one another;
- to assess risks;
- to consider possible settlement options; and
- to resolve voluntarily their dispute.

"impartial" means being and being seen as unbiased toward parties to a dispute, toward their interests and toward the options they present for settlement.

"conflict of interest" means direct or indirect financial or personal interest in the outcome of the dispute or any existing or past financial, business, professional, family or social relationship which is likely to affect impartiality or reasonably create an appearance of partiality or bias.

III. Principle of Self-Determination

1. Self-determination is the right of parties in a mediation to make their own voluntary and non-coerced decisions regarding the possible resolution of any issue in dispute. It is a fundamental principle of mediation which mediators shall respect and encourage.
2. Mediators shall provide information about their role in the mediation before mediation commences, including the fact that authority for decision-making rests with the parties, not mediators.
3. Mediators shall not provide legal advice to the parties.
4. Mediators have the responsibility to advise unrepresented parties to obtain independent legal advice, where appropriate. Mediators also have the responsibility to advise parties of the need to consult other professionals to help parties make informed decisions.

IV. Impartiality

1. Mediators shall serve only in those matters in which they can remain impartial.
2. Mediators have a duty to remain impartial throughout the course of the mediation process.

3. If mediators become aware of their lack of impartiality, they shall immediately disclose to the parties that they can no longer remain impartial and shall withdraw from the mediation.

V. Conflict of Interest

1. Mediators have a responsibility to disclose to the parties in dispute any conflict of interest reasonably known to the mediator, as soon as possible.
2. Mediators who have disclosed a conflict of interest to the parties shall withdraw as mediator, unless the parties consent to retain the mediator.
3. Mediators or their associates or partners shall not establish a professional relationship with any of the parties in a matter related to the mediation which could give rise to a conflict of interest, without the consent of all parties.
4. Mediators' commitment is to the parties and the process and they shall not allow pressure or influence from third parties (persons, service providers, mediation facilities, organizations, or agencies) to compromise the independence of the mediator.

VI. Confidentiality

1. Mediators shall inform the parties of the confidential nature of mediation.
2. Mediators shall not disclose to anyone who is not a party to the mediation any information or documents that are exchanged for or during the mediation process except:
   (a) with the mediating parties' written consent;
   (b) when ordered to do so by a court or otherwise required to do so by law;
   (c) when the information/documentation discloses an actual or potential threat to human life;
   (d) any report or summary that is required to be prepared by mediators; or
   (e) when the information/documentation is non-identifiable (unless all of the parties otherwise authorize identification), and is used for research, statistical, accreditation, or educational purposes and is limited only to what is required to achieve these purposes.
3. If mediators hold private sessions (breakout meetings, caucuses) with a party, they shall discuss the nature of such sessions with all parties prior to commencing such sessions. In particular, mediators shall inform parties of any limits to confidentiality applicable to information disclosed during private sessions.

4. Mediators shall maintain confidentiality in the storage and disposal of mediation notes records and files.

VII. Quality of the Process

1. Mediators shall make reasonable efforts to ensure the parties understand the mediation process before mediation commences.
2. Mediators have a duty to ensure that they conduct a process which provides parties with the opportunity to participate in the mediation and which encourages respect among the parties.
3. Mediators shall inform parties to a dispute that mediation is most effective when the parties with full authority to settle are in attendance and when they are willing to consider options for settlement.
4. Mediators who are lawyers shall not represent any party(ies) to the mediation.
5. Mediators have an obligation to acquire and maintain professional skills and abilities required to uphold the quality of the mediation process.

VIII. Advertising

In advertising or offering services to clients or potential clients:

1. Mediators shall refrain from guaranteeing settlement or promising specific results.
2. Mediators shall provide accurate information about their education, background, mediation training and experience in any representation, biographical or promotional material and in any oral explanation of same.

IX. Fees

This section has been deleted for the purposes of the Mandatory Mediation Program and replaced by the fee regulation under the *Administration of Justice Act* and Part 3 of the MMP Code of Conduct.

X. Agreement To Mediate

Mediators shall ensure before the mediation commences that the parties understand the terms of mediation whether or not they are contained in a written agreement/contract to mediate, which terms shall include but not be limited to the following:

(a) confidentiality of communications and documents;
(b) the right of the mediator and parties to terminate or suspend mediation;
(c) fees, expenses, retainer, method of payment and what, if any, fee there is for cancellation, lateness or delay; and

(d) the fact that the mediator is not compellable as a witness in court proceedings by any parties to the mediation.

XI. Termination or Suspension of Mediation

1. Mediators shall withdraw from mediation for the reasons referred to in paragraphs IV.3 and V.2.
2. Mediators may suspend or terminate mediation if requested by one or more of the parties;
3. Mediators may suspend mediation if in their opinion:
   (a) the process is likely to prejudice one or more of the parties;
   (b) one or more of the parties is using the process inappropriately;
   (c) one or more of the parties is delaying the process to the detriment of another party or parties;
   (d) the mediation process is detrimental to one or more of the parties or the mediator;
   (e) it appears that a party is not acting in good faith; or
   (f) there are other reasons that are or appear to be counterproductive to the process.
4. Mediators shall terminate mediation if the conditions referred to in XI.3(a)-(f) are not rectified.

XII. Other Conduct Obligations

Nothing in this Model Code of Conduct replaces, supersedes or alienates ethical standards and codes which may be imposed or additionally imposed upon any mediator by virtue of the mediator's professional calling.

REFERENCES

Abel, R.L. (1982). *The politics of informal justice. Vol. 1* (pp. 267–320). New York: Academic Press.

Alcock, J.E., Carment, D.W., & Sadava, S.W. (1998). *A textbook of social psychology* (4th ed.). Scarborough, ON: Prentice Hall.

Armstrong, M.J., & Hurley, W.J. (2003). A comparison of arbitration procedures for risk neutral disputants. In *Proceedings of the eleventh annual conflict resolution symposium* (pp. 221–238). Ottawa: Carleton University Department of Law.

Azar, E. (1990). *The management of protracted social conflict*. Aldershot, UK: Dartmouth Press.

Bailey, M. (1989). Unpacking the "rational alternative": A critical review of family mediation movement claims. *Canadian Journal of Family Law*, *8*, 61–96.

Benjamin, R. (1995a). The constructive uses of deception: Skills, strategies, and techniques of the folkloric trickster figure and their application by mediators. *Mediation Quarterly*, *13*, 3–18.

Benjamin, R. (1995b). The mediator as trickster: The folkloric figure as professional role model. *Mediation Quarterly*, *13*, 131–149.

Benson, H. (1975). *The relaxation response*. New York: Avon Books.

Bianchi, H. (1994). *Justice as sanctuary: Toward a system of crime control.* Bloomington, IN: Indiana University Press.

Bingham, L. B., & Pitts, D.W. (2002). Highlights of mediation at work: Studies of the national REDRESS evaluation project. *Negotiation Journal*, *18*, 135–146.

Birkhoff, J. (2000). Gender, conflict and conflict resolution. http://www.conflict-resolution.net/articles/birkhoff.cfm.

Bishop, P. (1995). *Winning in the workplace: ADR strategies for employment disputes*. Scarborough, ON: Carswell.

Bodtker, A.M., & Jameson, J.K. (1997). Mediation as mutual influence: Reexamining the use of framing and reframing. *Mediation Quarterly*, *13*, 237–249.

Boulding, K.E. (1962). *Conflict and defense: A general theory*. New York: Harper & Row.

Boulle, L., & Kelly, K.J. (1998). *Mediation: Principles, process, practice*. Toronto: Butterworths.

Braithwaite, J. (1989). *Crime, shame and reintegration*. Cambridge, UK: Cambridge University Press.

Bronson, S. (2000). Improving mediator competence through self-assessment. *Mediation Quarterly*, *18*, 171–179.

Brooks, N. (1976). The judge and the adversary system. In A. Linden (Ed.), *The Canadian judiciary* (pp. 86–118). Toronto: York University.

Bunker, B., Rubin, J., & Associates. (1995). *Conflict cooperation and justice*. San Francisco: Jossey-Bass.

Burr, V. (1995). *An introduction to social constructionism*. New York: Routledge.

Burrell, N.A., Zirbel, C.S., & Allen, M. (2003). Evaluating peer mediation outcomes in educational settings: A meta-analytic review. *Conflict Resolution Quarterly*, *21*, 7–26.

Bush, R.A.B. (1989). Mediation and adjudication, dispute resolution and ideology: An imaginary conversation. *Journal of Contemporary Legal Issues*, *3*, 1–35.

Bush, R.A.B., & Folger, J.P. (1994). *The promise of mediation*. San Francisco: Jossey-Bass.

Chornecki, G., & Hart, C. (1996). *Bypass court*. Toronto: Butterworths.

Christie, N. (1977). Conflicts as property. *British Journal of Criminology*, *17*, 1–15.

Church Council on Justice and Corrections. (1996). *Satisfying justice*. Ottawa: Church Council on Justice and Corrections.

Cloke, K. (2001). *Mediating dangerously: The frontiers of conflict resolution*. San Francisco: Jossey-Bass.

Cobb, S. (1994). A narrative perspective on mediation. In J. Folger & T. Jones (Eds.), *New directions in mediation: Communication research and perspectives* (pp. 48–63). Thousand Oaks, CA: Sage Publications.

Cobb, S., & Rifkin, J. (1991). Neutrality as discursive practice: The construction and transformation of narratives in community mediation. *Studies in Law, Politics and Society*, *11*, 69–91.

Cornelius, H., & Faire, S. (1989). *Everyone can win: How to resolve conflict*. East Brookvale, NSW: Simon & Schuster.

Coser, L. (1956). *The functions of social conflict*. New York: Free Press.

Coser, L. (1968). *Continuities in the study of social conflict*. New York: Free Press.

Covey, S.R. (1989). *The seven habits of highly successful people*. New York: Freeside.

Crawford, S.H., Dabney, L., Filner, J.M., & Maida, P.R. (2003). From determining capacity to facilitating competencies. *Conflict Resolution Quarterly*, *20*, 385–401.

Currie, C. (2003). Conflict and mediation: A framework for justice. In *Proceedings of the eleventh annual conflict resolution symposium* (pp. 92–120). Ottawa: Carleton University Department of Law.

Della Noce, D. (2001a). Mediation as a transformative process: Insights on structure and movement. In J. Folger & R.B. Bush (Eds.), *Designing mediation: Approaches to training and practice within a transformative framework* (pp. 71–84). New York: Institute for the Study of Conflict Transformation.

Della Noce, D. (2001b). Recognition in theory, practice and training. In J. Folger & R.B. Bush (Eds.), *Designing mediation: Approaches to training and practice within a transformative framework* (pp. 96–111). New York: Institute for the Study of Conflict Transformation.

Deutsch, M. (2000). Justice and conflict. In M. Deutsch & P. Coleman (Eds.), *The handbook of conflict resolution: Theory and practice* (pp. 41–64). San Francisco: Jossey-Bass.

Deutsch, M. (1973). *The resolution of conflict*. New Haven, CT: Yale University Press.

Eckhoff, T. (1969). The mediator and the judge. In V. Aubert (Ed.), *Sociology of law* (pp. 171–181). London: Penguin Books.

Emond, D.P. (1989). Alternative dispute resolution: A conceptual overview. In D.P. Emond (Ed.), *Commercial dispute resolution* (pp. 1–25). Aurora, ON: Canada Law Book.

Family Mediation Canada (1999). *Practice, certification and training standards*. Ottawa: Family Mediation Canada.

Faure, G.O. (1995). Conflict formulation: Going beyond culture-bound views of conflict. In B. Bunker, J. Rubin, & Associates (Eds.), *Conflict, cooperation and justice* (pp. 39–57). San Francisco: Jossey-Bass.

Fisher, J. (2000). Symbol in mediation. *Mediation Quarterly*, *18*, 87–107.

Fisher, R., & Ury, W. (1981). *Getting to yes: Negotiating agreement without giving in*. Boston: Houghton Mifflin.

Fisher, R., & Ury, W. (1991). *Getting to yes: Negotiating agreement without giving in* (2nd ed.). New York: Penguin Books. Copyright © 1981, 1991 by Roger Fisher and William Ury. Reprinted by permission of Houghton Mifflin Company. All rights reserved.

Fiss, O.M. (1982). The social and political foundations of adjudication. *Law and Human Behavior*, *6*, 121–128.

Fiss, O.M. (1984). Against settlement. *Yale Law Journal*, *93*, 1073–1091.

Flanagan, J. (1997). Insight. In *Quest for self-knowledge: An essay in Lonergan's philosophy* (pp. 16–31). Toronto: University of Toronto Press.

Fletcher, G.P. (1996). *Basic concepts of legal thought*. New York: Oxford University Press.

Folger, J., & Bush, R.B. (1994). Ideology, orientations to conflict, and mediation discourse. In J. Folger & T. Jones (Eds.), *New directions in mediation: Communication research and perspectives* (pp. 3–25). Newbury Park, CA: Sage Publications.

Folger, J., & Bush, R.B. (1996). Transformative mediation and third-party intervention: Ten hallmarks of a transformative approach to practice. *Mediation Quarterly*, *13*, 263–278.

Folger, J., & Jones, T. (Eds.). (1994). *New directions in mediation: Communication research and perspectives*. Newbury Park, CA: Sage Publications.

Folger, J.P., Poole, M.S., & Stutman, R.K. (1993). *Working through conflict* (2nd ed.). New York: Harper Collins College Publisher.

Folberg, J., & Taylor, A. (1990). *Mediation: A comprehensive guide to resolving conflicts without litigation*. San Francisco: Jossey-Bass.

Fuller, L.L. (1971). Mediation: Its forms and functions. *Southern California Law Review*, *44*, 305–339.

Fuller, L.L. (1978). The forms and limits of adjudication. *Harvard Law Review*, *92*, 353–409.

Galanter, M. (1975). Why the "haves" come out ahead: Speculations on the limits of legal change. *Law and Society Review*, *9*, 95–160.

Galaway, B., & Hudson, J. (Eds.). (1996). *Restorative justice: International perspectives*. Monsey, NY: Criminal Justice Press.

Gergen, K.J. (1999). *An invitation to social constructionism*. Thousand Oaks, CA: Sage Publications.

Gilligan, C. (1982). *In a different voice: Psychological theory and women's development*. Cambridge, MA: Harvard University Press.

Goleman, D. (1995). *Emotional intelligence*. New York: Bantam.

Gordon, T. (1977). *Leader effectiveness training*. Toronto: Bantam.

Goundry, S., Peters, Y., Currie, R., & Equity Matters Consulting. (1998). *Family mediation in Canada: Implications for women's equality*. Ottawa: Office of the Status of Women Canada.

Gourley, C.B. (1994). Mediator differences in perception of abuse: A gender problem? In A. Taylor & J. Beinstein-Miller (Eds.), *Conflict and gender* (pp. 73–92). Cresskill, NJ: Hampton Press.

Grey, B. (1994). The gender-based foundations of negotiation theory. *Research on Negotiations in Organizations*, *4*, 3–36.

Grillo, T. (1991). The mediation alternative: Process dangers for women. *Yale Law Journal*, *100*, 1545–1610.

Gudykunst, W.B. (1991). *Bridging differences: Effective intergroup communication.* Newbury Park, CA: Sage Publications.

Gulliver, P.H. (1979). *Dispute and negotiation: A cross-cultural perspective*. New York: Academic Press.

Harrington, C. (1985). *Shadow justice: The ideology and institutionalization of alternatives to court*. Westport, CT: Greenwood Press.

Hillenbrand, L. (2001). *Seabiscuit: An American legend*. New York: Random House. Copyright © 2001 by Laura Hillenbrand. Used by permission of Random House, Inc.

Himes, J. (1980). *The nature of social conflict in conflict and conflict management.* Athens, GA: The University of Georgia Press.

Hocker, J., & Wilmot, W. (1995). *Interpersonal conflict* (4th ed.). Madison, WI: WCB Brown and Benchmark.

Hofstede, G. (1980). *Culture's consequences: International differences in work-related values*. Beverly Hills, CA: Sage Publications.

Honeyman, C. (1990). On evaluating mediators. *Negotiation Journal*, *6*, 23–36.

Hudson, J., Morris, A., Maxwell, G., & Galaway, B. (Eds.). (1996). *Family group conferences*. Monsey, NY: Criminal Justice Press.

Irving, H.H., & Benjamin, M. (1987). *Family mediation: Theory and practice of dispute resolution*. Toronto: Carswell.

Janis, I.L. (1982). *Groupthink: Psychological studies of policy decisions and fiascos* (2nd ed.). Boston: Houghton Mifflin.

Jones, T.S., & Bodtker, A. (1998). Satisfaction with custody mediation: Results from the York county mediation program. *Mediation Quarterly*, *16*, 185–200.

Katz, N.H., & Lawyer, J.W. (1994). *Resolving conflict successfully: Needed knowledge and skills*. Thousand Oaks, CA: Corwin Press.

Keashly, L. (1994). Gender and conflict: What does the psychological literature tell us? In A. Taylor & J. Beinstein-Miller (Eds.), *Conflict and gender* (pp. 167–190). Cresskill, NJ: Hampton Press.

Kolb, D.M. (1983). Strategy and the tactics of mediation. *Human Relations*, *36*, 247–268.

Kolb, D.M. (1993). Her place at the table: Gender and negotiation. In L. Hall (Ed.), *Negotiation strategies for mutual gain* (pp. 138–150). Newbury Park, CA: Sage Publications.

Kolb, D.M. (1994). *When talk works: Profiles of mediators*. San Francisco: Jossey-Bass.

Kolb, D.M., & Coolidge, G.G. (1991). Her place at the table: A consideration of gender issues in negotiation. In J.W. Breslin & J.Z. Rubin (Eds.), *Negotiation theory and practice* (pp. 261–279). Cambridge, MA: PON Books.

Krauss, R., & Morsella, E. (2000). Communication and conflict. In M. Deutsch & P. Coleman (Eds.), *The handbook of conflict resolution* (pp. 131–143). San Francisco: Jossey-Bass.

Kressel, K., Frontera, E., Forlenza, S., Butler, F., & Fish, L. (1994). The settlement-orientation vs. the problem-solving style in custody mediation. *Journal of Social Issues*, *50*, 67–84.

Kressel, K., Pruitt, D., & Associates. (1989). *Mediation research*. New Brunswick, NJ: Centre for Negotiation and Conflict Resolution at Rutgers, State University of New Jersey.

Kruk, E. (1997). *Mediation and conflict resolution in social work and the human services*. Chicago: Nelson Hall.

Kruk, E. (1998). Family mediation in Canada: The state of the art. *Interaction*, *10*, 12–14.

Kydd, J. (1996). Language and family: The poverty of English. *Family and Conciliation Courts Review*, *34*, 351–372.

Lakoff, G., & Johnson, M. (1980). *Metaphors we live by*. Chicago: University of Chicago Press.

Lang, M., & Taylor, A. (2000). *The making of a mediator*. San Francisco: Jossey-Bass.

Law Commission of Canada. (1999). *From restorative justice to transformative justice*. Ottawa: Law Commission of Canada.

Law Commission of Canada. (2003). *Transforming relationships through participatory justice*. Ottawa: Law Commission of Canada.

Lax, D., & Sebenius, J.K. (1986). *The manager as negotiator*. New York: Free Press.

LeBaron, M. (1997). Intercultural disputes: Mediation, conflict resolution, and multicultural reality: culturally competent practice. In E. Kruk

(Ed.), *Mediation and conflict resolution in social work and the human services* (pp. 315–335). Chicago: Nelson Hall.

LeBaron, M. (2002). *Bridging troubled waters: Conflict resolution from the heart.* San Francisco: Jossey-Bass.

LeBaron, M. (2003). *Bridging cultural conflicts: A new approach for a changing world.* San Francisco: Jossey-Bass.

LeBaron Duryea, M. (1994). The quest for qualifications: A quick trip without a good map. In C. Morris & A. Pirie (Eds.), *Qualifications for dispute resolution: Perspectives on the debate* (pp. 109–129). Victoria, BC: University of Victoria Institute for Dispute Resolution.

Lederach, J.P. (1995). *Preparing for peace: Conflict transformation across cultures.* Syracuse, NY: Syracuse University Press.

Lederach, J.P. (1997). *Building peace: Sustainable reconciliation in divided societies.* Washington, DC: United States Institute of Peace Press.

Leymann, H. (1997). *The mobbing encyclopaedia.* http: //www.leymann.se/.

Llewellyn, J.J., & Howse, R. (1998). *Restorative justice — A conceptual framework.* Ottawa: Law Commission of Canada.

Lonergan, B. (1957). *Insight: A study of human understanding.* New York: Philosophical Library.

Love, L., & Stulberg, J. (1996). Practice guidelines for co-mediation: Making certain that two heads are better than one. *Mediation Quarterly*, *13*, 179–189.

Lynch, J. (1997). *RCMP: Revitalizing culture, motivating people: Innovations in conflict management system design at the Royal Canadian Mounted Police.* Ottawa: RCMP.

Macfarlane, J. (1995). *Court-based mediation of civil cases: An evaluation of the Ontario Court (General Division) ADR centre.* Toronto: Ministry of the Attorney General.

Maggiolo, W. (1971). *Techniques of mediation.* Dobbs Ferry, NY: Oceana.

Maslow, A. (1987). *Motivation and personality* (3rd ed.). New York: Addison-Wesley.

Maxwell, D. (1992). Gender differences in mediation style and their impact on mediator effectiveness. *Mediation Quarterly*, *9*, 353–364.

Mayer, B. (2000). *The dynamics of conflict resolution.* San Francisco: Jossey-Bass.

McCurdy, C.W. (1976). Stephen J. Field and public land law development in California, 1850–1866: A case study of judicial resource allocation in nineteenth century America. *Law and Society*, *10*, 235–266.

McKay, M., Davis, M., & Fanning, P. (1983). *Messages: The communication skills handbook*. Oakland, CA: New Harbinger Publications.

McLaren, R.H., & Sanderson, J.P. (1995). *Innovative dispute resolution: The alternative*. Scarborough, ON: Carswell.

McThenia, A.W., & Shaffer, T.L. (1985). For reconciliation. *Yale Law Journal, 94*, 1660–1668.

Melchin, K.R. (1998). *Living with other people*. Ottawa: Novalis.

Menin, B. (2000). The party of the last part: Ethical and process implications for children in divorce mediation. *Mediation Quarterly, 17*, 281–293.

Merry, S.E. (1990). The discourses of mediation and the power of naming. *Yale Journal of Law and the Humanities, 2*(1), 1–36.

Miglin v. Miglin. (2003). [2003] 1 SCR 303; 2003 SCC 24.

Minow, M. (1998). *Between vengeance and forgiveness: Facing history after genocide and mass violence*. Boston: Beacon Press.

Mnookin, R., & Kornhauser, L. (1979). Bargaining in the shadow of the law: The case of divorce. *Yule Law Journal, 88*, 950–997.

Mnookin, R., Peppet, S., & Tulumello, A. (2000). *Beyond winning: Negotiating to create value in deals and disputes*. Cambridge, MA: Belknap Press.

Moore, C.W. (1996). *The mediation process: Practical strategies for resolving conflict* (2nd ed.). San Francisco: Jossey-Bass.

Moore, C.W. (2003). *The mediation process: Practical strategies for resolving conflict* (3rd ed.). San Francisco: Jossey-Bass.

Morelli, M., & Morelli, E. (Eds.). (2002). *The Lonergan reader*. Toronto: University of Toronto Press.

Murray, M.M. (1995). *Artwork of the mind: An interdisciplinary description of insight and the search for it in student writing*. Cresskill, NJ: Hampton Press.

Nader, L. (1988). The ADR explosion — The implications of rhetoric in legal reform. *Windsor Yearbook of Access to Justice, 8*, 269–290.

Nichols, M. (1995). *The lost art of listening*. New York: Gilford Press.

Patton, B., & Downs, T. (2003). *Decision-making group interaction: Achieving quality* (4th ed.). Boston: Allyn and Bacon.

Payne, J.D., & Payne, M.A. (2001). *Canadian family law*. Toronto: Irwin Law.

Peachey, D. (1989). What people want from mediation. In K. Kressell & D.G. Pruitt (Eds.), *Mediation research* (pp. 300–321). San Francisco: Jossey-Bass.

Perry, M. (1998). Deindividuation. In *Living in a social world.* http://www.units.muohio.edu/psybersite/fans/deindividuation.shtml.

Picard, C.A. (1994). The emergence of mediation as a profession. In C. Morris & A. Pirie (Eds.), *Qualifications for dispute resolution* (pp. 141–164). Victoria, BC: University of Victoria Institute for Dispute Resolution.

Picard, C.A. (2000). The many meanings of mediation: A sociological study of mediation in Canada. PhD dissertation. Ottawa: Carleton University.

Picard, C.A. (2002). *Mediating interpersonal and small group conflict* (2nd ed.). Ottawa: Golden Dog Press.

Picard, C.A. (2003). Learning about learning: Value of insight. *Conflict Resolution Quarterly*, *20*, 477–484.

Picard, C.A. (2004). Exploring an integrated framework for understanding mediation. *Conflict Resolution Quarterly*, *21*(3), 295–311.

Picard, C.A., & Saunders, R.P. (2002). The regulation of mediation. In M. MacNeil, N. Sargent, & P. Swan (Eds.), *Law, regulation and governance* (pp. 223–238). Toronto: Oxford University Press.

Pruitt, D., & Carnevale, P. (1993). *Negotiation in social conflict.* Pacific Grove, CA: Brooks/Cole.

Putnam, L.L., & Roloff, M.E. (1992). Communication perspectives on negotiation. In L.L. Putnam & M.E. Roloff (Eds.), *Communication and negotiation* (pp. 1–17). Newbury Park, CA: Sage Publications.

Raifa, H. (1982). *The art and science of negotiation*. Cambridge, MA: Harvard University Press.

Reeve, C. (1998). The quandary of setting standards for mediators: Where are we headed? *Queen's Law Journal*, *23*, 441–474.

Report of the Ontario Courts Inquiry. (1987). Toronto: Ministry of the Attorney General.

Retzinger, S., & Scheff, T. (2000). Emotion, alienation and narratives: Resolving intractable conflict. *Mediation Quarterly*, *18*, 71–85.

Riskin, L. (1996). Understanding mediator orientations, strategies and techniques: A grid for the perplexed. *Harvard Negotiation Law Review*, 7, 25–35.

Rubin, J., Pruitt, D., & Kim, S.H. (1994). *Social conflict.* New York: McGraw-Hill.

Rubin, J., & Levinger, G. (1995). Levels of analysis: In search of generalizable knowledge. In B. Bunker, J. Rubin, & Associates (Eds.), *Conflict, cooperation and justice* (pp. 13–39). San Francisco: Jossey-Bass.

Rummel, R.J. (1976). *Understanding conflict and war: Vols. 1 and 2*. New York: Wiley.

Sander, F.E.A., & Goldberg, S.B. (1994, January). Fitting the forum to the fuss: User-friendly guide to selecting an ADR procedure. *Negotiation Journal*, 49–67.

Sargent, N. (2002). Is there any justice in alternative justice? In M. MacNeil, N. Sargent, & P. Swan (Eds.), *Law, regulation and governance* (pp. 204–222). Toronto: Oxford University Press.

Satir, V. (1988). *The new peoplemaking*. Palo Alto, CA: Science and Behavior Books.

Schellenberg, J.A. (1996). *Conflict resolution: Theory, research and practice*. Albany, NY: State University of New York Press.

Schlabach, J. (1998). In-group, out-group bias. In *Living in a social world*. http://www.units.muohio.edu/psybersite/fans/inoutbias.shtml.

Schon, D.A. (1987). *The reflective practitioner*. San Francisco: Jossey-Bass.

Schwerin, E.W. (1995). *Mediation, citizen empowerment and transformational politics*. Westport, CT: Praeger.

Scimecca, J.A. (1991a). Conflict resolution and a critique of alternative dispute resolution. In H. Pepinsky & R. Quinney (Eds.) *Criminology as peacemaking* (pp. 263–279). Indianapolis, IN: Indiana University Press.

Scimecca, J.A. (1991b). Conflict resolution in the United States: The emergence of a profession? In K. Avruch, P.W. Black, & J.A. Scimecca (Eds.), *Conflict resolution: Cross-cultural perspectives* (pp. 19–39). Westport, CT: Greenwood Press.

Shaffer, M. (1988). Divorce mediation: A feminist perspective. *University of Toronto Faculty of Law Review*, *46*, 162–200.

Sharpe, S. (1998). *Restorative justice: A vision for healing and change*. Edmonton: Edmonton Victim Offender Mediation Society.

Silbey, S., & Merry, S.E. (1986). Mediator settlement strategies. *Law and Policy*, *8*, 7–32.

Spence, G. (2002). Toward a pluralist approach to mediation practice in a legalistic, problem-solving culture. MA thesis. Ottawa: Carleton University.

Sternberg, R., & Davidson, J. (1995). *The nature of insight*. Cambridge, MA: MIT Press.

Stitt, A., Handy, F., & Simm, P.A. (1996). Alternative dispute resolution and the Ontario civil justice system. In *Rethinking civil justice: Research studies for the Civil Justice Review: Vol. 21* (pp. 449–490). Toronto: Ontario Law Reform Commission.

Stone, D., Patton, B., & Heen, S. (1999). *Difficult conversations: How to discuss what matters most.* New York: Penguin.

Stuart, B. (1996). Sentencing circles: Turning swords into ploughshares. In B. Galaway & J. Hudson (Eds.), *Restorative justice: International perspectives* (pp. 193–206). Monsey, NY: Criminal Justice Press.

Stuart, B. (1997). Sentencing circles: Making real differences. In J. Macfarlane (Ed.), *Rethinking disputes: The mediation alternative* (pp. 201–232). Toronto: Emond Montgomery.

Taylor, A. (1997). Concepts of neutrality in family mediation: Contexts, ethics, influence, and transformative process. *Mediation Quarterly, 14*, 215–235.

Thomas, K.W., & Kilmann, R.K. (1974). *Conflict mode instrument.* New York: XICOM.

Ting-Toomey, S. (1985). Toward a theory of conflict and culture. In W.B. Gudykunst, L.P. Stewart, & S. Ting-Toomey (Eds.), *Communication, culture and organizational processes.* Thousand Oaks, CA: Sage Publications.

Tjersland, O.A. (1999). Evaluation of mediation and parental cooperation based on observations and interviews with the clients of a mediation project. *Mediation Quarterly, 16*, 407–423.

Umbreit, M. (1994). *Victim meets offender: The impact of restorative justice and mediation.* Monsey, NY: Criminal Justice Press.

Umbreit, M. (1995). *Mediating interpersonal conflicts: A pathway to peace.* West Concord, MA: CPI Publishing.

Umbreit, M. (2001). *The handbook of victim offender mediation.* San Francisco: Jossey-Bass.

Ury, W., Brett, J., & Goldberg, S. (1988). *Getting disputes resolved: Designing systems to cut the costs of conflict.* San Francisco: Jossey-Bass.

Ury, W. (2000). *The third side: Why we fight and how we can stop.* New York: Penguin Books.

Van Ness, D., & Strong, K.H. (1997). *Restoring justice.* Cincinnati: Anderson Publishing.

Waldman, E. (1996). The challenge of certification: How to ensure mediator competence while preserving diversity. *University of San Francisco Law Review, 30*, 723–756.

Watson, C. (1994). Gender differences in negotiating behavior and outcomes: Fact or artifact? In A. Taylor & J. Beinstein-Miller (Eds.), *Conflict and gender* (pp. 191–210). Cresskill, NJ: Hampton Press.

Weingarten, H.R., & Douvan, E. (1985). Male and female visions of mediation. *Negotiation Journal*, *1*, 349–358.

Welsh, N. (2001). The thinning vision of self-determination in court-connected mediation: The inevitable price of institutionalization? *Harvard Negotiation Law Review*, *6*, 1–96.

Wheatley, M.J. (1999). *Leadership and the new science*. San Francisco: Berrett-Koehler Publications.

Winslade, J., & Monk, G. (2000). *Narrative mediation*. San Francisco: Jossey-Bass.

Wright, M., & Galaway, B. (Eds.). (1989). *Mediation and criminal justice: Victims, offenders, and community*. London: Sage Publications.

Zehr, H. (1990). *Changing lenses*. Scottdale, PA: Herald Press.

INDEX